M. W. (Marmion Wilard) Savage

The Lights and Shadows of Real Life

M. W. (Marmion Wilard) Savage

The Lights and Shadows of Real Life

ISBN/EAN: 9783337054861

Printed in Europe, USA, Canada, Australia, Japan

Cover: Foto ©ninafisch / pixelio.de

More available books at **www.hansebooks.com**

THE
LIGHTS AND SHADOWS

OF

REAL LIFE.

BY

M. W. SAVAGE, ESQ.,

AUTHOR OF "THE BACHELOR OF THE ALBANY," "MY UNCLE THE CURATE," ETC.

NEW-YORK:
A. A. KELLEY, PUBLISHER.
1860.

CONTENTS.

BOOK THE FIRST.

CHAPTER I.
Birth and early education of Reuben 8

CHAPTER II.
In which several friends of the family are introduced to the reader 11

CHAPTER III.
The night before Reuben went to school: how his hair was cut, and who was the hair-cutter 16

CHAPTER IV.
Mrs. Medlicott borrows Mrs. Winning's French maid. Reuben leaves home, and other important incidents . . . 25

BOOK THE SECOND.

CHAPTER I.
The school at Hereford. Reuben renews an old intimacy and makes several new acquaintances 35

CHAPTER II.
Mrs. Barsac's ball 41

CHAPTER III.
More festivity at Mrs. Barsac's 47

CHAPTER IV.
The vicar's account of the Barsacs. Reuben shows a talent for music. His first and his last pugilistic contest . . . 54

CONTENTS.

CHAPTER V.
A chapter of good advice and of good intentions . . 63

CHAPTER VI.
Chiefly occupied with the ill behaviour of an old gentleman and the discomfort it occasioned a young one . . . 67

CHAPTER VII.
Reuben spends a memorable Sunday with his grandfather, and all the Barsacs 71

CHAPTER VIII.
Reuben sits to a fair artist for his picture. Who interrupted the sittings 81

CHAPTER IX.
An afflicting discovery, which ought to have been made sooner . 85

CHAPTER X.
Reuben gets an insight into the private life of his grandfather . 87

CHAPTER XI.
How Reuben celebrated his grandfather's marriage . . 96

BOOK THE THIRD.

CHAPTER I.
Chapter of retrospects. Reuben is bored: his parents are Pigwidgeoned 103

CHAPTER II.
Reuben's recovery and the joy it occasioned . . . 112

CHAPTER III.
A bold stroke for a dinner. How the apothecary got back to the vicarage, and how he turned the vicar out of it . . 119

CHAPTER IV.
A few pleasant days with the doctor. Reuben receives the honours of a prima donna, and the whole party set out on a tour . 124

CHAPTER V.
The Medlicotts on their travels. Reuben buys a Welch grammar, makes the acquaintance of a Welch bard, and falls in with some fair friends 128

CONTENTS.

CHAPTER VI.
Henry Winning and Hyacinth Primrose join the expedition . 135

BOOK THE FOURTH.

CHAPTER I.
Departure for college 145

CHAPTER II.
Hero worship 152

CHAPTER III.
Mrs. Medlicott has a lucid interval. A storm succeeded by a calm . 157

CHAPTER IV.
The dean at the table 162

CHAPTER V.
A new employment 169

CHAPTER VI.
The sermon on conscience. An episode . . . 173

CHAPTER VII.
Mr. Medlicott meets one who is as versatile as himself . . 177

BOOK THE FIFTH.

CHAPTER I.
Burlington Gardens 184

CHAPTER II.
Not important, but not long 191

CHAPTER III.
A social revolution 195

CHAPTER IV.
The school of rhetoric 203

CHAPTER V.
The Professor's wife 209

BOOK THE SIXTH.

CHAPTER I.
A glimpse of glory 215

CHAPTER II.
Thoughts that breathe and words that burn . . . 221

CHAPTER III.
The apostasy 225

CHAPTER IV.
The tremendous demonstration 280

CHAPTER V.
A chapter of consequences 287

BOOK THE SEVENTH.

CHAPTER I.
Mr. Medlicott quarrels with the church . . . 242

CHAPTER II.
Mr. Medlicott is called to the bar 247

CHAPTER III.
A rival orator 251

CHAPTER IV.
Mr. Medlicott sympathises with the Poles, and is naturally led from one sympathy to another 258

CHAPTER V.
How Mr. Medlicott fell among the Quakers . . 266

BOOK THE EIGHTH.

CHAPTER I.
The tobacconist of Chichester 280

CHAPTER II.
A summer evening's walk 286

CHAPTER III.
Pleasure before business 292

CHAPTER IV.
Friends in council 297

CHAPTER V.
Sirach, the raven 501

CHAPTER VI.
In which a discovery is made that surprises everybody . . 803

CHAPTER VII.
Mr. Medlicott receives the deputation 811

CHAPTER VIII.
Mr. Medlicott gives his friends a treat 819

CHAPTER IX.
Wheels within wheels 827

CHAPTER X.
How the contest was conducted 830

CHAPTER XI.
The conquering hero comes 837

CHAPTER XII.
A chapter of outrages on all sides 845

CHAPTER XIII.
A political victory followed by a domestic triumph . . 851

BOOK THE NINTH.

CHAPTER I.
The ascent of a sky-rocket 859

CHAPTER II.
Airs and affectations. Discords and reconcilements . . 865

CHAPTER III.
A scene in Kensington Gardens 873

CHAPTER IV.
Mr. Medlicott visits the New World 380

CHAPTER V.
Peace proves more fatal than war 385

CHAPTER VI.
In which Fortune promises to compensate the vicar for her treatment of his son 391

CHAPTER VII.
Mr. Medlicott in office 396

CHAPTER VIII.
Mr. Medlicott renounces the errors of beef and mutton . . 401

CHAPTER IX.
In which another bubble bursts 408

BOOK THE TENTH.

CHAPTER I.
The last effort of genius 419

CHAPTER II.
Folly interrupted by sorrow 425

CHAPTER III.
Progress of mental infirmity 431

CHAPTER IV.
The last folly and the last speech 436

THE
UNIVERSAL GENIUS;
OR, THE COMING MAN.

BOOK THE FIRST.

> "Uno ore omnes omnia
> Bona dicere, et laudare fortunas meas
> Qui gnatum haberem tali ingenio præditum."
> — *Terence. Andr.* Act I. Sc. I.

> All the world
> With one accord said all kind things, and praised
> My happy fortune, to possess a son
> So good, so liberally disposed.
> — *Coleman's Translation.*

ARGUMENT.

IF the world is a stage, and human life a drama, a prefatory chapter to a biography must be as proper as a prologue to a play. The object in both cases is much the same; to establish a fair understanding between the author and his audience; in other words, by a little art and gentle preparation, to bring the spectator, or the reader, into a state of mind akin to what professors of mesmerism mean by being *en rapport* with their patients. In the opera, this is accomplished by the device of the overture, which gives a sort of musical abstract of the sentiments and passions of the coming performance; now melting in harmony with the amorous scenes of the story, again swelling into unison with its sterner passages; then, with a full orchestral crash, vaguely foreboding a certain catastrophe, either of a tragic or a comic nature. Upon the same principle of composition, the overture or preface to a human life ought to aim at representing, in some allusive, slight, rapid, and sketchy way, its leading vicissitudes and characteristics. Adopting the idea of an overture, we should request the reader of the following pages to imagine the orchestra thronged with a greater variety of instruments, of all sorts, than Nebuchadnezzar had in his band:—harps, dulcimers, flutes, sackbuts, psalteries, and all kinds of music, ancient and modern, which must farther be conceived to play to the mind's ear as miscellaneous a concerto as was ever composed, consisting of snatches of very many tunes, with a profusion of variations. Should this illustration not be sufficiently illustrative, let a pantomime be supposed to follow and harlequin perform his series of Christmas tricks and transformations. The motley necromancer himself typifies perpetual motion and endless variety; let the freaks of character and the changes of fortune be ever so numerous, he is knight of the shire, and represents them all.

Or the reader may, if he please, or thinks it worth the trouble, summon up and cause to pass in procession before him, all the innumerable images, types, and figures of versatility and mutability, such as chameleons, rainbows, weathercocks, kaleidoscopes, Joseph's coat, or a herald's tabard, the clime of England, the constitutions of France, a Brougham, an opal, a woman, or the moon. He may spin out the pageant, if he like, until it is tedious as my Lord Mayor's show; only let it be equally noisy, with plenty of drums and trumpets, especially speaking-trumpets; for, as Montaigne saith truly, "this is a world of babble," and our Coming Man had more than his fair share of it.

By way of argument to our first book, let it suffice to say, that the subject of our story (whom we deliberately refrain from styling its hero) is born herein; nor can there be a doubt that he made a speech upon the occasion, and one that was exceedingly well received by the audience, although it was altogether unpremeditated, and no report of it has been preserved. Escaping all the fatalities that often cut the mysterious thread of life while it is yet a short one, he graduates in the nursery with *éclat*, and, arriving at the green age of thirteen or fourteen, is sent to a public school, to him a momentous event, though, in itself, no startling or extraordinary occurrence. Among our earliest acquaintances, as well as his, will be a reverend father and an accomplished mother; we shall pop upon the gentleman cultivating his cabbages, and surprise the lady in her white dimity, green spectacles, and blue stockings. Possibly, if the father had cultivated his cabbages less, and his son more, the latter might have succeeded as well as the early York did, or the brocoli. Possibly, too, if the mother's hose had been of another hue, it might have changed the complexion of the boy's fortunes. But a truce to possibilities. It is time for our overture, or prologue, to end, and the curtain rise upon the performance, such as it is; for we know not well how to describe it, unless in the words of Polonius: "Comedy, history, pastoral, pastoral-comical, comical historical-pastoral, scene undividable, or poem unlimited."

CHAPTER I.

BIRTH AND EARLY EDUCATION OF REUBEN.

Mr. REUBEN MEDLICOTT, whose variegated life we are about to relate in the following pages, was the only son of a clergyman in the neighbourhood of Chichester, who, neither possessing powerful connexions, parliamentary interest, or any higher talents than some classical taste, and a modicum of dry humour, enjoyed no richer preferment in the Church than the vicarage of Underwood, worth about three hundred pounds a-year, including the value of the glebe, and a small, but pretty and comfortable house upon it. The Vicar was a better gardener than theologian, and more a respecter of learning than a learned man himself. He considered himself, however, a good, plain, classical scholar, and was disposed to prize that species of erudition more than any other. His wife, indeed, had the advantage over him in point of variety of attainments. She was the daughter of Doctor Wyndham, an eminent dignitary of the Church, who had been distinguished when a young man at Cambridge among men of science, but having subsequently deserted the serene study of mathematics for the more exciting pursuits of controversial divinity, was supposed to have been making a push for the mitre; and some people thought he had not yet withdrawn his eyes from that captivating and brilliant object. Dean Wyndham, however, had not been very unsuccessful in his professional career, even as things were, for besides the deanery of a cathedral town in the north of England, he was incumbent of a good living near Hereford: and the additional possession of a fair sinecure in the diocese of Chichester, completed his resemblance to those prosperous sons of the Church, who are described by Dryden as

> "bearing on their shield,
> Three steeples argent on a sable field."

The veteran pluralist was now a widower, and led a sort of vagrant life, to and fro among his various preferments, something like the wandering shepherds we read of in Arabia, or the steppes of Tartary. When he was supposed to be at Hereford, he was away in Northumberland, and when a letter was addressed to him in Northumberland, an answer was returned from Chichester

Besides he kept up his ancient connexion with the University, where he generally spent a month or two in the height of the academic season, with one or other of his old cronies.

But to return to the mother of our Reuben: she had erudition on both sides of the house, for her mother had been one of the *femmes savantes* of her day; she had written a book on education, corresponded with Hannah More, and left an unfinished treatise behind her on the Academic Institutions of the Spartans. It was surprising Mr. Medlicott made the choice he did between Catherine and Elinor Wyndham, the two daughters of the Dean by this learned lady; for Catherine was more suited to him, and better qualified in every respect for the wife of a simple country clergyman; but the fact was, that Catherine Wyndham, having nothing to recommend her but her good looks and sweet disposition, was neglected by her mother, or rather systematically kept in the background, while Elinor, who walked in the maternal footsteps, and resembled her both in mind and person, was trotted out and trumpeted upon all occasions. However, she made a bad hit after all in the matrimonial way; for with her literary pretensions, she ought at least to have netted a senior wrangler, or trapped a regius professor, and she was therefore considered to have actually thrown herself away upon Mr. Medlicott, who had neither university reputation, nor interest in the Church. She married him, too, against the wishes of both her parents; by her mother she was never forgiven, and her father did not relent until her husband obtained his small living through the influence of a patrician schoolfellow, which did not happen until after he had been married for several years.

Catherine Wyndham remained single until she was no longer in her *première jeunesse*, and then she married Mr. Mountjoy, a man of considerable fortune, who dying in the third year of their union (which had not been blessed with offspring), left her blooming and independent, in the possession of a handsome income, which no woman in the kingdom deserved better, for no woman could have made a more amiable and liberal use of it.

But poor Mrs. Mountjoy was, in literary attainments, a mere nobody; she knew a good deal about men, but little or nothing about books. It was here that her sister outshone her. The difficulty is to say what Elinor Wyndham, or Mrs. Medlicott, did not either know, try to know, or wish to seem to know. She knew twenty times as many things, or something about them, as the Vicar, her husband; but so far was this superiority on her part from impressing him with due admiration of the female faculties, that he began to entertain something approaching to contempt for them, before he was many years a married man. He was particularly disposed to this way of thinking when he found his wife meddling with the ancient authors, and used to say sarcastically to his intimate friends, that to see a woman reading Greek or Latin, filled him with spite and envy; "for it was evident she must have exhausted all the stores of knowledge and entertainment to be found in the living languages, before she was reduced to the necessity of resorting to the dead ones."

The Vicar divided his time, for the most part, between his parish, his garden, and his small collection of books: a few standard works on divinity, from which there is reason to think he purloined his sermons, and now and then a play of Terence, or a dialogue of Lucian, to keep up his knowledge for the benefit of his son. Horticulture was perhaps his favourite occupation, and he did not addict himself to it the less because his wife considered it beneath her attention. In spite of the diversity of their tastes however, and a certain quiet conjugal contempt for one another, they did not live inharmoniously together. Sometimes Mrs. Medlicott would even relent from her stern pursuits and take a transitory interest in the flowers, or stoop to pick a strawberry; and again, as a meet return for her complaisance, the Vicar would sit for a quarter of an hour hearkening, with more patience and gravity, than admiration or profit, to his wife's far from luminous elucidations of the secrets of the universe, such as polarised light, or the process by which a nebula developes itself into a world. It was very provoking, however, that he himself never was tempted to plunge into any of the dazzling abysses, into which Mrs. Medlicott led the way, for his encouragement. Such occasional *séances* generally ended by the Vicar's quoting a verse of the nineteenth psalm, and taking up his hoe to earth his kidney beans.

The Vicarage was as charming a spot as you could wish to be born and bred in, if you had a voice in the matter. It had that modest, sequestered, pastoral character, which agrees so well with the notions we form in the guileless and unsuspecting days of our youth, of the life of a Christian shepherd. If it was not very ancient, there was an air of antiquity about it which made you think of the beautiful old times, when architecture was a province of the kingdom of poetry, and they knew how to build cottages as well as cathedrals. You might have assigned the incumbency of Chaucer's "good parson" as the probable date of its erection: or, if belonging to a much later period, at least have guessed it to have been planned by Milton and built expressly for Lycidas. It stood close to the roadside, not one of your broad, level, dusty, glaring causeways, but a zigzag, up-and-down, primrosed by-road, always surprising you with some new picturesque peep at every rapid turn. The house in its structure was a very jewel of irregularity, with such fantastic gables, such quaint grey chimneys, and windows, such a curious jumble of wood, brick, and stone, mossed over in one place, ivied in another, matted with roses in another, and upon one flank quite overhung with a wilderness of laurels, chestnuts, hawthorns, and laburnums, that had a company of young poets and painters, in the heyday of their imagination, turned masons and carpenters in a freak of fancy, they could scarcely have produced anything more exquisite in the Anglo-Arcadian style. It was just the sort of house which youthful couples, newly united by Holy Church, heigh-ho'd for as they passed, and vowed they preferred a thousand times to any castle, hall, or mansion in the land. Older people, weary of the world, coveted precisely such a peaceful nook to close their days in. The veteran soldier desired no better fortune than to recline in his old age under those superb laurels; nay, even the passing lawyer in the height of his business and reputation, mused with himself, and doubted whether he would not have had a happier lot as Vicar of Underwood, and the humble tenant of so sweet an abode.

When Master Reuben came into the world, you may imagine with what intense anxiety a woman like Mrs. Mellicott must have watched the growth of his little faculties. To prepare herself to preside properly over his early instruction, she went through a course of study that would frighten many a hardworking scholar of the Universities: and she laid down a course of reading for her husband also, but she might as well have spared herself the trouble, for the Vicar had no original views whatever upon the subject of education, and thought John Locke had said every thing that was to be said about it. There was, however, one point in which the parents were agreed, namely, in praying that Reuben, when arrived at years of maturity, would take after his grandfather, rather than his father. The Vicar had an extraordinary and almost servile veneration for Dean Wyndham, who was in his eyes the greatest divine and almost the greatest man in England. He had written profoundly when a very young man upon some abstruse mathematical subjects; later in life he had published a learned commentary on the dialogues of Plato; and he was now, in his green and vigorous old age, hurling his thunderbolts at the Church of Rome, and rousing the Protestant spirit of the country to resist the admission of Roman Catholics into the legislature. Nor ought it perhaps to be left altogether out of account that the Dean was supposed (as we have already intimated) to have pretty fair prospects of advancement to a bishopric, which could not but be a joyful event to all his kindred and connexions in holy orders.

Happy it unquestionably would have been for the Vicar's son, had some hard-headed man like Doctor Wyndham been the director of his studies and the moulder of his character. For the early education of our hero was a curious hash of all conceivable methods, systems, theories and régimes. In short there was no system in it at all, or it had the defects and inconveniences of all systems. This misfortune would probably not have befallen him, had either the Vicar, or his wife ruled the roast, for then the ideas of one or the other would have prevailed, and something like a system, right or wrong, would have been the result; but the energies of this respactable couple were so nearly balanced that neither had the ascendancy for any considerable length of time; now the father was supreme, now the mother had her way; in fact the scale of authority and influence went up and down like a game of see-saw played by two urchins in a saw-pit. When Mr. Medlicott was up, Latin and Greek went up with him, grammar and prosody, Alexander, Scipio, Scylla and Charybdis. When the mother's end of the beam was aloft, came the turn of modern languages and what she called the arts and sciences; a splash of French, an occasional twist at German, sometimes even a bout of geology and astronomy, and every now and then a great hullabulloo for a few days about arithmetic. Mrs. Medlicott had a crotchet in her head (which she got from the Phrenologists, who were great oracles with her), that as the organs or the faculties were many in number, the provisions or exercises for them ought to be equally numerous: in fact that the best system of instruction was the most diffused and multifarious. Mr. Medlicott on the other hand was all for concentration; and each had a copious collection of authorities and dogmas, "wise saws and modern instances," 'n support of the doctrine that each held. Thus the boy was in fact pulled backwards and forwards, from one parent to the other, the lessons of neither making an impression of much value or permanence; except that between them both he early laid in a wonderful stock of words and phrases, the foundation of the character he subsequently acquired as a talker of the first magnitude. And there was just the same regular irregularity in hours and habits. In the dark months, Mrs. Medlicott would sometimes conceive a sudden and irresistible passion for early rising, and the maids were called up at cock-crow of frosty mornings, to kindle the school-room fire, or a fire in some other part of the house, for not even the room where Reuben received his education was a settled place. He remembered having learned his Latin grammar in all manner of chambers, and he recollected having once been lectured on geography in the kitchen, the cook asking his father to show her one of the West Indian islands on the globe, where her son who was a soldier, was serving in his regiment. On the other hand, in the middle of summer, the business of the day would often not commence until the dew was off the grass. Then, there was a continual shifting of Reuben's meal-times; the hours that suited the mother's convenience never accommodating the father, and the regulations insisted on by him during his brief period of authority, being invariably reversed the moment the next counter-revolution placed the dynasty in her hands. The effect of all this was that to the eye of a visitor in the house for a short period, it seemed the very model of order and discipline, so that people who were not deep in the secrets of the Vicarage used to leave it mightily pleased; extol Mr. and Mrs. Medlicott highly, and wish they could manage things with half the regularity in their own houses.

But the education of Reuben was at the mercy of other influences besides those already mentioned, and still with the same unlucky tendency to distraction. At certain intervals his parents would both suddenly discover that neither one nor the other was the proper person to conduct his education, and that he ought to go to school, or have a tutor or governess. Between eight and nine he was the scholar of an old Quaker schoolmistress, named Hannah Hopkins, who kept an infant seminary in Chichester, where she taught small children of both sexes to knit and sit upon forms, as mute as if they were at meeting. She may have taught Reuben the former art, but as to silence, he never was very proficient at it, either under her or any of his other instructors. Then Mrs. Winning, of Sunbury, a lady of considerable fortune in the parish, had a tutor at one time for her nephew, Henry Winning, and she was glad to allow Reuben to join him in his studies, partly out of friendship for the Vicar, and partly to afford her nephew the advantage of a companion, although Reuben was his junior by two or three years. This was a very desirable arrangement (particularly as Henry Winning was a boy of great promise), but it did not last many months; Mrs. Medlicott interfered in the course of tuition in a way that Mrs. Winning disapproved, and the wind also happening to shift to the rainy point, Reuben caught a cold one day, returning from Sudbury, and domestic education was resumed again.

Had there been coercion in any of these diversified processes, our hero would probably have hated books of all kinds, and disliked all his teachers in turn; but his love of learning escaped this very common danger. He was of so teachable and ductile a disposition that he profited to some extent by all the lessons he received, and bent like an osier to all the shifting breezes to which parental vacillation exposed him. It was equal to Reuben whether the parlour was his study, or the pantry; he got up cheerfully at six, and he got up cheerfully at nine; he could conjugate *amo*, or decline *musa*, with Nell churning at his elbow, or copy a French exercise while Mopsa was making his mother's bed.

In truth, he had a strong natural appetite for knowledge, which made it the more deplorable that the craving was not satisfied with method and judgment. The system of variety and diffusion was unquestionably that for which the boy himself would have voted, for even his mother's range was not wide enough for his taste, or his ambition; he read, or dipped into every book within his reach, not positively interdicted; and as to interdicts in such a disorderly place as the Vicarage, they were too often revoked, or modified, to be much respected, or very punctiliously obeyed.

In short, there was not a branch, or a twig, of the tree of knowledge, within the reach of his feeble wing, on which Reuben Medlicott had not perched and prattled long before he was fully fledged. Far from needing the stimulus of the least severity, he outran every expectation of diligence entertained by his friends. A still temperament and a delicate frame inclined him to prefer even a task by the fireside to almost any amusement out of doors. He made toys and bedfellows of his books, and, except to force him to take exercise absolutely necessary for his health, his parents had never occasion to say a cross word to him.

1*

The sweetness and pliability of character which are so graceful in a child, and often so much commended, are virtues leaning to the side of faults, and beauties with a principle of weakness in them. There was visible early in Reuben's life a deficiency of the spirit, and daring so proper and so promising in boyhood; there was more of the female than the masculine type in his constitution; his tongue was the most active of his members; he might rival his grandfather in his stores of learning, but, unless some signal revolution took place, there seemed very little prospect of his equalling either the mental energies, or the physical strength of Doctor Wyndham.

In person the boy, who was now in his thirteenth year, had not taken very decidedly after either of his parents. His mother was a tall woman, with a pretentious carriage, a high colour, and regular, though somewhat hard features, to which the blue spectacles she always wore gave a didactic, and decidedly masculine expression. The Vicar was a short, thick man, of a florid complexion, and slightly inclined to corpulence, both probably the effects of the healthy, but inactive life he led—a life in which it was hard to say whether his pastoral labours, his classical studies, or his gardening relaxations, were the most or the least fatiguing. Reuben, at the age we speak of, was disposed to be tall; but he had none of the father's or mother's florid complexion in his cheeks: he was pale, though the hue was not sickly; his face was long, and almost preternaturally placid; for, instead of the hard expression which he might have taken from the female side of the house, Reuben's physiognomy had inherited a certain tone of indecision from his father's features, and particularly about the mouth, which was large and pendent. His hair was fair and abundant, still permitted to fall in girlish profusion on his shoulders: and his eyes were of his mother's speculative azure, with a touch there, too, of the Vicar's too quiet and indeterminate character.

CHAPTER II.

IN WHICH SEVERAL FRIENDS OF THE FAMILY ARE INTRODUCED TO THE READER.

It was not until Reuben had reached the age when, according to the custom of England, boys of his position in life are sent from home to receive the benefits, and run the risks of a public school, that his grandfather began to manifest any interest, either in Mrs. Medlicott, or her son. The Dean had, indeed, been gradually softening for some years, but it was a slow process; he sometimes invited the Vicar and his wife to spend a dull Christmas or Easter with him, and occasionally paid them an abrupt visit, when his business brought him to Chichester and it suited his convenience to quarter himself somewhere in the vicinity. Latterly, however, the parties had been on more cordial terms. The Dean had the feelings of a father *au fond*, and he was also won by the simplicity of the Vicar's character, though he despised his abilities most heartily. What, however, had probably the greatest effect in reconciling him to Mr. Medlicott, was the veneration in which the latter held him. It was the delight of Doctor Wyndham to receive homage, and inspire awe; he was never very fond of anybody who did not either fear or flatter him, and the Vicar possessed the two passports to his favour.

The first concern the Dean showed in his grandson's welfare, betrayed itself in the curt postscript to a letter which the Vicar received from him on some indifferent matter of business. "So you have not sent your son to school yet, how long do you mean to coddle him at the fire-side? Send him to school at once, or you'll be sorry for it. There is a very good school at Hereford —kept by Mr. Brough, related to my friends the Barsacs—at least it is as good as any other I know."

The Dean's word was law, and it happened that the Hereford school was just the one his parents would probably have selected for Reuben, had they been left to themselves. It was not as expensive as the great seminaries, such as Eton and Winchester; the Dean had a living within ten miles of Hereford, which he had latterly favoured with his presence more than his other preferments; and, moreover, Mrs. Winning's nephew, who has been already mentioned, was a pupil of Mr. Brough's at present, and was considered a creditable specimen of that gentleman's efficiency as a tutor. The Medlicotts knew something already of the Barsacs (the family mentioned by the Dean), through Mrs. Mountjoy, who was connected with them by marriage. They were wealthy people in the wine-trade, resident at Hereford, and would probably be civil and perhaps useful to Reuben, for the sake of the Dean.

The expense, however, was a grave consideration, for the Vicar's mode of living was of the simplest, and there was no very large margin for retrenchment. However, every practicable reduction was resolved on, and a variety of presents (marking the interest which his friends took in him), materially diminished the cost of the boy's outfit. Mrs. Mountjoy would gladly have contributed handsomely to so important an object as her nephew's education, but Mrs. Medlicott was always averse to receiving assistance from her more prosperous sister, with whom she was not indeed upon the most cordial terms. As to the Dean, he was generous enough of his advice, which he tendered, as we have seen, with much more freedom than delicacy; but though he had a large income, as good as that of some bishoprics, and was also a widower with his children disposed of, he was the last person in the world to whom the Medlicotts would have applied, even in a case of serious embarrassment. Not that he was a grasping, or illiberal man either, for he had done bountiful things in his time, though apt to diminish the effect of a kindness, by an inconsiderate and harsh manner of doing it. But the fact was that Doctor Wyndham was one instance, among a thousand others, of a rich man who was always more or less involved in pecuniary difficulties. He was afflicted with an ungovernable mania for building, which, perhaps, has involved more men in embarrassed circumstances than any other passion, except gaming. His propensities in this way were very well known to his relations and friends, but not the extent to which he indulged them. Commencing with villas he advanced to terraces, and from terraces his passion was beginning to transport him to more spacious projects of crescents and squares. As to the houses in his own immediate possession, of which he had several, besides his ecclesiastical residences, he was always altering, enlarging, or entirely remodelling them. Indeed he never could pass a night in any house, whether his own or a friend's, without planning its reconstruction, or alterations still more expensive. Bricks and mortar, in short, never left him the command of a fifty-pound note, and when his pockets were drained to the last shilling, he borrowed with as much spirit as he engaged in his other enterprises.

At the very moment when Mr. Medlicott was what is termed "hard up" for a small sum of money to meet the first expense of his son's schooling, his seemingly opulent father-in-law was actually in the neighbourhood, without the knowledge of his relations, negotiating a loan of several thousand pounds from a wealthy citizen of Chichester.

The Medlicotts discovered this by the merest accident only a few days before Reuben left home for Hereford. The Vicar, in fact, wanted a sum of twenty pounds at the moment.

"Probably," said Mrs. Medlicott, "Mr. Cox could accommodate you."

"With much less difficulty," said the Vicar, "than I shall have in asking him."

Matthew Cox was a remarkable man of his class, and a steady friend of Mr. Medlicott, as he was of many a worthy man besides in his city and neighbourhood. He had carried on the trade of a tobacconist in Chichester for many a year, until having made a considerable fortune there, he extended his business to London, where his shop in the Poultry was well known in the early part of the present century. At a later period of our story we shall make the acquaintance of this fine specimen of the British tradesman; it is sufficient to add here that he was wealthy, influential, benevolent, and liberal. As a tobacconist he was chiefly celebrated for his snuff, with which the bishop of the diocese filled his box weekly, and which it was even said had made his Majesty George III. sneeze upon the throne. Matthew had married a quakeress, a relation of Hannah Hopkins, the schoolmistress already mentioned; this, indeed, was the origin of his acquaintance with the Vicar, and of his early knowledge of Reuben, who had few older recollections than his infant sports with Mary Hopkins, Hannah's daughter, among the canisters.

"I have a mind to ride into town this evening," said the Vicar.

He mounted a steady mare he had, and Reuben, (who had weighty business in town with his trunkmaker and his tailor,) mounted his small pony, and rode into Chichester with his father.

It was a charming zig-zag ride, alternately sunny and shady, from the Vicarage to the part of Chichester where Mr. Medlicott's affairs led him. There is probably now a much straighter road; nay, in all likelihood a railway, which if the present incumbent of Underwood prefers to a succession of green lanes, he would probably also prefer a station-house for his residence to the picturesque parsonage described in the foregoing chapter.

Mr. Cox was in London. This the Vicar learned, without entering his shop, from another devoted friend of his, Mr. Broad, the cutler, who was in his usual place at that hour of the evening, on a stone bench, under a canopy of laburnums, immediately opposite to the tobacconist's, and not far from his own house.

"This very afternoon, to Lunnun, sir," said the cutler, jumping up to salute Mr. Medlicott and his son, which he did in a manner which nobody could see for the first time without being extremely diverted. He was a little fellow, about fifty, of a dry yellow complexion, and as brisk as a bee. He wore a white hat, an enormous mass of white cravat, a swallow-tailed blue body coat, the skirts of which almost touched the ground, and breeches of nankeen, with long strings of buff ribbon dangling at the knees. His stockings were white, and his shoes had steel buckles, so that altogether it was a neat costume, although a queer one. When he saluted the Vicar, he twitched off his hat with one hand, revealing a powdered head of hair, carefully brushed up into a peak, like the top of the Jungfrau; whilst at the same time, with the other hand under the skirts of his coat, he performed the oddest possible antic by way of a bow.

For so small a rate in aid as the Vicar wanted, Mr. Broad suited his purpose as well as anybody else; so while Reuben trotted off to the places where his little affairs led him, Mr. Medlicott transacted his business with the cutler, and that having been settled, the Vicar desired to know what news was stirring in Chichester.

"I presume," said Mr. Broad, "your reverence knows that the Dean is in the neighbourhood."

"No, indeed, I did not," said the Vicar; "we know very little of the Dean's motions; he comes and goes like the wind, I think. He is staying, I presume, with Oldport as usual."

Mr. Oldport was a Canon of Chichester, and an old chum and crony of Dean Wyndham's.

"So I am informed," said Mr. Broad.

"Have you seen the Dean?" said Mr. Medlicott.

"I saw him no later than yesterday, sir, at Mat Cox's; they

were transacting business together, and I was called in to witness the signing of the papers."

"Building is not to be carried on without money," said the Vicar, with a smile and a sagacious nod to Mr. Broad.

"I'm afraid the Dean is very deep in the mortar," said the cutler.

"Do you say so?" said Mr. Medlicott.

"Matthew has advanced him five thousand pounds, sir;—a large sum, sir, five thousand pounds."

It appeared even larger to the Vicar than it did to the cutler, but he made no remark, and changed the subject of conversation by asking Mr. Broad whether he had had any argument with the Dean on politics, or anything of that kind. Reuben had now rejoined them, being just in time to hear a curious illustration of his grandfather's character, rendered still more singular by the oddity of the narrator's appearance and gestures.

"The Dean had no argument with me, sir," said Mr. Broad; "but he had a grand one with Matthew Cox; they had a battle royal in Mat's shop, sir."

"Were you present?"

"Aye, that I was, sir; and so was old Hannah Hopkins; it was all about the coronation oath; the Dean said that if the King was to consent to an act for admitting Roman Catholics to sit in Parliament, he would be guilty of flat perjury, and ought to lose his ears, sir, as well as forfeit his throne. He thumped the counter, sir, till the snuff flew out of the canisters, and made Mrs. Hopkins and her daughter sneeze and run out of the shop; but they were frightened, too, I believe, by the Dean's loud voice and the way he thumped the counter."

"Well," said the Vicar, "and what did Matthew say?"

"Mat was very respectful, sir, as he always is to people above him, and to the clergy particularly; but he was very firm also, and stood up for his own opinions like an honest man; he kept his temper, sir, which I am sorry to say the Dean did not; for he ended with calling Mat a Papist, and went away without so much as wishing him a civil good morning."

"Was this before the pecuniary transaction, or after it?" inquired Mr. Medlicott, with his modicum of dry humour twinkling in his eye.

"After it, sir, after it; the Dean, sir, had the five thousand pounds, (or the order for the money, which was just as good,) in his pocket, sir, at the moment he was abusing Mat, and calling him twenty Papists."

"That was too bad," said Mr. Medlicott, looking at his watch, and extending his hand to Mr. Broad to bid him a good evening.

The sun had set before the Vicar and Reuben were on the road home again through the winding lanes. The Vicar mused, the greater part of the way, upon the strange peculiarities and contrasts of his father-in-law's character, while Reuben, trotting by his side, speculated on the capacity of his new trunk for holding his clothes and his books, and packed and repacked it twenty times over in his busy imagination.

———•••———

CHAPTER III

THE NIGHT BEFORE REUBEN WENT TO SCHOOL: HOW HIS HAIR WAS CUT, AND WHO WAS THE HAIR-CUTTER.

The Dean was indeed the guest of Canon Oldport at the time, as Mr. Broad and the Vicar supposed. The Canon was an old bachelor, who had a tolerably good library, and kept only too good a table; for, between the sedentary habits of the student and the *bon-vivant*, he had generally two fits of the gout in the year; while, in the intervals, he was so afflicted with corns, that, in fact, he might be said to pass his whole life in his elbow-chair. Accordingly, being passionately fond of gossip and conversation, he was always delighted when a neighbour, or old college acquaintance dropped in to dine, or spend a few days with him. His greatest friend was Wyndham, and yet the Dean was so troublesome a guest that the Canon was generally as well pleased when he left his house as when he came to it. The Dean turned every house he entered topsy-turvy; but he provoked Oldport most by his unceremonious way of tumbling about his books, which kept the Canon in a continual fret, particularly as the Dean never restored a volume to its place, so that his friend was continually hobbling after him, to keep his library in order.

One evening, while the Dean continued Oldport's guest, it suddenly occurred to him to pay the Medlicotts a visit; and accordingly, leaving the Canon to drink his wine alone, (the thing of all others least agreeable to him,) Dr. Wyndham took up his huge gold-headed cane, and strode across the fields to the Vicarage. He was a man of huge frame and gladiatorial muscle

Nature seemed to have designed him for physical, as well as polemical conflicts. He valued himself, indeed, on his personal strength as much as upon his prowess in controversy, and was particularly proud of his pedestrian powers. He had such a pair of legs as Hogarth would have given to an Irish chairman, or Wilkie to one of the swarthy demon-like coal-whippers to be seen issuing from those black arches in the Strand, which might well be imagined to form the regular communications between London and the nether world.

The Vicar was watering his plants, apparently screened from public observation by a close hedge of beech, nearly six feet high, which separated his garden from the road, when he heard a well-known rough stentorian voice call out—

"Medlicott, you know no more of gardening than you do of Newton's Principia. I'll show you how to water, when you think proper to let me in."

The Vicar looked up, and beheld the broad pugnacious face of his wife's father, with an immense aquiline nose, and an acre of well-shaven skin, the whole overshadowed by a shovel-hat with a particularly intolerant cock, peering at him over the hedge, which he was well able to do without standing on tip-toe. Having hospitably welcomed his distinguished relative and visitor, he ventured to observe, good-humouredly, that he *did* presume to know something of a garden, though he was an humble vicar, and had all his life been ready to receive instruction from any one who was so competent to afford it, on most subjects, as the Dean. As he spoke, he hastened to open a small wicket door in the hedge to admit the dignitary, who instantly thrust himself in, stooping more than was necessary, and observing that it would not have cost five shillings more to have made the door a couple of inches higher.

The Vicar again meekly smiled, and excused the door by observing, that there was not such a tall man as Dr. Wyndham in the parish of Underwood, or, he believed, in the diocese.

"Give me the watering-pot," cried the Doctor, without noticing the Vicar's apology, although so flattering to his person, "and go you in and tell Elinor I am come to take tea."

"My wife is somewhere about the garden," said the Vicar.

"Go and find her," said the Dean.

The Vicar obeyed, and in a few minutes returned with his wife and son, who were followed at a cautious distance by Hannah Hopkins, the Quakeress, and her daughter Mary, a fair, round, cosy girl, with a most unquakerlike expression of mirth in her eye, and a trick of laughing equally unbecoming of her solemn sect. Hannah Hopkins, who had already (as we have seen) met the Dean in Matthew Cox's shop, and been so frightened by his violent deportment, felt very much inclined to make her retreat when she heard his name mentioned, but the Vicar had overruled her, as she had had a long walk and come expressly to take tea. Mrs. Medlicott, with Reuben, hastened forward to welcome her father, whose arrival was not entirely unexpected, as it was known he was in the neighbourhood. Both mother and son were proud to excess of the Dean's talents and reputation. You could see it in their faces; but you might also have perceived that they were fluttered as well as gratified by his visit. They found him, however, a little crest-fallen, and somewhat in the state that is called a pickle. He had got himself into a scrape by his conceited meddling, for stooping too low to replenish the watering-pot in the well, his shovel-hat had fallen into it, and he was now fishing for it with a rake. Mary Hopkins laughed most irreverently. Old Hannah shook her head at her. She was a tall, gaunt, elderly woman, with the parched brown complexion of an ancient gipsy; she wore steel spectacles on her nose, and her bony hands were furnished with knitting-needles, which were never idle, making or mending some garter, mitten, or worsted stocking.

She shook her head at her daughter when she laughed, and it was an awful sight to her scholars when Hannah Hopkins shook her head, though by no means an infallible cure for laughter in other cases. The Dean, however, took no notice of either mother or daughter, but having recovered his hat commenced whirling and swinging it about, without thinking much of the sprinkling he gave any of the party. As to poor Mrs. Medlicott, she got so much of the cold spray, that she was forced to cry out for mercy, and cover her face and bosom with her hands. Mary Hopkins caught some of it too, and it set her laughing again, though she did her best to repress it.

"The hat's not much the worse," he said, bluffly shaking hands with his daughter and grandson; he was evidently quieted by his little mishap, and said no more of watering or of gardening that evening. The room where the tea was prepared was a small one, and the table where it was spread was small likewise. When the great churchman was seated, it seemed as if there were no room for anybody else. Yet two of the party had disappeared. What had become of the Quakeresses?

"What has become of Hannah and Mary?" asked the Vicar, looking all round about him.

"They were just behind us," said Mrs. Medlicott.

"They came to tea," said Reuben.

Reuben was greatly concerned, and, running in all directions, searched the garden for them, but he searched in vain; for the timorous Quakeresses had slipped away unperceived through the wicket in the hedge; Hannah Hopkins dreading another untimely explosion of mirth on the part of the fair fat Mary, and not knowing what awful consequences might follow, should the formidable Dean suspect that he was the subject of it.

"Gone without their tea!" said the Vicar, when his son returned from his unavailing search.

"And without their flowers," said Reuben, who had gathered an immense nosegay for his old schoolmistress and her daughter.

The Dean now, addressing himself to nobody in particular, launched out into a philippic on the Quakers, their habits, and their doctrines, belaboring Fox and Penn without mercy, and promising to administer a still more elaborate castigation to the whole Society of Friends upon some future occasion—a promise which he lived to redeem. Poor Medlicott had generally a good word to say for the Quakers, but he rarely ventured to controvert any opinion of Dr. Wyndham's, and upon the present occasion he observed a most servile silence.

Some time elapsed before Mrs. Medlicott succeeded in drawing her father's attention to Reuben, and to the interesting fact that the very next day was fixed for his departure for school.

"So you are taking my advice at last; you ought to have taken it long ago," he cried, addressing both parents, but looking at neither, which was no deviation from his ordinary manners in society. He then fell upon the eatables on the table, as if his friend the Canon had given him no dinner, talking loudly and volubly, on the subject of public schools in the necessary intervals of eating, and sometimes during the process, relating his own exploits at Harrow, and further, to encourage Reuben, giving lively and forcible descriptions of the discipline which, at that period, was in vogue in most English seminaries of any notoriety.

"Quorum pars magna fui," said the Doctor. "It was through the birch I made my way to the laurel. It was whipped into me." Reuben blushed, and felt excessively uncomfortable all over. His mother felt uneasy also; yet she could not but reflect with pleasure that her son's passion for study would necessarily enable him to reach the laurel without passing through the other grove alluded to by his grandfather.

"I was a Goth when I was a boy," continued the Doctor, still stufling himself. "I hated books; I was a foe to learning; I was a Goth and a Visigoth. It was whipped out of me."

"But Reuben does not hate books, or learning, father," said Mrs. Medlicott with a sort of nervous playfulness, for she was always timid in her father's presence, and spoke in a subdued way, which she was not so much in the habit of using with her husband.

"Perhaps it would be better if he did: boys are boys, a learned boy is as great a monster as an ignorant man. I am afraid, Elinor, you have been stufling your son's head with too many things. I have known men ruined by cleverness, but I never knew a man ruined by dulness." The Vicar shrugged his shoulders and expressed his full concurrence in this opinion.

Mrs. Medlicott was now moved: she took off her blue spectacles, as she always did when she was about to do or say anything with particular energy or seriousness (probably lest they should fall from her nose), and laid them beside her on the tea-table. This done, she remarked with some spirit, and even a little irritation, "that it was rather hard she should now be blamed for misdirecting her son's studies, as she had never acted on her sole responsibility, and particularly as Reuben was quite as forward as other boys in his Greek and Latin, while over most children of his age he had a decided advantage in many other branches of knowledge, which she had often heard her father himself say, were too much neglected in public schools."

"The boy will do well enough, I dare say," cried the Dean, cutting his daughter short. Then turning to Reuben, he added —"you must do your grandfather credit, sir."

"That's what I often tell him," said the Vicar.

"I trust, father, he *will* do you credit," said Mrs. Medlicott more emphatically; "it is my prayer that he may, and I believe it is his own earnest wish. Is it not, Reuben?"

"It is, mother," answered her son very frankly and handsomely. His manner pleased even the rugged dignitary, who called the tall bashful boy over to him, patted his fair head, and gave him a great many valuable pieces of advice for his conduct at school, both in his behaviour to his teachers and his fellow-scholars, ending by reminding him that he had nothing but his talents and industry to depend on for his advancement in life.

"What can your father do for you—a poor church-mouse of a vicar?"

"He can only leave you his blessing and the family Bible," added the Vicar humbly.

"We must rely upon Providence," said Mrs. Medlicott, with a sigh, but at the same time with a complacent smile on her son, as if she had not much doubt of his success in life.

"Very right," said the Dean, "but Providence only provides for the provident; never forget that."

"Very true," said the Vicar.

"Very striking," said his wife.

"I'll have another cup of tea," said Dr. Wyndham, pushing his cup towards his daughter. He drank tea like Dr. Johnson when the tea-drinking fit was on him, but he was sometimes equally violent in his love of coffee.

"Well," said the Vicar cheerily, after a moment's halt in the conversation, "if Reuben goes into the Church, which he probably will, he won't want a friend there to give him a push in the world."

"Let nobody expect to rise by holding my skirts," said the Dean dryly and pompously; "my head is as hard to be fitted with a mitre as parson Yorick's."

"Nothing is impossible," said the Vicar, somewhat maladroitly.

"Nothing's impossible, of course," rejoined the Dean; "if you go to possibility, you may be a bishop yourself one of these days."

"The Vicar laughed at this rude speech, as if it was a capital joke, while the old gentleman began abruptly to talk a great deal about his friends the Barsacs, abusing their house and their society, but extolling the people themselves, especially one of the Miss Barsacs, whose name was Blanche, and whom the Dean called a sensible good girl twenty times over, and more than once an angel. The Barsacs, he said, were only too attentive to the Finchley boys: they would be kind to Reuben as a matter of course.

The sun was now setting behind a row of great old yews which stood at the top of the sloping garden of the Vicarage, separating it from the church-yard, and as the level beams fell on the fair hair of young Reuben, they attracted the attention of his grandfather to its feminine beauty and abundance.

"Come, Elinor," he cried to his daughter, "you are not going to send the boy to school with this ridiculous head of hair; why, his school-fellows will use him for a Pope's head."

"It *is* too long," said the Vicar. Mrs. Medlicott herself could not dispute it. The hair was the colour of her own to the nicest shade, which perhaps was one of the causes of the favour in which she held, and the care with which she had cherished it.

"Is there no hair-cutter in the village, eh?" pursued the Doctor, looking furiously at the golden locks.

"Not nearer than Chichester," said Mrs. Medlicott, "indeed I should have had it cut before, but now it is too late."

"Too late, fudge! why don't you cut it yourself?"

"Oh, father," said Mrs. Medlicott, laughing, "I should be a very awkward *coiffeuse:* I wouldn't undertake it for the world."

"Undertake it! Where's the difficulty? hand me a pair of scissors; I'm a capital hair-cutter; I always cut my own at College—hand me those scissors, boy." Imagine a Roman dictator, Furius Camillus for instance, issuing his orders.

Reuben smiled, coloured, glanced at his mother, then looked fearfully at his grandfather, and finally handed the scissors. It was the affair of a moment. You know the sound that sharp steel makes passing through masses of crisp curls.

"Now don't, dear father; don't," cried Mrs. Medlicott, jumping up and running round the table. "I'll do it myself,—don't father, don't,—you might have allowed me."

The bright hair was tumbling on the floor in bunches, while the mother was thus interceding for it idly, for her father's huge hands wielded the shears as ruthlessly as those of Atropos.

The Vicar was pleased, but he enjoyed his satisfaction in silence. As to Reuben, he was man enough to have borne the loss of his superfluous ringlets, for in truth they were an incumbrance and inconvenience to him; but when he saw that his mother was really agitated and vexed at his grandfather's violent proceedings, the tears stood in his eyes, and it was with some difficulty he prevented them from joining his hair on the carpet.

The Vicar accompanied the dignitary for about a mile of the way back to the house were he was quartered, the latter walking with immense strides, talking volubly and vehemently all the time; and the former a short-winded pursy little man, trying ineffectually to keep the pace, and equally unsuccessful in his efforts to take part in the conversation. At length they came to a point where the Dean was to cross a stile to take a short cut through the fields; and here he suddenly missed some papers, no less important than a sermon which he was to preach in the Cathedral of Chichester the following Sunday. The papers ought to have been in his hat, and as they were not there, the probability was that they were in the pond, or well, in the Vicar's garden.

"Have you ducks?" cried the Dean, astride on the stile.

"No," said the Vicar laughing; "it's not a pond, only a well."

"Well, there's one well in the world," said the Dean: "one at least that realises the old proverb, and you may now boast, Medlicott, that you have got it in your garden."

"I'll recover the sermon," said the Vicar; "it won't be a dry discourse at all events."

"I make you a present of it," said the Dean. "Preach it to the people of Underwood."

"I'll take you at your word, sir," said the Vicar, "and the present is very acceptable, for I have been so engrossed by sending Reuben to school, that I have had no time to compose a sermon of my own for next Sunday."

Mrs. Medlicott and her son had strolled forth also to enjoy the remnant of a beautiful evening more agreeably in the fresh air, and neighbouring fields, than in the feverish atmosphere of a room, which had been twice heated by the steam of the tea-kettle, and the presence of a great controversial divine. Mrs. Medlicott had of course many prudent maternal cautions to impress, and many sage injunctions to impose upon the young adventurer who was about to quit her side for the first time; and Reuben, on his part, had promises to make, resolutions to form, and projects, enterprises, visions, speculations, hopes, and dreams to communicate. One of the pledges now exacted by Mrs. Medlicott, with the greatest earnestness, was that the boy would not over-tax his strength by too much anxiety to improve himself, or even to please his parents; he was young, and there was time enough before him for all the purposes of life; he was highly intellectual—she might venture now to tell him so—and the drudgery, which with inferior faculties might be indispensable, was in his case not only needless, but was calculated to defeat the very object of study.

"But there will be time enough for every thing," said Reuben; "I need not forget my French, or my German, or my geology, or my botany, or anything you have taught me, mother; although I promise you I will attend chiefly to my school business, and not neglect my health."

"That is all that I ask, my love," said the tall matron, looking down with maternal pride upon her son through her blue spectacles, and bitterly sighing when she missed his hyacinthine curls.

"I should not be happy, mother," pursued Reuben, "if I were to feel myself forgetting anything you have had the trouble of teaching me."

"My dear boy," said his mother, after a pause, during which she collected herself for one of her speeches, "now that I am satisfied you will be prudent, believe me I do not want to disguise from you the immeasurable extent of the field of human knowledge, and the innumerable provinces of the mind, (for really they are innumerable,) in which the triumphs of literature and science are to be won. I have often told you—have I not?—I think I have—the opinion I entertain of the vast capacity of our intellects, and my conviction that there is infinitely more than enough room in your brain, for example, Reuben, or in mine, for all the learning that ever was acquired, and all the sciences that ever were invented. Our minds, my dear, you must never forget, are not only immortal, but infinite. When you have read Locke's Essays and Browne's Philosophy of the Mind, you will have clearer notions of what immortality and infinity mean. There is nothing so important, dear Reuben, as to have clear and precise ideas upon every subject; but to return to what I was saying, I am inclined to believe that Plato, the divine Plato, held pretty much the same opinions that I have expressed, or tried to express, on the vastness and variety of the human capacity. I have really sometimes thought of comparing the human mind to an infinite kaleidoscope."

"I long to read Plato," said Reuben.

"He is a glorious writer and philosopher," said the blue lady; "you will study him at College."

"Not till then," said Reuben, with a sigh; "but tell me, mother," he added, "was my grandfather so very dull at school as he says he was? Was he a Goth, and a Visigoth?"

"Your grandfather, my dear," said Mrs. Medlicott, smiling, "like most very energetic men, sometimes speaks in a strain of exaggeration; you must receive his statements, therefore, *cum grano*, or with a grain of allowance for this peculiar feature in his idiosyncracy;—no, my dear, he was, I believe, one of the very cleverest boys at Harrow, though idle and refractory perhaps at times, which accounts for the experience he told you he had of the severities of academic discipline." Here a winged beetle gave Mrs. Medlicott a bob in the face, and brought her prematurely to a stop.

"I will make it my study, mother, to resemble him," said Reuben, solemnly.

"Not in being idle and refractory, I hope," said Mrs. Medlicott, smiling;—she was seldom so jocular—"but who is this approaching us? it has grown so dark that we shall scarcely have light to get home. Those coleopterous insects are exceedingly annoying: it is owing, you may remember, to the peculiar structure of their visual organs."

The personage thus dimly descried in the twilight, was the Vicar who, while he accompanied them back to the glebe, informed them of the watery doom of the Doctor's papers. Mrs. Medlicott was greatly excited at the thought of the possible loss of any production of her father's, and her excitement was caught by Reuben, who ran forward with impetuosity to procure a lantern from the kitchen, to guide them to the well, where indeed the papers were found floating, as was anticipated, just where they had tumbled out of the shovel-hat. Mrs. Medlicott, herself, took possession of them, and dried them carefully with her handkerchief, and afterwards at the kitchen fire, before she went to bed. The Vicar entertained a momentary design of sitting up to read the sermon, of which he was now the owner, but whether it was the reflection that it was his own property, or that he was unaccustomed to reading by candlelight, he gave up the task after nodding over it for a few minutes, and retired to his pillow likewise.

We shall not hear of this sermon again for some years. When it came to the point, the Vicar found it no easy matter to reconcile it with his conscience to palm his father-in-law's learning and eloquence upon his parishioners as his own.

CHAPTER IV.

MRS. MEDLICOTT BORROWS MRS. WINNING'S FRENCH MAID. REUBEN LEAVES HOME, AND OTHER IMPORANT INCIDENTS.

ALL the incidents of that evening made a deep impression on the mind of young Reuben,—the sudden panic flight of the old Quaker and her daughter,—the cutting of his hair by his rude and eccentric grandfather,—the rescue of the sermon from drowning, but his last walk and conversation with his mother more than all the rest.

The boy loved his mother with more than ordinary tenderness; they had indeed been fellow-students more than pupil and preceptress, and his attachment to her was almost identified with his ardour for the various studies into which she had not very discreetly initiated him. The worst of such instruction was that his lights were taken upon most subjects from one whose own mind was far from being luminous enough to undertake the enlightenment of others. Mrs. Medlicott was not at all more logical in her habits of reasoning, or precise in her notions, than the large majority of woman-kind, although the range of her reading was so general and so ambitious. Her understanding at the brightest was but a sort of shining mist. The knowledge she possessed, or what she called knowledge, was nine parts out of ten either an affair of the memory, or the imagination. These were also, of course, the provinces of Reuben's intellect, which had been most industriously cultivated; so that in his case, unquestionably, it would have been better if the old routine of instruction had been adhered to, and if the white paper, to which Locke compares the human mind before the reception of ideas, had not been so extensively scrawled over with hieroglyphics, by the hand of a vain self-opinionated woman. Let a woman, however, be ever so blue, she is still a woman. She does not put off her own sex, when she encroaches on the prerogatives and pursuits of ours. Of this Reuben's mother now afforded a remarkable example. Among many other subjects of maternal solicitude which harassed the mind of Mrs. Medlicott that night, the rape of her son's locks was not forgotten, and the uncouth figure he now made haunted her imagination, and even disturbed her rest. She was apprehensive of making matters worse if she tried with her own hands to mend them, but was there no other resource? Must Reuben actually go to school with that shocking head of hair, looking as if he had been trimmed with a hatchet, as Charon in Lucian was accustomed to trim the beards of the philosophers? Reuben's departure stood fixed for a late hour on the following day, so there was time left for a little management, if she could only think what to do There is nothing like thinking perseveringly and doggedly when you are in a dilemma. Things are very desperate when nothing comes of persevering dogged thinking. Mrs. Medlicott thought so long

that she thought at length of her neighbour, Mrs. Winning of
Sunbury, and recollected that she had lately returned from a continental tour, bringing with her to England a treasure of a young
French *femme-de-chambre*, who was already celebrated in the
neighbourhood, both for her cleverness and her beauty. Mrs.
Medlicott jumped out of bed in the morning long before the Vicar had given any signs of life, and wrote a long note to her
friend, detailing the misfortune that had befallen Reuben, and
begging a loan of her maid for a few hours to help her out of
the difficulty, for Mademoiselle was of course an expert *coiffeuse*.
This note was entrusted to an out-door servant, who was ordered
to take the Vicar's mare to convey it, and to furnish the animal
with a side-saddle for the accommodation of the French maid,
the distance being something too much for a walk. The clock
of Underwood Church, (the tower of which was just visible above
the line of the old yews,) had just gone seven, when the servant
with the mare and side-saddle set out on his odd commission.

There was great excitement that morning at the Vicarage,
and it commenced at an early hour, many of Reuben's old friends
coming to bid him adieu, and present him with little tokens of
affection, to keep themselves green in his memory when he was
far away.

First to arrive were the simple Quaker school-mistress and
her cosy daughter, no longer daunted—poor timid hares—by the
overbearing Dean, with his thundering voice, and church-militant
manners. As they came early and stayed long, we have time
to observe them better than when we met them last. One was
never seen without the other; they were inseparable even in
thought, like chicken and tongue. Two bees were never more
industrious. Their business was teaching, their relaxation needlework. If they had a passion, it was for flowers, grasses, and
peacock's feathers. If Mary had a fault, it was that she was too
merry for her sect, and too plump for her stature. If Hannah
had her imperfections, they leaned to the side of literature, like
Mrs. Medlicott's. Mary was plain in her attire only; the mother
was plain in every sense, including plain-speaking and plain-dealing. Her school, in the management of which Mary now
bore her part, was her principal means of subsistence; it yielded
them but a scanty income, for they were extremely modest in
their terms, and taught the children of people who were as poor
as themselves, for almost nothing at all.

What she taught would not be important enough to mention, if she had not been one of Reuben Medlicott's early teachers.

Her course included reading, writing, and arithmetic as far as long division; she never puzzled her pupils with the rule of three, or maddened them with fractions. Her system of geography was much shorter and simpler than Humboldt's. In history she taught how Alfred burned the cake, how Clarence was drowned in the malmsey, and who founded the state of Pennsylvania. In short, she taught many things superficially, and stocking-knitting profoundly. But she was perhaps more in repute as a moralist, than for merely enlightening the mind. In ethics she taught that honesty is the best policy, that wilful waste makes woful want, that idleness is the mother of mischief, and that there is a time for all things under the sun. There is reason to think she considered this last maxim the corner-stone of the edifice of virtue, she repeated and insisted on it so very frequently. Neither of the Quakeresses came empty-handed. Mary brought a silken purse, of her own manufacture, in which she had curiously interwoven Reuben's name, and very tenderly, as well as a little nervously, did she present him with it, whispering, while she placed it in his hands, that she trusted he would be happy where he was going, which appeared to be very far away. Hannah had her gift also, a large segment of a certain economical species of plum-cake, made with her own hands from a receipt handed down in her family for generations. It was called the "cut-and-come-again cake," and was particularly in demand for the quarterly and yearly meetings.

There now appeared another visitor, one, however, who came to take rather than to give, as the world is divided between people of the two propensities. The new comer was a tall, awkward, heavy animal of a boy, somewhat senior to Reuben, the son of Mr. Pigwidgeon, the family apothecary, who, not being able to come himself, sent his son Theodore with a present of a box of stomachic pills, and a commission to say what was proper on his part, which perhaps the lad would have tried to do, had not the sight of the cake driven all other thoughts out of his mind. His arrival was evidently a bore to Reuben, who had to request him to keep his intrusive hands out of his trunk, which was packed, but still open, while he willingly accepted Mary Hopkins's offer to put the things in order again which had been deranged by such unmannerly meddling. Master Pigwidgeon then kept hovering, like a great fly, about the "cut-and-come-again," and at last ventured to pick at the enamelled sugar with which it was overlaid. In all probability he would soon have taken much greater freedom with it, if old Hannah had not suddenly laid hands on him, and, drawing herself up to her full height, addressed him with a severity which not more appalled the object of it, than it vastly entertained the Vicar.

"Go thy ways," she cried, shaking her head, and shaking the delinquent at the same time, "the cake is not for thee; hadst thou been a scholar of mine, I would have taught thee betimes to keep thy hands from that which is not thine."

The tall lubberly youth slunk away from the table where the cake lay, and looked so abashed and frightened that Mrs. Medlicott pitied him, and gave Reuben a hint to offer him a piece of the cake, which the generous boy did in the promptest and most good-natured manner. Nor was Master Theodore Pigwidgeon too proud to be appeased in this way, though he preferred enjoying his share of the cake in private, and stole away home, scarcely bidding his benefactor a good-bye, and utterly forgetting the pills, for which Reuben perhaps had no reason to be seriously offended with him.

Among the hours and half-hours that are most irksome to pass in this world (such as the half-hour before dinner, or before the rising of the curtain at the play), must certainly be enumerated the interval that elapses between the completion of the preliminaries of a journey and the moment of the last embraces and adieus. It is an interval which cannot be too much abridged for the comfort of all parties; for the tenderest leave-takings do not admit of being protracted for more than a few minutes; sighs cannot be drawn out beyond a limited length, and the tenderest eyes will not secrete tears at discretion. The visits of even common acquaintances therefore, have their value on these occasions, provided they do not come to pry into our boxes and eat up our plum-cakes. Mrs. Medlicott nevertheless was not sorry when the considerate quakeresses gave Reuben the last proofs of their affection—Hannah with kisses which he would gladly have dispensed with, and a parting speech containing the cream of her proverbial philosophy—and went their way in sympathy and silence. In fact Mrs. Medlicott had for some time been extremely fidgetty, looking out for the arrival of the French maid, and not wishing her to come until the Hopkinses had departed. It happened exactly as she wished. The quakeresses were not gone five minutes when Mademoiselle arrived, not on the Vicar's mare (for she shuddered at the notion of riding), but in a little phaeton of Mrs. Winning's. Louise (so she was called), was very young, extremely pretty, exceedingly well-dressed, thoroughly Parisian, and the most lively, ardent, and obliging creature in the world. In a neat basket, which hung from her arm, she carried her scissors and her tongs, her oils, marrows, and pomatums, in short all the instruments and appliances of that luxurious and ornamental art in which her compatriots of both sexes leave the rest of the world immeasurably behind them. The exquisite arrangement of her own hair was enough of itself to prove her capacity for the delicate mission she came to execute. In a word, she seemed a very sylph of the toilet, an actual Crispissa, as she alighted from the carriage and tripped into the Vicar's parlour. What a contrast, except in being obliging and good-natured, she presented to poor Mary Hopkins!

"Ah, mon Dieu; ah, mon Dieu;" Mademoiselle exclaimed, when the state of poor Reuben's tresses was shown her, "que les prêtres Anglais sont des ignorans!" as if she had expected to find the ecclesiastics of England particularly expert at hair-cutting.

Mrs. Medlicott talked French reasonably well for an English woman who had never been abroad; but Reuben had not yet reached that degree of proficiency, so that Mademoiselle, who spoke English prettily, employed that tongue chiefly during her visit. She had a nice operation to perform, but she executed it with such dexterity that, although she could not replace the lost curls, she soon left little or no trace of the Dean's clumsy hands behind her. Mrs. Medlicott stood by delighted and thankful, rewarding every clever touch with a profusion of acknowledgments and a mint of smiles. Reuben himself had no words to express what he felt; gratitude was the least of it. Though but a boy of thirteen, he was far from insensible to the prodigious difference between the small tapering rosy fingers of the pretty sparkling young French woman, and those of his last hair-dresser. She touched him so delicately, so playfully, made such a number of artless flattering little speeches, had such bright eyes, and such a musical voice, seemed so happy to please his mother, and every now and then came out with such pretty little exclamations, and adjurations (which were always in her own language), that the boy was utterly confused and bewildered, and experienced emotions which poor Mary Hopkins had never inspired. In fact it was fortunate he had so many other occupations for his thoughts at the moment, for otherwise he might have actually fallen in love.

When Mademoiselle heard that he was on the point of starting for shcool, she cried out that he was too young, too fragile, and began to implore his parents to change their purpose. She even offered to come over herself twice a week from Sunbury, and teach him French. His clever father and mother could teach him every thing else; "voilà mon projet d'instruction pour Monsieur Reuben."

Mrs. Medlicott could not but laugh, while in the most courteous terms she thanked Mademoiselle Louise for her project and all her civilities.

"C'est mon projet," she repeated curtseying, while she sheathed her scissors, and prepared to take leave, which she was not permitted to do without luncheon. While that was preparing, she tripped over to a piano, which happened to be open, and without sitting down, played and sang one little lively air after another, with such grace and sweetness that the Vicar himself was greatly taken with her.

"I will come encore, and pay you a visit, when you come back for de holidays, Monsieur Reuben," she said, when luncheon was over, "and remember, if your méchant grandpapa cut your beautiful hair again, you always send for Mademoiselle Louise."

Before she went, she gave him several admirable precepts for the care of his hair and the improvement of his person generally, and presented him with a flask of Eau-de-Cologne by way of an impromptu souvenir; so that Reuben carried with him to school substantial pledges of regard from a great many friends and acquaintances.

At length the parents were alone with their son, and now many a maternal caress was repeated, many a paternal counsel reinforced; many a time Mrs. Medlicott was sure she had left something unsaid of the utmost consequence, and, with her hands clasped over her eyes, laboured in vain to recollect herself, for in fact she had said everything important and unimportant ten times over. The Vicar had all along confined his instructions to but a few points, but to these he had returned frequently, and even now at the eleventh hour, he inculcated once more the few short moral lessons into which he tersely divided what he called the whole duty of a schoolboy.

The final tendernesses may be left to the reader's imagination—who has not either experienced or witnessed them? "Tears have streamed through every age" for this commonest of causes, but fortunately though such tears are natural, we "wipe them soon," as our first parents did, after a scene of more bitter leave-taking. The Vicar's resource in every grief was his garden. He pulled his hat down over his face, and went forth to commune with an old raven he had of the name of Sirach. Mrs. Medlicott hurried to her room. Reuben mounted the top of the stage-coach with his eyes still red with weeping. The precise number of hours his journey occupied is not recorded; all that is certain is, that on the third day after leaving home he was duly enrolled as a scholar at Hereford, having in the course of the journey met with the usual varieties of ups and downs, rough and smooth, according as nature had diversified the country he travelled through, or the overseers of the roads had performed or neglected their duties.

BOOK THE SECOND.

> "*Mi perdonate*, gentle master mine,
> I am in all affected as yourself;
> Glad that you thus continue your resolve
> To suck the sweets of sweet philosophy.
> Only good master, while we do admire
> This virtue, and this moral discipline,
> Let's be no stoics, nor no stocks, I pray;
> Or so devote to Aristotle's checks
> As Ovid be an outcast quite abjured."
> *Taming of the Shrew.*

ARGUMENT.

A MAN on first coming into the world is very much in the position of a minor whose affairs are altogether in the hands of his guardians and his lawyers; he has nothing at all to do with what he is most concerned in, but is entirely at the disposal and mercy of other people. We are not at liberty to choose our own fathers and mothers, or even our pastors and masters; and perhaps, on the whole it is so much the better—it is easy to imagine what would happen were such a privilege accorded us. Mr. Hudson, for instance, would probably have more sons than Priam of Troy; the Duke of Wellington would have a prodigious Christmas party at Strathfieldsay; and our gracious Queen would soon find herself in the same domestic difficulty with the notorious little old woman, who, whilom, lived in the shoe. Cobblers and curates would be childless, and infants of the most moderate ambition would be born with silver spoons in their mouths. These points are settled for us; and not only are we provided with ready-made parents, but with complete sets of relations, friends, and acquaintances,—not made to any order of ours, and with respect to whom we have not so much as the melancholy choice of Hobson.

There is no help for this state of things any more than there is for our not being nearer neighbours to the sun than we are, or qualified to promenade our ceilings like the flies. It is the common law of the world as much as gravitation: we are free to grumble, but not at liberty to disobey.

Fortune is but another name for the infinite mass of circumstances in the midst of which we seem to be flung, like Bligh's boat on the Pacific, or the infant Moses in his cradle of rushes upon the flood of the Nile. An unseen Providence steers the ark; but as far as regards the little crew himself, he is absolutely at the mercy of the current and the crocodiles. Or we may be said to be as molten metal poured into the mould of ten thousand pre-existing facts and relationships, all influencing us, and more or less, determining what manner of men we shall be. We take their form and pressure most submissively. There is no option but to take it.

Circumstance is like a she-bear who licks her cubs into shape. Some are licked too roughly, some too delicately; a few receive the proper moderate licking which forms the fine animal. After a certain period we come to be old enough to take a part in the process, and lick or educate ourselves; one energetic man in a hundred will recast himself altogether; the majority continue to the end of the story much what nurseries, schools and colleges, parents, pedagogues and priests, conspired to make them in life's introductory chapters.

The second book of our "poem unlimited," contains something about learning, but a great deal more about love. More than one personage will be transported by that passion who ought to be thinking of graver things. When grandfathers fall in love, grandsons may well "sigh like a furnace." We shall presently (to employ again a former illustration) be spectators of some of the pantomimic changes of real life. With our eyes fixed on a grammar-school, we shall see it turned into a drawing-room; and the study of a grizzly old divine will be transformed with equal suddenness into a myrtle-bower. Our Reuben is here advanced a stage on his journey nowhither; he extends his acquaintance with authors, adds largely to his stock of words, and commences an intimacy with a young lady, and to all other books prefers the Book of Beauty. The good old people of Chichester have a very imperfect notion of the sayings and doings of the gay young people at Hereford, or, indeed, of the gay old folk either. While one sort of instruction is liberally paid for, another is generously afforded gratis; for all that influences a man is part of his education; our friends and companions are unsalaried tutors; the houses we frequent are so many academies of easy discipline; the girl we dance with imparts a great many new ideas;—in short, what is the wide world but a seminary, where the youth of both sexes are promiscuously educated by mistresses as well as masters, and under the fan as well as the ferula.

In short, for a model-school (taking the world as it is), commend us to that kept by Professor Biron in the park of Navarre, where the scholars forswore their books when they took a vow of study. A man, however, may, like Reuben Medlicott, be at once amorous of books and studious of beauty. It would not be amiss if the sculptors of gems would sometimes give Cupid the beard of Plato, and transfer the wings and arrows of the profligate little god to the founder of the Academy.

CHAPTER L.

'SCHOOL AT HEREFORD. REUBEN RENEWS AN OLD INTIMACY AND MAKES SEVERAL NEW ACQUAINTANCES.

There was a modified system of fagging established, or permitted, in the school at Hereford where Reuben Medlicott was now a pupil. The aim of Mr. Brough, the principal, (a pompous, but kind man,) was to preserve the system itself without permitting the gross abuses usually attending it, and in the main he was successful in effecting this object. Mr. Brough was a good schoolmaster, had some natural gift for teaching, and considerable sagacity in discovering the characters and measuring the capacities of his boys, taking their altitudes and sounding their depths, as he used to call it. He was not long in taking the measure of Reuben, with tolerable accuracy, and finding him a clever boy, rather deficient in force, and at the same time not of a very robust physical conformation, he considerately assigned him as vassal to his old friend Henry Winning—an arrangement very pleasant for Reuben, and one that gratified his parents extremely when they heard of it. Henry Winning was not only clever, but remarkable for steadiness and perseverance. He was also a brave, generous fellow, so that all apprehension of tyranny was soon banished from the mind of his new subject.

Reuben was on his knees unpacking his box of books the morning after his arrival, and Winning was standing over him, wondering in silence what the boy could want with so many more volumes than he had ever possessed himself. As Reuben placed them one after another on the floor, the other stooped and looked at their titles in succession. The first was a Latin Grammar, which was quite right; next came a Delectus, also indispensable. Then there appeared the Discourses of Sir Joshua Reynolds.

"The Bodleian in a box," said Winning: "come we don't learn that at Finchley;" and he pitched the Discourses aside.

"I read it with my mother," said Reuben, looking up timidly, and colouring.

"An Arithmetic?—no harm."

"This is the History of France."

"It will be no use here," said Winning, "we only read Roman and Grecian History."

Reuben coloured again,—"It's only to keep up my knowledge," he said: "I learned it at home."

"And it appears you learned Geology at home, too, Medlicott. Your mother must be omniscient.—What is Geology?—pray enlighten me."

Winning was holding the book in his hand, turning the pages rather disdainfully, and smiling while he asked the question. The smile and expression of ridicule confused poor Reuben, and he gave a very confused account of the objects of Geology, very like one of his mother's precise definitions.

"It seems much the same as Geography," said the elder, "by your account of it. We do not neglect that at Finchley; but, of course, we have nothing to do with anything but the ancient world—Attica, Asia Minor, the Islands in the Ægean Sea; we learn all about them of course."

"And nothing about America," cried Reuben, with subdued amazement, "or the British dominions in India?"

"This is not a mercantile school, Medlicott; it's a classical school. We have nothing to do with America or India. I suppose they read about India in the East India College."

"That's very odd," said Reuben. "I thought every part of the world was equally desserving of study."

"And perhaps you may be right in the abstract, Medlicott," said Winning, looking intently at his new acquaintance, and struck at once by his modesty and precocious enlargement of views; "but we cannot learn everything at school, or anywhere else. Certain studies are appointed here, and it is expected that we shall devote ourselves to them, not perhaps exclusively, but at least so closely, that I can tell you, Medlicott, there is not much time to do a great deal besides, unless we could manage to do without food, sleep, and cricket."

"Not much time, I dare say," said Reuben, "but you admit there is some: when I have a leisure moment I suppose I may read any of my books I please."

"Under my rule you may.—Now that's magnanimous, is it not?" said Winning, "for I can tell you, Medlicott, there are some men here, who, while I have been quietly looking over your motley library, would have weeded it without the least compunction, and consigned your French History, Botany, and Geology, *Veneris marito*,—do you know who that is?"

"Vulcan," replied Reuben promptly.

Winning now clapped him good-naturedly on the back,

called him a promising fellow, only a little too desultory in his habits of reading, and ended by telling him that he might read what he liked, on condition only that he did not neglect the business of the school, or defraud himself of the time necessary for sleep and exercise.

"But did you come from Underwood and bring me no letters, messages, or anything?"

"Oh, I quite forgot,—I have a parcel for you," said Reuben, greatly fluttered, and ransacking the bottom of the box.

"Stupid: and why did you not give it to me the first thing you did?—from whom is it?"

"From your aunt Winning, of course."

"And did she send me nothing else?"

"Nothing but a letter."

"Do you call that nothing?—you are a fine fellow,—as to the letter, I presume you have lost it—come, let me try—if it is in the box, I'll soon ferret it out."

"Permit me," said Reuben, eagerly but humbly.

He was uneasy lest Winning should discover the silk purse, and still more afraid of his finding the plumb-cake, which he felt quite ashamed of, and had only carried with him out of his affection and respect for old Mrs. Hopkins. But Winning was resolved to search for himself, and he soon found the letter, for he tossed about Reuben's shirts and other things, without much ceremony, but he lighted at the same time, not on the plumb-cake, but upon Mademoiselle's little present of the flask of Eau-de-Cologne.

"What have we got here?" he cried, holding it up to the light: "eh, what is this?—is it wine?"

"Eau-de-Cologne—a scent," said poor Reuben, in wonderful trepidation.

"Oh, a scent, is it?—do you know what we do with scents at Finchley?"

"No," said Reuben.

"Come to the window, and I'll show you what luxurious fellows we are."

Winning walked over to the window, followed by Reuben, very curious to see the use his friend was going to apply the Eau-de-Cologne to.

The room was on the third story, and there was a paved court beneath the window. Winning desired Reuben to look at a particular stone, and then holding the flask between his finger and thumb, he dropped it critically over the spot, where, of course, it was shattered in some thousand pieces, sprinkling the court for some yards round with that agreeable perfume to which a thousand flowers are said to contribute.

"Are we not luxurious fellows, eh?—to water our pavement with Eau-de-Cologne!"

Reuben looked extremely chagrined.

"My dear fellow," said Winning, patting him on the back, "the scent is much better there than in your box. If the fellows here were to find out that you scented yourself, or had scents in your possession, you would never hear the end of it. Now go and put your things in order—I must read my good aunt's letter."

The boys soon became cordial friends; Henry Winning exercising a mild protective despotism, and Reuben reasonably abstemious from supernumerary pursuits, for which in truth the routine of the seminary, (its amusements as well as its business,) left him but little leisure. The example and influence of Winning were signally useful to young Medlicott, who not only prosecuted his classical studies with almost uninterrupted assiduity for the greater part of a year under the auspices of his judicious and spirited friend, but following his footsteps also in other things, began to take pleasure in gymnastic exercises, which materially improved his health and added to the attraction of his person. Winning stimulated his ambition upon these points by dwelling on the vast importance attached to them by the ancient Greeks, who were at the same time the most literary and intellectual people in the world. This was a view of the matter which seized hold of Reuben's imagination powerfully. In conjunction with two boys named Primrose and Vigors, aided by a few admiring followers, he projected a revival of the Olympic games on the play-ground of Finchley, and they actually commenced putting the design experimentally into execution by hiring two donkey-carts belonging to a coster-monger in the vicinity, and starting them against each other, by way of a chariot-race. Reuben dubbed himself Phaeton; Vigors was Salmoneus. The donkeys were named after the horses of the Sun. This aspiring piece of puerility ended in the two charioteers being left sprawling in the dust of the mock hippodrome; Salmoneus getting a broken nose, and Phaeton coming still worse off with a violent sprain of his ancle. Primrose took no very active part in this Olympic experiment, but he composed a

Pindaric ode in celebration of it, the concluding stanza of which, with a serio-comic allusion to the catastrophe, obtained the applause of Mr. Brough himself.

But Reuben's social experiences are perhaps better worth relating than his experiences as a schoolboy; the acquaintances he made, and the connexions he formed at Hereford, had full as much influence upon his future career as the Latin and Greek he learned, and the nonsense verses he composed.

He heard a great deal of the Barsacs from Winning and other boys, but for one reason or another, much to his disappointment, a considerable time elapsed before he received any of that civility and attention from them which his grandfather's talk had led him to expect. At length, as if they had suddenly heard of him for the first time (which may have been actually the case) he was included in a very general invitation of Mr. Brough's scholars to a juvenile fête, or ball; the event excited him greatly; he recollected accurately every word of what the Dean had said about the Barsacs, in praise or abuse of them; and in Blanche, whom his grandfather had so repeatedly and energetically pronounced "an angel," Reuben almost expected to find that flattering description true to the letter.

The elements of dancing he had learned, as such things are to be learned in a place like Chichester; but he had brought no dancing shoes with him from home, so he consulted his chief, and was strongly recommended by him to a little shop kept by a Frenchman, who sold wonderful nice shoes, and wonderfully cheap.

"You and I, Medlicott," added Winning, "must look sharp to economy; neither of us have very splendid allowances; indeed I believe neither will have much but his industry and talents to depend on through life."

"So I have heard my father often say," said Reuben.

"Well," said Winning, "you will find Monsieur Adolphe's shoes excellent and dog-cheap; the shop is at the corner of one of the closes—I forget the name—but it is on the east side of the Cathedral, between a pastry-cook's shop and a cutler's: remember the name is Adolphe."

It was a fine summer evening, and the shadow of the great square tower of the Cathedral of Hereford was thrown like a broad sombre mantle over the cluster of lanes and buildings to which Reuben had been directed by his friend. This shop was easily ascertained, for the name of Adolphe was freshly painted in sufficiently large letters over the door. Reuben entered and found a pale handsome young man, with shining black moustache, sitting without his coat on the little counter, and playing the flageolet. He had heard the air before: it was certainly one of those charming ones which Mrs. Winning's obliging French maid had sung at the Vicarage on the day he left home. The young man jumped down, bowed with his national grace and politeness, and in very good English tendered his services and manufactures to his customer. The shoes seemed to justify Winning's eulogies, and Reuben was soon fitted with a pair which promised both in shape and polish to make a pretty figure at Mrs. Barsac's ball. While M. Adolphe was putting them up in paper, Reuben took up the flageolet to examine it, for he had never seen one before.

"Did Monsieur play the flageolet?"

"No, but it seemed a very sweet instrument."

"It is very easy," said Adolphe: and taking it up again, played another little air, which was also one of those which Mademoiselle Louise had played and sung at Underwood. The musical shoemaker saw that his customer was very much pleased with the performance.

"Ah! but I cannot sing, Monsieur; it is the voice that makes the little romances of my country charmant; I have a sister who sings them like a nightingale."

Reuben lost no time in informing the shoemaker that he had heard the very same airs sung by a countrywoman of his at a house in the country near Chichester.

"Ah, oui! Chichester—Madame Winning—sans doute c' étoit mademoiselle ma sœur:—elles chante ces petits romans là à ravir."

Our hero thought he had made some wonderful discovery in finding that Mrs. Winning's French maid was the shoemaker's sister, and he communicated the fact to Winning with the utmost gravity.

"Is it not very singular?" said Reuben.

"Why," said Winning, smiling at his simplicity, "if a Frenchman and his sister live in England at all, and do not live in the same place, I see nothing prodigious in one living at Hereford and the other at Underwood."

"Why no," said Reuben, "I see there is not, on reflection."

But the occasion for wearing the shoes soon put the maker of them, and all connected with him, out of Reuben's head for the time being.

CHAPTER II.

MRS. BARSAC'S BALL.

The long-expected evening came at last, and Reuben found himself transported into the midst of a tumultuous assembly of well-dressed people, in the gay house of which he had so long desired to penetrate the interior. Except his school-fellows, he was acquainted with nobody. There was nobody to tell him the name of any one. Which of the company were the Barsacs, or whether they were present or not, he was in their house for an hour, without knowing more than the man in the moon, as the saying is. He knew the ball had commenced by hearing the music, feeling the floors vibrate, and finding himself swayed to and fro occasionally by the movements of the dancers, though he could scarcely see them. He wondered what had become of Winning, and paid close attention to the ladies in white dresses, among whom alone he expected to find Miss Blanche Barsac, so strongly had his grandfather's description of her affected his imagination.

Suddenly his shoulder was tapped behind. He turned about and found Winning at his elbow.

"Why are you not dancing?" said his friend. Reuben replied, with a faltering voice, that he would rather not dance; he knew little more than the steps—had scarcely a notion of a figure.

"Not dance?—then why did you buy the dancing-shoes?"

"Besides, I have no partner. I know nobody—at least, no lady."

"Oh, I'll soon settle that;—come, will you dance with brown sherry, pale sherry, or dry sherry?"

"You are joking," said Reuben, his gravity overcome by his friend's question.

"No,—don't you know that those are our names for the three Miss Barsacs? There is Brown Sherry, the prettiest, dancing with the officer; that cross-looking girl, talking to Mr. Brough yonder, is Dry Sherry; and, stay, there's Pale Sherry actually looking at us, asking us with her eyes. You shall honour her with your hand."

"What is her name?" asked Reuben, in great excitement.

"Blanche," replied Winning, little guessing Reuben's interest in the answer.

Pale Sherry was pale; but, at the same time, very pretty; she was what people commonly call an interesting girl. She had soft grey eyes, which had a particularly earnest and devoted expression in them, when she was talking to you, which was very flattering and very fascinating. Besides, she had a nice figure, and a demure and composed manner, which corresponded admirably with her pale complexion and soft eyes. None of the Barsac girls were mere girls: the eldest was probably twenty-seven, and there was not more than three or four years' difference in standing between the eldest and the youngest. Of course it was condescending of the angelic Blanche to dance with a boy of thirteen; but he was tall for his age, and she acted her part with perfect good-humour and good-nature, keeping him right in the figure as far as she could, and trying to put him as much at his ease as possible. Both were difficult things to do; not only was Reuben's nervous ambition to excel of itself sufficient to lead him astray, but every time his partner's mild, earnest eyes encountered his, he experienced the strangest sensations, and felt himself blushing, he knew not why or wherefore; in fact, he was in love with Blanche before the second part of the dance was over.

"Medlicott dancing!—I should as soon have thought to see Xenophon in a quadrille," said De Tabley—one of the senior boys,—who, being a noodle himself, took a special pleasure in tormenting Reuben for being too wise.

"An ignoramus made that remark," said Winning in his ear; "you ought to know that Xenophon was one of the gayest cavaliers of his time, as well as one of the ablest men."

De Tabley was extinguished, and skulked off to the refreshment-room to console himself with the sandwiches and jellies, for which his capacity was first-rate.

Winning had given Reuben one direction at starting, which was just to observe his partner, and do whatever she did. This rule answered pretty well to a certain extent; but when it was pushed too far, it was not so successful; for whenever Blanche danced, Reuben, being quite bewildered, insisted upon dancing also, and, when she checked him, he was utterly at a loss what to do, and, consequently stood stock-still when it came to his turn to move. This, however, was of no great consequence; but there came a period in the course of the figure when it was Miss Barsac's cue to advance to him, which she did most graciously and encouragingly, holding her frock with the tips of her fingers on each side in the usual manner of ladies dancing alone. It was unnecessary for Reuben to imitate this part of the action, but he was too confused to make very nice distinctions, and, accordingly, when his turn came, he seized his trousers at the hips with both hands, and holding them out as far as he could make them go, advanced in this unusual manner to meet the lady, who found it very hard, of course, to refrain from smiling, particularly as he kept his eyes intently fixed upon her all the time. Others, however, were not so well able or so well disposed to refrain as Blanche was; so that there was a good deal of laughing at poor Reuben's expense, though some of the company thought he had done it out of pleasantry, and gave him credit for being a grave-faced, waggish little fellow.

Happy fellow he was when that quadrille was over, and Miss Barsac suffered him to lead her to a seat. Then Reuben, being more at his ease, thought it his duty to ask her a series of questions, though he could scarcely muster up the courage to do it, or indeed to address her at all. Did she play the piano? She did. Did she sing? Pale Sherry did not sing. Did she draw? Yes. Landscape? No. Flowers? No, no—how could he suspect her of drawing flowers? and she looked at him in that peculiar way of hers, which incontinently brought the foolish rose to his cheeks, as he apologised for such an unlucky guess, and, trying again, hit upon portrait-painting, which could not well have been anything but right. It was then the lady's turn to ask questions, and she was still more catechetical; for she commenced by asking his name, and being a better adept at the art of conversation by queries than he was, she soon distilled from him a multitude of particulars and details about his parents and his early education, in which she certainly seemed to take a great interest, whether she felt it or not. He was drawing her a picture of the Parsonage, and beginning to recover his fluency and feel tolerably comfortable, when Winning came up and asked Pale Sherry to dance. She left Reuben with a smile, and he saw no more of her the whole evening.

It was not a house for books, though in other respects amply and even luxuriantly furnished, or he would have known how to dispose of himself in a corner, while everybody else was thinking of nothing less than reading. After sitting for a while just where Blanche Barsac left him, with his hands before him, just in the way his old Quaker mistress considered the perfection of good manners, he took courage to creep into a room adjoining the ball-room, where there was a whist-party made up; Mr. Brough, his master, and Mrs. Barsac, against Mr. Barsac and an old lady whom he did not know.

That whist-party would have made a good picture. Mr. Brough was a tall man, with regular features, florid complexion, powdered hair, a solemn manner, and, though not a clergyman, dressed like one—in the glossiest black suit and the whitest cambric. Opposite to him was a very old lady in black velvet, with a profusion of old lace hanging about her, and as intent upon the points of the game as if her eternal welfare depended upon the two by honours, which she had just marked with old guineas of the reign of George the First. Barsac, who was now shuffling the cards in canary-coloured gloves, looked social and good natured, but unmistakeably purse-proud; he carried his head consequentially, with his chin cocked up almost in advance of his nose; displayed a superb bouquet in his button-hole, and wore a jet-black wig, which was intended to pass for his own hair, but the fraud was too palpable to impose upon anybody. His wife was a mellow, motherly, brisk and shrewd woman, with sparkling eyes, showy and bustling manners, and worldly all over; you saw at a glance that a ball with her was a business; even a juvenile *fête* had its ulterior practical objects; indeed, Mrs. Barsac was fertile in every sense—she had lots of sons and daughters, of all sizes and ages, and as many projects for every one of them as any mother in Mrs. Gore's novels. She was superbly dressed, like her husband; a diamond star blazed on her forehead, and the rustling of her wide-spread amber brocade was like a breeze in a shrubbery.

Reuben had not been standing there very long, watching the fortunes of the game, of which he was not entirely ignorant, when Mrs. Barsac noticed him, asked him had he been in the refreshment room, and recommended him to go there. He went very obediently, although he did not want refreshment; took something because he thought he was under some sort of obligation to do so, and then returned to the ball-room, where a new dance had in the meantime formed, which included everybody he knew, and left him again to his own meditations. He soon felt himself growing sleepy, and was rubbing his eyes to keep himself awake, when the eldest Miss Barsac—a tall girl, with a supercilious and austere countenance, justifying the nickname the boys had given her,—observed him in passing with another lady, and said, in a tone perfectly audible—

"That child ought to have been in bed an hour ago."

This remark piqued Reuben exceedingly, and had the same effect as if Dry Sherry had thrown a glass of cold water in his face. Determined to show that he was not in the state Miss Barsac supposed, he went immediately and took his place behind Henry Winning, who was now dancing with the bustling and rustling Mrs. Barsac herself, though she protested her dancing days were over.

She probably noticed him again, for Reuben could perceive that she put a question to his friend, in reply to which he was near enough to hear Winning say—

"He is a very clever fellow, and has a wonderful fund of knowledge for his age."

"He knows Latin, Greek, Spanish, French, Arabic, and Persian ; Botany, Zoology, Mathematics, Conchology, Phrenology, and Syntax," said De Tabley, volubly, just returned from stuffing himself with the jellies.

Mrs. Barsac was amused and said—"You boys are so funny and so ill-natured."

Winning looked thunderbolts at De Tabley; but out of consideration for the lady of the house, repressed the indignant repartee that was on his lips.

Reuben could not but suspect that it was for him all these compliments were intended, and not liking his present position he went off again to the refreshment-room, merely because he might as well go there as anywhere else. Before he had been there two minutes, Mr. Brough, his master, perceived him, and concluding that Reuben had been refreshing himself ever since Mrs. Barsac sent him from the card-table, he beckoned him to follow him into a quiet corner, where he read him a severe and solemn lecture upon intemperance, which Reuben endeavoured in vain to save him the trouble of delivering, by trying to explain that he had taken nothing the whole evening but some tea and a Naples biscuit.

Mr. Brough never liked to be interrupted in the course of his admonitions, which were very grave and pompous. Every time that Reuben attempted to speak, he was silenced by the lifted finger and austere regard for the glossy pedagogue, who, when his harangue was over, immediately rose and went back to the whist-table. As Mr. Brough left the room, he met De Tabley returning to it. Mr. Brough patted him playfully on the head, —presumed he had been dancing all the evening.—and told him to go and have some refreshment,—an order which the young gourmand received with profound respect, and proceeded to obey implicitly; but as soon as the schoolmaster was out of hearing he burst out laughing, and told Reuben that this was his fourth visit to the jellies and sandwiches.

But on this occasion there was a formal supper at an early hour, to suit the habits of the juniors, who were the principal part of the company. Reuben had never before seen anything so gorgeous as Mrs. Barsac's supper-table. The plate—the lights—the variety of dishes, substantial and unsubstantial—the piles of fruit—the multiplicity of wines of all colours and vintages—the miracles of pastry—the wonders of confectionary—towers, castles, pyramids, and pagodas—a profusion and splendour which he had never seen in the quiet parish of Underwood—astonished, dazzled, and confused him. At the head of the table presided Mr. Barsac, standing up with a dish of roast ducks before him, which he carved with ostentatious dexterity, still wearing his canary gloves, and pausing at intervals to take wine with this person or that, making little jocular prepared speeches, suggesting madeira to one, hock to another, champagne to a third, and sometimes recommending one of his sherries, which invariably set Mr. Brough's pupils tittering, winking, and nudging each other, for they generally herded together upon these festive occasions, getting as far beyond the ken of the master as they could.

Reuben, however, still attached himself to the side of Winning, who had no object in avoiding Mr. Brough's neighbourhood, and the consequence was, that when Reuben was seated he found himself close to his master, who ruled the roast at the foot of the table, as pompously, but not so rhetorically, as Mr. Barsac at the other end. He was not the boy to eat a surreptitious supper, or he might have managed it easily; so that, to avoid again attracting Mr. Brough's unjust suspicions, he affected to have no appetite, and went to bed supperless that festive night, although, in truth, the poor fellow was very hungry. Nor did he sleep the better for having nothing but his wrongs to digest, but occupied himself alternately with concocting twenty little speeches which he felt he ought to have made to Miss Barsac, and framing a spirited retort to demolish De Tabley the next time he should renew his impertinences. These were probably his earliest efforts in eloquence, and it is not unlikely that his model-orator that night was Mr. Barsac with his canary gloves.

CHAPTER III.

MORE FESTIVITY AT MRS. BARSAC'S.

"REUBEN," said Winning, the next morning, "a ball is thrown away on you; you can't expect Mrs. Barsac ever to invite you again."

"Why so?" said Reuben.

"Why, you neither danced nor eat supper; Mrs. Barsac keeps a list of the men who don't dance, and Mr. Barsac takes a note of those who despise his suppers."

"I shall dance more," said Reuben, "when I am familiar with the figures; I think I shall soon understand the principle at all events."

Winning laughed at the principle of a quadrille; and Reuben said he thought there was a principle in everything, to which Winning assented, though he laughed again.

"But you surely had no difficulty in catching the principle of supper. What have you to say for yourself on that head?"

Reuben then related what took place the preceding evening between himself and Mr. Brough; how he had been lectured and reprimanded for *gourmandise*, when in fact he had taken next to nothing.

Winning was distressed at this story, and undertook to set his friend right in Mr. Brough's opinion. This he took an opportunity of doing that very day, and Mr. Brough sent for Reuben and very handsomely expressed his regret at having hastily misjudged him, adding some profound common-place remarks on the hazards of circumstantial evidence, by which the safety of innocence had often been compromised, even under the direction of the ablest men that ever adorned the bench. Reuben went his way with a high opinion of his preceptor's magnanimity and enlightenment. Mrs. Barsac's ball gave him a great many new ideas; he had only heard of balls before as young Norval had heard of battles; in a long letter to his mother he gave her as minute an account of the *fête* as if it had been the first thing of the kind ever known in England; and amused her exceedingly by his innocent remarks on the ladies' dresses, his mistakes in dancing, and the absurd names of the three Miss Barsacs. Of Blanche he said wonderfully little, only observing that in his opinion she seemed to justify all that his grandfather had said about her. There was good reason to think that he had originally intended to say much more, for there was an extensive erasure in this part of his letter, as if he had not found words suitable to express certain ideas in his mind. In fact, the entire letter was written altogether to gratify his mother, because she had expressly requested him to give her a full account of his first introduction to the Barsacs; no doubt he had tried to convey the feelings uppermost in his mind in connection with the ball, and had either failed to do so, or clothed them in language only too forcible.

The Barsacs had another gay party shortly after, but it was not especially juvenile, and the only boys formally invited of Mr. Brough's school were Winning, Vigors, and De Tabley. Reuben was seriously afraid his name had been inserted in those awful lists of which Winning had told him: he received an invitation, however, at the eleventh hour, for which he was accidentally indebted to the interest he took in Gothic architecture, and a smattering he had of drawing. On the evening of the party, to console himself for Mrs. Barsac's omission to include him in her select list, he determined to execute a design he had formed some time before, to make a sketch of the cathedral for his mother; so taking his portfolio and pencil, he posted off to that venerable pile, and having chosen what he considered the best point of view, he was so busily engaged at his work that he took very little notice of the circle of urchins, which the oddity of his employment in so public a place gathered about him in a few moments. However, before his sketch was quite finished, another class of spectators were amongst the observers of his artistic enthusiasm, for hearing some female voices close by him, and one or two pleasant tittering laughs, he looked up and found the whole family of the Barsacs (at least the female portion of them) standing within a yard of his elbow. Fortunately his sketch was nearly complete, for to have put another touch to it that evening would have been utterly impossible. He put up his pencils in a hurry, not without some blushing, and answered confusedly the numerous little questions with which the ladies overwhelmed him, without indeed giving him much time to reply, had he been ever so self-possessed. Mrs. Barsac was gracious and encouraging; her daughter, the brunette, was good-natured too, but it was her laugh which had originally attracted Reuben's attention, and she had scarcely done laughing yet. The eldest girl said very little, but what she did say was supercilious and unpleasant.

Blanche alone of the sisters regarded the young artist and his work with interest; she commended his drawing highly, said it was executed with spirit and cleverness; and induced her mother and her good-humoured sister to concur in the same opinion. Reuben soon revived in the warmth of this agreeable approbation, and he was completely set up again when Mrs. Barsac invited him to join her party, politely apologizing for not having asked him before. He walked palpitating by the side of Blanche discovering new fascinations in her every moment, and did not recollect in the first happy flutter of his spirits that she was an artist as well as himself; but this community of tastes soon became a fertile topic of conversation, and Reuben was soon so deep in the subject of the fine arts as to ask if Miss Barsac had read Sir Joshua Reynolds's Discourses. She smiled very sweetly, as she frankly owned she had never even heard of the work, upon which Reuben with *empressement*, offered to lend them to her,— an offer she graciously accepted just as they reached the house.

Reuben went back to Finchley to put himself in ball costume, and there he found a letter from home awaiting him, which, impatient as he was to be at Blanche's side again, he read conscientiously to the last syllable. The reading of his letters, and the making of his toilette, occupied a considerable time, and when both operations were performed, he had to hunt for Sir Joshua Reynolds's Discourses, which detained him a good deal longer, for he was not in the habit of keeping his things very methodically. The result was that he found the festivities already commenced when he returned to Mrs. Barsac's: one dance had already taken place; another had just been arranged, and when Reuben entered he made a great sensation, greater indeed than he was ambitious of making, for with his books in his hands he had to traverse the whole circle (hemmed in by the dancers awaiting the signal to move), in order to find the fair lady for whom so unusual a ball-room offering was intended.

He probably did not observe the smiles of which he was the occasion, but he could hardly have failed to hear some of the little jocular remarks which accompanied them; however, his enthusiasm, and singleness of purpose, carried him through all, and he presented Blanche with the volumes, under a perfect conviction that no bouquet of the most rare and exquisite flowers would have been half so acceptable to her. While she was depositing the books in a corner, sedulously attended by Reuben, Mrs. Barsac happening to pass at the moment inquired what books they were, and when Reuben told her they contained Reynolds's Discourses, she probably mistook Reynolds for a divine, for " I doubt very much," she observed, with a gracious smile on Reuben, " if they are to be compared with the discourses of your grandpapa."

Reuben would have enjoyed this second party much more than he did, if there had not been a whisper in the room that the Dean was expected in the course of the evening. None of his school-fellows were fond of meeting his grandfather at Mrs. Barsac's. The Dean in a drawing-room was always like an eagle in a dove-cot; he looked at a ball like a clerical magistrate about to disperse a mob; but it was not to the dancing he objected particularly, for he was rather in favour of all such innocent pastimes; the music was what he hated, because it prevented him from holding forth, or drowned his voice when he raised it. If there could have been dancing without music, he was willing to let the young people dance till morning, provided he was satisfied of the strength of the rafters, and not jostled by the waltzers, which made him furious. The Dean was rough with most people, sometimes even with women, but he was invariably rough with school-boys; he knocked them about without ceremony, examined and catechised them in all companies, and in the middle of dinner, or at a tea-table, would question them in the Horatian metres. When he saw any of the scholars of Finchley at Mrs. Barsac's, talking to one of her daughters, for instance, and particularly ambitious to shine and to play the man, he was sure to flout him; and above all if the poor boy happened to wear white gloves and was asking a lady to dance. Then the Dean would make the most unpleasant observations, sometimes turn upon Mrs. Barsac, abuse her roundly, and declare that she was destroying the discipline of Mr. Brough's school, and ruining the rising generation.

But the gaieties of the present occasion were not interrupted by his grandfather, further than the damp which the continual apprehension of his appearance threw over some of the company. Mrs. Barsac herself seemed nervous. Blanche declined to dance, but she permitted and even encouraged Reuben to sit beside her and talk about books, which she seemed to like to talk about; or rather to hear him expatiating on, for in truth her share in the conversation was little more than that of an attentive and flattering listener. Sometimes, however, she appeared to have little short fits of abstraction, and now and then glanced like her mother anxiously at the door. Reuben easily guessed who the ogre was, whose expected arrival alarmed the fair Blanche as it did other people. He felt extremely vexed at his grandfather; yet sometimes he was almost half inclined to allay Blanche's apprehensions, by apprising her of the high opinion the rough old gentleman had of her. Wanting the courage to do this, he asked her in what part of the house the library was; he had not yet seen it.

Blanche smiled at the notion of a library, and said, "her papa had very few books indeed."

Reuben did not conceal his surprise at this confession as well as it would have been polite to do.

"I feared it would shock you," continued his fair friend, "but we are not at all intellectual or reading people in this house:— of course you have a nice library at home."

"Well, indeed," said Reuben, "I cannot exactly say we have any particular library, but we have a great many books in one place or another; there are some in the parlour, some in the hall, and a good many in my mother's room. But my grandfather has a superb library at Westbury;" and then he asked Blanche had she ever been there.

She had been at Westbury, and expressed her surprise that Reuben had not.

"My grandfather has been making extensive alterations," he said.

"So I am told," said Blanche absently.

Reuben desired to know the nature of the improvements the Dean was making.

"I understand very little about building," said Blanche, rising, "but here comes papa who will tell you all about it;" and so saying she rather abruptly handed Reuben over to Mr. Barsac, who, with great pomposity, led him into a room called the music-room, where there were lying on a table a set of maps and plans, not only of the Dean's improvements at Westbury, but also of the more extensive projects in which he was engaged jointly with the rich wine-merchant. Reuben surveyed these charts with the utmost astonishment and curiosity. He had heard vague statements of his grandfather's connection with Barsac in building speculations, but he had no notion of the extent of them. The Hereford plans included a terrace called Wyndham terrace after the Dean, and a square not yet named, which Mr. Barsac said he hoped would be called Wyndham likewise.

"I hope so too," said Reuben.

"At all events, I trust it will not be called Barsac Squa e: that would never answer," added the merchant, pronouncing the words "Barsac Square," with an evident relish and enjoyment which showed that he coveted nothing so much as the honour and glory which he professed himself so anxious to avoid.

"I trust so, too, Sir," said Reuben.

"But I trust it will," said De Tabley, coming up: "Barsac Square sounds a thousand times better than Wyndham Square, but Medlicott would call everything Wyndham; Wyndham Square, Wyndham Terrace, Wyndham Lane, Wyndham everything."

"No, indeed," said Reuben, mildly, "I should do no such thing; I am not so foolish."

"I must say I agree with Mr. Medlicott in this instance," said Barsac; but though he agreed with Medlicott, he smiled upon De Tabley, and graciously conducted him to the refreshment-room, leaving the too candid Reuben to shift for himself.

"What will you have?" asked the merchant.

"What do you recommend?" said De Tabley.

"Well, suppose we begin with the pâté de Perigord." And he helped him handsomely.

"A very good pie," said De Tabley; "I should think Perigord must be a delightful place to live in, wherever it is."

"Near Bordeaux," said Mr. Barsac; "you have heard of the celebrated Talleyrand, Prince of Perigord.—So a glass of claret will be very proper along with it. That's the comet vintage; by-the-by, I should be glad if your uncle knew we had some of it left, it is a great favourite of his."

"I shall be writing to him to-morrow," said De Tabley; "I'll take care to mention it."

"Some ham and chicken?" said the merchant: "I shall have some myself: and now, if you please, let us take a glass of champagne together."

"A very good notion," said De Tabley, and when he had dispatched the ham and chicken, he returned the compliment, and proposed a glass of champagne to the merchant.

"You take champagne," said Barsac, "I'll join you in a glass of dry sherry."

De Tabley laughed, and looked about him for Winning or Vigors to wink at. Barsac thought he was amused by the epithet "dry" applied to the sherry, and gave him a little lecture upon wines, to which the promising young gourmand listened with the gravest attention,—helping himself meanwhile, however, to a lobster salad within his reach. Hearing that there was such a wine as dry champagne as well as dry sherry, he was curious to taste it, but there happened to be none upon the table.

"I dare say you have some in the cellar," said De Tabley; and he pressed Barsac to such a degree, that he actually went to his cellars and brought forth a flask of dry champagne to gratify the curiosity of his impertinent guest, whose vanity made him pronounce a high panegyric upon it, though in truth he liked the sweet wine better.

Barsac soon saw the necessity of drawing De Tabley away from the temptation into which he had led him; and this was no easy matter to accomplish. At length he effected it, but not until the incorrigible young gourmand had returned to the sweet champagne, and was beginning again to ogle the Perigord.

"See what you lost by your simplicity, and I must say by your rudeness," he whispered Reuben, whom he immediately went in search of. "I thought Barsac Square just as absurd as you did, but I had the wit and good manners not to say so."

"What did I lose?" asked Reuben.

"Dry champagne," said De Tabley, with an air of great importance, "though I confess I think the other pleasanter stuff; but the best of it was that I made the old cock go down to the cellar for it: he brought up a flask expressly for me. At the same time, I know very well he wanted me to recommend the wine to my uncle, who gets the house immense custom in the clubs he belongs to in London."

"Then all I lost was the dry champagne?" said Reuben.

"Old Barsac gave me such a magnificent supper. I had ham and chicken, lobster salad, two goes at a Perigord pie. Perigord is a place in Bordeaux, famous for its pies; they are made by a celebrated fellow of the name of Tally—something: Tallyho, or Talleyrand, a prince—you may laugh, but Mr. Barsac himself told me so. I had a magnificent supper; I have got a capital head."

"For wine," said Reuben.

"Yes, for wine, as every great man ought to have," replied De Tabley. "I have heard my uncle often say so; I wish you could hear the anecdotes he tells of Pitt, and Fox, and Lord Eldon, and all the most celebrated characters in English history."

"Not all," said Reuben.

"All the jolly fellows," said De Tabley.

Reuben said something disparaging of the pleasures of the bottle.

"Don't abuse wine in this house," said De Tabley, "or perhaps you will never be invited again; the Barsacs have an eye to the main chance, let me tell you, every one of them, even Pale Sherry herself, sentimental as she looks."

Reuben boiled with indignation.

"I can tell you more," said the other, excited by the wine he had drunk; "you made a monstrous ass of yourself to-night, coming here with your hands full of books, as if it was the Philosophical Society. Everybody laughed at you, even Pale Sherry herself—I saw her; she would have preferred a bouquet of roses and pinks, I can tell you."

Reuben was greatly provoked by these remarks, and would perhaps not have controlled his feelings sufficiently, if Winning had not fortunately approached at the moment, conducting Blanche to the refreshment-room. As Winning passed, he good-naturedly proposed to Reuben to join them, remembering the Lent he had kept on a former occasion, and determined he now should have compensation. Seated between his considerate friend and the young lady he so greatly admired, Medlicott was in high spirits, and ended his evening with a good supper.

CHAPTER IV.

THE VICAR'S ACCOUNT OF THE BARSACS. REUBEN SHOWS A TALENT FOR MUSIC. HIS FIRST AND HIS LAST PUGILISTIC CONTEST.

THE following day, another chronicle of the gay doings at Mrs. Barsac's was faithfully dispatched to the Vicarage. Mrs. Medlicott was charmed by the attention paid to her son; but the Vicar recollected the Dean's observations, and wanted to know how balls and suppers were to be reconciled with the business of the school. Mrs. Medlicott wished her son to receive the education of a man of the world; her husband shrugged his shoulders, and said he had sent his son to school to Mr. Brough, not to Mrs. Barsac.

Reuben's correspondence with his mother recalls us for a few moments to Underwood opportunely, for we shall hear the Vicar giving old Hannah Hopkins an account of the Barsacs, which will help us to a better acquaintance with that worthy family. The reading of Reuben's letters was not always an affair of the strictest domestic privacy, which may serve as his excuse if he did not upon every occasion unbosom himself on paper, even to his father and mother. Sometimes Mr. Pigwidgeon, the apothecary, was invited to the reading of a letter from Hereford; sometimes it was only Hannah and Mary Hopkins, or old Matthew Cox, the tobacconist. The Quakeresses were present when the letter arrived with the account of Mrs. Barsac's second fête, and Hannah was interested and inquisitive about the people who were so good to her old pupil. Possibly, though belonging to such an unworldly sect as the Quakers professedly are, and a woman who had even been a minister, and lifted up her voice in the Meeting, old Hannah had not thoroughly divested herself of all human sympathy and womanly concern in its gay doings and wicked ways. There will still cling some little portion of earth about us all, even about the disciples of Fox and sisters of Mrs. Fry.

"I'll tell thee all I know, Hannah, and it's not much," said the Vicar. He had fallen into the habit of thee-and-thou-ing it with his Quaker friends, without the least approach to mockery of their personal pronouns.

Hannah Hopkins was sitting rigidly perpendicular on a rustic seat in the garden, beneath a walnut-tree, knitting, as usual, most industriously. It was an employment she seldom intermitted during the day, except when she was eating her meals, or collecting flowers and grasses. Mary was not far off, knitting also. There was a little table near Hannah, with a plate of strawberries upon it, and Reuben's letter, which his mother had just been reading.

"I am ready to hear thee, friend Thomas," said the Quaker mother; "thou art always instructive or entertaining."

"Generally both, mother," said Mary, who was burning in secret to hear the promised revelations, notwithstanding the plainness of her bonnet.

The Vicar, thus complimented and encouraged, proceeded to say that the Barsacs were the people who understood the art so well of making pleasure and profit go hand in hand.

"Merry and wise," said Hannah.

Mrs. Barsac's system, the Vicar went on to state, was (as far as he understood it), to give balls to marry her daughters, while her husband gave sumptuous dinners to advertise and recommend his wines. What would be extravagance with other people was thrift with the wine-merchant of Hereford. For every glass of champagne that sparkled at his board (here the Vicar digressed on the subject of champagne, to explain it to the Quakeresses), Mr. Barsac sold a flask, or perhaps a case of it. People had a decided interest in dealing with a wine-merchant who gave them handsome entertainments; it was an abatement in the price of the wines; in fact, a dinner was both an advertisement and a description of discount. The balls were more to advertise the daughters, an article of which Mrs. Barsac had a large stock on her hands, as her husband had wine in his vaults; but there was a great difference, said the Vicar, between the two commodities, for the older the wine grew it was the more in demand, whereas with the girls it was not precisely the same thing.

Here Mary Hopkins laughed. I believe it was the cautious way in which Mr. Medlicott put the distinction between women and wine that overset her gravity, but it was never very difficult to do it.

"Laugh and be fat," said old Hannah, an injunction which she repeated a dozen times a day, and very superfluously, inasmuch as her daughter had already very dutifully complied with it.

"Well, Hannah," said the Vicar, "I have now told you what the world says of Mr. and Mrs. Barsac."

"There are wheels within wheels," said the old Quakeress, shaking her head horizontally several times.

"Dost thee believe all the world says, friend Thomas?" said Mary, recovering her sobriety.

"The world, Mary, has a very lively fancy, and a very busy tongue," said the Vicar. "My private opinion is that the Barsacs are very good-natured people, and if their good-nature and gaiety make them richer instead of poorer, I don't see that any body has a right to complain. For my own part, theirs is just the house where I should feel myself most comfortable, for I never could enjoy myself anywhere, when I had reason to think my friends were committing a folly, or involving themselves in difficulties to entertain me."

"And I am sure," added Mrs. Medlicott, "it is the purest good-nature to invite the boys, who neither buy Mr. Barsac's wine, nor are likely to propose for his daughters."

The truth was, however, that the attentions paid to Mr.

Brough's scholars were chiefly in furtherance of the system which the world very justly imputed to the wine-merchant and his wife. Their invitations were by no means indiscriminate, but confined to those boys whose fathers were customers of the firm, or with whose families the managing Mrs. Barsac thought it would promote her interest to be acquainted or connected. Thus De Tabley was never omitted, because he was nephew of Sir John De Tabley, a beau and bon-vivant of the old school, whose influence procured for Barsac the profitable custom of the Noodle's, and Boodle's, and one or two other London clubs. Winning was nearly related to a Mr. St. Stephen, who was a bencher of the Inner Temple, through whom it was not impossible but that Barsac might some day or other be appointed wine merchant to that honourable and learned society. Several of the lads (Vigors for instance) were sons of beneficed clergymen in the neighbourhood; and as to Reuben, he had the double claim of being nephew to Mrs. Mountjoy, connected with the Barsacs by marriage, and grandson of Dean Wyndham, who besides being actually a customer, was from his rank in the Church a man whom Mrs. Barsac would have probably courted upon that account alone. Of course if any young man was particularly handsome, amusing, or recommended by Mr. Brough, he was noticed by Mrs. Barsac without reference to the mercantile interest. Winning would probably have been a favourite under any circumstances. There was Hyacinth Primrose too, who had nothing to support him but his good looks and his flow of spirits. There were also one class of boys who were seldom or ever countenanced by Mrs. Barsac, and these were the sons of families who were in any trade which she considered less dignified than traffic in wine. The Vicar understood the Barsacs very imperfectly, although he undertook to give Mrs. Hopkins an account of them.

A shower now began to patter among the leaves of the walnut tree, which served the purposes of a green umbrella for some time tolerably well, but when the drops began to increase in weight and number they forced their way through the canopy, and one at length falling on Mrs. Hopkins's knitting, and another with a splash on Reuben's letter, the *séance* was broken up, and the party retreated into the house as fast as they could, Mary running with the plate of strawberries and laughing all the time. Let us take the same opportunity of returning to Hereford, where we shall find Reuben increasing the number of his accomplishments by picking up a few notes of music.

3*

Meeting the French shoemaker in the streets one day, Adolphe gracefully saluted him, hoped his shoes gave him contentment, and asked when he would do him the honour of calling again and listening to an air on the flageolet. Reuben said he would call the next day. He kept his engagement, and the result was that from a listener he became a learner, and commenced flageolet-playing himself. After a few clandestine lessons, during which he improved his knowledge of French also, our hero began to reproach himself with concealing his new accomplishment from Winning, and also with occupying the time of a poor tradesman without reward; but when he mentioned the latter scruple to Adolphe, there was an end of it; he professed shoemaking, not music; but even if it had been otherwise, the glory of having so promising a scholar would pay him for his pains twenty times over; besides Monsieur Reuben would recommend his shoes; and through him and M. Vinning, the custom of all the school would be secured for his little commerce.

The first intimation Winning had of Reuben's flageolet-playing was unfortunately not from his friend and *protégé* himself. De Tabley was jeering at Medlicott one morning on the now threadbare topic of his multifarious acquirements, when Winning came up and told him impetuously that he would suffer no more of his impertinence upon that point; that Medlicott was under his protection, and protect him he was resolved to do. It would be long enough before any one would taunt De Tabley with knowing too many things, or knowing any one thing decently. "By the by," he added, "I recollect your insolence at Mrs. Barsac's ball; if I had not had a lady on my arm, I would have called you then to a severe account."

"I only said what was true," said De Tabley, moving to some little distance from Winning, for his courage was of that kind that is commonly called pot-valiant.

"It was not true," said Winning, drily.

"It was," repeated De Tabley, "and I might have added music into the bargain."

"You would then have added another falsehood," said Winning.

"Why Medlicott is taking lessons on the flute," retorted the other.

"De Tabley, I shall be obliged to thrash you."

De Tabley moved a little further off, muttering—"It's true nevertheless, and you know it as well as I do."

Winning heard the muttered speech and dashed at him; but he had only given him one blow, which merely knocked his hat down over his eyes, when Reuben Medlicott rushing forward caught his arm, crying—

"Stop, Winning,—let him alone—what he says is true—at least nearly true—only it's the flageolet, not the flute."

Winning turned round amazed upon Medlicott, and glaring on him like a tiger.

"Flute or flageolet, how do you come to be learning it without my knowledge and permission,—who's your music-master? answer this moment—the truth, the whole truth, and nothing but the truth, or I'll give you what I was going to give De Tabley, whose pardon I beg most humbly."

"Hear me patiently," said Reuben, "and I'll tell you all about it; I was going to tell you all, when I was anticipated."

"Don't make your case worse than it is," said Winning; "it's bad enough as it stands,—follow me, I'll examine you in private."

De Tabley had heard of our hero's proceedings from the very best authority, namely Adolphe himself, from whom Winning would have heard the same story himself, had he chanced to have wanted a pair of shoes.

Winning was very much disposed, upon the whole of the matter, to give Reuben a drubbing for want of straightforwardness and candour. However, he was as merciful as he was strong, and spared his delinquent subject; ordering him, however, either to give up the flageolet forthwith, or obtain the principal's sanction for continuing the shoemaker's pupil. Reuben chose the latter side of the alternative, and obtained the permission without much difficulty, no other conditions being imposed than an inquiry into the moral character of M. Adolphe, and the equally proper step of applying for the consent of his parents.

His acquaintance with the French shoemaker occasioned a ludicrous mistake, and involved him in one of the few personal rencontres he was ever so unlucky as to be engaged in. A group of boys were standing talking under a colonnade one showery morning, waiting for the weather to clear up. They first talked of their fathers, and then of their grandfathers—at least as many as had grandfathers to talk of. De Tabley said his grandfather had been a judge. Vigors said his was a physician, and other boys made similar statements. The light-hearted Primrose said his father was a painter, and his grandfather a poet.

"Is a poet a profession?" said another.

"It's a bad trade, I believe," said Primrose, laughing; " at least my grandsire found it so, for he left my father nothing but his poems, which with my father's pallet will descend to me; so that at all events I shall have two estates, such as they are."

After the boys had laughed at this speech, one of them named Peters, looked excessively knowing, and said there was a boy in the school whose grandfather was a barber. Some laughed doubtingly, and some cried, "name, name." Peters at first refused, but upon being taunted with being afraid to speak out, for fear of being thrashed by the barber's descendant; he declared that he meant Medlicott. De Tabley called instantly to Reuben, only too happy to tell him of the serious charge brought against him by Peters.

Reuben laughed, and said he thought they all knew that Dean Wyndham was his grandfather.

"That we know very well," said De Tabley; "but I presume you sport two grandfathers;—at least I do."

"So do I," said several boys, chuckling at De Tabley's wit.

Now it happened that Reuben knew very little of his paternal grandfather, except that he had been in trade; so when he was pressed to say what station in life that venerable gentleman had filled, the only answer he could think of was that he had been in business.

"Then Peters is right enough, I have no doubt," said De Tabley, insolently.

"He is not," said Reuben, glowing like a live coal.

Peters repeated his assertion; Reuben repeated his contradiction.

"Give him the lie," said a friendly boy at his elbow.

Reuben, altogether unused to rude language, hesitated.

"He has the barber's blood in him, for a thousand pounds," said De Tabley.

Reuben was now stung to the quick, and instantly pronounced the decisive monosyllable.

They fought three awkward rounds, Reuben with the disadvantage of being new to such encounters, and having only one boy to back him; while Peters, with little more experience in pugilism, had the advantage of being the general favourite. In the second round one of Reuben's blue eyes was metamorphosed into a black one, but Peters in return received a random salutation on the nose, which was a fair exchange for the damage he had inflicted. Winning came up just as the third commenced,

There was no time to inquire how the quarrel originated. Winning merely took his place among the spectators, but that was a great point for Reuben, who, being now supported by the presence of his patron, as well as by the justice of his quarrel, speedily vanquished his antagonist, who had no great stomach for blows.

"Now," said Winning, "what has all this been about?"

De Tabley told him the whole story, and Peters said that his authority was Adolphe, the French shoemaker.

"I think," said Winning, "Medlicott himself is a better authority on a matter of the kind than Adolphe or any one else can possibly be. The whole affair is supremely ridiculous; let us go to Adolphe, and find out how the mistake arose."

The matter was easily explained. It arose out of a confused account the shoemaker had received from his sister Louise, of the hair-cutting scene at the Vicarage the night before Reuben left home for school.

Adolphe was so profuse of apologies for having retailed the story to Peters, and in such an abyss of affliction at the consequences of his indiscretion, particularly when he saw his pupil's black eye, that Reuben's resentment lasted a very short time indeed.

Yet his black eye was a serious disaster, for while his face was still disfigured with it, the Barsacs invited Winning and him to a family dinner. Reuben repined bitterly at not being in a condition to accept an invitation which flattered him more than any he had yet received, and over and over repeated his injunctions to his friend to assure both Mr. and Mrs. Barsac that the written excuse he had sent, pleading the effects of an accident, was a *bonâ fide* one. What he secretly dreaded most was that Blanche Barsac should think he preferred any pleasure in the world to the light of her sweet eyes, which would, indeed, have been doing him great injustice; for the saint in the song was not more diligent to shun the eyes of the hapless Kathleen than Reuben had been to pursue Blanche's, ever since he had first basked in their lustre. He had not, indeed, been often successful. The hours of business seemed often to have been expressly arranged to cross his more agreeable occupations; nay, even those of recreation were unaccommodating enough; for he was as much at Winning's disposal as Mr. Brough's, and the two taskmasters appeared on some occasions in a conspiracy to thwart him. Since the second ball at Mrs. Barsac's, he had never seen Blanche but twice,—once in the dusk of the evening, walking with a bevy of ladies and an old gentleman, very like his grandfather; and again, coming out of the Cathedral after divine service, when he even touched her dress, though in the crowd she was not aware of his presence. Nothing provoked Reuben more than the stupid system Mr. Brough had of taking his boys to the Church of All Saints instead of the Cathedral, where the service was so much more solemnly performed, and where the Barsacs invariably went.

Misfortune, indeed, may be said to have persecuted Reuben at this epoch; for when the next festivity took place at the wine-merchant's, and there was no black eye to prevent him from sharing it, Blanche was from home, on some visit to relations, as she had often been when poor Reuben was running in all directions to catch a glimpse of her.

It was most probably about this period that Reuben's young brain, excited by the action of his susceptible heart, began first to secrete that particular humour called poetry, a certain quantity of which (be the quality what it may) is supposed by some philosophers to exist in the head of every man born of woman. It is not very clear, however, whether he wrote poetry before he wrote prose, or whether the productions came forth in the reverse order. Probably the two fountains within him began to flow much about the same time; for Hyacinth Primrose had unquestionably commenced distinguishing himself both in prose and rhyme, and it was not likely that the versatile and imitative Reuben was far behind him in the one accomplishment more than the other. Reuben and Primrose fraternised early. Among other enterprises, they established a manuscript magazine, of which they were joint editors, and almost the sole contributors; so that, between the business of the school and the business they made for themselves, they had work enough on their hands for their leisure hours, especially Reuben, who had his flageolet to practise and Blanche to think of into the bargain. The business of the school, however, was not neglected, for both Reuben and Hyacinth loved the classics. Reuben's first essay of any length in verse was a translation of the story of Pyramus and Thisbe, which, in point of merit, challenged comparison with the drama of the same name, enacted by Mr. Bottom and his company,— a drama which is believed, upon valid grounds, to be the work of Shakspeare himself. Neither Mr. Brough nor Henry Winning, therefore, had any ground for complaint, and neither of them did complain,—Mr. Brough because he knew nothing about the literary labours in question, and Winning because he was extremely busy himself, and his good sense pointed out the folly of interfering too much in the character of a Mentor, even with a boy whom he loved as he did Reuben.

CHAPTER V.

A CHAPTER OF GOOD ADVICE AND OF GOOD INTENTIONS.

THE time, indeed, soon came for Henry Winning to leave school for college. A brilliant career was evidently before him; for to talent he united industry, and to both high principle and frank popular manners. He had a manly person, moreover, a good constitution, and a good voice, so that he possessed the physical as well as the intellectual qualities which the bar requires; for that was the profession upon which, no less by his own inclination than by the advice of his relative and guardian, Mr. St. Stephen, he had fixed his choice. Winning was sorry to part with Reuben, appreciating his amiable disposition, and recognising his abilities while he perceived the radical faults of his character, and had done all in his power to correct them.

"You are too versatile and too squeezable, my dear fellow," he said, as they strolled in the fields together the day before their separation; "those are your defects, if it is not presumptuous in me to tell you of them."

With the greatest sincerity, Reuben thanked him for taking so friendly a liberty.

"You take impressions too readily, and pursue too many objects, not reflecting that life is so short that there is no more than time for a fair degree of success in some one leading pursuit. *Ars longa, vita brevis*—you remember that pregnant aphorism of Hippocrates. What I now say to you is not any wisdom of my own, for I possess none and I pretend to none; it is what my guardian, Mr. St. Stephen, one of the ablest and most successful men of the day, has always impressed upon my mind, and firmly believing in its truth and importance, I would be glad, my dear fellow, to impress it in turn upon yours. I have observed, although I have said very little to you on the subject, how Primrose has been influencing you of late; you have been writing essays and making verses because he does so, just as you took up the flageolet because your shoemaker played it; in fact, you possess a great many talents, a facility for picking up almost everything that you see done by any body; and pardon me if I add, that you seem more disposed to hearken to the praises of shallow people who call you a clever fellow for all this, than to believe me, for example, when I try to show you the dangers of it."

Reuben pleaded guilty to every charge but that of swallowing the sort of compliments alluded to by his friend; but probably his conscience smote him that there was something even in that accusation not altogether unfounded in truth.

Reuben had as yet scarcely thought of a profession. The Church had always been his father's plan for him, but the subject had not received mature consideration, either from himself or his parents. There seemed time enough to discuss the question in the case of a boy under sixteen. Winning, however, now spoke of it in his direct practical way, wishing to discover whether Medlicott had any strong leaning towards any particular vocation, and hoping that, like himself, he would decide in favour of the Law. But neither law, physic, nor divinity had as yet seized hold of Reuben's imagination. He thought it likely that the Church would eventually be his destiny; but he was equally disposed to the bar, and he had no decided dislike to the notion of physic. Such ideas of a career as Reuben had were of the most confused, but most high-flown and disinterested character. He had no notion of emolument at all, or of prosecuting any pursuit with a view to make money by it. Winning, although his character was ingenuous, and had even a noble strain, had already caught the worldly spirit, without which worldly success is not very easily attained; but Medlicott had not a conception of lucre. In his pure romantic mind, divinity was indeed divine, and every other calling was almost as ethereal as divinity: when he thought of the law, it was only as the science of justice, unpolluted by the notion of a fee; and when medicine took its turn in his cogitations, the notion he had of a physician's life was a sort of Quixotic ramble through the world, tilting with disease and pestilence, out of mere unadulterated philanthropy.

It was very clear that the time was not yet come for coupling the wisdom of the serpent with the innocence of the dove in young Medlicott's understanding. Winning, however, was far from ridiculing or despising him for this. On the contrary, he could not help thinking to himself how few boys he had ever met with who were not more or less infected prematurely with the sordid spirit of life; and though he would have wished Reuben's head a little harder, he found an attraction in his rare simplicity, and parted from him with a feeling of strong and tender attachment.

"Well, Reuben," was his last observation, "as to the profession, you have lost no time; it is a subject on which the minds of most people waver a considerable time before they fix; your present business is the knowledge and preparation equally necessary for all professions. Mind that steadily. *Hoc age*—another pregnant maxim; let me hear from you; I shall be backwards and forwards a good deal between Cambridge and Lincoln's Inn."

The young men parted affectionately, in a few hours after the preceding conversation, and the next day, in the same place, Reuben was sauntering with Hyacinth Primrose, the poet's grandson, repeating to him the sage counsels he had received from his friend; resolving himself to be guided by them rigidly and unswervingly for the future, and deeply impressed with the duty of making Primrose a convert to them also. Hyacinth was, indeed, profoundly impressed for a minute or two with the sound wisdom of Winning's remonstrances, and pulling out a pocket Shakspeare, introduced Reuben to that splendid passage in "Troilus and Cressida," where Ulysses, in a strain so wise and eloquent, recommends the virtue of perseverance:

> "Perseverance, dear my lord,
> keeps honour bright. To have done is to hang
> Quite out of fashion. Take the instant way,
> For honour travels in a strait so narrow,
> Where one but goes abreast. Keep the path,
> For emulation has a thousand sons
> That one by one pursue: if you give way,
> Or hedge aside from the direct forthright,
> Like to an entered tide they all rush by,
> And leave you hindmost."

Reuben, to whom the works of the great dramatist were yet an unworked mine, was delighted with the aptness of this quotation, and borrowed the book from Primrose to make himself master of the entire of the play containing it. Hyacinth was enthusiastic on the subject of Shakspeare, and had a rhapsody in his praise at his fingers' ends; how he was an encyclopædia of poetry, an armoury of philosophy, a library of knowledge, a magazine of thought, a body of divinity. Reuben soon fell into the same transports. Primrose and he were proofs that a man may be mad about wisdom without being wise, just as he may be wild about poetry and wit, without being either a wit or a poet.

As an invalid, when he dismisses one doctor, usually sends for another, or as a sultan, having bow-stringed his vizier, promotes some one else to the post, so did Reuben Medlicott, after the loss of Winning, finding a bosom friend and bookmate indispensable, select the light-hearted and literary Hyacinth Primrose, to fill those important offices about his person; an unfortunate choice, but a very excusable one, as Primrose was one of the most intellectual boys in the school,—in fact, the only boy of abilities and tastes akin to Reuben's, after Winning had left Finchley.

The volatility of the new minister was of a livelier description than Reuben's, who at this period of his life was rather a *penseroso*, and except when he was in his loquacious mood, enjoyed the mirth of his companions in a sort of passive melancholy way, that was partly his temperament, but not altogether, perhaps, free from affectation. Primrose was always gay, always *riant;* full of pleasantry sometimes malicious, generally good-natured; he saw every object in a rose-coloured light; and was determined to prosecute literature to please himself, while he studied the law to please his relations.

"I'll read law," he said. "I'll make myself a lawyer, a black-letter lawyer; I don't at all despair of being a judge; but I don't pretend that I have any love for the profession. However, a profession is necessary, and a profession I must have. I'll make my bread by the bar and my character by the pen. That's my plan, Medlicott; is it not a good one?"

"Remember Winning's maxim," Reuben would say gravely; "remember the wise aphorism of Hippocrates."

"But, Medlicott, I have been reading about Hippocrates lately, and I find he was not a mere physician, but a brilliant and almost universal genius. I shall probably write his life one of these days."

CHAPTER VI.

CHIEFLY OCCUPIED WITH THE ILL BEHAVIOUR OF AN OLD GENTLEMAN AND THE DISCOMFORT IT OCCASIONED A YOUNG ONE.

The school at Hereford had been selected for Reuben partly on account of the benefice which his grandfather had in the neighbourhood; but of so little use to him was the circumstance, that he had now been nearly three years at Finchley without seeing his venerable relative scarcely the same number of times. Dean Wyndham appeared there occasionally, just as he did at Chichester and other places, arriving unexpectedly and departing abruptly, as comets were wont to do before the astronomers got their motions under proper control. When the Dean did show himself in this part of his orbit, he did not altogether neglect his grandchild, but his attentions were little more than a chuck under the chin at one visit, and a question in prosody or Roman antiquities at another. About the period of Winning's departure, however, the old gentleman was beginning to be seen at Hereford more frequently; the new squares and terraces were making rapid progress; and a report now began to prevail (greatly to the annoyance of the Dean's relatives) that he was not indisposed to marry for the third time, if he could induce one of the Barsac girls (the eldest, of course) to assist him in so extraordinary and promising an undertaking. Nobody gave this rumour so little credit as Reuben; at the same time, he could not but observe that his grandfather was daily becoming more intimate and absolute in the Barsac family. He dictated their dinners, regulated their hours, selected their society, discountenanced their pleasant evening parties; in fact, he appeared to be turning their once agreeable house topsy-turvy. Reuben's special grievance was, of course, that he was no longer invited there himself as often as before. It was mostly by hearsay he was aware of the unexampled tyranny exercised by his despotic ancestor over the household of a freeborn British merchant. He saw, however, quite enough to make all accounts that reached him only too worthy of credit. On several occasions, for instance, he observed the Barsacs going about shopping, or walking of an evening, with the Dean; nor was it to Mrs. Barsac that the preposterous old dignitary seemed to be paying his attentions: he preferred the daughters to the mother, and generally had one upon each arm, though once or twice it happened that but one of the girls was of the party, and this hard lot fell upon Blanche. Reuben marvelled that he had never heard her complain of being forced to perambulate the streets and precincts of Hereford, with so extraordinary an escort; but when he recollected in what a near relation the Dean stood to himself, he admired the delicacy that dictated her reserve.

The only wonder, indeed, was that the design of the Dean upon one of the three sherries had not been suspected sooner, —he lived so much and so openly with the Barsacs, and was so notoriously connected in large speculations with the father of the family. It soon became current enough. The gossips of Hereford had not had so rich a subject of discussion for a great many years. It set a great many heads shaking, tongues wagging, and eyes winking; caused infinite nodding, whispering, tittering, giggling; and if it did not occasion much wit, it had certainly a decided tendency to promote the consumption of tea. The boys of Finchley shared in the general excitement; and Reuben was exposed to so much annoyance on the subject, particularly among his school-fellows, that he was beginning to think his grandfather was destined to be the plague of his life, instead of being a comfort and a blessing to him, as a respectable grandfather ought surely to be.

The rumour of the Dean's matrimonial views was treated at the Vicarage as utterly unworthy of attention; but Mrs. Medlicott was seriously displeased when she found that Mrs. Barsac was beginning to be so neglectful of Reuben's education for a man of the world. The Vicar, on the contrary, was gratified; for he thought the cricket-ground became boys better than the ball-room, and hoped Reuben would relax himself with a little regular study, now that he had a good spell of vacation from balls and parties. And indeed his son was not idle at this period, although the business of the school was by no means sufficient to occupy the time he now had on his hands. He stood in the same rank in point of scholarship with Hyacinth Primrose; they topped the school in the classics without the least drudgery, and had ample leisure for a course of the English poets, into whose distinguished society Primrose introduced Reuben, who found in their charming circle some little consolation for the exile to which he was doomed from the sweet bright eyes of Blanche. De Tabley, although his strongest tastes were for the table, discovered some taste for poetry also; and, having ceased to sneer at Reuben's accomplishments, he was occasionally the companion of him and Primrose in their rambles on the banks of the Wye, when they repeated their favourite passages alternately, and discussed, with the rash criticism of boys, the beauties and the blemishes of the poets. Now and then, in these literary walks, De Tabley's ruling passion would come out amusingly in connection with some sublime or sentimental quotation. One day that some doves were heard plaining in a grove of trees hard by, Reuben repeated the hackneyed lines of Shenstone—

"I have found out a gift for my fair,
I have found where the wood-pigeons breed."

De Tabley, after a few minutes' silence, diverted his friends exceedingly by gravely observing that he did not much fancy pigeons, except in a pie. It was a standing joke against him with Primrose all his life.

The tender verses of Shenstone, and amorous and elegiac verse generally, pleased Reuben most in these early days. He had Prior's "Henry and Emma," no short poem of this class, every line by heart, and probably often wished the heroine had been a blonde like Blanche, instead of a brunette like her sister.

But the time came when Primrose followed Winning to college. De Tabley left school about the same time. Reuben was virtually left alone, for his only remaining friend was Vigors ; but Vigors had no more poetry in him than a Master in Chancery: his heart and soul were in gymnastic exercises; he was a good fellow and a good boxer, but no companion for an intellectual and sentimental youth like Medlicott. This was a dreary, melancholy time. The golden days of our youth have many a leaden hour. Reuben, in fact, ought to have been removed from Hereford along with his friends whom he had kept pace with in his studies. The Barsacs were not designedly inattentive to him, but they had not recovered their hospitable habits. Even when the Dean was absent they lived in the quietest way. Barsac himself was said to be in London much of his time, and his wife and daughters were frequently from home whole weeks together on excursions or visits. Our poor Reuben had but two resources—the library of the Cathedral, where he moped a great deal among the old books, and his flageolet, which he continued to practise with the French shoemaker occasionally.

Suddenly, however, he was deprived of this resource also, though fortune soon made him handsome amends.

Dropping into Adolphe's little shop one evening, he observed a pink satin shoe lying on the counter, and taking it up he complimented the maker on its shape and workmanship.

"Ah!" cried Adolphe, "that is beautiful; but do not admire the shoe, although it is my *chef d' œuvre*—that is nothing; admire the foot, it is the foot that is beautiful: it is the foot of a lady of your *connaissance*, Mademoiselle Blanche Barsac."

Reuben acknowledged that he knew her, with a degree of confusion and a quantity of carmine that would have disclosed the foolish state of his mind, had Adolphe been the obtusest of human beings.

"*Ah! oui;* you know the foot itself. I am a judge of feet; it is my profession; there is no foot so beautiful as hers in this town; it is perfection. I have a theory on feet, Monsieur Reuben: when the foot is pretty all is pretty. I reason from the foot up, up, up to the crown of the head: it is my philosophy of feet; I have studied, I have *approfondi* this subject. In the foot there is character, *esprit*, talent, heart, soul, genius, everything. When it walks, it is eloquence; when it dances it is poetry; when it stamps it is power. What do you think of my theory? Ah, that foot is the foot of an angel!"

A few days elapsed. Reuben heard a rumour in the school that, notwithstanding the custom it afforded Adolphe, he was not very flourishing in his trade, or likely long to find Hereford an eligible place for carrying it on. With a generous instinct Reuben flew to him directly this report reached his ears, resolving to raise money to assist him, either by the sale of his superfluous books, or the mortgage of his flageolet, for other sources of wealth were not very abundant with him. But it was too late; the little shop was shut up. Reuben knocked repeatedly, but there was no reply save the hollow echo of the sound he made with his knuckles, and when he applied at the cutler's, next door, for an explanation of these facts, he heard quite enough to satisfy anybody, whose mind had not been completely prepossessed with admiration and sympathy, that the French shoemaker had not been particularly attentive to his landlord's interests before he made up his mind to abandon Hereford.

Reuben went his way melancholy, his thoughts full of the poetry of bankruptcy; and, connecting the misfortunes of Adolphe with his talents and accomplishments—his genius shown even in his humble trade, his philosophy of feet asd his sister Louise—he formed a most romantic picture in his mind of the struggles and calamities of an ambitious French shoemaker.

The next day was a holiday; I think it was the martyrdom of Charles the First. While the rest of the scholars amused themselves with the soaring kite, the bounding ball, or the rolling marbles, Reuben recreated himself with his pen, collecting all the cases and anecdotes he could find of laureate shoemakers and cobblers of immortal genius, such as Bunyan, Gifford, Hans Sachs, "the cobler-bard" of Nuremberg, and others, ending with a sketch of his friend Adolphe, whom his enthusiasm placed in the same memorable class. The poor artist's mysterious fate gave a melancholy interest to this part of the essay, and Reuben ended his speculations with suggesting suicide by charcoal, under most poetical circumstances, as the too probable close of his career.

The simple truth was, that Adolphe had not prospered in his trade because he did not mind his business. He was too fond of talking, theorising, and playing the flageolet. The very shoes upon which he had built his philosophy of feet had been returned to him by Miss Barsac as a misfit. In point of probity, however, he was not more unjust to his landlord than he had been to himself, for he absconded without taking the trouble of collecting a number of small sums that were due to him. Mrs. Barsac, among others, owed him some money, and, thinking that Reuben might be able to inform her what had become of him, she wrote him a note requesting to see him one morning.

Wings could scarcely have borne him swifter than he flew in obedience to this summons. The nature of Mrs. Barsac's business with him was a sad disappointment, but that was forgotten before he left the house. Mrs. Barsac was particularly gracious, told him that his grandfather was to preach in the Cathedral the following Sunday, and offered him a seat in her pew, if he desired to hear him.

CHAPTER VII.

REUBEN SPENDS A MEMORABLE SUNDAY WITH HIS GRANDFATHER, AND ALL THE BARSACS.

THE Barsacs, who were what is commonly called a fine family, never looked so fine as when they were assembled together in their spacious and prominent pew on a Sunday morning. The spectators had then an opportunity of seeing several junior members of the firm, whom he did not commonly see at their parties, except when a juvenile ball was given, or round about a Christmas tree, dropping bon-bons. Though their pew was the largest in the church, it was not more roomy than they required, particularly as the ladies occupied much more space with their spreading silks and muslins than their mere persons required. As to Mrs. Barsac and her eldest daughter, they took up room enough for four reasonable women. Perhaps it was to do due honour to Dean Wyndham's discourse that they were attired with more than usual splendour upon the present occasion, but certainly poor slender Reuben, whose lot it was to get wedged in between them, almost disappeared between the gorgeous shawls, floating veils, and pompous petticoats, that hemmed him in upon either side. Mrs. Barsac vouchsafed him some attention, and extended her superb prayer-book now and then to accommodate him, but her daughter seemed unconscious of his proximity, arranging her dress when she sat down, without the slightest reference to his existence, and when she stood up, eclipsing him altogether. Opposite to him sat the fair Blanche and her brown sister, divided by their purse-proud and pompous father, dressed in a light blue frock, with a forest of geraniums in his button-hole. It was a goodly sight to see Barsac at his devotions; he performed them in such an exemplary, determined, imposing manner; so loud in his share of the responses, that the services of a clerk might have been dispensed with in whatever parish he resided, and ostentatiously observant of every little ceremony and genuflexion which usage or the rubric required. The grandest thing of all was his bow at a certain passage in the creed. Mr. Barsac always prepared himself for this solemn act by a previous arrangement of his countenance and disposition of his person; he drew himself up to his full height, threw back the breast of his coat with the enormous bouquet, and bowed in the manner of a man who seemed to feel that he was conferring an honour upon the Christian religion, rather than humbly expressing his reverence for its truths.

But even Barsac sank into insignificance, when the principal actor of the day, the mighty Dean, marched from his stall to the pulpit, preceded by the officious verger, perspiring under the weight of a huge silver mace. If Dr. Wyndham was a giant in his ordinary clothes, you may fancy what a man-mountain he was in his canonical raiment. It needed no great effort of fancy to conceive that there was not only a dean but a whole chapter beneath a surplice which might certainly have made a set of shirts for the entire corporation, down to the minor canons.

This huge body of divinity had no sooner mounted the pulpit than Mrs. Barsac requested Reuben to change places with Blanche, in order that she might have a better view of the preacher. Barsac made a like exchange with two of his younger children, and similar movements took place all over the cathedral, proving the great interest excited by the expectation of a sermon from a theologian of such renown. Reuben would have willingly made a much greater sacrifice for the gratification or convenience of Blanche, but, in fact, although it would have pleased him to see as well as hear his grandfather preaching, he was glad to emerge from the ladies' dresses, and by the new arrangement he had Blanche opposite to him still, which was a very fair compensation for the face of old Dr. Wyndham. A pin might have been heard to drop as the Dean in his loud, dry, grating voice gave out his text, and commenced his discourse, which was, in fact, a pamphlet more than a sermon, consisting of an undoubtedly eloquent, but unnecessarily violent, denunciation of the doctrine of political expediency, the fiercest anathemas against the statesmen of the day, who were supposed to be governed by it, and tremendous warnings to the nation to beware of permitting the corner-stone of its Protestant constitution to be removed a single inch from its place, out of any false complaisance to Romish errors or sophistical ideas of toleration. The only change the Dean's harsh, monotonous voice underwent, was when he came to utter these awful comminations, when it fell into a kind of hoarse growl, like that of a bear apprehensive of a design against her cubs, or a mastiff prepared to defend his bone. Many parts of the sermon were ably and acutely reasoned, supporting the Dean's reputation thoroughly; but the contrast of argument, sometimes as fine as Mechlin lace, with language often as coarse as Norwich drugget, was exceedingly curious and occasionally almost diverting. In fact he kept his audience alternately admiring the force of his positions, and scandalised by the scurrility of his language; they would, indeed, have been divided in their judgments of the discourse upon the whole, had he not wound it all up with a peroration upon the value and dignity of principle, as opposed to expediency, so beautiful, as well as vehement, that all the previous blemishes of his composition were forgotten, and he dismissed his hearers, not only with the highest possible opinion of his ability in the pulpit, but with a profound and consolatory conviction that there was at least one man in the Church whom no temptation of wealth or rank could seduce from the path of duty. The Barsacs were variously affected throughout the sermon, or rather expressed in a variety of ways the feelings with which it impressed them. Mrs. Barsac intimated by numerous little gestures, intended to be critical, sometimes to her husband, sometimes to one or other of her daughters, that she had never in her life heard a discourse that so entranced her. Barsac kept nodding at the preacher at the close of every passage, to testify his approbation of every syllable. Miss Barsae looked particularly cross, which was perhaps a mood rather in unison with the general tone of the Dean's observations. The brunette paid the usual respectful attention, but nothing more; in fact she was not much of a theologian, and nothing of a politician at all; very few brunettes are, and not many blondes either. Blanche seemed to be an exception, for she kept her deep, quiet, devout eyes rivetted on the pulpit from first to last, never suffering them to wander to any object nearer the earth, not even once upon Reuben, who sat directly over against her, marvelling at her intense interest in subjects which had but little interest for himself, and of which he had indeed at that period but very imperfect and confused notions.

After the service, as they stood in a group at one of the doors, waiting for the Dean, who had some ecclesiastical business to transact and to disencumber himself of his robes, when everybody had said everything that was to be said in admiration of the sermon, Mr. Barsac said something aside to Mrs. Barsac, who immediately addressed Reuben, and made him as happy as a king by inviting him to their family dinner.

They still waited for the Dean; not impatiently, however, for he was a man whom the Barsacs considered it an honour to dance attendance on, which was fortunate, as he was not likely to hurry himself upon their account. There was no carriage waiting for them, for it was a rule with the Barsacs to walk to church when the weather was propitious. The distance was nothing, and they managed to go to church on foot with as much parade and ostentation, as if they had gone in a coach-and-six.

At length the Dean joined them; he instantly seized Mrs. Barsac's arm, and commenced walking at his usual great pace, taking no more notice of Reuben than of the sparrows that were hopping in the streets. Barsac and his daughter Blanche fell into the second line, followed by the rest of the party in open order, Reuben not very well knowing to which division to attach himself, but keeping as near Blanche as he possibly could. Mrs. Barsac would have said twenty handsome things of the sermon, if the Dean had allowed her to speak at all, but he knew perfectly well what she had got to say, so that his vanity was no loser; and having just as little doubt on his mind that Barsac was heaping on incense as fast he could behind his back, he gave himself just as little trouble to catch the precise words in which the consequential merchant was expressing his sentiments.

"It is commonly remarked," said the Dean, after he had said more than enough in commendation of his own discourse, " that an author is not the best judge of his own compositions; I don't know how it may be with other men, but the remark does not hold in my case. I was never yet wrong in my opinion of any work of my own. When I write a good book, or compose a good sermon, I know it; when I write a bad thing, or a weak thing, I know it also. No critic can criticise me better than I can criticise myself. No living author has been the subject of such ridiculous criticism as I have. My best works have been abused by the reviewers, and, on the other hand, there are some of those fellows always ready to tell the public that any trash bearing my name is worthy of being written in cuneiform characters on pyramids."

"I believe, sir," said Barsac, "you have written very little, if anything, that is not."

"I have written trash in my time," said the Dean, "like other men; not so much, perhaps, as ———, or ———, or my Lord Bishop of ———, but I have written trash in my time, as arrant trash as ever was printed."

"What you call trash, Dean, would make the character and the fortune of any other man in the Church!"

"Perhaps you are not very wrong in that," said the Dean; "I know very well there's a difference between my trash and other men's trash. What is your dinner hour?"

"Five, sir, on Sundays," replied Mrs. Barsac, blandly and obsequiously, to this abrupt question.

"Why five?" demanded the Dean.

"Dinner shall be at any hour you please, Dean," cried Barsac, who was even more supple than his wife. "Would you prefer six, or shall we say seven?"

"As you have named five to your company, let it be five," answered the Dean; "don't consider me in your domestic arrangements. Never change your hour to please anybody. It's unfair to your cook, and it's unjust to your company."

"I am sorry to say," said Barsac nervously, "we have no company to meet you to-day, sir, only our own family, with the exception of our young friend here, and, possibly, my brother-in-law, Mr. Brough."

"Where was Brough to-day?—where was your master?" demanded the Dean, turning sharply round upon Reuben, whom he now honoured with his notice for the first time. Nothing was more usual with Dr. Wyndham than to put a question like this, and instantly change the conversation, without caring, or seeming to care, whether it was answered or not. While Reuben was endeavouring to explain or excuse the absence of his schoolmaster, by stating that it was not the custom of the school to attend divine service at the cathedral, the Dean was proposing a visit to the buildings in which he and Mr. Barsac were concerned, by way of filling up the interval between luncheon and dinner. The walk was too much for Mrs. Barsac and her eldest daughter. The rest of the party, however, as soon as luncheon was over, sallied forth again, and had not proceeded far before they were joined by the glossy Mr. Brough, who approached the Dean with something almost servile in his manner. The Dean, who had now taken Blanche under his arm, never looked at him, or, rather, he looked through-him, as if he had been a ghost. This was to punish Mr. Brough for not having been at the cathedral to hear his sermon, and it evidently did punish him, for he was visibly abashed, and falling into the rear, began to converse in a very subdued tone with Barsac, who increased his brother-in-law's confusion by telling him aloud all he had lost, and assuring him that the loss was totally irreparable, as it was out of all human probability that so splendid a specimen of pulpit eloquence would ever again be heard in England.

Possibly the Dean did not hear this flourishing speech of the merchant, although it was intended that he should, for he was now mounted on one of his favourite hobbies, and talking at a prodigious rate of granite and limestone, the timber of different countries, and building materials of every kind. He seemed to Reuben to be boring Blanche excessively. They were now arrived at Wyndham Terrace, which was in a state of considerable forwardness. The square, not yet named, was adjacent to it. The ground was laid out, the foundations of the houses laid, but only one house had been erected, and even that was little more than a skeleton of wood and brick. The ground all round about was strewed over with blocks of stone, piles of bricks, timber, iron railings, and a thousand other things of the same kind; but none of these obstructions impeded the Dean's progress; he strode over and through them all, making Blanche follow, or rather pulling her along after him, without the least consideration either for her shoes or her ankles, the latter of which were really now and then in danger from the spikes of the railings, and the points of pickaxes. Reuben was very angry, but could do nothing to help her, though he showed by his looks amusingly enough how eager he was to do so. But Blanche herself was very good-humoured about it, and so was her sister the brunette, who was compelled to traverse every inch of the same rough ground in company with her father and uncle, whose complaisance to the Dean would have supported them through much more dirt and many more difficulties than they actually had to go through. Their trials, however, were only commenced, for as soon as Dr. Wyndham reached the house which was in a comparatively advanced state, he insisted on the merchant and the schoolmaster accompanying him through it from top to bottom, a journey which was one of not a little hazard, as a great deal of it had to be performed along rafters over which the flooring was not complete, and up and down inclined planes formed of loose boards, which at present represented the staircases. The Dean's activity was surprising; none of the masons or carpenters could have done what he did with more self-possession, and he never ceased talking the whole time, alternately lecturing upon the principles of ventilation and sewerage, and ridiculing Barsac and Mr. Brough, who were scrambling reluctantly after him, with imminent risk to their limbs at every step. When, at length, this perilous survey was over, it was diverting to observe the annoyance of both at the state in which their clothes were with the mortar, dust, and whitewash; Mr. Brough was in the worst pickle, for he was the awkwardest climber, and besides he was dressed, as usual, in a complete suit of the newest and glossiest black, looking as if he had been polished all over with Day and Martin. Reuben goodnaturedly assisted in restoring his preceptor to his original lustre, and Blanche performed the same little service for the Dean when he came forth, but he had suffered much less than the others, because he had been so much more agile.

He now seated himself on a square block of Portland stone, and the rest followed his example, some sitting on other blocks,

Mr. Brough on an inverted wheelbarrow, which he first carefully dusted with his handkerchief.

"This will be the finest square in England," said the Dean, "when it is finished."

"That it will, sir," said Barsac.

"That it certainly will," said Mr. Brough.

"Of course I don't include London," said the Dean.

"Of course not," said Barsac and his brother-in-law together.

"Barsac," said the Dean, "this square was my idea, not yours."

"For which reason," said the merchant, "it must be called after you, sir."

"No," said the Dean; "and to prevent any more argument on that point, I now christen it Barsac Square, and we must consider how to adorn the centre of it. What is your opinion?" This was addressed to Blanche, who sat on the next block to him.

"A fountain, sir, would be pretty," she replied.

"Fountains are very well in some climates," said the Dean, "but the skies of ours afford us water enough without artificial supplies."

"A just and happy observation," said the schoolmaster on the wheelbarrow, in a timid tone, but hoping to be heard by the object of his slavish veneration.

"The square, sir, was your idea," said Barsac, "and therefore I don't think any thing would be so appropriate, if I might venture to offer a suggestion, as a statue of the Very Reverend Dean Wyndham."

"Colossal," added Mr. Brough as before.

"Mr. Brough," said the Dean abruptly, now that the schoolmaster had forced himself on his notice, "you were not at church to-day. That was wrong, Mr. Brough; doubly wrong, for as an individual, you neglected the duty of attending divine service, and, as a preceptor, you set an example of the same neglect to your scholars; you, of all men, are bound to be scrupulous in these matters; you are *in loco parentis;* you should not only have been present yourself, but you should have come at the head of all your pupils and assistants. You must not be offended with me for speaking to you plainly on a subject so important. I hope and trust you do not make a practice of turning your back upon the Church."

Mr. Brough was in the greatest state of excitement during this speech, wriggling on the wheelbarrow as if he was frying, and every moment jumping up and endeavouring, but all in vain, to get in a single word; for a single word would have shown the Dean that his accusation was most unjust, and his lecture most uncalled-for. The Dean's loud, fluent, and commanding mode of speaking overbore all attempts at interruption, so that the pedagogue was exactly in the same predicament in which he had formerly put Reuben, by harranguing him on intemperance at the ball, while the poor fellow was actually supperless. And when at last the Dean came to a pause, and Mr. Brough was allowed to defend himself, the former made him very slight amends for the wrong he had done him.

"I am very glad to hear it," he said, in the driest way, as again he took Blanche under his mighty wing, and announced that it was time to return to dinner.

At dinner Reuben sat next to Blanche, but his grandfather sat on the other side, and, as usual, kept the conversation exclusively to himself. When at the second course Mrs. Barsac recommended some dish to Reuben, the Dean said she was cockering him too much; when he was a boy he never had such delicacies.

Mr. Barsac shortly after asked Reuben to take wine.

"Wine too! what does a schoolboy want with wine?"

"One glass of sherry, Dean, will do no harm.- Pale or brown, Master Medlicott?"

Reuben was crimson; he fancied it was an indirect way Mr. Barsac took to discover which of his daughters he preferred. In his confusion, however, he made the wrong answer, and said brown, when he meant pale. This utterly discomforted him, and he sat silent and abashed the rest of the dinner.

Barsac was carving a duck. The Dean told him he knew nothing of carving fowl; that few people did but himself, and ordered a servant to bring the dish to him. He certainly carved better than Barsac, as far as it depended on strength; but he lopped the wings and legs from the duck with so much energy, that he sprinkled Blanche's dress all over with gravy. Blanche bore it with great equanimity, but Reuben was very much incensed, and again had occasion to admire the delicacy with which she refrained from appearing annoyed by any part of his grandfather's behaviour.

When the ladies had retired, Reuben did not wait for one of

his grandfather's hints, but followed them very soon. He was now compensated for his annoyances at dinner, and had more discourse with Blanche than he had ever yet had an opportunity of enjoying. Mrs. Barsac and her other daughters were present, but they were reading, and took little part in the conversation. After some time Blanche fixed her earnest eyes on Reuben, and smiling said she had a great favor to ask him; but she hoped he would not hesitate to refuse her if she was going to trespass upon him too much.

"I know so well what Blanche is going to say," said one of her sisters aside to the other, looking up from her book.

"So do I," said Mrs. Barsac, also aside.

How Reuben was agitated at the thought of Blanche asking him to do her a favour! What would he not do for those persuasive eyes?

The favour was this,—to sit for his picture. Blanche, as we have already mentioned, was an amateur portrait painter; she took pretty good likenesses in water-colors, and when a face particularly pleased her, she felt an irresistible inclination to reproduce its features with her pencil.

"Now you must be very candid with me," she repeated, looking intently into the face of the handsome bashful boy, studying its lines and favours with the license of an artist, to whom beauty is only a theory.

"Blanche," said Mrs. Barsac, beckoning to her daughter.

Blanche went to her mother.

"Are you sure, my dear, the Dean will be pleased? I very much question it."

Reuben only imperfectly caught what was said. Blanche returned to him with a thoughtful expression, and, after sitting silent for a moment, with the tip of her finger to her lips, she suddenly brightened again, and said, with the air of a woman settling a point which she has authority to settle—

"The Dean shall know nothing at all about it."

"It is very kind of Mr. Medlicott to sit for you," said Mrs. Barsac; "I hope he has not promised out of mere politeness."

Blanche had no doubt that Reuben was dealing sincerely with her; and as to Reuben himself, his protestations to the same effect were amusingly eager. In fact he was delirious with joy, which nothing happened to interrupt for the remainder of the evening.

CHAPTER VIII.

REUBEN SITS TO A FAIR ARTIST FOR HIS PICTURE.—WHO INTERRUPTED THE SITTINGS.

The first sitting took place the very next day. There cannot be a more delicate or perilous situation,—one trembles to think of it. Boyhood sitting to Beauty for his picture! The proximity, the artistic licence we spoke of just now, the opportunities of conversing both with the lips and the eyes, the necessity the fair painter is under of continually settling and resettling her patient's attitude and position, often the tie of his handkerchief, the fall of his collar, or the arrangement of his hair; all these, and twenty more little circumstances and incidents of amateur portrait-painting, have a manifest tendency to promote that relative state of the sentiments and feelings, which possibly may yet be brought under the dominion of science, and proved to be nothing more than an invisible play of some species of galvanic fluid, between a pair of hearts under certain conditions of Paphian electricity.

Of the two, however, Blanche was the most practical and business-like upon an occasion when the temptations to be sentimental are so very numerous. Nothing could be cooler or more professional than the liberties she took with Reuben to place him in the proper light, to dispose his draperies for picturesque effect, and establish that sort of animated repose and speaking silence in his features, which she hoped to succeed in transferring to the carton before her. The subject himself was all in a tumult during the preliminaries, which the artist arranged without the slightest flutter of the pulse or loss of self-possession. Reuben often wondered afterwards how Blanche Barsac made such a good likeness of him as she managed to do in a few sittings; so difficult a task it must have been to catch the lines of a face, the owner of which was all the time in a state of such nervous excitement, and whose colour was for ever coming and going, with a decided tendency, however, to settle into a perpetual blush.

Conversation is of enormous service on such occasions. Blanche never talked so much as when she was painting, and she forced Reuben to talk too, asking him a thousand questions about his mother, his friends, his studies, his plans, and many a thing besides. They had been so long without seeing him; where had he been? Was it his fault, or was it theirs? When had he heard from Mr. Winning and his friend with the pretty name, Mr. Hyacinth Primrose, who was always so lively and entertaining? She knew he had been studying very hard, he was so pale. Had he any time for drawing? Had he taken any more views of the cathedral? And she hoped he had not given up the pleasant magazine of which she had seen one or two specimens. Had he been writing at all lately? He was not long in confessing his latest production, the essay on shoemakers of genius, and modestly yielded to the strong wish she expressed to read it, though stipulating that nobody should see it but herself.

Then she went on painting in silence for a few minutes, examining the lines of his countenance between the touches, as if it was but the statue of a boy that sat before her; then suddenly she paused, and feared she was detaining him too long, but she would soon release him.

He had no wish to be released; but Blanche had probably other engagements, for she now looked at her watch, rose hastily, wondered what had become of her sisters, and fixing a day for the next sitting, terminated the present one almost abruptly.

Reuben was extremely dissatisfied with himself for his behaviour upon this occasion. He had been so sheepish, so stupid, while Blanche had been so agreeable, so encouraging, so every way charming. He determined to act a more manly and gallant part the next time.

But the next sitting was not a *tête-à-tête* like the former. The sisters were provokingly present. Blanche was in her walking-dress, all but her parasol and gloves, which lay on a sofa beside her. Nothing could be more uncomfortable; and at last in bustled Mrs. Barsac herself, richly shawled and bonneted, nodded to Reuben, glanced at the picture, and swept away Blanche along with her so rapidly, as scarcely to give her time to put up her brushes and appoint a time for the third *séance*. He had brought his essay with him, but had no opportunity of placing it in her hands unobserved by the other members of the family.

The third sitting was pleasanter than the second, though not so private as the first. He presented her with his MS. She was now painting his hair.

"I wish," she exclaimed, "it were not cropped so very close, it is so beautiful; it would look so well suffered to fall down upon your shoulders like mine;" and as she spoke she touched her own hair, which was light brown and very bright and abundant. The compliment and the comparison together damasked Reuben's cheek very deeply indeed. With the slightest conceivable smile upon her lip, Blanche withdrew her eyes from him and fixed them again upon her work. After a few touches, she spoke again.

"Did you never wear it long?"

Reuben now made an effort to tell her the tale of the outrage which his grandfather had perpetrated with the scissors the day before he went to school. Blanche was evidently diverted, though she said she could perfectly understand how provoked his mother must have been. He must have looked a positive fright.

This extracted the sequel of the tale, all about Mademoiselle Louise, which Reuben told in so confused a way, and with so much stammering and blushing, that Blanche could not help raising her finger, shaking her head, looking mysterious, and then apologising for having betrayed him into making her the confidante of what was evidently a sentimental business.

He was seriously parrying this attack, when a maid entered the room and put a little slip of paper into Blanche's hand, which seemed to have an electrical effect upon her. She jumped up, hastily covered the unfinished portrait, and was running out of her studio, without fixing a day for Reuben to sit again, but he followed, and, overtaking her at the door of the drawing-room, with throbbing nerves reminded her of what she had probably only forgotten in her hurry. She was forced to stop, and was rapidly running over on her fingers her engagements for the few following days, when the door opened behind them, and forth came Mrs. Barsac, her eldest daughter, and his grandfather.

The Dean blew a terrific gale when he saw Reuben, although he had not a notion that he was there for any purpose but to pay an idle morning visit. That, however, was enough to raise the tempest, with the ideas he had of schools and schoolboys. He scolded Reuben, scolded Mr. Brough, and so abused Mrs. Barsac that she became quite disconcerted, and in her perplexity made matters worse by assuring the Dean that his grandson was not so much to blame as he seemed to be, and that she would explain every thing presently. On hearing this, the Dean blustered again, puffed his cheeks like Æolus, and after frowning like night upon every body in succession, but most upon Reuben, returned with Mrs. Barsac into the drawing-room. The three girls remained for a moment outside, the two eldest whispering and laughing together in a subdued tone, while Blanche, sincerely pitying Reuben's humiliation, shook his hand with the utmost good-nature, and even accompanied him part of the way to the hall-door.

The Dean's anger on trifling occasions like this was a very "short madness" indeed. Even when he heard from Mrs. Barsac how Reuben had been sitting for his picture to Blanche, he merely called them all a pack of fools two or three times over, desired to have no more such nonsense, and appeared to have forgotten all about it before dinner.

But Reuben did not so soon recover his composure. He had a more serious cause for anxiety than the humiliation he had met with from his choleric and eccentric relative. He had placed more that day in the hands of Blanche than one of his literary efforts—he had slipped into the folds of the MS. a full confession of the resistless power of her charms with a frank and honorable declaration of love.

He was not long without a reply, under her own hand and seal.

The lessons of the following day were disposed of, and Reuben was hurrying to regain his room, and bury himself in solitude, when he saw a servant of the Barsacs, and observed him inquiring for somebody or something. Reuben ran over to the man, who put a note and small paper parcel into his hand, touched his hat, and went away. In an instant Reuben was in his closet, and had already torn the parcel open.

It was his MS., with a few lines from Blanche, to the effect that she had read it with the greatest pleasure, and thought it exceedingly clever and interesting. With respect to a detached paper which she had found enclosed, she had read that also, but not with the same satisfaction; she begged him to excuse her for observing that it did not appear to her to be as well considered as his other essay.

The other note was from Mrs. Barsac, suggesting the expediency of discontinuing the sittings to her daughter, at least for the present; indeed, she was happy to acquaint him that Blanche was in hopes of even finishing it without giving him any further trouble, and was very thankful to him for the sittings with which he had favoured her.

CHAPTER IX.

AN AFFLICTING DISCOVERY, WHICH OUGHT TO HAVE BEEN MADE SOONER.

REUBEN was not long in ignorance of the overwhelming truth which the sagacious reader has probably already divined. Schoolboys are great proficients in the art of ingeniously tormenting The very next day, while the smart was fresh of the wounds received in the last chapter, Reuben overheard the following dialogue, which had in all probability been concerted expressly to be overheard by him.

"Think of dry sherry," said one, " being Medlicott's grandmamma! She will keep him in precious order, won't she?"

"That she will, and no mistake," replied another.

"I hear it's not dry sherry at all; it's brown," said a third.

"Pale, I say."

"So do I. The pale one, for a bottle of pop."

"Done," said the backer of one of the other ladies.

"Why, it's pale sherry he is in love with; to be in love with his grandmother would be capital fun."

This was the first hint. Confirmation followed quickly enough, and in only too great an abundance.

Reuben often laughed, in his maturer years, at the follies and miseries of this period of his life. It seemed to him, as it has done to most men, hardly credible that his puerile infatuation should have carried him to such preposterous lengths, and still harder to understand how he could have made himself so wretched as he did by his incomparable absurdities.

The notion of that grim old grandfather marrying the fair young Blanche, with those sweet, calm, bewitching eyes, almost overset his reason. The principal fact was so horrible, that he took little or no interest in the subordinate events connected with it. The marriage, although decided on, was not to take place for some time; there were delays and difficulties, as usual in hymeneal transactions, and rumour ascribed them to various causes, among others to the true one, the embarrassed state of the Dean's private circumstances, notwithstanding his rich preferments in the Church. Blanche Barsac went on a visit at this time to friends in London, and Reuben knew nothing of it for several weeks, during which interval his correspondence with his parents, and the letters he received from his Aunt Mountjoy, and his friends Winning and Primrose, helped to familiarise his mind, in some measure, with the subject that was most painful to reflect on, and gradually to extract the sting of his anguish. Primrose wrote him a very pleasant letter, in which he paralleled the Dean and his bride with Tithonus and Aurora, and discussed in a most amusing manner the singular passion which young women sometimes conceive for men who might be their fathers. Neither Hyacinth nor Winning had the slightest notion of their friend Reuben's competition with his grandfather for the lady's affections; and as they had both met Blanche in town, it was perfectly plain she had kept his secret with the most amiable fidelity.

The truth, indeed, was that Blanche was very fond of Reuben, and had the sincerest regard for him, which she afterwards showed upon many an occasion, as the course of this history will prove.

Meanwhile his schoolboy days were nearly numbered. He was actually now within three months of the period which had been fixed upon for his leaving Finchley, where he had learned as much as his preceptors professed to teach, and more a great deal than was necessary as preparation for either of the universities. The period of his departure, however, was precipitated by the good-nature of Mr. Brough, who, having noticed that Reuben was looking ill, mentioned it one morning to his grandfather, whom he chanced to meet, adding that change of air and relaxation for a week or two would (with deference to the Dean's better judgment) be of the greatest service to him.

"You think so," said the Dean, who was propitious at the moment, "very well, let it be so,—Chichester is a great way off, but I'm going down to-night to see how the alterations are going on in my house at Westbury, and I'll take him with me. He shall have a gun to shoot the rabbits, and Mrs. Reeves, my housekeeper, will make dandelion tea for him."

"No plan could be better," said Mr. Brough.

"But you had better," said the Dean, "give him a book of Virgil to get by heart; he can't shoot rabbits all the day long."

"With great respect, sir," said the complaisant but humane schoolmaster, "Mrs. Reeves and the rabbits will do him more good just now than a book of Virgil."

"Perhaps you are right," said the Dean, "and as the coach office is at hand, I'll book the boy now and secure his place."

So Reuben was booked like a parcel, without having a voice

in the matter, and he went down that night with the Dean to his place at Westbury.

CHAPTER X.

REUBEN GETS AN INSIGHT INTO THE PRIVATE LIFE OF HIS GRANDFATHER.

WHILE the following morning was yet grey, Reuben's sleep was broken by an infinity of discordant sounds, produced by carpenters, bricklayers, glaziers, and chimney-doctors, dispersed over all parts of the house, and all in turn occasionally drowned by the harsh thundering voice of his grandfather, dictating to the several tradesmen, and informing them all in rotation, that they were scandalously ignorant of their business; that he knew more of masonry himself than half the masons in England; that painters ought to know something of mixing colours, but he never saw a painter who did; that it was more noise than work with the carpenters; and as to the chimney-doctors, they were a pack of charlatans. Reuben, after rubbing his eyes, stole out of bed, and peeped over a balustrade close to the door of his bed-room, from whence he obtained a view of the Dean in a loose old trailing dressing-gown, alternately lecturing and abusing the mechanics, some of whom were quietly going on with their work without taking much notice of their eccentric employer, while others were suspending their hammers, their brushes, or their diamonds, and receiving his observations with affected gratitude and respect. Reuben stole back again to his bed, for it was still early; but he had scarcely laid his head on his pillow, when his door was thrown open with a clatter, and in stalked the Dean, followed by a couple of glaziers, to whom he was giving a torrent of instructions, in compliance with the first of which the only window in the room was chucked in a trice out of the frame; so that Reuben might as well have had to make his toilet *al fresco*. He dressed himself in presence of his grandfather and the glaziers, while the former commenced ransacking an old bookcase, the contents of which he had quite forgotten, mixing up running commentaries on the books as he tumbled them out, with odds and ends of advice to Reuben on the subject of rabbit-shooting and other similar sports, which naturally led him to his own exploits with the gun, some of them not much less amazing than the exploits of Baron Munchausen. Then he held forth on the various breeds of rabbits and their extraordinary fecundity, and told anecdotes of rabbits that made the mechanics grin, and even Reuben laugh, who had not laughed for weeks. He told them Bacon's story of the simple schoolboy who was astounded when the rabbits scampered off on his shouting in Latin to his comrade, never dreaming that rabbits were acquainted with the dead languages; and how Hobbs, when he lived at Old Sarum, humorously concluded, that a burgess in the English language was synonymous with a cony, as the conies were the only constituency which even in his time that ancient borough had to boast of. The glaziers thought the Dean omniscient, particularly when he made some just remarks on matters connected with their own trade. However, as he went down to breakfast he forfeited their good opinion to a certain extent; for, taking a hammer out of the hand of one of the carpenters' apprentices, to show him how to drive a nail with precision, he missed his aim by a quarter of an inch, and gave himself a smart rap on the thumb. He pretended it was nothing, but the apprentice knew very well what a sore thing it was, and quoted a familiar adage as soon as the old gentleman was out of hearing.

The Dean only remained a day or two, passing the time between odd discussions with his workmen, and researches in his library, chiefly among the fathers, to support some theological dogma or another which he was shortly about to propound to the world either in a sermon or a tract. Engaged in this latter occupation, he utterly forgot his engagement to Reuben to give him the gun, and set him down to copy long passages from Eusebius and Bellarmine, which filled up the interval between a straggling breakfast and a dinner of the same character. The house being in such confusion, everything was done in the library, which was, of course, not much behind the other apartments in point of disorder. The books lay on the floor in heaps, for the shelves had been just painted, and the Dean sat at his breakfast amidst a chaos of classics and divinity, simultaneously eating and reading with equal voracity; now and then striding to the door to shout directions to the painters, and bellowing to Mrs. Reeves for hot water to shave. He always used his library or study as his dressing-room, wherever he resided. In the present state of his house, his toilet was in perfect keeping with the general disorder of the establishment. He shaved himself in a little shattered looking-glass, which he set upon the mantel-piece, not even waiting until he had quite finished his meal, but travelling backwards and forwards between the breakfast-table and the hearth-stone, uttering all manner of strange noises and internal rumblings, to the consternation of his gentle grandson, who had never seen or heard so much of the private life of his maternal ancestor before.

Mingled, however, with the inarticulate sounds elicited partly by the difficulty of eating and shaving at the same time, partly by the embarrassment of seeing more chins than one in the mirror, came forth at intervals a multitude of sound, hard-headed maxims and receipts for success in life, intended for Reuben's use, and probably more likely to remain impressed on his memory, delivered as they were, than if they had been imparted with more dignity in any portico or academic shade.

"Aim at being a great man; there is something great in even failing to become great. Encourage the passions that lead to greatness; there are three of them; love of business, love of reputation, and love of power. But if you would be a good man, which is better than being a great one, you must love two things besides, you must love truth and you must love mankind. I put truth foremost; God forbid I should give man the precedence; nine men out of ten are scoundrels, not that we ought not to love scoundrels, or try to love them; but it is a difficult thing to do,— the cutler who made this razor was an arrant scoundrel." The Dean had prepared Reuben for this last remark by a series of grunts with which he had interpolated the latter part of his speech. He gulped down some coffee, soaping the edge of the cup in doing so, and resumed in a new track of observation, while Reuben sat imbibing his counsels, and gazing almost with terror at he bloody harvest which the bad razor was reaping.

"Preserve due order among the objects of your respect and veneration. Place them in your mind as you do pounds, shillings, and pence in your arithmetic. Respect piety and virtue first; genius and learning in the second place; rank and authority in the third, when they are not disgraced in the persons of their possessors—they often are."

Here he finished his operations on one s'de of his face, and refreshed himself with some coffee and toast before he proceeded to the other moiety.

"Wealth, and what is called blood, have no claims upon your

reverence at all. Birth is an accident. Wealth is odious when it is acquired by sordid methods, and when it is obtained by talent and industry, the industry and talent command our homage, not the fortune obtained by them. Before good men be reverent; before the wise be diffident; before the great be discreet; but never bow your knee, or bait your breath in the presence of the mere *millionnaire,* or the mere patrician."

He cut himself again, interpolated another attack on the cutler, and resumed—

"I never did. My 'learned pate'—if there is any learning in it—never 'ducked to the golden fool,' as Shakspeare has it. Hand me that towel."

Reuben obeyed, and in doing so took courage to say that he recollected another passage in Shakspeare, breathing the spirit of his grandfather's observations.

"I held it ever,
Virtue and wisdom were endowments greater
Than nobleness and riches."

"Well said and well remembered: who is the speaker?" asked the Dean, looking down with grim approbation upon his youthful companion, as he wiped his razor, having concluded his sanguinary work.

"The Ephesian lord, sir, in the play of 'Pericles,'" said Reuben, blushing at his little success.

"Shakspeare knew," said the Dean, "that there are lords as well as commoners who understand in what true greatness consists, and who draw honour from its proper fountains. Men cannot help being lords; they are neither to be respected for it, nor despised for it. Hand me that coat on the back of the chair yonder."

While Reuben was handing the coat, his grandfather was disembowelling the huge pockets of his dressing gown; and unquestionably it was a strange miscellany that he produced from those receptacles; letters, invitations, soiled handkerchiefs, odd gloves, keys, memorandums, notes of sermons, builders' estimates, a heap of copper coins, with here and there a sixpence shining among them, a great many bills, and very few receipts. All these articles he now thrust into the pockets of the coat, in doing which he dropped one of the notes and nodded to Reuben to pick it up.

Our poor Reuben! in picking up the note he glanced at the

writing, and recognised the hand of Blanche. Down it went, however, crushed among the other things, with no more ceremony or sentiment than if it had been a tavern reckoning. The heart of the susceptible boy felt crushed along with it, but, fortunately for him just at present, his grandfather's society was perfectly incompatible with the indulgence of tender thoughts. The Dean was no sooner dressed than he took Reuben with him to inspect the stables and offices, thence hurried him through the garden, over the farm, and round about the neighbourhood for a couple of hours, after which he returned to a lusty luncheon, had another altercation with the contractor, and sitting down to Eusebius himself, set Reuben to copy pages of Bellarmine until dinner.

At dinner he was equally instructive, though perhaps more vainglorious.

"Keep doing, always doing, and whatever you do, do it with all your heart, soul, and strength. Wishing, dreaming, intending, murmuring, talking, sighing, and repining, are all idle and profitless employments. The only manly occupation is to keep doing. I have been often told by wiseacres that building was a ruinous taste, but it is true of one kind of building, of castles in the air—a sort of castle that I never built. If I am a good example for anything, it is for energy; I study with energy, I exercise with energy, I sleep and I eat with energy."

Reuben had the proof of the latter assertion before his eyes, in the rapid consumption of the beef and mustard which his grandsire was making, while he had scarcely disposed of the first slice he had been helped to. The Dean at length observed his descendant's inefficiency with the knife and fork.

"Dine like a man, sir," he said, helping him a second time; "I don't approve of your dainty dastardly eaters; I don't like the man who does not like his dinner; that's one of my maxims; he may be honest but I am not sure of it. When I don't see a good appetite I am apt to suspect there is a bad digestion; and I cannot help connecting that with something amiss in the moral organisation. We are compound beings; we are not all body, neither are we all mind. The stomach and the conscience have a close affinity, take my word for it." The Dean paused, took a glass of port, pushed the water to Reuben, and hoped he was careful in the choice of his friends.

"Have you many?" he inquired.

"A good many, sir," said Reuben.

"You are a fortunate fellow," said his grandfather sneeringly;

"Achilles had only Patroclus; Pylades only Orestes, and you have a troop it seems. Who are they?"

"Henry Winning."

"I have heard of him; a promising young man."

"Hyacinth Primrose."

"Anybody else?—you have not come to the end of the list."

"Well, indeed, sir," said Reuben, "I had no notion how few friends I had, until I counted them."

"There is an important difference," said the Dean, "between friendships and intimacies. Intimacies are not friendships, but the tests of friendships. It is, unfortunately, only through intimacies we can discover how unworthy men are of possessing our friendship. We think we are deceived by our friends, when we have only discovered that they never were true friends at all."

Two or three days passed in this manner, and then the Dean left Westbury as abruptly as he came there. One morning after breakfast, having curtly recommended Reuben to the care of Mrs. Reeves, he thrust all his papers and things (that his pockets did not hold) into a carpet bag, grasped it by the lug, as a constable might do a thief, and strode away with the steps of Homer's Poseidon, to meet the coach for Hereford, which passed his gate at a certain well-known hour. Few ever deeply regretted the departure of Dean Wyndham. He usually left behind him the kind of feelings that people are conscious of when a storm has ceased which threatened to pull down their chimneys, and kept them awake the livelong night. The workmen were decidedly the happier when he was gone. Old Mrs. Reeves always tried to persuade herself that she was distressed upon such occasions, but in truth she was more comfortable in her master's absence, just because she was quieter; she expressed the exact state of her mind when she said that she "missed him very much," for we miss many a thing that we have no wish to have back again in a hurry—a truth well known to widows in particular. Reuben alone would have been better pleased if his grandfather had protracted his stay. The Dean's company had the singular effect of banishing from his thoughts the very subject which it might have been supposed it was particularly calculated to encourage. Reuben was carried away and interested in spite of himself, by a force and originality of character which, indeed, produced upon most people, a very strong impression. He was won too by the substantial kindness of the old gentleman's behaviour. In short he was more inclined upon the whole to gratitude than to resentment; he was probably too young to be furiously jealous; or perhaps it is not very easy or natural to be jealous of a man's grandfather.

In the way of rabbit shooting, our hero did as little as it was possible for him to do, for which there were several reasons, but the principal one was this,—his grandfather went away without giving him the gun he had promised him. This was a matter of less concern to the rabbits probably than it was to Reuben; but even to him it was of no great consequence, for he never had much enjoyment in any out-of-door occupation in which he had no associates. Had he made war upon the rabbits, therefore, it would probably have been over in a single campaign, and it is questionable if he would have killed a sufficient number of the enemy to entitle himself to the honours of a triumph. Failing the sports of the field, the resources at his command were the library, the workmen, and the society of the housekeeper. He was rather successful with Mrs. Reeves, because it was easy to be so, if you allowed her to be kind and attentive to you in her own fashion, tasted her gooseberry jams, pretended to give her dandelion tea a trial, and allowed her to go in and out and fidget about you, without snarling, or looking thunder at her. But Mrs. Reeves was not an Egeria with whom you could live in a cave or a desert. The silent library was more fascinating to Reuben, so he established himself there, and after some hours' deliberation commenced making a catalogue, and he labored so incessantly at this undertaking for several days, scarcely affording himself time for food and exercise, that Mrs. Reeves concluded it was a task set him by his grandfather, and never approached his table without heaving audible sighs and uttering various little ejaculations of a compassionate nature. At last he noticed these symptoms of mental uneasiness, and it was easy to bring the old lady to an explanation.

"It was a pity, so it was, to see so young a gentleman tied to the desk from morning till night, when it would do him so much more good to be diverting himself in the fields, or even assisting the haymakers in making the hay; she had heard stories of students growing double from moping too long over their books, and though her master was so old a man, few young men of the present day could do what he could do."

"There is a great deal of sense in what you say," said Reuben, "and I'll take your advice this instant. I have been working unnecessarily hard, but from this day forth, while I remain here, I will be ruled by you and divide my time more equally between business and relaxation."

If you want to win an old woman's heart, let her advise you, and either take her advice, or leave her under the impression that you will take it. The latter will do nearly as well.

Reuben, however, actually followed Mrs. Reeves's suggestions, so that he was soon in the highest favour.

The works going on in the house now began to engage his attention, particularly when the weather was unfavourable for walking. It was not only amusing but instructive to watch the processes of the different mechanics, who were employed in the extensive alterations going forward. The first acquaintance he made was with the young carpenter, whom the Dean had taught to drive a nail at the cost of bruising one of his own. From this intelligent lad he picked up nearly as much of the trade as he could have done in the greater part of a seven years' apprenticeship. He gained the carpenter's affections by playing the flageolet, and he was repaid for his strains by being instructed in the use of the saw and the chisel. Indeed, the flageolet soon became a great source of enjoyment to all the workmen, without at all hindering their labours, and Reuben was often prevailed upon to station himself in a central position on the principal staircase, perched on the bannisters, or on one of the painter's ladders, so that the music might be distributed as equally as possible over the whole house. The most popular airs were the cheerful ones, but there was one of the glaziers, a pallid pensive young man, who always begged for something sentimental, and Reuben afterwards found the name of Fanny in straggling letters upon a pane in his bed-chamber, which had most probably been scratched there with his diamond by the love-lorn artisan.

One evening after he had done a good day's work at the catalogue, while Mrs. Reeves was making his tea—not the dandelion—the young carpenter came with an humble petition to Reuben. There was dancing going on in the farm-yard, but the lads and lasses had no music except the whistling of one of the ploughmen, and if Master Medlicott would come down with his flageolet, and play them a few tunes, he would make the assembly happy and grateful beyond all expression. Reuben was easily persuaded to do a good-natured thing, so he very cheerfully consented to improve the rustic orchestra. Mrs. Reeves was at first adverse, but she was soon brought round, and would even have gone to the ball herself, only for certain infirmities connected with her feet, which always indisposed her to walking.

The farm-yard presented a gay sight, and there never wss a happier throng assembled in any ball-room, than was assembled there that evening under a full moon, which with the rosy remains of daylight afforded the revellers as much illumination as they cared to have. The excitement was at its height when Reuben appeared with his instrument, and the homestead rang through all the sheds and offices with the praises of his good-nature, cleverness, and condescension. It is not very common to witness so harmonious a union of husbandry and handicraft as was witnessed on the occasion of this impromptu festivity, for the masons, painters, plumbers, and other workmen employed in the house, were mingled with the ploughboys, dairymaids, and haymakers; the ball was opened by Reuben's friend, the carpenter, and Dorothy, the gardener's daughter, a full-blown rose of a girl, well able to dance down all the rest of the company, particularly the mechanical portion of it. Jenny, who held an office in the dairy, and was fair and mild as her own milk, danced with the chief of the masons; Molly, the under hen-wife, was led off by a plumber; Maria and Rebecca, two of the housemaids, consented to be the partners of a bell-hanger and a painter; the rest paired off as they best could, and whether it was a reel, a jig, a country dance, or a fandango, there never tripped a merrier group on the best chalked floor in London, than our hero put into motion by the first breath of his flageolet, just as if it had been an electric machine with a system of wires attached to the heels of the dancers. Reuben climbed by a ladder to the flat summit of an unfinished hay-rick, and seating himself in that commanding position shed his toe-inspiring melody upon the animated crowd beneath him. The love-lorn glazier, who would not dance because his Fanny was far away, was a pensive spectator of the scene from the topmost step of a wooden staircase which led to a granary; and various urchins about the farm, who were either too untaught, or too unclad, to be admitted into the circle (for there are exclusives even in the farm-yard), climbed into the boughs of a great tree, where, concealed from view by the foliage, they nevertheless managed to make their presence sufficiently known by the shouts and loud laughter with which they hailed all the little mischances and fatalities, liberties and necessities, incidental to rustic gaiety and moonlight mirth.

In short, the jollity was of the most exuberant description; nor, though the lance was not tipsy, was there wanting a supply of cider and brown ale from the neighbouring village to refresh the company, for the farm-people had clubbed half-a-crown to treat the tradesmen, and Reuben graciously contributed the same sum from the residue of his pocket-money, so that there was quite enough of the two beverages to promote innocent exhilaration, and not enough to stimulate it beyond the bounds of propriety. The first tankard was voted unanimously to the obliging Orpheus of the evening, who, after a moderate libation, descended from the rick, and graciously bowing to the revellers, and making them a dainty little speech, but quite long enough for the occasion, with something in it to please everybody, lads and lasses, rustics and mechanics, withdrew from the yard amidst loud plaudits, and carrying all hearts along with him.

CHAPTER XI.

HOW REUBEN CELEBRATED HIS GRANDFATHER'S MARRIAGE.

It was a great step towards Reuben's complete recovery, when he became composed enough to converse with Mrs. Reeves upon his grandfather's singular marriage. Mrs. Reeves had long been anxious to have a palaver with him on the subject, but she did not know how an allusion to it by her might be taken, and this consideration had kept her silent. But it was not in the nature of woman to endure such restraint for ever, so when the housekeeper found that Reuben would not take the initiative, she determined to take it herself, and when she once began it was a task beyond the power of Reuben to stop her.

"Well, wonders," she thought, "would never cease, and she did not know what the world would come to at last, for she remembered the time when gentlemen who were stricken in years, like her master, used to think of the burial-service more than the marriage-service. To be sure the Dean was hale and hearty, and a stout comely man for his years, but he was an old man nevertheless; for she was not a young creature herself, but she remembered the first day she ever laid eyes upon him, when she was only a giddy girl, and he was not a young man at that time. She had served two mistresses, and she never thought to be called on to serve a third, but if it was the will of Heaven, she was prepared to submit."

Reuben approved of the spirit evinced by Mrs. Reeves. It was necessary to say something, and this answered the purpose.

Mrs. Reeves then proceeded to say, that "she didn't see much use in sense and learning, since all the learning her master had in his head didn't make him wiser than other people after all: it was bad enough to marry at all, but if marry he must, he might have chosen some respectable elderly person, not a giddy, gay, inexperienced young lady, and handsome, she was informed, into the bargain.

This was painful to Reuben's ears, and he would have put an end to it, if he had been able.

"I suppose," he said, again in doubt what he ought to say, "my grandfather wanted a companion, somebody to manage his house for him."

This was rather a maladroit remark. "His house was not so ill-managed as all that," returned Mrs. Reeves, drily; "though she said it that should not say it; and as to companions, he had his books, he had his own writings and sermons; had he not as much company as he chose to invite?—and was not she always willing, when he was lonely, to bring in her knitting, or her ironing, or whatever little thing she was doing, if it was only an apple-dumpling she was making, and sit anywhere he pleased? he might talk to her, or let it alone, just as he liked; but he never was, to say, an affable sort of a gentleman at any period of his life; and since he began to dabble in mortar, it had not sweetened his temper. Then she hoped and trusted his new wife would prove a better match for him than the two who were in heaven; but perhaps Master Reuben could tell her something about the young lady, as he had come from Hereford where she lived."

Reuben had been apprehensive it would come to this, but there was no help for it, so he did his best to commad his emotions, and being once compelled to speak of Blanche, he could not do so except in terms the most laudatory, and even enthusiastic. In short, he was warmed by the theme, and ended by leaving Mrs. Reeves under the satisfactory conviction that if her new mistress laboured under the disadvantage of being young and handsome, she made some amends for those defects by being at the same time one of the most angelic of her sex.

The Dean's house presented now the edifying picture of a most diligent community; the workmen busy from morn till night at the repairs; Reuben labouring at his catalogue; Mrs.

Reeves manufacturing the fruits of the season into jams and conserves; in short, the bees were not a more industrious commonwealth. Catalogue-making pleased Reuben, because it not only exercised his ingenuity, but augmented his knowledge of the resources of literature. Reuben found numerous works in his grandfather's collection, of the very existence of which he had been ignorant; nay, he scarcely knew that there were such subjects as they treated of. Among others he found some curious old treatises on astrology, which seduced him for a day or two from his immediate pursuit. While interested in this idle study, he covered whole sheets of paper, and all the backs of his letters with diagrams, horoscopes, and calculations of imaginary nativities according to the rules which he found in the books. At length, having exhausted his paper, and wanting a more extended space for the working of a greater problem than he had yet encountered, he cleared the centre of the floor, drew his figures and circles with chalk, and began to realize to himself the actual operations of a cunning man of the middle ages. While he was occupied thus, his friend the carpenter came to him to solicit another favour, but it was a favour for the glazier, not for himself; in fact, the glazier wanted to send his Fanny a love letter, and wishing the letter to be a finer composition than he felt himself equal to produce, the idea had occurred to him of prevailing on our hero to compose one for him. The carpenter was indeed instructed to say, that there was little doubt of the heart of Fanny yielding to the pen of Master Reuben Medlicott, if he would kindly lend his genius for the occasion, and write the *billet doux* with a crow-quill. Reuben was interrupted and disturbed, but he was also flattered by this request. The crow-quill was easily found; the glazier, with his friend the carpenter, attended in the library after the work of the day, and an epistle was written, which (as Reuben long afterwards confessed), consisted for the most part of the identical tender thoughts and sentimental similies, which, arrayed in nearly the same words, had formed the materials of his letter to Blanche Barsac. "The fact was," he used to say, in his own excuse, "I was so engrossed by the astrology that original composition at the moment was out of the question." The gratitude of the glazier was unbounded; but give most men an inch and they will take an ell if they can get it. The carpenter re-appeared when Reuben was at breakfast, the next morning, and glancing knowingly at the figures and spheres with which the floor of the library was covered, he ventured to hint, after some circumlocution, that Mr. Medlicott could, if he pleased, form a tolerably shrewd guess as to the future fortunes of the glazier and his love.

Though Reuben declined to pry into the book of fate, even for the sake of comforting an affliction with which he could not but profoundly sympathise, it did not prevent his fame from spreading abroad for fortune-telling as well as letter-writing. Not many days elapsed before our magician, *malgré lui*, had two applications made to him, one for the discovery of a cow which had been stolen from a poor farmer, and the second, in another love case, to divine the success of a young man in the neighbourhood with Dorothy, the gardener's daughter.

In the middle of all this, and in strict keeping with the abruptness of everything connected with the life and movements of Dean Wyndham, down came the news of his wedding.

As it was to be, it was well it was over. Reuben's love was now his grandmother.

"After all," he said sensibly to himself, at the end of a solitary walk which he took to compose his spirits, "I am only eighteen, and Blanche is twenty-seven; she is certainly too young to be my grandmother, but she is also too old to be my wife." The same evening brought him a letter from home. Blanche had written his mother a charming letter a few days before her marriage, and sent her the picture she had drawn of Reuben, which had actually only required a few finishing touches, and those she had given from memory. The picture pleased Mrs. Medlicott extremely, and it was already placed over the chimney-piece of the dining-parlour, in a frame much too costly for what it contained, considered as a work of art.

When the Dean's wedding was noised abroad, it caused prodigious excitement, and as he had sent Mrs. Reeves a sum of money, to promote a little gaiety on the occasion among his people at Westbury, what form that gaiety ought to take became an immediate subject of deliberation. Another rustic ball was resolved on, and as the moon was no longer auspicious, the barn was selected for the scene of festivity. A box of candles was ordered from the nearest town, and the carpenters with a few hoops made some capital substitutes for chandeliers, all under Reuben's directions; for, without any formal appointment, or any ambition to obtain it, he found himself installed in the office of master of the revels. The walls had their nakedness handsomely clothed with festoons of evergreens and flowers; the floor was well rolled and made as smooth as it was possible to make it; a substantial supper was prepared; a hogshead of cider stood ready to be broached; all the fiddlers and pipers within reach were retained specially, and a Welsh harper, who was on his way to a meeting of the bards, was induced to sojourn for the night, and add his contribution to the music. The Dean had no idea of such doings, or he would never have sent the donation, for there was an end of all labour on the farm, and all work within doors for the two days preceding the *fête*. The greatest excitement of all, however, was among the girls, wondering and discussing which of them would be honoured with Reuben's hand, for the ball would, of course, be opened by him; and whether it was a nymph of the dairy, the garden, or the bedrooms, it was certain that the honour of being his partner would fall to the lot of somebody.

All would have gone well if they had been content with the dancing, but Reuben unluckily knew something about making fire-works, and the moment the word was mentioned, it became clear to everybody that without fire-works, the celebration of the nuptials might as well be abandoned altogether. Accordingly to work he went at the pyrotechnics, and, aided by the carpenter and glazier, who were now his most devoted servants, a quantity of rockets, squibs, crackers, and a few more ingenious devices, were produced in a wonderfully short time, as there was no difficulty about procuring gunpowder.

It was arranged that the fire-works should precede the ball and supper; had it been otherwise, they might have secured the latter enjoyments at all events; but the fire-works had the precedence, and the beginning of the display was most successful. Reuben let off the rockets with his own hands, and the wonder and delight of everybody was at the height, when an exclamation was heard that the great hay-rick had caught fire. Consternation soon took the place of mirth. The rick was in a blaze before the nimblest could reach the yard. All that could be done to extinguish the flames, by putting up ladders and carrying up buckets of water, was done with as much expedition and activity as possible, but in spite of every effort the fire continued to rage, and soon extending to other ricks and some stacks of corn, threatened the entire of Dean Wyndham's farm-property with destruction. Reuben behaved now like a hero, if he had not acted before like a philosopher. His exertions were beyond those of anybody else, except perhaps his friends, the mechanics, who supported him as well as men could do. The utmost, however, that could be effected was to save the buildings and the cattle. All the hay and corn in the yard, with many of the agricultural implements, were a heap of ashes before the sun rose the following morning; and as to Reuben, who considered himself the responsible person for the calamity, between the toil he underwent, the drenching of his clothes, and his mental-sufferings, when poor Mrs. Reeves (herself in a pitiable situation) put him to bed at four o'clock in the morning, he was in the first stage of a high fever.

BOOK THE THIRD.

"'Tis the Philosopher, the Orator, the Poet, whom we may compare to some first-rate vessel, which launches out into the wide sea, and with a proud motion insults the encountering surges. We are of the small-craft, or galley kind. We move chiefly by starts and bounds, according as our motion is by frequent intervals renewed. We have no great adventure in view, nor can tell certainly whither we are bound. We undertake no mighty voyage by help of stars or compass, but row from creek to creek, keep up a coasting trade, and are fitted only for fair weather and the summer season."—*Shaftesbury's Characteristics.*

ARGUMENT.

THIS brief book is an interlude between school and college. Returned to quiet Underwood, we shall make the acquaintance of some very disagreeable, impertinent, meddling and unconscionable people, happy in the name of Pigwidgeon, the only pleasant thing about them. They were none of Reuben's friends: his parents brought them upon him—his mother by being so clever a woman, his father by being so easy a man. In short, the Medlicotts were Pigwidgeoned, and we are not to pity them, for they brought the Pigwidgeoning on themselves. Pigwidgeoning will prove to be a social usage, nearly akin to sponging, although you will hardly find the word in the books of synonymes. Much is to be said against the practice, much also in its defence and favour; in particular how it leads to the development of numerous Christian graces and excellencies of the human character. Doth it not put into daily practice the noble virtue of self-abasement? Is not the spirit of martyrdom as much evinced in suffering the snubs and rubs, and all the thousand ills that sponging is heir to, as in roasting like Latimer, or being fried like St. Lawrence! There are men of such exemplary fortitude as to submit to be roasted themselves for the sake of a roast sirloin, and make themselves the butt of the company for a glass or two of wine. What infinite mortifications abroad does not such a man endure, nay court, which he might easily escape by dining selfishly at home upon a mutton chop? Can the spirit of self-devotion descend lower, or should we not rather ask, can this noble spirit be conceived to soar higher than this? To enter ungreeted, to depart amidst general satisfaction, to feel that he is the guest by sufferance of one who is a host of necessity, to know that an evil eye follows every motion of his fork, to feel that a bailiff or tax-gatherer would receive a more cordial welcome, would make ambrosia itself bitter, and turn a very cup of nectar sour. How then shall we ever enough admire the brave race which encounters these manifold evils undismayed. How strong must be their social yearnings! How great the warmth within, that counteracts the frigid look, the wintry reception, the cold shoulder! How genial the glow of that self-hospitality which sustains them in the arctic regions abroad, to penetrate which they leave the temperate climate of their own fire-sides with a gallantry like that of our Parrys and our Franklins.

But this will be found not only a book of tribulations but a book of travels. There is no room in the Welch inns with our friends the Medlicotts, the Hopkinses, the Primroses, and Winnings. Reuben must have his travelling physician, too, for he travels for health, while the rest travel for pleasure—except the Vicar, indeed, with whom it is a matter of necessity, being turned out of his house, and in the condition of the badger whose hole has been seized by the fox, or of the eagle, whose unguarded nest the sneaking weasel has invaded. Reuben is popular in the principality, where he learns the Welch tongue and the Welch harp, and breaks the hearts of the Welch maidens. As to his own, it is again in some slight danger; we shall now detect the winged mischief lurking in a plump Quaker's bonnet to launch another of his frivolous bolts at the boy's heart; for there are hazards incidental to learning the guttural Welch as well as the liquid Italian in company with a fair young friend —perils not less formidable perhaps than sitting for one's picture. Yet nothing serious is immediately to be apprehended; Reuben will probably reach Cambridge heart-whole.

CHAPTER L.

CHAPTER OF RETROSPECTS.—REUBEN IS BORED; HIS PARENTS ARE PIGWIDGEONED.

LEAVING the subject of our history for a short time to the tender care of Mrs. Reeves and the skill of Dr. Page, the physician of the neighbourhood, we fly back to Underwood with the alarming news of Reuben's illness; and having arrived there it will not be amiss to put the reader briefly in possession of what had been doing at the Vicarage since we left it to go to school.

People of passive character often exercise surprising influence in domestic life, just as the most yielding substances, such as a snail or a branch of fern, will often leave their stamps for many centuries in the solid rock. Thus the absence of Reuben from home made a serious change at Underwood. The Vicar, becoming more and more absorbed in his pinks and strawberries, having no further motive to keep up his Greek and Latin, was less a companion for his wife than ever, and the little fund of wit he possessed would have become rusty indeed but for the occasional burnishing he gave it when he met a pleasant party at Mrs. Winning's, or chatted with Hannah Hopkins, or a brother parson, beneath the walnut-tree, or under the mahogany.

Mrs. Medlicott's spirits had been deeply affected by the separation from her son, and she missed, even more than her husband, the favourite and engrossing occupation of twelve anxious years. But she had more consolations and resources than her spouse. In the first place she had the solace of continually writing to her son, and receiving his dutiful and minute letters; then her mind (you know) if it had any fault, was only too richly caparisoned; and, lastly, she possessed in a very strong degree that womanly yearning towards her species, which made solitude absolutely intolerable to her, particularly in the prosecution of her intellectual pursuits. She had long been an ardent phrenologist, but now she cultivated that subject with redoubled spirit, pronouncing it decidedly one of the inductive sciences, and questioning whether Dr. Spurzheim was not as illustrious a philosopher as Sir Isaac Newton. Her great ally in the prosecution of her craniological studies was a certain slovenly, sycophantic, gossipping apothecary, of the name of Pigwidgeon, father to that interesting youth whose attempt to appropriate a certain cake belonging to Reuben was related in an early chapter. This Mr. Pigwidgeon had some reputation for skill, and would have had more business if he had not been so painfully negligent of his personal appearance, and so addicted to sponging upon his patients. He had a tincture of learning, just enough to pass for erudition with people who were not erudite, and being conceited in proportion to his real ignorance, he was inordinately vain of his acquaintance and intimacy with Mrs. Medlicott, though the run of the kitchen was that which he still more valued. A few years had made considerable change in the personal appearance of his son Theodore; he looked as much a booby as ever, but he was tall, had good features, a fresh florid complexion, abundance of black hair, and lively boisterous spirits, which made him an insufferable bore to all who were not for some reason or another excessively partial to him. The father had already announced his intention to make a physician of him, and to show what a natural genius he had for that profession, Mr. Theodore Pigwidgeon never heard a complaint or disease mentioned, but he had a trick of exclaiming—" I wonder what's good for that." The apothecary pronounced the measurements of the lad's cranium magnificent, and of course predicted for him a career of the most dazzling description, while the little public of Underwood, on the contrary, relied upon Lavater's system more than Spurzheim's, and the effect of the father's over-weeningness was that the son got only more generally laughed at, and went in derision by the name of "the Doctor." Mrs. Medlicott was one of the few who took young Pigwidgeon's part; but commanding intellects are the most tolerant of mental inferiority in those about them; besides the apothecary never pretended that the Doctors developments were altogether equal to Reuben's, which might have excited a mother's jealousy. Between Mr. Pigwidgeon, indeed, and Mrs. Medlicott, the great bond of union was the inexhaustible subject of Reuben's skull. Mr. Pigwidgeon had long ago taken its measurements in due form, with the brass gauge or craniometer, which he always carried about him in one pocket of his coat, to balance the stethoscope which he carried in the other, and had made an exact inventory of the organs, a copy of which Mrs. Medlicott possessed, and nobody can conceive what a comfort it was to her, when the head itself was no longer near her. But with Pigwidgeon junior she had other and wider associations; her profound study of the mind enabled her to discover that his seeming obtuseness was only the temporary dormancy of very respectable talents, if not of actual genius, and the next step brought her to the point of feeling that it was her duty to awaken that somnolent state of the brain of so nice a young man into life and activity. Thus her didactic abilities came into play again, just when she was beginning to fear that her maternal mission was concluded. She now had somebody, or rather something to lecture and belecture as before; and dull, or rather dormant as the Doctor's faculties were, he was not insensible to the honour of being the pupil or fellow-student of the Minerva-like matron, who laid herself out to improve and develope him.

The first occasion upon which Reuben noticed the growing domestication of the Pigwidgeons at the Vicarage, was once upon returning home for the vacation, in the beginning of the dogdays. His father happened not to be at home on his arrival, but his mother seeing him approach, bustled out to receive him, and after tenderly embracing him on the little close-shaven lawn, led him into the cool shady room where she had been sitting, and where Reuben, not without some surprise, found the apothecary's son, with whom he had never been on intimate terms, and whom of late years he had never heard mentioned without ridicule. Reuben was always shy, and young Pigwidgeon was nothing short of a lout in his manners. The meeting was anything but cordial, nor were matters much improved when Mrs. Medlicott went about her domestic affairs, and left the young men to "entertain one another."

Reuben hardly knew whether it was his office to amuse Pigwidgeon, or Pigwidgeon's to amuse him; Reuben was at home certainly, but really the other looked very much at home too, to judge from his unceremonious dress, and the graceful New-England freedom with which he had extended his lubber length upon the only sofa in the room.

Pigwidgeon yawned and said it was a hot day.

Reuben agreed in the briefest possible terms.

The former expressed his surprise that Reuben did not wear a broad-leafed straw hat like his own, as everybody did in the country.

Reuben said he had not got one, at which capital jest Pigwidgeon laughed in his facetious way, ho, ho, ho, &c.

"How many boys are there at the school?"

"Sixty."

"Are any of them ever sick?"

"Sometimes; there was one boy very bad with the croup when I left."

"I wonder what is good for that," said the Doctor.

The conversation ended as it had begun, with Pigwidgeon yawning freely, after which he got on his legs, and said he would go and have some strawberries, at the same time politely inviting Reuben to have some too.

When Mrs. Medlicott returned she found her son where she had left him, and looked displeased that he had not accompanied Pigwidgeon to the strawberry beds. She took that opportunity of letting Reuben know the lively interest she felt in the young man, and expressed an anxiety that they should become friends and companions.

Reuben made a dutiful effort to like Pigwidgeon, because his mother was anxious about it, but friendship will obey a mother no better than love. The thing was not to be done. It was out of the question to take an interest in him, unless you were engaged, as Mrs. Medlicott was, in developing his faculties.

The enjoyment of several vacations was marred to Reuben by the almost daily presence of a booby whom he despised, but from whose society in a limited rural circle there was no means of escaping. The vicar despised him too, and though little given to be satirical on his friends or his guests, could not help making himself merry now and then in a guarded way at Pigwidgeon's expense, particularly at his favourite exclamation — "I wonder what's good for that." But neither father nor son had the moral courage to express their sentiments freely. They received the Pigwidgeons as a visitation of Providence, and submitted to it with as much fortitude as they could muster.

The only holidays Reuben thoroughly enjoyed were while Theodore Pigwidgeon was running the London hospitals, as the phrase is; but that stage in the young man's medical education only rendered him more ridiculous and offensive when he returned to Underwood after it. He returned wearing moustaches, turning down his shirt-collar, and talking of the eminent physicians and surgeons of the day, as if they were his playmates. Reuben marvelled how his father, easy as he was, tolerated such a creature, and as to his mother, who actually admired him, Reuben could only account for her conduct by believing her under the influence of some possession. He now seldom enjoyed a ramble in the fields with her, without the "Doctor" accompanying or joining them. It was Pigwidgeon who helped her over the stiles, Pigwidgeon who arranged her shawl when it slipped from her shoulders, Pigwidgeon who held her spectacles when she was energetic, Pigwidgeon here, Pigwidgeon there, Pigwidgeon everywhere.

Then after the infliction of the son for the greater part of a day, would follow only too often the visitation of the father at the close of it. Evening came on anything but sweetly when it brought the apothecary with it, and he made himself particularly disagreeable to Reuben by volunteering an opinion that his chest was not strong, and that playing the flageolet was not good for him. His parents had not consented to his learning that instrument without consulting Mr. Pigwidgeon in the first instance. The apothecary had then made no objection, but when Reuben was at home, our Pill Garlic (who was generally meddling with people's lungs when he was not measuring their skulls) began to change his mind, and talk of sounding his chest with the stethoscope one of those days.

Reuben was sent for by his mother one morning, and found her seated under the walnut-tree, reading. The book was a scientific book on the Diseases of the Chest and Lungs, which the apothecary had lent to her.

The following dialogue then took place:

"Well, mother," said Reuben, sitting down at her side.

"What I am about to say," she said, after preparing her voice and assuming a serious manner, "is of considerable importance. Mr. Pigwidgeon, you must know, who is very friendly, extremely skilful, and very much attached to you, my dear Reuben, has been talking to me a good deal lately about the state of your chest."

"My chest, my dear mother!" exclaimed Reuben, not able to refrain from laughing.

"Yes, my dear, he thinks your lungs are not quite as strong as he would wish them to be, and as he hopes to make them."

Reuben again smiled at the notion of anything being the matter with his lungs. Well he might; for nature had made him only too vigorous in that part of his constitution.

Mrs. Medlicott took off her spectacles, and said that medical men were not infallible of course, but that their opinions were not to be despised, particularly when it was manifest that their opinions were perfectly disinterested.

"Let Mr. Pigwidgeon be ever so disinterested, mother, and ever so skilful, I am not the less satisfied that there's nothing amiss with my lungs. What could have put such a notion into his strange head?"

"I trust you are right, my dear Reuben; but I hope you will not be obstinate on a matter of such vital importance. I am sure, Reuben, you would even make some little sacrifice to make my mind easy."

"I conclude, mother," replied Reuben, "you wish me to submit to be stethoscoped; if so, you shall be gratified, although the prospect of undergoing that, or any other operation at Mr. Pigwidgeon's hands, is not the most agreeable in the world."

"I was not alluding merely to the stethoscope," replied Mrs. Medlicott, a little drily; "Mr. Pigwidgeon has his doubts whether playing the flageolet is good for you."

"Really, mother," said Reuben, standing up, "this is too bad; who asked his opinion on the subject? When people want opinions on their lungs they don't consult country apothecaries."

"Theodore fully concurs with him," said Mrs. Medlicott.

"Which, I am sure, mother," cried Reuben, with unusual impatience, "adds very little weight to his authority. Mr. Theodore Pigwidgeon is neither a doctor nor an apothecary—as yet."

Mrs. Medlicott was greatly displeased at the tone taken by her son, but she commanded her feelings; and the interview ended by Reuben's amiable consent to have his chest examined, feeling, indeed, too confident in the soundness of his lungs to be apprehensive about the result.

There was one spot in the garden which Reuben in his imaginative boyhood had always thought the prettiest, and where it had been his wont in the days of domestic instruction often to establish himself in fine weather, with the birds warbling and hopping about him, the flowers scenting the air, and the butterflies sometimes perching on his books. There was a rustic bench fixed there, and a massive round table, of the same rough construction, which answered the purposes of study and occasionally those of tea. A few evenings after the conversation with his mother which we have just related, Reuben, entering this favourite spot, found his father and the apothecary there, sipping something, he knew not what, only that the drinking-vessels were not tea-cups. The sweet smell of the garden was lost in the vapour of the negus or the toddy. His bower was turned into a sort of *cabaret*. The circular marks of the glasses were visible all over the rustic table, as you see them in the casinos and suburban tea-gardens.

When Reuben appeared, Mr. Pigwidgeon shuffled about, invited him to take a seat by his side—a civility which Reuben declined with the driest acknowledgment, for nobody ever sat by the side of the apothecary who could avoid it. He smelled of senna in the morning, and of tobacco in the evening; besides he took snuff in enormous quantities, and scattered it about him so liberally in the act, that it was almost impossible to be in the same house with him without continually sneezing. Reuben was turning away to seek his mother, when she saved him that trouble by appearing at the moment, attended, as usual, by her medical student. Tea was ordered in the bower, and while it was preparing, the apothecary fumbled in his pockets, produced his stethoscope, and said it was a very good opportunity for making a little examination of Reuben's chest. Reuben submitted with as much patience as he could muster, while his mother stood by, looking on with the greatest interest and anxiety, and watching the apothecary's countenance, to try to find out what opinion he was forming as he proceeded with his soundings. The Vicar had taken up a newspaper, and paid no attention whatsoever to what was going forward. When Mr

Pigwidgeon was done he pronounced the sort of ambiguous judgment so commonly pronounced by medical practitioners—that there was nothing, he hoped, decidedly wrong about the lungs, but that there were indications of weakness which he thought ought not to be neglected; he might, however, be mistaken, and, as two heads were better than one, he wished his son would take the stethoscope, and say what he thought on the subject. This was too much for Reuben's patience, amiable as he was. When the Doctor, with his usual "ho, ho," took the instrument and advanced to manipulate him, he repelled him with very little ceremony, and the Vicar at the same time looking up from his paper, was evidently pleased to see an end put to operations which he considered absurd and superfluous.

Young Pigwidgeon himself seemed to mind the repulse exceedingly little; his attention was strongly solicited at this moment by the cakes and the fruits with which the maids were spreading the tea-table, and he laid the stethoscope aside with a "ho! ho!" as he took it up; but the paternal vanity of the apothecary was visibly wounded, and he was as bitter as rhubarb the rest of the evening, though he was not less devoted than his son to the repast before him. Indeed, even if the Doctor had been ever so angry with Reuben for the disrespect shown to his medical skill, the redoubled favours of Mrs. Medlicott would have amply compensated him, for she made him sit by her side, and, loading him at the same time with compliments and other sweets of a more substantial nature, effectually prevented him from falling the tenth of an inch in his own estimation.

Another circumstance, which occurred at a later period, and arose out of the incident just related, tended still more decidedly to generate a malignant feeling towards Reuben in the mind of the elder Pigwidgeon, though the animal interests he had in maintaining friendly relations with the Vicar and his family made him very careful not to display his real sentiments. The magazine has been mentioned which Reuben and his friend Primrose established at Hereford. On the return of the former to school, after the annoyance which he had experienced from the apothecary and the stethoscope, he entertained his nimble-witted friend with an account of the affair, and gave him a description of Mr. Pigwidgeon, which Primrose thought so comical that he made it the subject of an article in the next number of the periodical. The paper was entitled "A Portrait of a Country Apothecary," and, except that the name was changed, nobody who had ever seen the subject of it could, without extraordinary obtuseness, have mistaken the aim of the writer. The magazine went down to Underwood as usual, for Mrs. Medlicott had made Reuben promise to send it to her regularly. It was winter; dinner was over; the Vicar and his wife, the apothecary and his son, formed a small semicircle about the fire (not, however, to the exclusion f a table with a bottle of port upon it, and a plate of walnuts), when what should arrive but the packet from Hereford, with the last new number of the "Mirror," for so the magazine was designated. The apothecary was the first to petition most earnestly for a specimen of Master Reuben's essays in polite literature, but the paper entitled the "Country Apothecary," looked so piquant that the Vicar said they must have that first, and the Pigwidgeons were equally anxious to have it.

The Doctor was the reader upon such occasions; he read as if he had a walnut in his mouth, and was not very punctilious about the stops, but Mrs. Medlicott said he read with feeling, and there was nobody to dispute her opinion. He had not read a couple of pages before the Medlicotts were horribly alive to the design of the paper; neither of them dared to look at the apothecary, or they might have seen by the contortions of his strange physiognomy that he too shrewdly guessed who had sat for the picture. Nor did they venture to stop the reader, much as they burned to do so, while he, being too dull to perceive anything in the world less palpable than a door-post, mouthed the libel upon his father to the last syllable, and laid the paper down with a protracted yawn, by way of a general critique, which was probably a very just one upon the performance.

The letters H. P. however were subscribed to the article; that was the only comfort the Medlicotts had, for they did not entertain the slightest doubt that the apothecary had recognised his own image in the "Mirror."

Let this be no disparagement to Mr. Pigwidgeon's merits as a hypocrite of considerable ability, or, perhaps, we should rather say, as a sensible man of the world, for he was never louder in his flatteries of Reuben than he was that same evening; and the better to mask what probably passsed in his mind, he made no change in his conduct, but continued to drop in at the Vicarage in his usual unceremonious fashion, to dine one day and sup another, just as if nothing had happened to hurt his feelings.

This state of things continued up to the period of Reuben's illness at his grandfather's country-house, when the paternal pride of the apothecary received another blow which he did not stomach so easily as the wound to his *amour propre*.

CHAPTER II.

REUBEN'S RECOVERY AND THE JOY IT OCCASIONED.

"The young incendiary!" said the Vicar, when he heard of the events at Westbury.

Mrs. Reeves was slow at writing and walking, but she had employed the parish clerk to write to Underwood, and had thus informed Reuben's parents of his serious illness and the causes that led to it. The same letter mentioned that the best medical advice in the neighbourhood had been provided, which was that of a Doctor Page, who turned out to be an old acquaintance of Mr. Medlicott's.

The Vicar was unable to leave home at the time, owing to the pressure of his pastoral duties, so the anxious mother determined to set out immediately. While she was making her little preparations, Mr. Pigwidgeon dropped in, and no sooner did he hear of Reuben's illness, and Mrs. Medlicott's intended journey, than he proffered the services of his son to accompany her to Westbury, and save the expense of a regular physician. The escort would have been extremely agreeable, but with all Mrs. Medlicott's high opinion of her friend Theodore, her regard for her son was too strong to allow her to think seriously for a moment of the latter part of the apothecary's proposal. It placed her, however, in a difficulty, which she tried to evade by thanking the father, and saying that "the company of Theodore would no doubt be a great comfort to her on the road."

"And a greater comfort to you," said Pigwidgeon, "when you come to the end of your journey."

"What do you allude to?" asked the Vicar, who just came in at the moment and only heard the last words.

Mrs. Medlicott repeated the offer which the apothecary had so kindly made.

"It will save you some guineas, let me tell you," said Pigwidgeon, accompanying the coarse speech with an equally coarse action, a little punch under the ribs with his forefinger.

The words and the action together made the Vicar forget himself for a moment, and he thanked Mr. Pigwidgeon in a manner so little gracious that it provoked from that gentleman a still less becoming observation on the slight to his son's medical skill, which he said he could not but take as a slight to himself. The Vicar replied as softly as he could that it was nonsense to say he had offered a slight to either father or son; at all events he had meant to do no such thing; he felt that Mr. Pigwidgeon's proposition was a very kind one, but he could not think of putting his son to the trouble and expense of such a journey, particularly as Reuben was fortunately already in the hands of a very skilful local physician, his old friend Dr. Page.

Directly the Vicar named this gentleman he saw that it had the same effect upon the apothecary that oil has upon fire. Mr. Pigwidgeon had evidently some bitter personal enmity to the physician of Westbury, for he lost the command of his temper when he was mentioned, and went away in high dudgeon, saying as he went "that his son Theodore, although he had not got his diploma, had more knowledge in his little finger than a whole college of Dr. Pages; he called Page twenty quacks and mountebanks; vowed he would not trust him with the life of a kitten, much less the life of one of his children; but he had done his duty, and now he washed his hands of it."

This was a favourite phrase with Pigwidgeon, and nobody could hear him use it, without wishing him to perform the operation literally, for his hands always looked as if they required washing extremely, though this was in some measure owing to the colour of the skin which was precisely that which arises from a chronic neglect of soap and water.

Mrs. Medlicott left the Vicarage that night, not even taking a maid with her, for she was not one of those women who can do nothing for themselves, and the Vicar's small means made even a small increase of expense a matter of serious consideration. At starting she was the only inside passenger, but the coach stopped at Mrs. Winning's gate and took in two gentlemen. Mrs. Medlicott recognised neither of them; indeed it was too dark to distinguish their faces, even if they had been old acquaintances. They were polite to her; left the best seat to her exclusive occupation, but only conversed with one another. They had been laughing before they entered the coach, and they were still in the same vein, whatever it was that diverted them, and this was not very long a secret from their fair fellow traveller, for the elder said to the younger—

"Of all the preposterous marriages I ever heard of, this of Dean Wyndham is the most preposterous. There is an account of it in the 'Times' of yesterday, copied from the 'Hereford Express'—why the Dean must be near seventy."

"So they say."

"You know him, I think."

"I have often met him, but I can't say I know him; he keeps fellows like me at an awful distance. There was a grandson of his at Finchley, a great friend of mine. We were all intimate with those Barsacs. Your nephew George, Primrose, Medlicott, and myself, were invited to all their balls;—but you have not heard the most amusing circumstance about the marriage in question."

"No!"

"Medlicott, I hear, was in love with the girl who turned out to be his grandfather's flame, and who is now of course his grandmother."

"Capital!"

"The girl herself may have behaved indiscreetly, but I have no doubt my susceptible friend acted as sentimental and soft a part as possible."

"With his grandfather's example before his eyes, what less could he do?"

"Yet Medlicott is a very clever and promising fellow; too clever in fact; 'tis almost the only fault he has."

"He takes that from his mother. Do you know her? Very blue, I am told."

"Blue as Minerva," said the younger.

Here Reuben's mother, who had been listening to the dialogue with the greatest interest and curiosity, gave a little cough, which whether intended to be admonishing or not, had the effect of recalling the attention of her companions to her presence, and suggesting the imprudence of carrying their personal remarks further. Indeed the conversation ceased at this point; the elder gentleman (who was Sir John de Tabley, uncle to the young epicure of Finchley) drew out a sort of travelling night-cap and sank into his corner where he soon fell asleep. Henry Winning who sat opposite the lady, folded his arms and probably courted repose also. In a few minutes Mrs. Medlicott was the only waking person of the three; she would probably not have slept a great deal under any circumstances, but in addition to her former anxieties about Reuben, the conversation she had just heard gave her fresh grounds of uneasiness upon his account. Towards morning, however, she yielded a little to slumber herself, for maternal solicitude will sometimes nod as well as the father of poetry, and when she awoke she was the only passenger in the coach. She reached Westbury greatly fatigued, on the evening of the second day of her journey, from which it may safely be inferred that England was not covered with railways at the period of our story, as it is in the days we live in.

Reuben was still seriously ill, but had already been pronounced out of danger. The sleep in which his mother found him, when she first entered his room, would alone have satisfied her that he had got through the worst of the attack. She knelt down at the side of his bed, and thanked Heaven for his preservation; then went down to the library to write immediately to her husband, and in the library she found Dr. Page. He was standing gazing at the circles and figures which still remained on the floor where Reuben had traced them, and Mrs. Reeves was at his elbow making an ineffectual attempt to explain the doctrines of judicial astrology.

As Mrs. Medlicott was accustomed to country doctors, she was less surprised at Dr. Page's exterior than if she had spent her life in London. You might have taken him for a farmer, or a horse-jockey, but he was as little like a doctor as possible, unless indeed the veterinary art was his branch of the profession. He was a short, florid, confident man, with a good expression of countenance, but forward and blunt manners; it was his dress, however, that would have led you astray as to his profession, for he wore a short green coat with gilt buttons, waistcoat and breeches of white cord, a crimson silk cravat, and gaiters of yellow buckskin which came up to his knees—a costume which nobody surely would adopt at a masquerade if he intended to impersonate a physician. However, as "honour peereth through the meanest habit," so do knowledge and skill through any habiliments, however singular; and Dr. Page had not been five minutes in company with Mrs. Medlicott before he convinced her that he was a man of sense and experience, whose confidence in himself was not without good grounds, though perhaps a little too ostentatious.

"Madam," said Page, making a low and too flourishing obeisance to the lady as she entered, "I should have been most happy to have saved you the fatigue of your long journey, but that was out of my power. I did my best, with the assistance of

Mrs. Reeves, to make your trouble superfluous, but you won't be displeased with us for that, particularly when I have the pleasure of adding that we have succeeded in our endeavours, and that your amiable, talented, and accomplished son has decidedly turned the corner."

"Believe me, sir," said Mrs. Medlicott, "my husband and I will never forget your services to our dear boy upon this occasion. Under Heaven we are indebted to you for his life; but unless I could make you conceive all a mother's feelings, I should fail to convey all a mother's gratitude."

"I have had the greater pleasure," replied the Doctor, "in affording your son the benefit of such little skill as I possess, because, from what Mrs. Reeves informs me, I am inclined to believe that I had formerly the pleasure of enjoying his father's friendship."

"My husband was struck by the name of Page," said Mrs. Medlicott; "I am delighted indeed to find that you are his old acquaintance and schoolfellow."

"Yes, ma'am," rejoined the rural doctor, "Page and Medlicott were Pylades and Orestes; his vocation was the cure of souls, mine was the cure of bodies; we took different courses; he sailed east, and I sailed west; but he was the wiser fellow of the two, for he had the sense and the taste to pick up a companion on his voyage, and I must say he could not have made a discreeter choice."

Mrs. Medlicott was too weary to do more than smile languidly in reply to this, while she threw herself into the nearest chair. The Doctor took the hint, became practical in a moment, apologised for having kept her standing so long, prescribed a cup of tea and an early bed, and after giving some brief directions to Mrs. Reeves, made another flourishing bow and took his leave for the night.

It was a short illness, but a tedious convalescence. Several weeks elapsed before Reuben's strength was restored even enough to enable him to walk down with his mother to the farm-yard, and give her the details of the conflagration. The Dean had gone to Switzerland immediately after his wedding. He was at Frankfort when the news reached him of the memorable manner in which his grandson had celebrated his nuptials; and whether it was that distance made him less sensitive to the loss he sustained, or that his young wife softened his feelings, or that the damage was covered by a fair insurance, he surprised everybody by the patience with which he bore the consequences of Reuben's indiscretion.

"If it had been the library," said the Dean, "I never should have forgiven him."

This was the harshest observation he made, or, at least, the harshest that was reported in England. From one of Mrs. Wyndham's letters, it appeared that he was sometimes even jocular upon the subject, and observed that his grandson had very early begun to illuminate the world.

If Mrs. Medlicott was not surprised at the popularity of Reuben with everybody at Westbury, it must at all events have delighted her. Wherever she went she heard nothing but the praises of his amiable disposition, and his various talents and accomplishments. She received congratulations from everybody on being the mother of such a clever son. It was the universal opinion that there had never been such a wonderful patient, such a wonderful fever, or such a wonderful recovery. The young carpenter and the sentimental glazier took care to throw themselves in her way, and give vent to their feelings; while Dorothy, the gardener's daughter, with her flowers and fruits, Jenny of the dairy, with her creams, and Molly, the sub-henwife, with her new-laid eggs, more than satisfied Mrs. Medlicott that Reuben stood as well as it was desirable that any young man should stand with his fellow creatures of the softer sex. Finally, Dr. Page pronounced the highest possible eulogium upon our accomplished hero,—

"Madam," said he to Mrs. Medlicott, "until I knew your son, I always thought myself a cleverer man than my patients, but, by Jove, since I have attended him, I have come to the conclusion that the patient is a cleverer fellow than the doctor. He talks like an angel, ma'am; by Jove he does. He'll astonish the world some of those days."

"I do so wish you were settled in our neighbourhood, Dr. Page," replied the gratified mother.

"You would see a great deal of me at the Vicarage, madam, if I were," replied the Doctor.

"We could never see too much, sir," said the lady; "but perhaps, when my husband comes to take us home, which, now that Reuben is so strong, will be in a few days, he will be able to induce you to accompany us back to Underwood, and pay us a short visit."

"That I shall do with pleasure, madam," said the Doctor; "but until your husband arrives, I must insist upon your being my guest, for I perceive that the painters are approaching this side of the house, and the smell of the paint would not accelerate my young friend's recovery."

"We are very thankful to you, indeed," said Mrs. Medlicott.

"Not at all," said Page, "I am only prescribing sweet air for you; you will find my bachelor's house fresh and clean at all events; only tell your son not to expect such a library as he has here, for I have only three books in the world,—a Bible, a Shakspeare, and the Pharmocopœia."

CHAPTER III.

A BOLD STROKE FOR A DINNER.—HOW THE APOTHECARY GOT BACK TO THE VICARAGE, AND HOW HE TURNED THE VICAR OUT OF IT.

Mrs. Medlicott had very little notion of the state of things at the Vicarage when she was inviting Dr. Page to pay her a visit. The Pigwidgeons seemed to have been placed by Providence in the parish of Underwood to be the plague of the Vicar's life; for as to his wife she was no more to be pitied than people in general are who bring their own troubles on themselves.

For a considerable time after his wife left him the Vicar v little or nothing of his friend the apothecary. In nourishing L s resentment so long, Mr. Pigwidgeon was probably not more influenced by his wounded feelings, than by the consideration that during the serious illness of Reuben, and the absence of the mother of the family, there was likely to be a suspension, or at least a marked diminution of the good cheer which no man loved better than he did, when it was not at his own expense. Once or twice during this period, Mr. Medlicott met Pigwidgeon about the neighbourhood accompanied by two dumpy red-faced daughters of his, treasures which the Vicar knew the apothecary possessed, for he had christened them, but he had scarcely ever seen them since that ceremony, the young ladies having been at an economical school in Yorkshire, from which they were now just returned. Nothing could well be colder than Mr. Pigwidgeon was upon these occasions; his voice was husky when he enquired for Reuben, and he looked as bitter as if it would have been a satisfaction to him to have heard of some serious mistake made by Dr. Page in his treatment of the case. The Vicar was, indeed, beginning to think that the breach was irreparable; sometimes he would reproach himself with having unnecessarily wounded the self-love of an old acquaintance; then again he would sum up, as he worked in his garden, or sat at his solitary meals, the advantages and disadvantages of Mr. Pigwidgeon's friendship, the balance being always of a nature to console him under the apprehension of having offended past reconciliation.

While he was musing on this very point one morning after his breakfast, walking about his garden, he heard a smart tap at the green door in the hedge. Opening it with reasonable haste, he found that his visitor was the Rural Dean of his district, who, was on his tour of inspection, and who made it a rule to dine at Underwood whenever he came there—a rule which Mr. Barber extended to most of the parsonages which he visited in his peregrinations. The Vicar was a hospitable little fellow to the extent of his means, even when he was in mental trouble, as he was at present; accordingly, after the transaction of some trifling business with Mr. Barber, he went through the usual and expected formality of inviting him to dinner, adding that there was a bed for him also, if it would suit his convenience to accept it. These prelimininaries settled, Mr. Medlicott begged his guest to excuse him during a short absence, and after warning his cook-maid that increased activity would be necessary that day in her province, he sallied forth into the village to provide the things needful, and to pick up, if he could, a couple more guests to make the party a square one. He had not gone far before he met one of the churchwardens, a farmer of the better class, with whom he was on friendly terms, and he booked him without much difficulty, for the farmer having a termagant wife never spent an evening at home when he could avoid it. Now, if only a fourth could be found, all would be right. The Vicar first called on the lawyer of the village, but he was engaged to an election dinner at Chichester. .

"That's unlucky," said Mr. Medlicott.

"Very unlucky for me," said the lawyer, "I would a thousand times rather dine with your reverence upon bacon and beans than with those noisy fellows in Chichester upon turtle and venison."

The Vicar was a simple man, but he did not implicitly believe this strong assertion nevertheless. However, he thanked the lawyer for the civil speech, and proceeded elsewhere in search of what he wanted. It is highly probable there were several people

that morning in the parish who would gladly have profited by
Mr. Medlicott's hospitable intentions, had it pleased Providence
to throw them in his way, but it was otherwise ordered; so that
the Vicar at length made up his mind for an odd number, and
turned his attention to the necessary provision for them. Attended
by a boy carrying a hand-basket, he went to and fro in the village, until the basket was nearly as full as it could conveniently
hold of the various articles which he considered proper for a plain,
substantial, pastoral dinner, and which his own small farm did
not supply. During these marketing transactions he had to pass
and repass the apothecary's house repeatedly, but the numerous
phials in the windows, with the coloured globes, would have prevented him from distinguishing anybody in the shop, had he
been ever so desirous to do so. The same obstructions, however,
did not prevent Mr. Pigwidgeon from accurately observing every
motion of the Vicar; and he observed them the more accurately
on account of the contents of the basket, which became more
interesting every moment, as they increased in variety and bulk.
The basket, indeed, was of such a construction as to afford too
clear a view of the good things deposited in it, amongst which a
fat goose and a leg of Southdown mutton fascinated the apothecary particularly. There must certainly be something in good
cheer and hospitable preparations, which melts the human heart
and disposes it to kindly feelings, for unquestionably the good
Vicar with his basket of provisions had not passed more than two
or three times before Mr. Pigwidgeon's, when his breast began
wonderfully to relent towards his old friend, and he commenced
examining himself for the first time, whether he had not been too
hasty in taking huff at a hasty word, uttered too at a moment
when the poor Vicar was agitated by the news of his only child's
dangerous illness. In a very few moments (so rapidly did the ice
melt when the thaw had once set in), the apothecary had so far
got the better of the paltry little grudge which he had been
cherishing towards the Medlicotts, that he felt not only prepared
to resume convivial relations with them, but actually conceived
the idea of seizing the earliest opportunity of putting that truly
Christian principle into practice. In short, he figured to himself
a charming little love-feast, consisting of the fat goose and the
joint of Southdown which he had seen, eked out with other
toothsome additions which he was well able to fancy. In this
tender frame of mind he made the circuit of his counter, displayed his slovenly person at his shop-door just as the Vicar went

out of sight, returning home after completing his purchases. There the apothecary stood musing for nearly a quarter of an hour, leaning against one of the posts, debating with himself what steps he should take, and also whether the dinner in contemplation was to be given that very day, or on some succeeding one. At length a sudden thought seemed to seize him, for he withdrew hastily, and appeared instantly again with his broad-brimmed, slouched white hat on. Beyond a doubt (judging from his well-known habits) he was going to the butcher's or the poulterer's to file a bill of discovery to ascertain the day fixed for the cooking of the goose and the mutton. But a certain phenomenon of a meteoric kind, partly terrestrial and partly celestial, saved him the trouble of making the inquiry. This was a spiral column of deep blue smoke which began at that very moment to ascend over the trees in the direction of the Vicarage, the bearings of which the apothecary knew as well as if he had taken an Ordnance survey of the parish. Nay, he knew the smoke at once to be that of the kitchen chimney, so nice an observer was he, for this was not the first time that similar indications over the same trees had determined his course of proceedings for the day. No time was to be lost. Mr. Pigwidgeon struck a bold stroke for a dinner.

The Vicar's dinner-hour was five o'clock, and at a little before four, as he and his brother parson were sauntering about, talking of tithes and dilapidations, and sometimes of better things, he was not a little surprised by the arrival of Mr. Pigwidgeon's apprentice with a present of a fresh trout from that gentleman, accompanied with a message to the effect that he had been prevented by his professional engagements from calling at the Vicarage for some time, but he would look in the first evening he had an hour to spare, as he was most anxious to hear from Mr. Medlicott's own lips the latest account of his son. The Vicar was trapped. There seemed to him no alternative but to accept the present, or come to actual daggers-drawn; and to have eaten the trout without inviting the giver to partake of it would have been against all Mr. Medlicott's notions of the fitness of things. Besides, he bore no ill-will to the apothecary, although inclined to despise him, and finally he wanted somebody to make a fourth at dinner, a point which was the more important in his eyes, as his table was a square one.

Mr. Pigwidgeon was invited, after which it was needless to say that Mr. Pigwidgeon came; and it was something like getting in the end of a wedge, for the apothecary had no sooner arrived and re-established himself in his old position at the Vicarage, than he made a push and a successful one to introduce his dumpy daughters, the pretext being that in Mrs. Medlicott's absence they would be useful in the evening to make tea for the party. In yielding this point the Vicar made a mistake which he very soon deeply regretted, yet what else could he well have done? The Misses Pigwidgeon were sent for, and ere the dinner was half over they were seen waddling up the principal walk of the garden, approaching the house in muslin frocks, prettily spotted with peonies, and every now and then dropping into the form of cheeses, or rounds of beef, to pick the gooseberries or currants, just as a pair of ducks, though bent on a journey to the pond, will halt every now and then to gobble up a snail in the grass. "My poor girls," cried the apothecary with paternal rapture; he was seated so as to have a full view of the corpulent nymphs to whom he was so nearly related. The churchwarden, who was the gayest of the party, paid broad compliments to their personal charms, although he could only see them over his shoulder. As to the Vicar and the Rural Dean, they were content with the side-long prospects their places afforded them, and took a glass of port together, while the apothecary was recounting to the farmer the gifts and accomplishments of his girls. After all, it was the churchwarden and Mr. Pigwidgeon who redeemed the dinner from stupidity; for though neither was a pleasant fellow himself, the collision between them, as it often happens, proved a source of some little amusement. The conversation having casually turned upon domestic arrangements, the farmer began talking of his house, and the apothecary must do the same.

"You know my house," said Mr. Pigwidgeon.

"I know the *outside* of it," said the churchwarden.

The Vicar and the Rural Dean looked at one another, and both enjoyed the visible elongation of the apothecary's already sufficiently long face.

"Well, Pigwidgeon," continued the churchwarden, "now your daughters are come home to take care of you, you will be showing your friends the *inside* of your house some of these days."

"Aye," said Pigwidgeon, wriggling in his chair, and making a vigorous effort to look good-humoured, "we must soon be thinking of doing something to keep the house warm."

"The best way of doing that is by keeping good fires in the kitchen," said Mr. Barber; "I look upon the kitchen as the heart of the house, and I need not tell a gentleman of Mr. Pigwidgeon's profession the importance of keeping up the caloric in that region."

"Pigwidgeon," said the farmer, "you must not let it be said you have a cold heart, which you see his reverence considers as bad as a cold kitchen."

The apothecary again tried to laugh; but made the worst attempt possible.

"There is not a more hospitable fellow alive than I am," he said, "or one that loves more to have his friends about him, but the misfortune of my profession is, that it leaves a man no time to think of hospitality; sometimes not a moment even to get a comfortable bit of dinner."

"That's a very hard case," said the churchwarden, with affected commiseration.

"There is no doubt," said Mr. Barber, benevolently coming to Mr. Pigwidgeon's rescue, "there are many men so situated, either professionally or domestically, that they are not in a position to be as social and convivial in their own houses as they would wish to be. Sometimes a man is very hospitable and generous himself, but is cursed with an unsocial or stingy wife."

"Or he may have a sickly family," added the Vicar, thinking of the apothecary's vigorous brood of children.

"However," pursued Mr. Barber, "what I was coming to is this, that there are two ways fortunately of being social and convivial; one is being convivial at home, which means giving dinners, and the other is being convivial abroad, which means accepting them."

"A just view of hospitality," said the Vicar, smiling, "and a classical one, being strictly in harmony with the two senses of the Latin word *hospes*, which signifies guest as well as host."

"I don't understand Latin and Greek," said the blunt churchwarden, "but I hope I understand plain English, and my notion is that a man ought not to dine with his friends and neighbours if he can't or won't entertain them in return."

Here Mr. Barber, observing that the farmer's tone was serious, while himself and the Vicar had been only jocular, and remarking also that Mr. Pigwidgeon was sore at the turn the conversation had taken, rose from the table and gave Mr. Medlicott's proposition of another bottle a decided negative.

The Vicar himself was relieved by the adjournment to the tea-table. Only one of the fair Pigwidgeons was there. The other, it appeared, had been taken suddenly ill, and had retired to another room. The apothecary hastened to see her, and soon returned, saying that it was nothing serious; she would be well presently and able to walk home. When tea was over, Mr. Pigwidgeon went up again, and the other sister with him. He now was absent for about a quarter of an hour, and when he came back it was to announce that his daughter was rather seriously indisposed, and that he feared he must trespass on the Vicar's goodness to allow her to remain where she was just for the night. It was only common humanity to accede to such a request, but the consciousness of that virtue was Mr. Medlicott's only reward, for before he was out of bed the next morning, Mr. Pigwidgeon came to inform him that his poor girl was in a very bad way, though whether it would end in scarletina or small-pox he had not yet formed a decisive opinion. It proved to be malignant scarletina, and no sooner did one sister begin to recover than the other thought proper to catch the same complaint; nor was this all, for the young doctor, who had been absent for some days previous, quartered himself at the Vicarage on his return in the capacity of resident physician, so that the Vicar now saw his house in the absolute possession of the Pigwidgeons, and turned into a regular infirmary.

Luckily, this unpleasant occurrence took place just at the moment when it was proper for him to set out for Westbury, but he must have gone on his travels under any circumstances, for he was nervous on the score of infection, and to have remained at home would probably have endangered his life.

CHAPTER IV.

A FEW PLEASANT DAYS WITH THE DOCTOR.—REUBEN RECEIVES THE HONOURS OF A PRIMA DONNA, AND THE WHOLE PARTY SET OUT ON A TOUR.

"It will cost you a barrel of vinegar and a ton of potash, at the very least," said Dr. Page; "I recollect that Pigwidgeon well. When I commenced life as physician to one of the London hospitals, he was the manager and resident apothecary there. We quarrelled originally on the subjects of ventilation and ablution.

The governors sided with me; and the cause of cleanliness triumphed in my person over Pigwidgeon and the opposite principle. There was a case of moral dirt against him also—jobbing in drugs and wine for the patients—you understand me—I might have pressed the charge if I had wished to ruin him, but I was as merciful as I was strong; so I gave the poor devil the alternative of resigning his place, or being exposed and probably prosecuted; he resigned and settled in your neighbourhood, it seems; probably because he heard your larders and cellars well spoken of."

"That accounts," said the Vicar, "for the feeling he displayed when he heard your name mentioned."

"Oh, he hates me as he hates soap and water," said the Doctor.

"He has turned us out of our house at all events," said the Vicar; "I don't expect to be settled there again for three weeks."

"Not for twice that time," said Dr. Page, "independently of the fear of infection. By Jove, a wise man in your circumstances would burn the house down; there's a young gentleman yonder would do it in no time."

This was a pleasant hit at Reuben, who was lying reading on a sofa at some distance, after returning from one of his first walks.

"What are you reading, my dear?" asked his mother, who had just finished a letter to Mrs. Wyndham, to acquaint her with the improvement in Reuben's health.

"Shakspeare, or the Pharmacopœia?" added the Doctor.

"'I do remember an apothecary,'" said Reuben, smiling and holding up the play of "Romeo and Juliet."

"I believe," said the Vicar, "there is something in Shakspeare pat to every subject one can talk of."

"A very just observation," said the Doctor; "I have often made it myself; only the other day I prescribed for a patient out of Henry the Fourth. I'll tell you about it. An old lady, a neighbour and patient of mine, was plaguing me lately about her complaints (all imagination, you must know): Well, madam, said I, how do you feel to-day? She said she felt—she didn't know how she felt—at last she said she felt hurt inside. Try parmaceti, ma'am, said I. Spermaceti! said she; sure that's only applied externally. Then you know better than Dr. Shakspeare, said I, for he tells you, 'there's nought like parmaceti for an inward bruise.'"

"Very pleasant," said the Vicar, "if you didn't lose your patient by your joke."

"No great loss, if I did lose her," replied the Doctor; "she was a bad patient; she had none of the virtues of a patient, not a single one of them."

"I never before heard of those virtues," said Mr. Medlicott; "pray enumerate them."

"If you consider a moment," said the Doctor, "you will see that several excellent qualities are necessary to make a good patient; candour in the first place,—a patient must be perfectly candid with his physician, or how can the physician understand his case? Then obedience; he must be thoroughly obedient, or what is the use of prescribing for him? Faith comes next, unbounded confidence in his doctor's skill, or the pills and potions won't do their duty, for medicine works morally as well as physically, let me tell you. The moment I find a patient either deceiving me, disobeying me, or doubting me, I leave him to the quacks and Pigwidgeons."

"Your list of virtues is far from complete," said the Vicar; "methinks you have omitted two very important ones—gratitude and generosity."

"As to gratitude," said the Doctor, "I hold that to be a virtue as incumbent on the physician in a great many cases, as on the patient,—if my young friend here (for example) is grateful to me for doing my best to bring him round, I am no less grateful to him for the opportunity of making his acquaintance, and renewing my old friendship with his worthy father."

With this civil speech on his lips, the Doctor went to his cellar, to bring up an old bottle of wine to treat his old friend with, for it was near dinner time.

"I am inclined to think," said the Vicar to his wife, "though the doctor and patient may divide the gratitude, the former will insist upon having the virtue of generosity all to himself."

"What do you propose to do?" said Mrs. Medlicott; "I suppose you will offer him a suitable sum of money."

"I'll follow the golden rule," replied the Vicar, after a moment's deliberation. "I would not like to have money offered me by an old friend myself, and I'll treat Page as I should wish to be treated by him."

"It would be a golden rule, indeed, father," said Reuben, "if we could often make such advantageous applications of it."

"I think so, Reuben," said his mother, highly pleased at her son's acute observation.

The following morning came letters to every body from every body else. Reuben had three, one from Hyacinth Primrose, another from his aunt, Mrs. Mountjoy, who was in Scotland, and a third from Mrs. Wyndham, at Geneva, playfully subscribed "his loving grandmamma." Mrs. Medlicott had a very long letter from her friend Theodore, and her husband a communication from the apothecary, both coolly dated from the Vicarage, and giving the minutest details of the progress of the interesting patients, what medicines they were taking, how many blisters had been applied to each, how the father and son had differed once or twice on questions between the leech and the lancet, and how Rose was expected to be the first of the two ladies to leave her chamber.

"The apothecary's Rose," said the Vicar.

"I think," said Dr. Page, "the other girl might appropriately be called Scarletina."

Reuben smiled; he never made a pun himself, but he sometimes graciously encouraged that weakness in others.

Breakfast over, the Doctor went about his professional avocations, which were very extensive, and left his friends to dispose of themselves at their pleasure until evening. The Medlicotts had business to transact also. A very important matter was settled that morning, namely, Reuben's preferment to Cambridge in the autumn, and that having been agreed on, the Vicar thought a quiet economical tour in Wales would for the present be the best thing they could do.

"Let us hear what the Doctor says," said Mrs. Medlicott, when the dinner hour came round again.

"The Doctor thinks very well of it," said Page, "if he cannot induce you to stay where you are, but there must be no long marches, and no climbing after Cadwallader and his goats."

"We shall only creep," said the Vicar; "is there any chance of your creeping with us?"

"I have a mind to join you," said the Doctor; "I think my young friend is not strong enough yet to travel without his physician, and by-the-bye, I have got a little carriage, which I think will hold us all comfortably, four inside and one on the box."

An early day was fixed, and the interval was agreeably spent; Reuben took his father over to Westbury, to pay his respects to Mrs. Reeves, and to show him the place where the great hay-rick stood no longer.

The Vicar had now an opportunity of hearing repeated all

the flattering things of his son, which Mrs. Medlicott had heard before, and though he was not so fondly credulous as his wife, it would be underrating paternal vanity to suppose that he was not pleased on the whole with the *vox populi*. When it was announced that Reuben was on the point of starting on a Welch tour, the effect produced was nearly as electric as if he had been going up in a balloon, or out in the "Hecla" with Captain Parry.

The great proof, however, of the popularity which our hero had earned by his music, his astrology, and his good-nature, was reserved for the day which was fixed for leaving the neighbourhood. The Doctor's carriage, as it stood at his door, was surrounded with the people from Westbury, all waiting to see Reuben for the last time, and give him and his parents a parting cheer. Nor were some of them content with that easy mode of testifying applause and gratitude. The tradesmen had all joined in the expense of a neat box of carpenter's tools, which he was entreated to accept, as a token of their feelings towards him. The blushing Dolly stood there with a basket of fruit as ripe and glowing as her own rustic charms, and as the carriage drove off amidst general hurrahs, she and the other maidens threw bouquets into it, and pelted him with flowers like a Prima Donna.

"This is too absurd," said the Vicar, receiving a volley of cabbage roses upon one of his ears.

CHAPTER V.

THE MEDLICOTTS ON THEIR TRAVELS.—REUBEN BUYS A WELCH GRAMMAR, MAKES THE ACQUAINTANCE OF A WELCH BARD, AND FALLS IN WITH SOME FAIR FRIENDS.

THE tour in the Principality was a very agreeable one, though not so easy and comfortable in point of travelling as it is at present. When Reuben Medlicott first visited North Wales, that mountainous region was not quite as easily traversible as the fens of Lincolnshire or Salisbury Plain. The roads climbed the hills and ran down again into the valleys: for one mile of dull straight route there were twenty of charming zig-zag. Far from shrinking from the edges of ravines and precipices, the wild Cambrian engineers seemed to delight in conducting travellers to them. As to the by-ways, they appeared to have been constructed by the goats and sheep; and there were numerous glens, gorges, hollows, and passes, which you may now penetrate in a Bath chair, if you please, but through which you must then have travelled on horseback or on foot, if you were not content to imagine their beauties.

The Vicar and the Doctor, being both advanced on the shady side of fifty, affected to have very lively fancies when they came to romantic places of this description; but neither Mrs. Medlicott nor her son were so imaginative. It was easy to say that mountains have all a family likeness, and that one valley must bear a striking resemblance to another, as the elements of all mountain scenery must generally be pretty much the same: Reuben had no notion of travelling through Wales without actually and thoroughly seeing it; and his mother took the same view of the matter, modified only by her prudent consideration for her son's health and her respect for Doctor Page's advice. On the score of health, however, there soon ceased to be any reasonable ground of anxiety, for the mountain air, with the novel excitement and delight of travelling, had such a beneficial effect on our hero, that after about a week's easy progress, at the rate of about twenty miles a day, he felt and looked as strong as ever he had been in his life, while, as to his appetite, it was such as to gratify his father and mother more than the Cambrian inn-keepers, whose interest in the subject was the reverse of parental. But no host or hostess with a grain of amiability could look at Reuben Medlicott and harbour a hostile feeling towards him, because he picked a leg or shoulder of small mutton almost bare for his dinner. He was the incarnation of good-humour, and continued to make himself popular wherever he came, without the slightest ambition or thought of popularity, for you may suppose he had no sinister object in winning the hearts of the ancient Britons. But everything amused and interested him, and his countenance faithfully reflected the happiness which he enjoyed from morning to night, and which increased with every new scene he visited and every additional mile he travelled. There was no occasion to "bid him discourse." He was always ready to "enchant the ear." He talked to the Welch people, when they happened to be able to converse in English, as if he felt under personal obligations to them for having such a picturesque country,—such fine lakes, streams, and waterfalls. When conversation was impossible, he looked at them so talkatively, particularly at the women, and paid such a number of sincere little silent compliments to their faces when they were fair, and when it was otherwise, to their costumes, their cottages, their children, or the scenery of their neighbourhood, always to something or another interesting to them, that had the whole Principality been one borough, and had Reuben aspired to represent it, his success would have been highly probable, at least if universal suffrage had been the system established. Mrs. Medlicott would gladly have understood the remarks which were made on her son in return for his various amenities, but her leash of tongues, unfortunately, did not comprehend the ancient one in which those remarks were generally uttered, and she was, therefore, under the necessity of interpreting them by the looks and smiles of the speakers, which were in general quite a sufficient key to the meaning.

They travelled for some days without falling in with anybody of whom they had the slightest knowledge, although Reuben turned over the pages of the travellers' books at every inn where they stopped; volumes, by-the-bye, which amused the Doctor and the Vicar greatly, and which they generally perused in the evenings over their wine or negus. At Aberystwith, however, among the very latest entries, in the freshest ink, the party found, to their great satisfaction and no small surprise, the names of Hannah and Mary Hopkins, both evidently written by the hand of the latter, but in so hasty and scratchy a way that the Vicar had no doubt she was laughing heartily while she wrote them.

"Hannah Hopkins in Wales at last!" cried Mrs. Medlicott. A trip to Wales had for many a long year been to the Quakeresses the great desire of their hearts, but one which they had scarcely dared to dream would ever be gratified.

"Are they not happy?" cried Reuben.

"They will not leave a sprig of heath or fox-glove behind them in the Principality," said the Vicar. The Quakeresses were wild about flowers, and the wilder the flowers were the wilder were the Quakeresses about them: wherever they rambled (for they had lived all their lives in the country) they gathered brooms of them, which were, indeed, the only ornaments of their humble apartments, except the feathers of peacocks and other domestic birds, of which Hannah especially was a zealous collector.

Reuben made enquiries, and it turned out that the Hopkinses had left the inn only that morning; their destination was not certain, but it was in the direction which the Medlicotts were taking, so that there was a fair chance of a happy reunion at some point or another,—the more unexpected, the more agreeable. We have already mentioned how kind the Vicar always was to old Mrs. Hopkins. Mrs. Medlicott had a sincere regard for her also; and as to the cosy, laughter-loving Mary, she was a favourite everywhere except at meeting, not being half grave enough for the Obadiahs and Rachaels, though she was always dressed as sadly and severely as any of them, which perhaps, however, only made the incorrigible gaiety of her nature the more conspicuous.

Reuben was not long content to be ignorant of the language of the country he was traversing. At Aberystwith he bought a Welch grammar and vocabulary, in a neat little shop on the skirts of the town, at the door of which, overhung by an elm of great age, was a wooden bench, upon which the old bookseller, a seedy but venerable man, was taking his ease; and Mr. Medlicott got into chat with him, while his wife and son were bargaining for the grammar. He proved to be the parson of the parish as well as the librarian. The Vicar little suspecting this, had been asking him questions about the state of the clergy in Wales, of which he had heard surprising accounts, and among other enquiries had asked what might be the value of the parish they were then in.

"Twenty pounds a year," said the old man.

"A small living for a man of education and a gentleman," said the Vicar.

"There are smaller in the Principality," said the bookseller.

"Selling books must be a more profitable profession," said Mr. Medlicott.

"My shop is the best part of my benefice," said the old man.

The Vicar went into the shop and communicated to his wife and Reuben the strange discovery he had made, for such it appeared to him. The purchase of the grammar had been effected, but they could not leave the reverend bookseller abruptly, and accordingly, as there was room enough on the bench, they sat down, at his courteous invitation, and passed an interesting half-hour in conversation with him. They found that he was an author and a poet, in addition to his other kindred vocations; he was too simple a man to hide any chapter of his history, and when Reuben questioned him about the bards and their lyric rhapsodies, it soon elicited the confession that in his greener days he had attempted a poetical translation of some of the wildest. Being greatly struck with Reuben, and flattered by the interest he felt in the bards, a member of whose sacred corporation he considered himself, he rose from the bench, when he saw his customers about to take leave, and, hobbling into his shop (for he was infirm, though not gouty), hunted out a copy of his "Cambrian garland," and, with a trembling hand and a bad pen, wrote on the title-page—

"The gift of the Reverend Hugh Evans, an old poet, ———," he paused for our hero to tell him what he should add.

"To Reuben Medlicott, a lover of poetry," said Reuben; and the inscription was completed accordingly.

"Very neat and very modest," said the old man, as he laid down the pen.

"Modest on Reuben's part," said the Vicar, when they were at some distance from the shop. "I cannot say so much for the modesty of Mr. Evans, in dubbing himself a poet so confidently."

"Yet he published anonymously, you observe," said Mrs. Medlicott.

"Probably," said Reuben, "when he published this volume of poems, he dreamed of afterwards producing something very superior, and never realised his expectations. But why, sir, did you not let the poor old gentleman know that you were a clergyman, like himself?"

"Because he had told me his income, and he might have desired to know mine."

"You need not to have been ashamed of it, father."

"No," said the Vicar, smiling, "two hundred a year is nothing to be ashamed of, but the Reverend Hugh Evans would have concluded me to be a second Dives, and the report might have reached the inn, and influenced the landlord in drawing out his bill."

Before he left Aberystwith, Reuben took a very good sketch of the little book-shop, the ancient tree, and the group under it, the old man himself being, of course, the principal figure. The union of the pastoral and poetical character with the humble though congenial business of bookseller was skilfully managed; at least, so thought those eminently impartial judges, the father and mother of the artist. But, indeed, Mrs. Hopkins and her daughter recognised the likeness the moment they saw the drawing, for at Barmouth the Medlicotts overtook them. The Doctor, who had been visiting an hospital, while the Medlicotts were visiting the bookseller, was not pleased when he saw the Welch grammar: he thought study of any kind unseasonable on an excursion of pleasure. But the name of the bookseller pleased him excessively when he heard it, for he was the first of the party to remember the pedagogue in "The Merry Wives of Windsor."

"By Jove," said Doctor Page, in great glee, "if the bookseller is so very old as you say, perhaps he is the very man who taught a distinguished ancestor of mine his *hig, hag, hog.*"

"Aye," said the Vicar, "you bear a Shakspearian name also."

"And very proud I am of it, I assure you," said the Doctor.

Proceeding from Aberystwith to the Goat Inn at Barmouth, they were at breakfast the morning after their arrival, in a little room, looking out upon the sands, and adjoining another with the same aspect, but separated from them by too thin a partition to render it safe to speak in a loud tone, particularly if you were maligning your neighbours, or speaking ill of the powers that be. Voices were audible in the next apartment, which gave rise to some speculation as to the speakers, but presently rang out the merry laugh of the young Quakeress, which removed all doubt upon the subject. In five minutes the two breakfasts were consolidated, and Hannah Hopkins was telling the Vicar a long story to explain how the great object of her life, an excursion in North Wales, came to be realised, just when she and Mary were beginning to despair of ever accomplishing it.

The tourists, now a party of six, were not long without concerting a very nice plan of operations, for that day and several to follow it. But when breakfast was over, it was raining, and it rained very doggedly for several successive days.

The Vicar and his friend sat down equally doggedly to backgammon, Mrs. Medlicott had brought a volume of metaphysical sermons with her from her father's library; Hannah Hopkins was soon engrossed by her everlasting knitting; Reuben and Mary had no resource but the Welch grammar, and to it they went spiritedly in a corner.

"The climate is in your favour," said the Doctor to Reuben, during a pause in the game, upon the third day of the captivity at the Goat.

"Is the grammar difficult?" asked the Vicar,—"vowels scarce, consonants plenty, eh!"

"Now don't set Mary Hopkins going," said Mrs. Medlicott.

"Friend Thomas always makes my Mary laugh," said old Hannah, looking gravely up from her needle.

"Not to say difficult, not as difficult as some other languages," said Reuben, replying to his father's question. "At least there is no difficulty to stop us."

"It would be too bad to be stopped by the elements both indoors and out of doors," said the Vicar.

Mary laughed again,—and again the old woman raised her eyes solemnly from her work, but this time she addressed the Doctor.

"Dost thou consider laughing wholesome, friend Page?" she inquired.

"I never had a patient that died of it," replied Page, rattling the dice.

Mrs. Medlicott now pretended that she could not read, her husband and the doctor were so facetious, but the fact was (and her husband suspected it shrewdly) that the sermon was beyond her depth, and she was glad of an excuse to lay it down.

The back-gammon ceased soon after they had played two-and-twenty hits; it was time to think of luncheon.

The name of Jones was on the spoons. Mary Hopkins had been laughing all through the Principality, at the fertility of the race of Jones.

"What a remarkable name it is," said the Vicar,—"There is Inigo, the great architect; Sir William Jones, the orientalist; Paul, the celebrated pirate; Tom, the hero of the great novel."

"Don't forget Davy," said the Doctor.

"Davy of the navy," said the Vicar.

"But Tom and Davy are ideal personages," said Mrs. Medlicott.

"Davy an ideal personage!" cried the Doctor, "I am sorry to hear a clergyman's wife broach such a heresy."

"Heresy reminds me of fire," said the Vicar, "go, Reuben, and order one to be lighted."

While Reuben was absent there was a little dry altercation between Mr. and Mrs Medlicott about the necessity for the fire.

"The fire would not be lighted half-an-hour before he would wish it extinguished again, and then, a fire at midsummer was so ridiculous."

"It was better to be too warm than too cold," was the Vicar's rejoinder.

"It was like madness ordering a fire at that season of the year."

"The thermometer, my dear, ought to decide the question, and not the almanac."

For once he had the last word.

Mrs. Medlicott, however, rose from her seat, which was near the fire-place, and removed with great state and dignity to a chair at the window, where, after trying to no purpose to penetrate the mystery of the hills through the clouds of vapour that shrouded them, she put on her spectacles, and made a similar effort at the Welch grammar, with not much greater success. As a last resource, she undertook a phrenological survey of the heads of the company, which occupied a considerable time, and would have occupied more, if the Doctor had not adroitly slipped out of the room, before his turn came, and, wet as it was, set out to explore the medical institutions.

CHAPTER VI.

HENRY WINNING AND HYACINTH PRIMROSE JOIN THE EXPEDITION.

MEANWHILE Reuben gave the order to a smiling maid at the bar, who passed it to a maid in the kitchen, where a numerous group, composed of travellers, servants, postboys, harpers, and miscellaneous hangers-on were collected in a confused circle round a capital fire; the travellers desirous of drying their clothes, and all clearly of opinion (in direct opposition to Mrs. Medlicott) that the heat of the dog-days in Great Britain occasionally stands in need of some artificial reinforcement. "A fire for No. 3," said Peggy Roberts.

"His reverence is chilly," said somebody from the chimney-corner.

"One of your country parsons, I suppose," said a young man, one of those who were trying to dry themselves.

"No, sir, an English gentleman," said Peggy Roberts.

"Parson Medligoat," said a post-boy.

"Medlicott!" cried the young man who spoke before to another who was at his side; "can it possibly be our Medlicott?"

"Not very likely."

"Is the parson travelling alone?"

"No, sir, he has an elderly lady and a young gentleman with him."

"That tallies."

"The young gentleman, what is he like?"

A dozen voices burst forth immediately with as many commendations of Reuben.

He was the nicest young gentleman Peggy Roberts had ever seen.

"And the civilest," said the post-boy.

Jenny Jones had seen as handsome, but he was as handsome as any young man need be, and had the beautifullest head of hair in the world.

A third damsel vouched for his scholarship, for she was the chambermaid, and had found his room strewed over with books.

"Our friend, to a certainty," said the young man who spoke first; "I wonder what can have brought the Medlicotts here; one would as soon have expected to have met the Greenwich pensioners mountaineering it."

"Come away," said the other.

"We are pretty well roasted, and so I think is that quarter of mutton which I suspect is designed for our dinner."

"I wish they had roasted the whole sheep; the higher I rise above the level of the sea, the more voracious I become. I think I could take the altitude of the mountains by my appetite."

"Do so, then, while I dine," said Henry Winning, taking his seat at a table spread for them in a little room, which Peggy Roberts assured them commanded a magnificent prospect of a dozen hills, with names unpronounceable, save by Cambrian lips.

"On the contrary, dining is the basis of the calculation," said Hyacinth Primrose, separating as he spoke the leg from the loin of the roast quarter of mutton. "Gulliver," he added, "must have brought this breed from Lilliput. Shall I send you the leg?—the mutton gets smaller as we get hungrier."

"No, help me to the loin; when I have disposed of that, if you want any assistance to manage the leg, let me know, and I. shall be ready to support you."

The loin sufficed Winning, and Primrose left very little of the leg to adorn the sideboard the next morning. Cheese and a glass of ale completed the repast.

"In fact," said Hyacinth, "the Welch sheep seem to be all lambs."

"Perhaps it is with mutton as with men. There are men who continue children all their lives."

"Since we grow philosophical we way as well go and face Mrs. Medlicott, for I suppose it must be done."

"It must," said Winning, rising reluctantly; "but after what I said in the coach that unlucky night, I have nothing to expect but the coldest reception."

"You compared her to Minerva," said Primrose; "why

man must be unreasonable if she was not flattered by

thought you knew the sex better," said Winning; "let a
resemble Minerva ever so much, she will infinitely prefer
sion to Venus or Juno. However, as you say, the thing
e done, so we may as well do it at once."
nning wrote his own name and his friend's on a card, and
Peggy Roberts to hand it to young Mr. Medlicott.
a moment Reuben was in their arms, and the next moment
Cambridge men were introduced to the Vicar and his
with the least possible form and ceremony. Mr. and Mrs.
ott now saw Mr. Primrose for the first time, though they
ard a great deal about him from Reuben, who never erred
side of undervaluing his friends, or praising them penuri-

nning saw at a glance that his unlucky remarks in the
had not yet faded from the memory of Mrs. Medlicott, al-
recollecting his friendship for Reuben, she was not defi-
n any of the civilities, which the occasion required. She
prominent part, however, for some time in the conversa-
the evening, greatly to the disappointment of Primrose.
l only, however, to look round the room to see that there
lack of subjects for curious observation. He fastened his
on the gaunt old Quakeress in an instant; an acquaint-
ith her fair fat daughter promised infinite satisfaction, even
he heard her laugh; and when he heard the gentleman in
en coat, white buckskins, and red cravat, addressed by the
Doctor, it completed his enjoyment, and gave him the no-
a cyclopædia of entertainment.
ry Hopkins made good tea; or if it was not good it was
lt of Jones, Roberts, or Williams, or whatever was the
f the landlord of the Goat. The Vicar talked, and so did
;, except the Doctor, who was dead tired after his rambles
pe the phrenological lecture, but nobody talked so much
irose. He was as lively as Mercutio, or Gratiano, who
l more nonsense than any man in Venice" of his time.
t tried to draw Mrs. Medlicott out, by touching upon the
c topics of the day, but failing in that, he laid himself out
enerally amusing, which he had the knack of being, even
ne talked of himself, which indeed was the subject upon
he was generally most fluent.
e Vicar desired to know whether either of the Cantabs·

were weather-seers; three days in the Goat had contented him, and he had had enough of the wiry music of the old harper in the hall, towards whom he was beginning to cherish the feelings that actuated the "ruthless king."

Primrose affirmed that he was superior to the skyey influences; he was above the clouds, and looked down upon the weather. In fact he preferred wet weather on a tour, particularly when he travelled with Winning, because Winning was too fond of the tops of the mountains for his taste. Another thing was that his luck in travelling was extraordinary. He was always sure to fall in with a charming intellectual party at every inn, and there was nothing like a long dismal wet day for enjoying their company.

The Vicar smiled (well knowing for whom the word "intellectual" had been thrown in), and said that fortune had, at least, been equally kind to himself and his friends in that respect.

Nothing escaped the keen, comic eye of Primrose, which rolled about the room, and penetrated every corner, taking in every object, no matter how minute, that was at all characteristic or illustrative of the company.

There was Mary Hopkins's enormous broom of wild flowers, containing so much of the fox-glove, or *digitalis*, that Hyacinth thought it must have been collected by the Doctor for his medical uses. Near it lay an equally large truss of dried grasses. Reuben saw Primrose surveying it with intense curiosity, and informed him aside that it was a whim of Mrs. Hopkins, who was a collector of grasses.

"Is she graminivorous?" whispered Hyacinth.

"I can tell you what that is," said the Doctor, pointing to the bundle, "it is the hay that was saved from Dean Wyndham's haggard on the night it was burned down by our clever young friend here."

"My poor Reuben," said his mother, "that will be a standing joke against him as long as he lives."

"It made us very merry in London," said Winning.

"And at Cambridge it kept us in good spirits for a week," said Primrose, who had now come to a table piled with books, and was turning over the Welch Grammar, the Hand-book to Botany, the Outlines of Geology, the Metaphysical Discourses, and the rest of the rather extensive travelling library.

"We have brought a good many books, you see, with us on our journey, Mr. Primrose," said Mrs. Medlicott.

"You are tolerably well provided," replied Hyacinth. "Winning travels with his law library. For my own part, I respect the law too much not to draw the proper distinction between term and vacation."

"Have you made much progress in your life of Hippocrates?" asked Reuben, slyly.

"Not very much," said Primrose laughing,—"but I have not forgotten it, I assure you. I shall certainly buckle to it some of these days, and it will be a great work let me tell you. I am a very hard-working fellow, but I hate labour mortally, that I admit."

"You have the more credit for being laborious," said Mrs. Medlicott.

"I work because I hate work," continued Primrose, "to have it all over early in life, and be in a position to devote the rest of it to the delicious *far-niente*. Labour was a curse from the beginning."

"A curse," said the Vicar, "with a blessing in it, as there is in all the divine judgments, if we apprehend them aright."

"Thou hast well spoken, friend Thomas," said Hannah Hopkins, who had all this time been sitting as mute as if she had been at her silent devotions, but hearkening to all that was said with amusingly earnest and profound attention. An argument that subsequently took place on the old question of concentration and diffusion particularly charmed her. Reuben and his mother, supported by Mr. Primrose, were pitted against the Vicar and Winning, the Doctor taking no part, nor even opening his lips, until Winning, overpowered by the fluency of his antagonists, pretended to want his support, on which Doctor Page shook himself and said he was "a physician, not a metaphysician," a pleasantry which put an end to the controversy, not before it was much to be desired.

Mrs. Medlicott, before she retired, invited the Cantabs to breakfast the following morning.

Primrose would have accepted the invitation unconditionally; but Winning, more steady to the plan of their journey, made his acceptance conditional upon the state of the weather in the morning, for if it was possible to travel it was necessary to proceed another stage.

"I almost hope for another wet day," said Primrose, when he and Winning were together again in the double-bedded room they occupied. "I have almost fallen in love with that merry quakeress."

"Falling in love is a bad way to rise in the world," said Winning, "so for your sake, as well as my own, I trust to-morrow will be fair."

"Falling asleep is the wisest course just at present," said Primrose, and he was soon steeped in slumber.

Winning sat down to a volume of "Coke's Institutes," and read until he could read no longer with the discordant music of a harp, which somebody was scraping most barbarously under his windows, converting it into an instrument of actual torture. Going to a window, and looking out, he very soon discovered to whom he was indebted for the interruption of his studies. Reuben was taking a lesson in the national music of Wales from the old harper of the inn.

Another wet day at the Goat—Primrose proposed, at breakfast, to change the sign of the inn from Capricornus to Aquarius. The Doctor wanted to know why Mrs. Hopkins had not given her opinion on the subject of last evening's conversation. Hannah shook her head, and told friend Page, that she loved to hear clever men and clever women arguing, and she did her best to understand what they were arguing about, but they were often too deep for her and her Mary, and this was the case, she confessed, with the argument of the preceding night.

"Thy faculties, Hannah," said the Vicar, " are finite, like my own and the Doctor's "

" My Mary and I," said Hannah, " have many an argument together, and we are sometimes not much wiser when we leave off than when we begin."

" A common case in controversies," said the Vicar.

A bee humming in the window set Primrose again going on the subject of himself and his views of study.

"There is no toil," he persisted, " lovely in my sight but the toil of the bee which works among the flowers, or of the man of letters (I mean the belles-lettres, not the black letters) who resembles the bee both in the varied field of his exertions and the nectared sweetness of their results."

" You have certainly taken a very exemplary insect for your model," said the Vicar.

"I observed a bee one day last summer in the Temple Gardens," said Winning, " he seemed very busy for a moment or two, but I suppose he had no great taste for the bitter sweets of the law, for he soon flew away up the river towards Richmond, and I never saw him in the Temple Garden again. That was Primrose's model bee, I suspect."

"Mary, canst thou repeat Letitia Barbauld's lines on the bee?" said Hannah Hopkins.

Mary obeyed and repeated the stanzas, happily not very numerous, with tolerable accuracy, all but one, in which Reuben most good-naturedly and condescendingly assisted her.

The Cambridge men were exceedingly diverted.

"Thou and Mary used to learn them together, when thou wert my scholar," said Hannah Hopkins, addressing Reuben.

"He learned many a useful lesson from thee, Hannah," said the Vicar.

"That I did, sir," said Reuben.

"Thank thee for saying so," said Hannah, "thou more than rewardest all my trouble—why dost thou laugh, Mary?"

Mary Hopkins had burst out into one of her constitutional and infectious fits of most unquakerly mirth. Primrose was in raptures with her.

"Because, mother, thou talkest of the trouble that Reuben Medlicott gave thee, as if he had been one of thy refractory scholars."

"Great men," said Primrose, "have been formed under the tuition of the fair sex; the great poet Pindar, for example, was the pupil of the charming poetess Corinna."

Winning now saw a fair opportunity for regaining the lost paradise of Mrs. Medlicott's favour, and adroitly availed himself of it.

"And the Gracchi," he said, "they were still more fortunate in having a woman of learning and genius for their mother."

"In these dull days Cornelia would have been called a bluestocking," said Primrose.

"The Romans understood some things much better than we do," said Winning, with consummate gravity.

Mary Hopkins, however, turned laughing to Reuben. "Thou seest," she said, "all that is expected from thee, thou shouldest be both a Pindar and a Gracchus, according to what thy friends say."

"Thou art thy mother's jewel at all events," said old Hannah.

The Vicar laughed heartily at the speeches of both mother and daughter, but what chiefly amused him was the notion of his wife being compared to the celebrated Roman matron, and Mrs. Hopkins bearing the laurelled name of Corinna.

Winning stood almost as high after this dialogue in Mrs. Medlicott's favour as Hyacinth Primrose. The rest of the day

passed as pleasantly as any wet day, perhaps, that was ever spent
in an inn. Winning had some private conversation with Reuben
about the University, in the course of which he soon discovered
that his friend seemed already to have almost made up his mind
to devote himself there to any but a definite course of study, either
with a view to mere academic distinction, or to the main business
of life. In fact, if a desultory career can be properly called a
career at all, Reuben Medlicott appeared bent upon pursuing one,
and Henry Winning was confirmed in the opinion he had hazarded more than once before, that his friend was much too clever,
or at least had too many friends about him, whose faith in his
genius was too implicit.

The following morning at five o'clock, Primrose opening his
eyes and drawing the curtains, saw Winning at the window
speculating on the prospects of the weather, in a dress very
similar to that formerly worn in acts of public penance. "Well,"
he said drowsily, "how does it look?—any sign of amendment?"

"Every promise of a glorious morning," said Winning.

"Then I suppose we must leave that dear merry quakeress behind us," said Primrose, with an affected sigh.

When the Vicar's party met at breakfast, the Cambridge
students were already some leagues from Barmouth, for the day
had kept the undertaking which the dawn had given, and was
all the lovelier for the contrast with the gloomy weather which
had kept the tourists in confinement. The Vicar would have
been happy, had his plans been consistent with those of his son's
friends, but that was not the case; and indeed it suited the Medlicotts better on many accounts to jog quietly along with the
quakers; and this accordingly they did in a very enjoyable manner; the only drawback being that the same vehicle was not
large enough to carry them all. This was remedied by the hiring of two rough surefooted ponies, upon which the Doctor and
Reuben rode generally, but now and then they picked up a side-
saddle for Mary Hopkins, who was probably the first quakeress
who was ever seen on horseback in England.

We cannot afford to travel at the tardy rate which they found
rapid enough for their pleasure and convenience. Slow, however,
as their progress was, the tour was completed, or at least they
had all returned to the house of Dr. Page, before Mrs. Medlicott
had fathomed the transcendental sermons, or Reuben perfectly
mastered the Welch harp and the language of the Llewellyns

and Cadwalladers. The Doctor made them all comfortable for near a week (during which Rueben preserved a strict incognito), and the worthy son of Esculapius would have willingly detained them much longer, pretending that at least a month's fumigation was indispensable to purify a house after the Pigwidgeons. But the Vicar argued that unless he was actually on the spot, the apothecary and his brood would never give up possession; and Hannah Hopkins, whose oft-repeated rule it was to be "merry and wise," had already exceeded the limits of the longest vacation she had ever enjoyed, and was inflexible in her resolve to return to her school with the greatest possible expedition.

Everybody was sorry to part with the kind Doctor, but nobody so much as Reuben, who would indeed have been ungrateful if he had not been attached to a man who had shown him so much hearty friendship.

The last thing Dr. Page said to him was in a tone of good-humoured warning—

"Beware of that laughing quakeress."

BOOK THE FOURTH.

Gratiano. Well, keep me company but two years more, thou shalt not know the sound of thine own tongue.
Antonio. Farewell, I'll grow a talker.
Gratiano. Thanks, i' faith, for silence only is commendable in a neat's tongue dried.

ARGUMENT.

WITH most men, as well as with Sindbad, or Captain Lemuel Gulliver, human life consists of a succession of ventures or voyages, literal or metaphorical expeditions; though it is only the luck of a few such pets of my lady Fortune to discover valleys of diamonds, or marvellous flying islands. But who has not his "travel's history," let it be prodigious as Munchausen's or dull as any modern tour in the Alps or Apennines? Which of us have not our voyages, on which we set out, when "the tide in the affairs of men" happens to serve, with more or less ballast in our hold, with more or less capital in money or brains to trade with, more or less of the breeze of hope to fan our sails; and from which (if we escape the perils of the deep) we return now and then to port with more or less reputation or profit? The first attempt is usually a little coasting trip to school, where we probably gain a small commodity of Greek and Latin, and think we have made pretty good merchandise; at least we have done as well as our neighbours, which ought in reason to content us. The second adventure is a little more adventurous: a cruise to one of the famous marts of learning, that time-honoured university, for instance, to which the young voyager of these pages—would he were a Jason for the reader's sake!—is now careering in his hopeful argosy,

with portly sail
Like signiors and rich burghers on the flood.

And now, if the prospect of the studious university daunts any timorous gentle reader, filling his imagination with notions of the endless jangling of bells, the tiresome and ponderous routine of lectures, not omitting "the stale, flat, and unprofitable" discourse of Commons, where punning takes rank as wit, and the dinner is often worthy of a better company; we desire and entreat of him at once to dismiss from his mind all such frightful apprehensions, for with none of these horrors will he be visited and afflicted. We shall not ask him to attend a single lecture, set him to work the slightest problem, nor throw in his eyes the minutest grain of the dust of the schools; in fact, it is for none of your hum-drum purposes our coming man has come to Cambridge. He has no notion of breaking his fine genius on the dull wheel of academic duties, and still less thought of bounding his aspirations with the winning of academic honours. He begins to be pricked with the spur of a loftier ambition, and to feel a craving within him which the glory of doubling the cube, or squaring the circle, will never satisfy. "*Sic itur ad astra*" is the direction of the only road he is inclined to travel, for the man that is destined to have a voice in the commonwealth, and make a noise, and a loud one, in the world, necessarily soars above the *curriculum* of his college, and scorns the low spheres of the mathematicians. The points we are now to carry in his person are neither the Hebrew points, nor those of geometry, which we leave to the mediocrities and the multitude. We hope to make a much finer figure than any in Euclid; and that is not to be done by listening abjectly and sheepishly when everybody is talking and haranguing, ranting and declaiming, or, at the very least, prattling and prosing round about us. In this talking world (for what better definition is it possible to give of it), how is a man to be distinguished but by out-talking it? It is for the plebeian spirits to "lend their ears," while men of nobler strain give tongue like Anthony; nor let it be said or insinuated that mighty talking is incompatible with mighty doing; for, surely, if it is true that "words are things," it follows, by all the rules of all the logicians from Aristotle to Whately, that the vulgar distinction between the man of words and the man of business is not to be maintained in solemn argument. Why, the tongue has ever been distinguished and exalted above all other parts of the human frame by the express title of "the busy member." Beyond dispute it is the busiest member of most Parliaments, to say nothing of its activity in the country at large, when Parliament is prorogued; or of its proverbial nimbleness in domestic discussions. In short, we question not but the reader is now completely satisfied of the truth of Gratiano's remark, that "silence is only commendable in a neat's tongue dried;" and has made up his mind to say with Antonio, "I'll grow a talker."

CHAPTER L.

DEPARTURE FOR COLLEGE.

"ONE would think," said the Vicar, "that nobody ever left this neighbourhood before to go to college."

"I think we may safely say," said Mr. Pigwidgeon, "that we never sent a young man up to either University with such splendid career before him. I'm a plain blunt man, who say what I think, and don't say what I don't think. That forehead of his is worth ten thousand a year; if it was mine, I would not exchange it for a dukedom."

Mrs. Medlicott thought of asking the apothecary home to dine; he had not dined at the Vicarage since he turned it into an hospital.

Somebody else who was present inquired what Reuben was intended for.

"Very little matter what he is intended for," said Mr. Pigwidgeon, taking it upon him to reply; "the young man is fit for anything; whatever profession he chooses, we'll see him at the tip-top of it before he is thirty."

This secured Mr. Pigwidgeon the dinner.

Mr. Pigwidgeon was a deliberate flatterer; he lived by it in part, as he lived by administering other less agreeable things: but the Vicar and his wife heard nearly the same language regarding Reuben from almost everybody about them, until it was not very wonderful that the mother's head was turned almost round, for it was as much as the father could do to keep his own steady.

If Reuben's departure for school made such a sensation among his relations and acquaintances, you may conceive the excitement caused by his setting out for the University. The fuss that was made about so common-place an event was absolutely ridiculous. Mrs. Winning, of Sunbury, gave a *fête champêtre*. Matthew Cox gave the heartiest of entertainments at his country-house, and made Reuben a present of the "Encyclopædia Britannica." Canon Oldport, who was always glad of an excuse for giving a dinner, invited Reuben and his father to a remarkably jovial party of eight; the effect of which upon the host was a fit of the gout, which confined him to his chair for the same number of weeks. Hannah Hopkins insisted upon every body drinking tea with her, and made one of her huge "cut-and-come-again" cakes for the occasion; and it was not without some management Reuben escaped being encumbered with half a ton of it on his journey to Cambridge. Every body did something hospitable but Mr. Pigwidgeon, who pretended that one of his daughters had a bad attack of influenza. The apothecary, however, showed not only the greatest willingness but the greatest anxiety to be included himself in all the festivities of the neighbourhood, and he never forgave Mr. Cox for not inviting him to the banquet he gave in honour of Reuben.

The object of all this interest, and the principal figure in these various festive scenes, was now nineteen; he had attained his full growth, not far beneath the six-foot standard; his figure was still slight, but showed a tendency to a larger development, and his countenance was most agreeable and prepossessing. His lip was no longer as smooth as Hebe's, and a manly graciousness was beginning to supersede the almost feminine softness of boyhood. Of his personal advantages he was not unconscious; he made the most of them by a scrupulous attention to his toilette, and no doubt he was much indebted to his graceful exterior, as well as to the amenity of his disposition and manners, for the favorable impression he made wherever he went; but nothing gained him so many admirers as his vivacity and fluency in conversation. In a narrow rural circle, where few could talk at all, and still fewer had anything to talk about, a young man who could speak with facility for a whole evening upon twenty subjects in succession, was regarded as little less than a prodigy. As Reuben could reason with his father on divinity, discourse with his mother on metaphysics, talk agriculture with the farmers of Underwood, commerce with the burghers of the neighbouring city, not to speak of poetry and botany with Mary Hopkins, it is not much to be wondered at that he was pretty generally believed to have all human knowledge at the ends of his fingers. He was, in fact, laying the foundation in local celebrity of that wide reputation which he subsequently acquired as a talker of the first magnitude. Several people of rank in the neighbourhood who met him at Mrs. Winning's and Mr. Oldport's, conceived the highest notions of his abilities, and as to the mercantile men and the farmers, they thought that nothing comparable to Reuben had ever appeared, at least since the days of Pitt, and freely talked of the biggest wigs in all the professions in connexion with his young head.

Upon the whole, what with his handsome person, his engaging manners, his voluble tongue, the acquirements he actually possessed, and those his fond friends so liberally gave him credit for, few young men ever left the paternal roof for the banks of the Cam or the Isis, leaving behind him a more general conviction that everything worth winning in the world would be won in a canter. He left behind him also several living proofs of his popularity, four little godsons all baptized by the name of Reuben, not only to do him honour, but with a prudent view to the future patronage and protection of so distinguished a sponsor.

Our very reverend grandfather was still abroad, Rhining and

Rhoning it with his young wife, or, notwithstanding the burning of his haggard, he would probably have appeared in person at a moment so critical to young Medlicott, and come handsomely down with some thumping lecture or discourse, on the duties and studies of a young collegian. Though absent, however, and absent upon such engrossing business as a honeymoon, he did not altogether neglect Reuben, but chalked out a course of reading for him, with a sort of chart appended to it for the entire voyage of life, all upon a loose scrap of paper, in the Dean's usual rough and hasty way of committing even his best considered views to writing.

The plan was this—Reuben was first to devote himself doggedly to mathematics, then he was to obtain a fellowship, after that he was to be ordained; pupils were all along to yield him a handsome income, but eventually he was to get a living; thus between collegiate honours and professional advancement he was, in fact, to tread as nearly as possible in his grandfather's steps, and a very fair road it was to wealth as well as to reputation; the more was the pity that it existed only on paper, like a Benthamite constitution.

The Dean made two egregious mistakes. The talent for doing anything doggedly was not among Reuben's gifts, various as they were. Besides, he had no ardent passion for mathematics; so the very foundation of his grandfather's scheme failed; it is to be hoped his houses on Wyndham terrace were considerably more substantial. It might have been hard to have chosen a path for Reuben, in which he would have steadily travelled, but he was unfortunate in being put in a track from which he was almost under a sort of necessity of wandering. Respect for his grandfather and the slip of paper, however, was too strong a principle not to govern his conduct for at least a year; accordingly for about that space of time he cultivated algebra, trigonometry, and the conic sections in that sort of heartless and desultory way which never made any man a senior-wrangler.

Towards the close of the year he began to grow weary of swimming against the stream, and had thoroughly convinced himself that he would never eclipse, or even equal Newton. The metaphysical and moral sciences suited him infinitely better than the exact ones; there was place in the former for the flowers that refused to twine with the triangles, and for the rainbow hues which the circles of geometry would have nothing to do with. Logic and Ethics were daughters of philosophy as well as Mathesis; and fame was to be achieved by courting them, if not at St. John's, at least beyond its walls. Reuben began already to despise his college for the narrowness and exclusiveness of its pursuits. Had the tree knowledge only one branch? Was the mind to march only in one contracted road? Why had learning so many provinces, why had the intellect so many faculties, why had the brain so many chambers, or the head organs? However, let the men of St. John's be as narrow as they pleased, was he to cramp his genius because they perhaps had none to be cramped; was he to degrade himself into a calculating machine, and pass the best days of his life extracting roots and solving equations? If these views had not readily occurred to his own mind, his friend Primrose was now at his elbow to suggest them strongly enough, and every letter from his mother tended also to confirm them. Mrs. Medlicott, in truth, had never much admired her father's ideas of a career for Reuben, and she had even been more hurt than she confessed at the slovenly informal way in which he had communicated them, upon a loose, and not over nice scrap of paper; in fact, it was the back of his bill at an hotel in Geneva. What she least liked in the plan was the notion of Reuben grinding. Were the fine talents of her son to be wasted in the most harassing and stupefying of all human occupations? Moreover, she was by no means satisfied of the absolute necessity of confining Reuben to the Church in the choice of a profession. In fact, in common with most of the Dean's family, she had ceased to flatter herself with the hopes of the mitre.

Mathematics having been thrown aside, a period followed in which Reuben seemed to lie dormant, like a boa who has made a vigorous meal, and reposes for months during the process of digestion.

After such vacations of his brain, Reuben generally surprised his friends by the development of a new talent; but the talent he developed now was not actually new, only a growth and expansion of an old one. Reuben became a member of the Union, and entered into its debates and political sham battles with his usual industry and ardour in pursuits irrelevant, or at best only collateral, to the main business of life. He soon attained a very considerable degree of success and celebrity as a debater on all sides of the questions commonly discussed in those juvenile schools of rhetoric, such as the assassination of Julius Cæsar, the public conduct of Coriolanus, and whether luxury ought or ought not to be permitted by the lawgivers of a wise community. In the course

of a few terms, it was surprising what an extraordinary command
he acquired of tropes and metaphors, and what a capital, telling,
and brilliant speech he was able to make upon any given subject
without boring his hearers with dry facts, or fatiguing himself
with extensive reading. He distanced his friend Winning many
a league. Winning could do no more than study the question
as attentively as his serious avocations permitted, and as his oratory was bounded by the extent of his knowledge, he made but a
poor figure against a competitor whose eloquence was only the
more copious and splendid, the less he knew about the real merits of what he was talking of. In fact, a man of a less generous
nature than Henry Winning, or of inferior understanding, would
have been mortified at the success of a rival who was so much his
junior as Medlicott; but Winning had still his eye steadily fixed,
as at school, upon the main chance, and only attended the meetings of the Debating Society to attain that degree of facility in
public speaking which is essential to distinction in the profession
of the law, though subordinate, of course, to the study of the law
itself. If he felt any pain at the sight of his friend's trophies, it
was purely on his friend's account; but he was now more economical of his advice than he had been at Finchley, not only because Reuben was of an age to think for himself, but feeling, as
all sensible men feel, the older they grow, that advice-giving is in
general a very presumptuous and a very unfruitful occupation.

It was the necessary consequence of Reuben Medlicott's victories in this new field that he began soon to think that the bar was
the profession best suited to his talents; and in this notion he was
warmly encouraged by the prudent Hyacinth Primrose, who saw
in our hero the embryo of an Erskine as clearly as he ever saw
any result in his life not actually present to his senses.

"Medlicott, you are not going to throw yourself away on the
Church?" said Primrose, one morning after one of Reuben's triumphs in mock debate,—" You are not going to bury those splendid oratorical powers of your's in a country curacy."

" As to your grandfather getting a bishopric, I look upon that
now as perfectly chimerical," said De Tabley, who was present.

" Whether my grandfather gets a bishopric or not, I shall certainly not go into the Church, without feeling a conscientious vocation for it," replied Reuben.

"That's an additional consideration," said Primrose. "You
have no more vocation to be a clergyman than I have. Very few
clever fellows have, unless when there is Church patronage in the

family. Men get a pastoral turn very early when they are born within view of a couple of handsome steeples, and their fathers possess the advowsons."

"I am not of age to be ordained yet;" said Reuben, musingly; "before that time arrives, I may possibly by study and reflection acquire the proper frame of mind."

"And if the frame of mind is not acquired, all the time passed in waiting for it will be thrown away."

"Why that is true," said Medlicott.

"Give the Church to the winds, my good fellow, that's my deliberate advice; turn your talents to account, and lose no time in entering your name at the Temple. What do you say, De Tabley?"

De Tabley was busy at a cold pie, but not so busy as not to assent to Primrose's opinion.

Reuben shook his head, and desired his friends to recollect that he was almost penniless; that his father had nothing to leave him, and that the bar was not a profession to yield an immediate income, even assuming success to be perfectly certain.

"My dear fellow," said Primrose, "neither Winning nor myself has any patrimony worth speaking of. In nine cases out of ten, a patrimony is a drag on the wheel of fortune; it is true of small patrimonies, at all events."

"But a man must live upon something before the fees begin to come in," said Reuben, arguing, as it were, for the Church, while he was greatly pleased and flattered by having the bar so strongly recommended to his consideration.

"No doubt, but you forget the never-failing and delightful resource of literature; you can write essays for the magazines, criticisms for the reviews, articles for the newspapers—there are the annuals, quarterlies, monthlies, weeklies, and dailies, all before you—in fact, you may make a little fortune with your pen, *attendant* the great one which you will afterwards make with your tongue. Recollect, too, that very little law will serve with eloquence rare as yours. Men get to the top of the wheel in these days much quicker by the tongue than the brains. The tongue is the substantial dish, the brains are only the garnish."

"Tongue and brains must have been a strange dish," said De Tabley; "I suppose it was a favourite one in Goldsmith's time."

Reuben smiled at De Tabley's incidental bit of gastronomy, and then said he thought there was a good deal of sense in the plan Primrose suggested.

"And it has this great advantage," continued Hyacinth, "that supposing the law to fail after all—"

"You have literature still at your back—"

"Exactly—two strings to your bow—decide for the bar, my boy; if our road will not be quite as short as Winning's, at least it will be twice as flowery, and twice as enjoyable."

De Tabley was again appealed to, and perfectly concurred with Primrose's views, adding, however, that he only dissuaded Reuben from the Church, because there was no prospect of Dean Wyndham being a bishop; "for," added he, "my opinion of the *summum bonum*, is a good living; which if a man can obtain, it must be his own fault if he does not keep a good kitchen, and a good cellar. I see no reason why he should not have a good library also."

"In the third place," said Primrose.

Many more conversations of the like nature tended rapidly to unsettle the views with which Reuben had arrived at Cambridge; but the question was too serious to be decided by the judgment of Primrose and De Tabley, or even of "the young man eloquent," himself, who, indeed, never contemplated upon this or any other occasion, flying abruptly or rebelliously in the face of his nearest friends and relatives, particularly his grandfather, the object of his earliest admiration and respect.

"Write to your father—break the matter to him," said Primrose, after the next rhetorical triumph in the mimic senate.

"I'll write to my mother," said Reuben.

CHAPTER II.

HERO WORSHIP.

He wrote to his mother accordingly, and to make his case in favour of the law as strong as possible, he accompanied the letter with two of his most elaborate speeches, one on Coriolanus and the other on the question of luxury, its effects on commonwealths, and whether lawgivers ought to restrain it or not by statutes. The oration on luxury pleased Mrs. Medlicott most; "it was so powerfully reasoned," she said, "and so philosophical;" but Doctor Pigwidgeon preferred the Coriolanus, without very accurately knowing who Coriolanus was.

Doctor Pigwidgeon was no longer a nickname. He had recently obtained a Scotch degree, and had now a right to the title. He and his father were on the old footing again at the Vicarage, dropping in at dinner two or three times a week, one or other of them, and sometimes both, upon the stale old pleas and pretences, which to be sure, as long as the object was gained, answered the purpose quite as well as new ones. As to the ladies of the family, however, Mrs. Medlicott kept them at bay inexorably, probably thinking that enough had been sacrificed to them already.

Doctor Pigwidgeon, as we have said, preferred the Coriolanus.

"Perhaps you are right, Theodore,—let us go sit in the garden, and you shall read it aloud to me."

The Vicar was planting out brocoli. It was not far from the usual dinner-hour, and a tapping was heard at the door in the hedge just before the reading of the speech commenced.

"That's my dad," said Doctor Pigwidgeon.

"Highly probable," said the Vicar, duly resting on his spade, and looking for the moment almost as sour as Timon in the same attitude.

Young Pigwidgeon went to the door; his conjecture was perfectly well founded.

"Dinner's over," said the son jocularly to the father, as he admitted him.

"You are come in the nick of time, Mr. Pigwidgeon," said Mrs. Medlicott, nodding to her never unexpected guest, the apothecary.

"Very good of you to say so, madam, but I can't even sit down. I only looked in, as I was passing by, to inquire if the hail yesterday injured your wall-fruit."

It would have been just the moment for taking the apothecary's picture. He was, indeed, a strange-looking animal. He was meagre, and would have been tall had he held up his head and shoulders, but he stooped so much that a string from his head to his heels would have made quite a bow of him. His limbs were so wandering and ill put together, that they seemed almost to be detached from his person, or as if the joints were made of some extremely soft gelatinous substance. This straggling and dropping character extended to his features. His eyebrows, which were grizzly and bushy, fell heavily over his small cunning eyes, which were never at rest, for he seemed to be always screwing and forcing them to see something more of everything about him than they were disposed to see of their own accord. His long, hooked nose (apparently a mere continuation of his high forehead) almost tumbled into his mouth when it reached it; the mouth in turn hung, or rather wagged, upon the chin, and the chin was in fact a flight of chins, descending shakingly to his chest. The morality which gave expression to this beauty was in unison with it. In short, the "music of his face," to use Byron's conceit, played an air very like "the Rogue's March." His attire (for he did not disdain "the foreign aid of ornament") consisted of a black suit, not very new, and which, like his limbs and features, seemed connected with him by associations of much too loose a kind. The coat would have held two such apothecaries, if his match could have been found in England. Upon the whole, there was something about the man that suggested a connexion with the *Pays Bas* of literature, or an existence in the back settlements of one of the learned professions. If a man of letters, he might have passed for a suburban writing-master; if connected with the Church, a parish clerk or a Welch curate; if in the medical department, you would have guessed him to be, what in fact he was, the shabby apothecary of a country village. Mrs. Medlicott used sometimes to say handsome things of his forehead. Positively it was a very fine one, but so much the worse for the science of phrenology.

"We should be very happy, Mr. Pigwidgeon, if you could stay to dinner," said Mrs. Medlicott, smiling, "but I was inviting you to a banquet of another kind,"—and she held up the paper that contained Reuben's thunder as if it contained the most tempting delicacy in the world.

"Ah!" said the apothecary, advancing, "that's a horse of another colour."

"And when I tell you what this is!" added Mrs. Medlicott, to pique his appetite.

As soon as the apothecary learned the nature of the threat that awaited him, he declared that he must postpone all other business to enjoy it; and accordingly the reading took place with due solemnity.

The Vicar went on planting his brocoli. He said he could hear very well, but Mrs. Medlicott thought it was quite impossible, so (to accommodate matters) Mr. Theodore Pigwidgeon climbed up into the fork of a pear-tree, from which rural rostrum his voice was easily audible in all parts of the garden. The apothecary seated himself on a rolling-stone, from which he could not only see his son in the tree, but the smoke of the kitchen chimney over it; while the proud mother occupied a rustic chair right in face of the doctor's perch, and the raven kept hovering and hopping near, as if he too was interested in the question of Coriolanus.

Between the orator and the majority of his critics there was not much difference in point of judgment. It would have been hard to decide whether Reuben's inflated sentences and redundant metaphors were more or less ridiculous than the plaudits which they drew forth from every one but the Vicar, for even the raven, after having heard the elder Pigwidgeon cry "hear, hear," half a dozen times, as if he had been at a parish vestry, mimicked the cry to admiration, and came out with "hears" in a manner quite parliamentary.

Before the reading was concluded, the tidy maiden, who filled the office of butler at the Vicarage, tripped forth to announce dinner. Mrs. Medlicott was for leaving the dinner to cool, and finish the speech, but the Vicar shouldered his spade, and marched into the house with the manner of a man who disdains to argue a plain question which he has in his power practically to settle.

As the apothecary sneaked after, we have an opportunity of observing him in motion. If he looked more comical at one time than another, it was when he walked, for he traversed the ground with ridiculously long strides, like the *step*-father in one of Hood's diverting sketches; and carried his hands plunged in the pockets of his nether garments, as a cheap substitute for gloves; keeping his eyes for the most part riveted upon his shoes, although neither in their shape nor their lustre was there anything to make them agreeable objects. This habit of walking with his eyes on the ground gave him a meditative air, and indeed Mr. Pigwidgeon was of a meditative turn; but I believe the general subject of his meditations was the contents of the Vicar's pot, or whatever might happen to be turning on the spits of such of his neighbours and customers as he was wont to sponge on.

"We are all partial," said Mrs. Medlicott, when the conversation returned to Reuben's oratory, after a tolerably smart exercise of the knife and fork, particularly by the apothecary and his son,—"We are all partial, and it is only natural I should, at all events, but I do think Reuben shows a decided talent for public speaking,—don't you think so, Mr. Pigwidgeon?"

Mr. Pigwidgeon thought that nobody could think anything else, after the speech he had had the pleasure and privilege of hearing.

"It is anything but surprising," proceeded the mother, " to find that the universal opinion of his college friends is, that with such talents, his success at the bar, if he was to go to it, would be beyond all question."

The apothecary only nodded ; he did not like openly to go to so great a length as this along with Mrs. Medlicott, without having some little inkling of the Vicar's sentiments.

Mrs. Medlicott saw that it was necessary to draw her husband out in order to prevent the conversation from dropping, so she asked him pointedly what his opinion was.

"About what?" said the Vicar. When Mrs. Medlicott took the trouble of informing him, all she got for her pains was sundry repetitions of the word "nonsense."

"Nonsense!" repeated his wife with asperity, "why do you say nonsense?"

"You wished to have my opinion," said the Vicar, "and I have given it to you frankly ; you know as well as I do that Reuben is to get a fellowship and take orders."

Then there ensued a disagreeable silence for a few moments.

"I must say," said the apothecary, breaking it, and trying to gratify the mother without contradicting the father, " after the very clever and very eloquent speech which I had the pleasure of hearing my son read before dinner (and I don't think he read it badly), nobody can wonder at the young man, who made it wishing to become a lawyer, nor would it be surprising if he were even to feel a desire to go into Parliament; on the other hand, when I think of what his prospects are in the other profession, with a grandfather who must be a bishop sooner or later—I have no more doubt of it than I have of my own existence—nothing is more natural than that his excellent father should have a very strong leaning in favour of the Church. And if the Church is to be my young friend's destination, what a comfort it is to think that his oratory will not be thrown away there ;—on the contrary, it will enable him to make a fine figure in the pulpit."

"That kind of thing," said the Vicar, meaning the specimen he had heard of his son's eloquence, " would do much better in the pulpit than at the bar, depend upon it."

"I can't think so," said Mrs. Medlicott Nor could Doctor

Pigwidgeon bring himself to think so either. The Vicar looked as if he cared very little what Doctor Pigwidgeon thought on the subject.

"I don't take it upon me to decide the point," said the apothecary; "but I'll take the liberty of proposing the health of my eloquent young friend. Let him choose what profession he may, he will be a credit to his parents and an ornament to his country."

Mr. Pigwidgeon wanted an excuse for another glass of port before he took his leave, which he did immediately after toasting Reuben. As it was growing late, his son rose at the same time to accompany his father home.

"The boy is just as fit for the bar, as he is to be prime minister," said Mr. Pigwidgeon senior to Mr. Pigwidgeon junior, as they walked home together, pretty well replenished with the Vicar's plain but excellent fare.

"But didn't you think it a beautiful speech?" said the son.

"Bah, flummery," said the father.

"I'm drowsy," said the Doctor, yawning with might and main.

"So am I," said the apothecary, making the same demonstration.

CHAPTER III.

MRS. MEDLICOTT HAS A LUCID INTERVAL — A STORM SUCCEEDED BY A CALM.

Mrs. Medlicott had her lucid intervals like other women, and in one of those which occurred the following day, she was providentially brought to see the folly of encouraging her son in the notions which Hyacinth Primrose and Caius Marcius Coriolanus had put into his head. She locked up Reuben's orations in a certain omnium gatherum press of hers which contained other treasures of the same kind, and wrote him one of the few really sensible letters which he had ever received from her. The Dean would never have heard a word of the matter if it had not been for Mr. Pigwidgeon's gossiping, in which, as usual, there was always a spice of malice, even when his best friends were the subject of his tongue. The only excuse for the apothecary was, that he was in the habit of making so free at table, that he never retained a very clear recollection of an after-dinner conversation. He soon noised it abroad that young Medlicott was to be a lawyer, contrary to his father's inclinations, and against his own advice. We have seen that among other branches of his profession he was a chiropodist, in plain English a corncutter. Among his patients in that line was Dean Wyndham's friend and crony, Mr. Oldport, and it happening about this time that the Canon stood in need of Mr. Pigwidgeon's services, the apothecary drove in his gig to visit him; and to beguile the time which his operations occupied, as well as the pain which they occasioned, what better could he do than to retail all the little parochial news he could collect, and it would have been strange if he had omitted the latest intelligence from the Vicarage, so likely to be interesting to a brother clergyman. In fact, the Canon introduced the subject himself by kindly inquiring for his friend the Vicar.

"Medlicott's falling into flesh, of late," he said, presenting his foot to the apothecary as politely as it is possible for one man to present another with that part of the person.

"He's too heavy an eater," said Mr. Pigwidgeon. "You ought to caution him against that," said the Canon. "So I do," answered Pigwidgeon, and so indeed perhaps he did, but it was altogether by precept, not at all by his example.

"And how is his clever son? I was greatly struck with him one day he dined with me. Talks a little too much, but promises to talk well. A little of Coleridge. Getting on well at the University?"

The apothecary wagged his head, and with all his chins shaking together gave his patient a ludicrous account of Reuben's oratory, and the discussion to which it had given rise on the subject of the bar, detailing especially, and with many little malignant exaggerations, the public reading in the Vicar's garden, of the great speech about Coriolanus, all which extremely diverted the Canon, who said he would have given a golden guinea to have been present, or to have had a peep over the hedge. In short, Mr. Pigwidgeon, partly through his blundering, and partly through his sycophantic eagerness to make himself agreeable to his patient, no matter at whose cost, left the Canon under the impression that Mr. Medlicott was so excessively weak as to be induced by the puerile effusions of his son in a debating society, to alter all his plans for the boy's career in life. From Mr. Oldport this intelligence spread to the Dean, by the most natural channel in the world, as they were regular correspondents. The Dean happened to be near Cambridge at the time; the first thing was to write a brimstone letter to the calumniated Vicar, and then in a tempest of indignation, after the true Sir Anthony Absolute fashion, he invaded Reuben's chambers.

Reuben had received his mother's letter of remonstrance several days previously, had acquiesced in her views most dutifully, and fully made up his mind to adhere to his original intentions of going into orders as soon as his academic race was run, always provided he felt the proper spiritual dispositions. He was particularly unfortunate in the moment his grandfather chose for paying him this visit, for a volume of Blackstone's Commentaries which Primrose had lent him was lying conspicuously on his table, and he was actually engaged in preparing a speech upon the feudal system, to be made at the next meeting of the society. The Dean, therefore, thought he had caught him *flagrante delicto*, and never did father or grandfather, either on the stage, or in real life, deluge an unlucky young man with such a flood of abuse and invective.

Reuben endeavoured to speak, knowing that in a few words he could dispel the misapprehension under which the old gentleman was labouring; but he might as well have tried to gain an audience in a West-Indian hurricane.

The Dean began by telling him he was no more fit for the law than he was to command the navy; then he asked him what single qualification for the bar he possessed?—had he the brain, or even the stomach, which that turbulent, laborious, and anxious profession required? No man knew better than he, the Dean, did what the requisites of a lawyer were. What private means had he to support him until there was the remotest likelihood of being able to support himself by his profession? A young fellow without a sixpence in the world! What possession was he under? Was he out of his senses? Were his parents in their senses? Here he snatched up the book that lay open on the table, and finding it was a Blackstone, flung it down with violence on the table, and resumed his tirade in a more exalted and passionate tone, like " Boreas talking to Auster," as Dr. Donne expresses it.

"You want the physical qualifications, boy, I tell you. There's nothing of the bull-dog in you. Who are your advisers? You don't know yourself. Who has stuffed your head with this nonsense? What business have you in debating societies? Mind your mathematics. What's Coriolanus to you, sir?"

"Nothing," replied Reuben, with a simplicity which took the choleric Dean by surprise, and checked his violence for a moment; but, noticing the papers that were strewed about, he snatched some of them up, and perceiving at once that they were notes of a speech, and a speech on a legal subject, he blew another gale stiffer than before, if that had been possible.

Reuben acted extremely well through a scene in which he had a difficult part to play. After this first unsuccessful interruption, he preserved a rigid but most respectful silence (only glowing with indignation when his grandfather most unjustly called in question his brains), until the time for reply was fully come, and then he quietly explained what, if he had been suffered to explain before, would have saved his grandfather the trouble and physical exertion of making such a hubbub about nothing.

——"I am glad to hear it," said the Dean, sitting down to rest himself, and at the same time wiping his broad forehead; for he had talked himself into a streaming perspiration.

Reuben showed him his mother's letter, which pleased him, and he even condescended to wish he had seen it before he had written to the Vicar under his erroneous impression.

"Who is Pigwidgeon?" said the Dean.

"Our apothecary," said Reuben.

"He must have read your speech, or heard it read," said the Dean. "I made a speech about Coriolanus myself, when I was a freshman."

Reuben smiled at this admission, and thought it not improbable his grandfather had made a speech on the feudal system also.

"But pray, sir." he asked eagerly, "was Mr. Pigwidgeon your informant?"

"He informed my informant," said his grandfather.

Reuben now saw to whom he was indebted for this unpleasant fracas with his venerable relative, and he did not allow the post to leave Cambridge without bearing a letter to his father; the effect of which was that the Vicar walked into the village within half an hour after he received it, and administered a bitter pill to the apothecary, in the form of a very severe rebuke for his unwarrantable violation of the confidences of private life. Mrs. Medlicott was highly incensed also; so that Mr. Pigwidgeon entirely lost the good-will of the Vicarage by his shabby behaviour in this affair, and never afterwards reinstated himself completely.

Reuben had never known his grandfather so gracious as he became, all of a sudden, on finding that his wishes were still as the laws of the Medes and Persians with his daughter and her husband. He insisted on Reuben dining with him at his hotel, and Hyacinth Primrose happening to drop in before he left the college, he extended the same civility to him. In the course of the day he strolled about a great deal with the two young men, like some redoubted peripatetic philosopher with his pupils dangling after him. To listen reverentially to Doctor Wyndham, receiving everything that fell from his lips as if it were honey of Hybla or gold of Ophir, was an infallible receipt for keeping him in good humour; and it was sometimes well worth while to pay him this sort of homage, for when he was serene and pleased with his company, no man discoursed more instructively or entertainingly, and for young men his conversation was particularly improving. On the present occasion, after making some excellent remarks upon debating societies, and balancing their advantages and dangers with great shrewdness and discrimination, he talked largely and eloquently upon the profession of the law, returning in good humour to the subject which he had handled shortly before in so termagant a fashion. His fluency, vigour, and knowledge of life, surprised and delighted Primrose, who was now in his company for the first time. The Dean recurred to his idea of the bull-dog, and when he heard that Primrose was designed for the bar, he hoped he had a dash of that pugnacious breed in him.

"A lawyer," he repeated, "is nothing without it; he wants it every day of his life, either to bully a witness, beard a judge, wrangle with his brethren, or thrust his own views of the case down the throats of the jury."

Primrose ventured to say that something of the spaniel seemed often to be a very useful element in the lawyer's character.

"The crown-lawyers, for instance," said the Dean, approving of Primrose's remark; "but what say you to a cross between the bull-dog and spaniel, perhaps that would be the best dog of all."

"I think, sir," said Reuben modestly, "a dog of that breed would make a good attorney-general."

"Very well," said the Dean, poking his grandson in the ribs with the end of his stick; "very well, indeed,—and now let us go to dinner."

CHAPTER IV.

THE DEAN AT THE TABLE.

The Dean had not said a word from which it was possible to infer that he was not quite alone at Cambridge, so the astonishment of Reuben may be imagined when, on entering the drawing-room, he found his grandmamma Blanche waiting to receive him. This totally unexpected meeting with his old flame, now placed in so singular a relation towards him,—one so utterly inconsistent with the slightest remnant of the feelings which she formerly inspired (even making such feelings absolutely ridiculous)—might well have fluttered a less susceptible young man than Reuben Medlicott. This was his first meeting with Blanche since she made her strange marriage; indeed since the day he left that unfortunate essay on shoemakers upon her table, in which he had but too incautiously disclosed the state of his heart. Fortunately the circumstances of the meeting prevented the embarrassment (which was in some degree mutual) from taking a sentimental turn. It was impossible to be sentimental in Dean Wyndham's company; and the near approach of dinner, with the presence of Hyacinth Primrose, had a further tendency to place the intercourse between Reuben and Mrs. Wyndham at once upon a rational and easy foundation. In fact, ere dinner was announced, Reuben's agitation was nearly over; and before the close of the evening, he was almost on the same terms with Blanche as he might have been with any other handsome young woman who had taken a fancy to marry the old Dean. Blanche was greatly improved by matrimony, but not so much in her person, perhaps, as in her air and manners. The little state of the matron became her; its independence and dignity had communicated a graceful firmness to her deportment; and though she still had that soft, earnest expression in her eyes, there was an animation in them now which was no doubt due to her enlarged experience of life, and a corresponding freedom and spirit in her conversation, to be attributed, of course, to the same cause. Her style of dress was altered considerably; as became the wife of a clergyman and dignitary of the church, she was attired with extreme but most becoming simplicity, no longer in the gayest hues of the season, as when she was one of the three Sherries.

Two bonnets were lying on a sofa, with other miscellaneous

female properties, seemingly thrown there, because, in an hotel, the bedroom was probably at a considerable distance. Mrs Wyndham saw Reuben's eye directed to the bonnets.

"I am not the only lady of our party," she said, smiling.

"Where's Catherine?" cried the Dean, almost at the same instant.

Reuben was alarmed, thinking that Catherine was in all probability the eldest Miss Barsac, of whom he retained a disagreeable recollection. But his alarm was only of momentary duration, for the door opened, and in came the woman, whom of all others, next to his mother, he would have wished her to prove—his bountiful and blooming aunt Mountjoy. She had scarcely time to embrace him, when the Dean seized her arm and led her into the dining-room, through a door which a servant had just thrown open. Primrose presented his arm to his old acquaintance, Mrs. Wyndam. Probaby a more agreeable party of five never met at a dinner-table. The Dean, no doubt, talked more than his share; but as he eat more than his share also, he left the rest considerable opportunities of conversing, and they were not neglected. Reuben, seated between his pretty grandmother and his charming aunt, from both of whom he had been so long separated, basking in the Dean's capricious favour, and with the most intimate and most brilliant of his university friends near him, could not have been much happier had he been at a feast of nectar and ambrosia in one of the Islands of the Blest. He appeared indeed that day to great advantage, confirmed the opinion of his talents which almost everybody was disposed to entertain, and pleased Mrs. Mountjoy so very much, that, although she was not in the habit of writing to her sister, she could not refrain the next day from doing so, for the pleasure of letting her know what she thought of her nephew, what a splendid future she predicted for him, and what an engaging young man he already was.

Mrs. Mountjoy was one of those women of whom it is impossible to speak in too flattering terms—impossible to think of without wishing to be near them—impossible to sit beside without extreme danger of falling in love with, unless, like Reuben, you happened to be a nephew, which alters the matter. Her beauties were ample, and her heart was large in proportion. In short, she was an angel all but the wings; and a stout pair of pinions it would have taken to have borne a seraph of her proportions through the empyrean.

The Dean, though he seemed sometimes to forget himself, and

treat Blanche on the footing of a child, patting her on the head, or chucking her under the chin, was manifestly influenced by her, and very much to his advantage, in more ways than one. Reuben could see at a glance that his grandfather was wonderfully softened since the period when he knocked the boys about at Mrs. Barsac's evening parties; and his aunt privately informed him that though she attributed the change partly to the society of his young wife, she considered it still more owing to the improvement of his circumstances by the addition of Blanche's fortune, and to a temporary withdrawal from his building speculations, by which he had burnt his fingers so severely. This was a mere conjecture of his daughter's, and not very well founded, as we shall soon have occasion to know.

"But hush, the Dean is talking, and we must listen, my dear," said Mrs. Mountjoy, stopping in the midst of her domestic explanations.

The Dean was talking of fluency as a result and a symptom of shallowness. "Full men," he said, "are seldom fluent. They are eloquent, but eloquence and fluency are different things. Young men discourse fluently in proportion to their ignorance, not to their knowledge, of a subject. There is no more worthless or more dangerous acquirement than eloquence in the vulgar sense of the word. Bruce remarked of the Abyssinians, 'that they were all orators,' 'as indeed,' he adds, 'are most barbarians.' The observation is extremely applicable to an unfortunate country not a thousand miles off, with which we are very closely connected. I have always thought the great misfortune of that country was that when the family of the Shallows settled there, the family of Master Silence did not accompany them."

All laughed—Primrose was particularly amused by this fancy of the Dean's, and said he had no notion so much about Ireland was to be learned from Shakspeare.

"His plays are full of Irish characters," said the Dean. "What do you say of such swaggering poltroons as Pistol and Parolles, or that facetious, foul-mouthed blusterer, Thersites? Are they not Irish to the back-bone? Can't you fancy Pistol member for Limerick, and Thersites representing the city of Dublin?"

"But, sir," said Reuben, "speaking of Homer's Thersites, is not that a very effective speech which he makes in the first book of the Iliad?"

"Very effective," muttered the Dean, "but only in bringing down the staff of Ulysses upon the speaker's shoulders. Homer makes Thersites the representative of talent without worth, eloquence without character. Pope well observes that had Ulysses made the same speech, the troops would have sailed that night for Greece. Character is to an individual what position is to a general. The world asks who a man is before it gives him an audience, or at least before it hears him a second time. We must not only take thought what we say, but from whence we say it. Even in society, the prosperity of a jest depends upon the consideration of the man who makes it, often upon his place at the table. Young men ought to reflect upon this, and take more pains to make themselves respected than admired."

Primrose tried to draw out the Dean on the question of Catholic Emancipation, but upon that subject he was reserved, and what he did say was oracular and ambiguous. He dropped it soon, and preferred giving an account of his varrious honeymoon expeditions, swinging himself about on his chair in his original manner, and threatening destruction to all the glasses and decanters within the reach of his arms. His last excursion, with Blanche, had been in Switzerland. Primrose was amazed at the feats of pedestrianism performed by a man considerably upwards of sixty, and could scarcely believe some of them, though solemnly attested by his wife. One of his walks was from Lauterbrunnen over the Wengern Alp, to the summit of the Faulhorn, "no journey that of a sabbath day." Blanche accompanied him on horseback. She had followed him also on another great excursion to the glaciers of the Rhone.

"I never saw a mountain in my life," said the Dean, "that I did not get to the top of it, if it was possible; when I was first in Switzerland, I was a very young man, and if I did not ascend Mont Blanc, it was not that the mountain was so high, but that my pockets were so low. The ascent is an expensive thing, for you must take a regiment of guides with you. Another passion of mine was for the sources of rivers. I have seen the sources of most of the great rivers of Europe. Had I devoted myself to it, I would have discovered the springs of the Nile long ago. I have no doubt of it."

"But you have been in Egypt, sir?" said Reuben.

"Yes, but not on a matrimonial excursion. I went further up the Nile than any man living, and I have seen more of Palestine than any man living either; I was on the top of Mount Sinai, which nobody in Europe has to say but myself. In fact, there is nothing that I have not done in the way of travelling; I rode everything rideable, shot everything shootable, swam everything swimmable, climbed everything climbable, and eat everything eatable, in every country I visited."

"I believe, sir," said Mrs. Mountjoy, "when you were first married you went to Scotland."

Mrs. Mountjoy and Mrs. Medlicott were the Dean's daughters by his second wife; his first marriage was very early in life; it bore no fruit, and seemed now even to himself an occurrence of ancient history.

"I was married in Scotland," said the Dean, in reply to his daughter's observation.

"Not at Gretna, I hope, sir," said Hyacinth Primrose.

"Not at Gretna; all was regular; but it was in Scotland, so that I took the tour of the Highlands. Nobody ever travelled so far north in Scotland as I did; I visited every lake, all the islands, and from the Calton Hill to the loftiest peak in the country, if it was a sin to do homage to nature on the high places, I committed that sin upon every one of them. But it is not nature we worship in such scenes, but the God of nature, and that is only the true religion. My second honeymoon I spent in the Pyrenees, so that there's a chain of mountains for you for every chain in which Hymen bound me."

"You will take your next wife to the Himalayas, sir," said Blanche quietly and pleasantly.

"Not further than the Andes," said the Dean, laughing, with a swing of one of his arms that knocked his glass of claret off the table.

"No," he added, with a vigorous sigh, never minding the glass, "I'll ascend no more mountains. My mountaineering days are over."

His young wife probably thought that he might have said his marrying days were over, but he cautiously confined his pledge to the ascent of mountains.

"Who will say or sing, henceforward," said Hyacinth Primrose to his friend the following morning, "that—

> Wint'ry age and youth
> Ne'er can well together?

I am heartily glad to see the Dean so happy with his young wife. What a fine old fellow he is!"

"Hyacinth," said Reuben, "you have been very successful in your gallery of personal sketches in the 'Cambridge Miscellany,' you ought to do my grandfather."

"A capital notion; I'll do it, Reuben, but I must see more of him. Is there a chance of his asking me to dinner again?"

"A very good chance, indeed," replied Reuben.

A note from Mrs. Wyndham within half an hour verified the prediction. The young men dined a second time with the Dean at his hotel, and Primrose had ample opportunities of studying the subject of his intended sketch in the bosom of private life. Hyacinth made rapid way in his favour, and in the graces of Mrs. Mountjoy also. On his return to his chambers he made some notes of the most remarkable things that fell from Doctor Wyndham. Among them was the following:—

Primrose had ventured flatteringly to allude to the bishopric which had not yet been conferred upon the Dean, though so long expected by his family, and which, in some respects, would have been only a just tribute to his talents and character as a Churchman.

"I'll tell you a tale of a prebend out of old Burton," said the Dean, "and you may apply it to a bishopric if you think it will fit."

The company were all curiosity and attention to hear the story, which the Dean related very nearly as it may be found in Burton's chapter on "repulses, injuries, disgraces, and contempts."

"In Moronia Pia, or Moronia Felix, I know not whether, nor how long since, nor in what cathedral-church, a fat prebend fell void. Many suitors were up in an instant. The first had rich friends and a good purse: every man supposed he would carry it. The second was my Lord Bishop's Chaplain, in whose gift it was: he thought it only his due. The third was nobly born, and he meant to get it through his great relations and allies. The fourth was the deceased Prebendary's son: his father died in debt (for the prebend, as it was said,) left a wife and many poor children. The fifth stood upon fair promises which had been formerly made to his friends for the next preferment in his Lordship's gift. The sixth had married a kinswoman of the Bishop, and he sent his wife to sue for him. There were several more, but the twelfth and last was a right honest man, an excellent scholar, a pious minister, and a painful preacher; but he had neither means nor money; besides he hated such courses; he could not speak for himself, neither had he any friends to solicit his cause, and therefore he made no suit, could not expect, neither did he hope for, or look after it. The good Bishop, perplexed among so many competitors, and not yet resolved what to do, at length of his own accord, mere motion, and bountiful nature, gave it freely to the excellent, pious scholar, altogether unknown to him but by fame. The news was no sooner published abroad, but all good students rejoiced, though some would not believe it, and some said it was a miracle. One among the rest thanked God for it, and said, 'Nunc juvat tandem Deo integro corde servire.' You have heard my tale of a prebend; but, alas, it is but a tale—a mere fiction; 'twas never so, and never like to be."

The Dean invited the young men again for the following day, but when the time came he had gone up to London on business, and Mrs. Wyndham and Mrs. Mountjoy remained to entertain the company. That was no difficult matter; but when the day was over, Mr. Primrose had his thoughts more engaged with Mrs. Mountjoy than with her father; in fact, he gave Reuben distinctly to understand that nothing could prevent his falling over head and ears in love with his aunt but her immediate departure from Cambridge. That event took place, however, sooner than he wished, for the Dean sent for his wife to join him in London, and Mrs. Mountjoy went up to town with her, having some law business there, and intending soon to go abroad, for she was a free British widow, might go where she pleased, and had made up her mind to use her liberty. She did not take leave of Reuben without the tenderest of adieus, giving him many useful little hints of the kind that women alone can give, and making him at the same time such a substantial present as her comfortable circumstances enabled her to afford, while those of Reuben made it most agreeable to him to accept. As to Mr. Primrose, if she had any sentiments towards him beyond those which most engaging young men inspire upon a short acquaintance, Mrs. Mountjoy kept them perfectly private, and they were not of a nature to alter her purpose of leaving England.

Twelve months elapsed before Hyacinth executed his purpose of sketching the character of Dean Wyndham for the Gallery of Eminent Living Divines, in the "Cambridge Miscellany." Probably his admiration of Mrs. Mountjoy, and the desire to please her, made him take unusual pains with this portrait, for it was done with great spirit and graphic ability, and made a considerable noise at the University and in the literary circles of London. The Dean was not long before he found out who the author was, and though a few of his faults were touched on, yet the censure was so adroitly mingled with praise, that upon the whole it gratified him extremely, and gave Primrose the first place in his favour, of all the young men at Cambridge. Reuben sent it to his aunt Mountjoy at Paris, where it was copied into *Galignani's Messenger*, a circumstance which added to the satisfaction of the Dean enormously.

CHAPTER V.

A NEW EMPLOYMENT.

But what was Reuben to do? His grandfather left Cambridge without taking the thought or the trouble of advising or instructing him upon that head. In fact, the old gentleman had enough of business on his hands, between his books and his bricklayers, without taking on himself the office of standing counsel to his grandson, and the only wonder was that he interfered in his affairs at all, even in the hasty, intemperate way that has been described.

But Reuben was too young to be left so much as he was, at this critical period of his life, to his own ingenious devices, or those of his friend Primrose. The Church was, in one respect, a most unfortunate choice for him. It left two or three years upon his hands, a space of time which it seemed impossible to fill up with mere theological studies, and which he was therefore only too much inclined and too much encouraged to fritter away in a variety of trifling and irrelevant pursuits. It seemed always time enough to sit down to study for ordination; and besides, until the time drew near, how could he be assured, upon anything like good grounds, that he was morally justified in entering a profession which, much to his credit, he had not brought himself to regard in the secular way in which he saw it regarded by most of the men about him. Thus, if he put aside the law, it was not so much to embrace divinity in its stead, as to give himself up to alternate fits of total indolence, or activity of a not much more profitable kind. He did not even cultivate literature with the energy of Primrose, who acquired not only character, but money, by his contributions to several periodicals. Reuben was too fastidious, too slow, and too uncertain, to produce with the rapidity indispensable to a journalist, or the punctuality of which only an editor knows the importance. At several intervals during these years he tried his hand at grinding, not knife-grinding, but grinding the edges of blunt intellects. This was lucrative, but it pleased his father more than it did his mother, and he did not stick to it very long; in fact, he discovered (no doubt with the aid of his mother's spectacles) that, whatever faculties he might possess for sublimer things, he was "little better than a dunce at grinding."

These were his own words in one of his letters home. The next day a letter from the Dean at Westbury informed him most unceremoniously, that he was nominated private tutor to a noble family in a northern county. His grandfather had settled all the preliminaries, the terms, the duties, the *quando* and the *quid pro quo*, in short everything; Reuben had only to pack his portmanteau and book himself for Westmoreland—an obedience which he rendered much against the grain, though he was not nearly so much hurt as his mother was by the arbitrary fashion in which an arrangement was made, in itself sufficiently distasteful.

The life, however, which Reuben led for several months with his pupils, Lord Appleby and Mr. Portly, was as easy a form of existence as can possibly be imagined. Their father, the Earl of Whitehaven, was a widower, resident abroad; and his sons, more studious of the pleasures of the chase and the table, than of those higher delights to which their preceptor would have led them, paid every attention to Reuben, except attention to his lectures. They left him in undisturbed possession of a good library during the day, and when the critical hour of dinner arrived, they took the best possible care of him, initiated him in many mysteries of the kitchen, and for gastronomic reasons, never imposed on him the duty of carving. The only way in which Reuben found it practicable to instil any classical taste into his noble pupils was by awakening their curiosity on the methods of hunting and cooking in use among the ancients. They were equally astonished and delighted to learn that there existed treatises on hunting and fishing by Greek and Latin authors, and that Mrs. Glasse and Dr. Kitchiner were not without their types and parallels in Rome and Athens. Upon these topics, and upon ancient wines, they would even draw their tutor out, and lead him to expatiate at breakfast or dinner.

When Reuben mentioned that the great Xenophon had written a work on sporting dogs, and another on horses, Lord Appleby would smile, and cry "indeed!" But though there was an English translation of the work on horses in the library, he never went so far as to take it down. Mr. Portly was partial to anecdotes of Apicius and Lucullus, and when Reuben told of those wonderful dishes of nightingales' tongues patronised by ancient epicures, the brothers invariably wondered whether there were nightingales enough in their neighbourhood to make a pie or a fricassee.

Reuben made no illiberal use of his own tongue in Westmoreland, but there was this excuse for him, that he had generally to find talk for the whole party, particularly during the labours of dinner, and after the fatigues of the chase. It was probably now that he first acquired the habit of lecturing in company, and considering a party collected round the dinner-table, or a group in a drawing-room, as an audience which it was his proper function to address, entertain, or enlighten. It was now likewise, that he devoted himself for the first time systematically to the study of words and phrases, independently of ideas and information. He began to keep a MS. book in which he gradually accumulated a prodigious stock of metaphors, similes, images, allegories, tropes, figures and allusions, taken from every work that fell in his way, and classified after a plan of his own, so as to have them ready for use upon every occasion, like the arms in a magazine. He made another book of quotations, marshalled according to subjects, and provided with an index for easy reference; nor was he content with any of the existing collections of synonymes, but commenced the formation of a very extensive one for his private purposes, so as to qualify himself (we may presume) to express everything he might possibly have to say in every form in which it was capable of being expressed; no doubt considering it a shabby thing in a speaker to have but one or two suits to clothe a thought in, although they should happen to fit it ever so well, and exhibit it to the best advantage.

Occasionally the disciples would leave their master for weeks together, to join a shooting-party in Scotland, or on some other excursion of pleasure. During one of these lonely intervals our opal-minded student devoted himself to a little course of reading in heraldry, a subject upon which the library at Appleby contained some very quaint and rare books.

Reuben commenced taking extracts from the works now at his command, originally with a view to illustrate the armorial bearings of the different English bishoprics; but his ideas extended as he advanced, and before his labours were over, his papers contained materials for a curious essay on heraldic zoology. This paper saw the light very soon after it was written; for, happening to meet, in a neighbouring country-house, an officious, but apparently good-natured little fellow, of the name of Griffin, who was an enthusiast on everything connected with heraldry, Reuben fell into conversation with him on the subject, and on mentioning his essay, Griffin offered to get it inserted in the "Gentleman's Magazine," if the author would entrust him with it. This Reuben did without hesitation, thanking him warmly for his kindness, and he very soon saw, by several laudatory notices in the newspapers, that Mr. Griffin had been as good as his word. The success of this essay, who actually benefited by it, and how shabbily the author was treated in the transaction, will appear in process of time.

A melancholy incident terminated this passage of Reuben's life, and made a deep impression upon him. He was induced one day to go shooting with his pupils and one or two other men. Reuben carried a gun, but with so little malice against the birds of the air, that after a single shot, which did no execution, he never loaded his piece again, but kept by the side of Mr. Portly, who was a keen sportsman, and never so good company as when he was in the field. Returning late in the evening through a close coppice, Reuben happened to be in advance of his friend by a few yards, when hearing a shot behind him, he turned about, and going back some paces, found Portly stretched upon the ground, life almost extinct, having received the contents of his own gun on one side of his head, which was mutilated and shattered in the most frightful manner. He expired on the spot where he lay. The spectacle appalled Reuben indescribably; a bloody apparition haunted his imagination for years, and for a considerable time not only were his spirits depressed, but his health sensibly affected. He left Appleby immediately after the funeral of his unfortunate pupil, and spent a short time with his parents, during which interval he was seen so frequently in the company of the cosy, fat quakeress, that people began to smile and gossip on the subject, although, after all, there might have been nothing in it.

There occurred one incident—and only one—worth relating during this visit to Underwood; but being of an episodical nature, we reserve it for a distinct chapter.

CHAPTER VI.

THE SERMON ON CONSCIENCE.—AN EPISODE.

It will be remembered that Mr. Medlicott had frankly and pleasantly accepted a present of the sermon which the Dean, his father-in-law, had dropped into the well several years before, on the night before Reuben went to school, and the Vicar had resolved to treat his congregation to it the very next Sunday. This resolution, however, he did not adhere to, being influenced chiefly by the integrity of his character, which disinclined him to deck himself with borrowed plumage, particularly with feathers which both his verdict and his judgment assured him were so much finer than his own. On several occasions subsequently, however, either when he was lazy, or otherwise indisposed, he used to say to his wife on a Saturday morning, that he had a great mind to give the parishioners her father's thunder; but still, when the Sunday came, he continued to shrink from what he considered a species of imposition; and one of his own old sermons on the vices of lying and slandering, or the bad habits of picking and stealing, was reproduced for the twentieth time. Latterly the Dean's sermon had been almost forgotten, and lay, with some others, in a sort of omnibus drawer in the bedroom, amongst the Vicar's shirts, flannel waistcoats, and loose miscellaneous papers. Mrs. Medlicott often remonstrated on the subject of that drawer, and suggested the expediency of putting its contents in order, particularly the papers; but the Vicar would shrug his shoulders and reply that they were quite as well arranged as the records of the kingdom itself; and moreover, his wife was open to a *tu quoque*, for there were drawers and shelves in her own chests and wardrobes, where similar confusion prevailed, and from which, when she drew a shawl or petticoat in a hurry, it was no uncommon event for one of Reuben's schoolbooks, French exercises, or her mother's unfinished tract on Spartan education, to tumble out on the floor. On the first Saturday evening after Reuben's arrival, the Vicar had been in one of his ordinary difficulties about a sermon; he had been too much occupied planting some new strawberries during the week, and had left himself little or no time for the more important duty of preparing a suitable discourse for the edification of his flock.

"I have a great mind," said he, "to read one of the homilies to-morrow. It is a pity they have fallen into disuse. Some of them are very fine compositions, and the worst is far better than any sermon I ever wrote, or shall write."

"You had better preach that sermon of my father's," said Mrs. Medlicott, and Reuben agreed with her.

"Perhaps so," said the Vicar, "I had almost forgotten all about it."

"Where is it?" said his wife.

"I suppose in the drawer with the shirts," said the Vicar.

Mrs. Medlicott said something to the effect, that the drawer in question was no place for her husband's sermons.

"I don't know," he rejoined, "whether it is the shirts that get among the sermons, or the sermons among the shirts, but they have pigged together in the same drawer ever since I was married."

After some more dialogue of this kind, he went to the drawer to look for Dean Wyndham's sermon, but it was not to be found. There was a sermon on drunkenness, which he had preached not many months before; the sermon on picking and stealing, which he had given two Sundays previously; and some other discourses on various moral duties, to every one of which either Mrs. Medlicott or Reuben had some objection to make.

"Perhaps it has got into some place of yours?" said the Vicar.

"How is that possible?" said his wife.

"Such things have happened," said the Vicar, "so we had better try."

Mrs. Medlicott was very averse to an examination of her stores, for she had been severe on the condition of her husband's, and was conscious that her own were not much better arranged. However, there was no help for it, and so her drawers in their turn were submitted to scrutiny. A French dictionary tumbled out of a bundle of dimities upon the Vicar's toe in the very beginning of the search.

"Upon my word," said he, stooping to rub his foot, "I am beginning to think that my drawers are not so very disorderly after all."

"The maids thrust everything into my shelves," said Mrs. Medlicott.

"Careless husseys!" murmured the Vicar.

"Well, the sermon is not here at all events," said his wife, pushing the dimities back into the press, and turning the key rather brusquely.

"We shall find it some day or another, when we are not looking for it," said the Vicar. "I suppose I must entertain them with 'the dinner of herbs and the stalled ox,' to-morrow."

This was a standard discourse of Mr. Medlicott's on the text, "Better is a dinner of herbs where love is, than a stalled ox and hatred therewith." It was really a very good plain sermon, and he had once indulged his peculiar vein of humour by preaching it before the corporation of Chichester, upon whose habits of good living it was a sly practical satire.

"I don't see what better you can do," said Mrs. Medlicott; and so it was settled on the Saturday night: but the following morning, when the Vicar took a clean shirt out of the drawer, the sermon that had gone astray turned up among the folds of the linen, and was preached that same day to the congregation of Underwood.

The subject was the office and authority of conscience in the moral constitution of man.

Never was a preacher more nervous through apprehension of being considered dull than Mr. Medlicott was upon this occasion, lest there should be anybody present capable of detecting and appreciating the originality and excellence of his discourse. In general, there was never a less critical audience than his parishioners formed, or one upon whose swinish judgments the pearls of eloquence or learning would have been so completely thrown away. He scrutinized them, however, upon this occasion very closely, and so did his wife and son, though Mrs. Medlicott's motive for doing so was mere curiosity to observe if by chance a single person present would be struck by the difference between a sermon of her father's and those which the congregation was in the habit of hearing. But not a being, in any corner of the little church, betrayed the slightest emotion, from first to last, of a nature either to alarm the Vicar, or to gratify the filial pride of Mrs. Medlicott. On the contrary, as the sermon was longer by about ten minutes, or rather more, than the ordinary standard in the parish, two or three of the farmers and shopkeepers were obviously affected by that peculiarity, as appeared by their yawning and fidgeting, and other symptoms of uneasy or weary listeners. Before the service commenced, however, both the Vicar and his family had made one observation which was important. One of the principal proprietors in the neighbourhood was an old nobleman, Lord Stromness, who only came there occasionally, and was very little known to anybody, except by his personal appearance.

He had a pew in Underwood church, and that was almost the only place where the Vicar had ever seen him: his lordship would appear there once or twice a-year, generally about partridge-shooting; he was in the habit of shaking hands with the Vicar and bowing to Mrs. Medlicott; that was all they knew about Lord Stromness. On this occasion he had come down after the rising of Parliament, and attended divine service as usual; but it was not his presence that attracted the Vicar's or Mrs. Medlicott's attention (for his lordship was no more of a critic than any of the farmers), but that of a stranger by whom his lordship was accompanied. Yet there was nothing at all extraordinary in the appearance of this gentleman, either: he was a grave elderly man, almost clerical in his dress. Mr. Medlicott merely noticed him as a stranger, and his wife (with her phrenological eye) because he possessed the recommendation of what she termed a highly intellectual forehead. When the Vicar came down from the pulpit, Lord Stromness paid him the usual civil attention, and the stranger made him a respectful obeisance also. This was all that occurred. The old nobleman and his friend were amongst the first who left the church. They had scarcely turned their backs before Mrs. Medlicott was all eagerness to find out who the strange gentleman was.

"Somebody shooting with Lord Stromness," said the Vicar.

"Do inquire who he is," said his wife.

"Ask the Sexton," said the Vicar, "while I take off my gown."

But all the Sexton knew was that Lord Stromness had a small party of sportsmen in the country with him, and he presumed the stranger was one of the number. The following day however, the Vicar met an acquaintance of his, who knew everything that was going on within twenty miles round in the sporting world, and who informed him that the Lord Chancellor was one of Lord Stromness's party, and was probably the stranger who had been at church with him, as the description answered the Chancellor's person perfectly. Mrs. Medlicott wondered how he could have left the church without testifying, in some way or another, his admiration of the discourse he had heard.

"It was not prolix enough to please him," said the Vicar.

"Something may come of it yet," said his wife, musingly.

"A Crown living!" cried the Vicar; "but could I conscientiously accept one, if it were offered me under such circumstances, particularly as conscience was the subject of the sermon?"

"Indeed, I think you might," said Mrs. Medlicott.

Reuben was of the opposite opinion.

"It's a nice point," said the Vicar, "but I shall probably have full time to consult the casuists, and consider it fully."

CHAPTER VII.

MR. MEDLICOTT MEETS ONE WHO IS AS VERSATILE AS HIMSELF.

REUBEN, returning to Cambridge, found that Primrose was flown. Hyacinth, though he had been so urgent with Reuben to embrace the profession of the law, seemed in no great hurry himself to enter it, for immediately after the appearance of his sketch of Dean Wyndham, he went abroad, and pursued his travels as far as Florence. Mrs. Mountjoy happened to be there at the time, which no doubt made the fair city on the Arno particularly agreeable to Hyacinth; it contributed, indeed, he frankly acknowledged, more to his contentment, than the presence of the Medicean goddess herself, "for which, I suppose," he said, in one of his letters home, "I shall be put down by your artists and artistic people as little better than a Hun."

Reuben was greatly scandalised (as well became him) at the truant life his friend was leading, when he ought to have been almost as far advanced in his profession as Henry Winning. Primrose, indeed, seemed now to be carrying into practice one of the many little playful theories which he was in the habit of broaching from time to time, to exercise his wit, and lighten the weight of an idle hour. Among other things, he was wont to maintain that for rising in the world there was no better plan than to do nothing, provided you have once got a general reputation for talent.

"My notion is," he used to argue, "that it is better to rest on the character one has, than expose it to hazard, by continually giving envy something to carp at. The men that succeed best are those who contrive to get a little clique about them, who cry them up not for what they actually do, but what they could do if they would only take the trouble. In those cliques, which are often exceedingly influential, active talent makes a very poor figure by the side of reputed cleverness. I was once of Shakspeare's opinion, that perseverance 'keeps honour bright;' but of late I am much inclined to think that honour is in more danger of being sullied than burnished by scouring. There are so many ways of disparaging anything actually done, and turning it against the doer. Any blockhead, for example, can deny one's originality, and affirm that he met, elsewhere, everything one has said or written, or even that he himself supplied the hints or the materials. If talent cannot be denied, what is so easy as to shake the head, and cry—'how indiscreet!' or come in with a 'yes, but that is all he can do.' But the most approved plan of all is, to exclaim, 'Ah, if such a one (the hero of the clique) had handled the subject, if such a one had spoken, or written on such a theme!' On the whole I conclude," said Primrose, "that intellectual activity is more likely to injure a man than to serve him; I am very much disposed in future to be more tender of my capital than I have been, and live like a great many prosperous fellows about me, upon the interest of my reputation."

This was precisely what Master Hyacinth seemed to be now actually doing, having fortunately, besides the interest of his reputation, the interest of a few thousand pounds to live on. Reuben was pained to see his friend so volatile, and had serious thoughts of writing him an admonitory letter—a step which it is to be regretted he did not take, as a remonstrance from him upon that particular subject would have certainly deserved a place among the curiosities of literature.

Primrose, however, was not the only acquaintance he had who stood much in need of a lecture on perseverance. As he was one day straying in the streets of Cambridge, probably moralising on this very point, he remarked a workman on a ladder painting an inscription over the door of a little shop, which seemed on the eve of being opened in some new line of business. While Reuben stood watching the operation, the name was completed, and to his astonishment it was ADOLPHE. Almost the next moment he had the pleasure of meeting his old acquaintance of Hereford again. Adolphe darted out of his shop, with a cigar in his mouth, not much changed, except that his moustache was larger, and his appearance that of a man who had been tossing about in this wicked world. Reuben was very happy to see the French shoemaker, and shook his hand cordially.

"Ah," said Adolphe, "you do not shake the hand like most d' your countrymen; you give your hand as if your heart was in it. I am happy to meet you again: you were always a kind friend to me."

Reuben presumed he was about to set up again in his former trade.

"Ah, no! he was now in the book line: he had at length, after repeated trials, discovered the career that suited his talents and his tastes; he had found in himself two passions—he loved literature and he loved merchandise; the true career of everybody was the result of his passions: this was his theory, and it had made him what he now was,—a bookseller."

"Where was mademoiselle his sister? was she still living with Mrs. Winning?"

"No, no; she was married, married to a distinguished comedian in London; she was settled in the world, and had a nice house at Bayswater."

"I shall not fail to visit her whenever I go to town," said Reuben.

"She will be proud to be visited by Monsieur."

It was a fortunate rencontre for Adolphe. Reuben deserved to have had his portrait taken by the first sign-painter in England, and hung over the door of the new shop, to reward the extraordinary pains he took to have it opened with *éclat*. He canvassed for customers; he even wrote Adolphe's advertisements for the newspapers; advised him as to the stock of books he should purchase; and incidentally put his name to one or two bills which were passed to the houses in Paternoster-row by which the orders for the books were taken.

Mr. Medlicott was also Adolphe's first customer. The book was a pocket edition of the poetry of Milton. It was a memorable purchase. Soon applying it to its purposed use, he took it with him the same evening in one of his lonely saunterings, and the first verses that met his eye stung him to the quick. It was the beautiful sonnet "On being arrived at the age of twenty-three:"

> "How soon hath Time, the subtle thief of youth,
>   Stol'n on his wing my three and twentieth year!
>   My hasting days fly on with full career,
>   But my late spring no bud or blossom shew'th.
> Perhaps my semblance might deceive the truth,
>   That I to manhood am arrived so near;
>   And inward ripeness doth much less appear,
>   Than some more timely happy spirits endu'th.
> Yet be it less or more, or soon or slow,
>   It shall be still in strictest measure even
>   To that same lot, however mean or high,

> Toward which Time leads me, and the will of Heaven:
> All is, if I have grace to use it so,
> As ever in my great Task-master's eye."

He read a great mass of divinity for a few weeks following the reading of that sonnet; he plunged deep into biblical literature and Church history; mastered the elements of Hebrew, and began to wonder at the little interest he had hitherto taken in sacred studies. In fact, many a young man is admitted to orders with a much scantier knowledge of divinity than Reuben acquired in this brief paroxysm of study. During a whole fortnight he never saw his *protégé*, the bookseller, except for an hour occasionally in the evening, when he would drop into his shop, by way of relaxation, or to inquire how the business was prospering. On one of these occasions, he found the lively young Frenchman sitting on his counter, playing the flageolet, just as he had found him at Hereford in the beginning of their acquaintance, when he traded in shoes. Some University men came in while Reuben was there; but, to his surprise, instead of asking for books, they inquired for cigars, and Adolphe supplied their wants from some boxes, which Reuben had not noticed before. There was a little theory ready to account for this union of trades. The literature of tobacco was very curious. Reuben thought it was possible it might be so; but he began to think, also, as he returned to his chambers, that his friend Adolphe was not much more constant to one pursuit than he was himself.

The three-and-twentieth anniversary of the nativity of Reuben came. The Vicar procured him a nomination to a curacy in Chichester. The Bishop of a neighbouring diocese, an excellent man, who had often been friendly to Mr. Medlicott, was soon to hold an ordination, and it was the earnest wish of Reuben's friends that he should sieze the opportunity, and present himself for admission into orders. But now came one of his fits of languor and indecision, unhappily much more frequent than his starts of energy and determination. He doubted the completeness of his preparation; there were many points on which he had not yet made up his mind; he had not examined himself with sufficient strictness and solemnity to discover whether he entertained that sincere desire for the pastoral office, and fitness for its duties, without which he had all along been resolved never to take the obligations of a clergyman upon him. In this there was some conscientiousness, but there was more indolence. The Vicar was morose; the Dean was violent, as usual, and intended to write his grandson a philippic, but, being otherwise much occupied, he devolved the duty on Mrs. Wyndham, through whose mild medium the indignation of his grandfather reached Reuben in a very diluted form. A pile of letters on the subject lay on his table from the different members of his family. There were two or three from his mother; at first she had been disposed to blame him with some asperity, in common with his father, but her later epistles were in an altered tone. It appeared that she had come round to her son's opinion, that the delay of a year or so could be of little consequence, as he was still so young a man, and could easily employ the interval to so much advantage in the cultivation of pulpit oratory.

In the midst of all this to-do about ordination, (for the subject made a great noise at Underwood, though very little in the world at large,) Mrs. Mountjoy had returned from the continent, and taken lodgings in London. Reuben shortly after went up to town to pass the season with her. This was his first visit to the great metropolis; and his mother trusted he would not neglect so good an opportunity for taking lessons in elocution from some of those experienced professors of that art, whose advertisements she had frequently observed in the public journals.

BOOK THE FIFTH.

Suds. "Why, I want to be made an orator on, and to speak speeches, I tell you, at our meetings, about politics and peace, and addresses, and the new bridge, and all them kind of things."
Foote. "Why, with your happy talents, I should think much might be done."
Suds. "I am proud to hear you say so. I did speechify once at a vestry concerning new-lettering the church-buckets, and came off cutely enough; and to say the truth, that was the thing that provoked me to go to Pewterer's Hall."—*The Orators.*

ARGUMENT.

If we were to offer advice to a reader, as Lord Shaftesbury has done to an author, we should begin by strenuously urging him to cultivate the excellent virtue of humility, so to avoid the too common presumption of cocking up his own little private opinions upon all occasions against the judgment of the writer, fancying if the pen had been in his own fingers how much better matters would have been managed, like a village politician pooh-poohing a cabinet minister; or as if a court of Pie-poudre were to review a decree of the Court of Chancery.

> "God bless thee, and put meekness in thy breast,
> Love, charity, obedience, and true duty."

A sensible reader will take things as he finds them in the book in his hand, very much as a wise man makes up his mind to take things as they are in human life, jogging along with the nymph Goodhumour hanging on his arm,—the best companion, rely upon it, for getting through a book as well as for getting through the world. We do not advise the reader, nor anybody else, to go to school to Diogenes in his tub; the seminary we do recommend is that where we were trained ourselves, that which was founded ages ago in Greece by that cheerful philosopher, who not only held, with Sir Toby, that "life consists of the four elements," but was much inclined also to Sir Andrew's opinion, that good fellowship entered largely into the composition, though perhaps he did not lay it down so broadly as the boozy knight in the inimitable play. Nor let it be thought that in recommending the school of Democritus we would wish to see the faces of our audience "wearing a universal grin," as that of Natus did upon the day of Tom Thumb's victory. The philosophy of Abdera consisted in the habit of looking at the sunny side of things, not in the idle trick of giggling like a girl, or laughing like a clown in a pantomime. Be as grave as you will, provided there is no sourness in your gravity, and you graciously receive what is honestly intended to please you. Let it be in chemistry as it may, very little, morally speaking, is to be done by the action of the acids. Hannibal is the only personage on record who ever gained an advantage by vinegar. If we authors are expected to have honey on our lips, that our periods may flow mellifluously, surely our readers ought to have honey in their hearts, that their judgments may run sweetly. Ah, that honey of the mind is a heavenly quality—

"Aerii mellis celestia dona."

You will not be the worse critic, if you must be of that quorum, for having all Hybla within you. As to write with bitterness is no mark of an able author, so to read with bitterness is as little a characteristic of the judicious reader. We are your hosts; you are our guests, and we pray you to remember the duties, obligations, and responsibilities incumbent upon you by virtue of that jovial relationship. You are bound to come to us with an unwrinkled brow and a bright eye, arraying your inner man in some festive suit made of cloth of sunshine, if it is to be had; all urbanity and complaisance, proving yourself a gentle and gracious reader in reality, as you undoubtedly are by the forms and courtesy of the world of letters. Away, then, with all exceptions to our story, or any chapter, or subdivision of it. We pronounce them ill-humoured and unmannerly. If our incidents are objected to, we declare it frivolous and vexatious; if anybody assails our characters, we call it calumny and detraction; while, as to the rate of our progress, we assert our indefeasible right to travel at what pace we please, whether by electric telegraph, or on the back of a tortoise. Nor do we sit here in our chair of state to answer inquisitive people, popping all manner of questions—our motive for this—our reason for that—in short, why we have written the present book and not a different one. Our book is our Republic, and we are President of it. Why, we might, if it so pleased us, strike a *coup-de-plume*, trample all human obligations under our feet, butcher one-half of our characters in cold blood, transport the residue to some equatorial swamp, producing only red pepper and yellow fever; leaving our "tale half told," like "the story of Cambuscan bold," or that other bard who

"broke off in the middle
Th' adventure of the bear and fiddle;"

and, if the book has had any subscribers, confiscating their purchase-money, or picking their pockets, with a sufficient number of "considerations," like the estate of the plundered house of Orleans.

CHAPTER I.

BURLINGTON GARDENS.

Mrs. Mountjoy resided in Burlington Gardens. Mr. Primrose, who had also returned from abroad, took chambers in the Albany.

Mrs. Mountjoy's opinion upon such a subject was perhaps not the best worth having; but she was decidedly of opinion that Reuben had acted wisely in postponing, for a short time, his entrance into a profession so very serious as the Church. Possibly she took rather a secular view of the matter, but she thought she was doing her nephew a solid service in giving him some little insight into the gay world, before his entrance into a profession which, to a great extent, must necessarily separate him from it for ever. The widow was fond of the world, it must be owned, but it was in as unworldly a way as ever the world was loved in; for she was much less anxious about enjoying its pleasures herself, than to make others partakers of them.

"I can't help thinking, Mr. Primrose," she said, "that a clergyman ought to be acquainted with life in all its varieties, even a little with its pleasures and amusements, if it were only to enable him to form a just estimate of their vanity; at the same time I am very far from thinking that the vainest things in this world are its enjoyments—at least the only class of enjoyments to which I would wish to introduce my nephew."

Primrose fully concurred in this opinion; and pushed it further, with his usual love of paradox, by observing that "he could not understand how a divine was to teach mankind to abjure the pomps and vanities of human life without having previously made himself perfectly master by experience of all that it was his duty to rebuke and discountenance. Of course," he added, feeling that he was overstraining the point, "I do not mean exactly to say, that a man ought to go through a formal course of dissipation to qualify him for the pulpit."

"Oh, of course not," said Mrs. Mountjoy, "I never could have dreamed you meant any such thing. At all events, the kind of dissipation I propose to practise and encourage, will, in my humble opinion, do no young man any harm. With your assistance I hope, while I remain in England, we shall manage to have a great many rational and agreeable evenings in this house."

"We must look after Henry Winning," said Reuben, coming in at the moment and joining the conversation.

There was no difficulty in finding Winning, for his chambers were now almost as well known at the Temple as those of His Majesty's Attorney General.

The gravity of his profession sat well upon Reuben's first friend and steadfast protector at Finchley. Winning was now a fair specimen of the rising young lawyer. His forehead was broad and fair, his well-opened eye was calm and penetrating, his manner was frank and bold, his voice was remarkable for distinctness, strength, and volume. His room was literally nothing but a hollow cube full of books and papers. The ceiling was the only side which was not covered with them. His table was well provided with briefs, though it did not yet groan beneath them; and finally he had arrived at the state and dignity of keeping a clerk and possessing an antechamber.

With all this, Henry Winning was a very agreeable member of society, conversed with spirit, kept up a tolerable acquaintance with the current literature and events of the day, was very economical of bar anecdotes, and never made a pun in his life. Mrs. Mountjoy received him cordially on Reuben's account, and was soon happy to know him upon her own.

That handsome and excellent lady had a very fair notion of enjoying existence, whether she lived in Paris, Florence or London. She would willingly have led a social and convivial life had Reuben been beyond the great wall of China, but his presence in the character of her guest made gaiety, in her opinion, a sort of duty, and accordingly she laid herself out to be more than usually hospitable and entertaining in Burlington Gardens. Quiet little jovial dinners were what she most delighted in, and she proposed to diversify them with suppers of the same character, after an opera or a comedy. Her desire was to have everything perfect, or as perfect as possible, which ought to be the object of all of us in other things as well as dinners and suppers, which, however, are none of the least interesting and important affairs of life.

"Would that De Tabley were here," cried Reuben; "he understands these matters infinitely better than I do, or, I believe, Primrose either."

Mrs. Mountjoy was curious to know who De Tabley was.

"One of our first men," said Primrose, "in gastronomic science. If cooking was honored like mathematics, he would take a first wranglership. Some men are destined to be pillars of the State, some of the Church: De Tabley was born to support, maintain, and defend the British Kitchen."

Reuben added the better points of the character, so that Mrs. Mountjoy could not but desire to make Mr. De Tabley's acquaintance as soon as possible.

There was no occasion, however, to invite him to London; he was in town at the time, having his eye upon a good sinecure place under government, which he hoped soon to enjoy, through the influence of his uncle and other parliamentary connections. In short, the gay widow soon had all the Hereford boys of her nephew's acquaintance about her, and a very attractive centre she made to the clever and agreeable group.

But, as this was not her novitiate in London, she had a large acquaintance already, and it included a number of humdrum people—very rich some, very respectable most of them—but none of them possessing the qualities suited to her present views, or rather those of her new ministry. Reuben's unsophisticated notions of men and of society were now of signal service. Now it was that he gave the first proof of his talents as a social reformer. In a very short time he succeeded in clearing his aunt's salons of a multitude of nobodies, whom she had fallen into the habit of cultivating merely because she saw them cultivated by other people. Reuben would ask who such a person was—some stupid formal old bachelor,—take Mr. Leadenhall, for example.

"That old gentleman, my dear," Mrs. Mountjoy would answer, looking extremely serious; "he is a director of the East India Company, enormously rich, made of gold; has a magnificent house in Park-lane; no end to his wealth—ingots, pearls and diamonds—quite incredible how rich he is."

"Will he give any of his ingots and diamonds to us, my dear aunt?"

"No, my dear, of course not; indeed, they say he is the most miserly old wretch in existence."

"But his house in Park-lane—I suppose that is always open to his friends; to you, for example," proceeded her nephew.

"Open to nobody living, my dear, but one or two old Sybarites like himself; he is the very personification of voluptuous selfishness."

"Well, my dear aunt, if you are neither the better for his riches nor for his magnificent house; if you admit that he is selfish and worthless; and if you do not pretend that he is agreeable or clever, pray why do you court his acquaintance? Of what earthly use is he to you, to me, or to anybody?"

"Well, indeed, Reuben, when you put it in that light, I do not know what to say: I ask him because everybody else does; I neither love him nor respect him. I'm sure—in short he is a very tiresome old man, and I shall never be at home to him again."

"He will be no loss," said Reuben.

"But then what is one to do?" continued Mrs. Mountjoy; "how is one to choose one's society?"

"On two principles, aunt—nobody is worth knowing except for his talents or his virtues—his moral grandeur or his intellectual celebrity."

"My dear boy," said the fair widow, "would you have me turn everybody out of my house but yourself and Mr. Primrose?"

Reuben smiled, thanked his aunt for so handsome a compliment, and said he feared his rule would indeed proscribe a great many persons of her acquaintance.

"I am sure," she said, "Sir Finch Goldfinch has neither virtue nor talent."

"He has got a box at the opera which he never lends you, and he gives a ponderous dinner now and then that bores you to death; in return for which favours you load him with all kinds of hospitable attentions, merely because he is Sir Finch Goldfinch."

"I must plead guilty, my dear; but I'll send him packing with Mr. Leadenhall."

"Do now, like a dear good sensible aunt, and cashier Sir Allan De Bray and Lord Greenwich at the same time; the latter is a mere lord, and the other a mere baronet."

"And only a baronet of Nova Scotia, my dear."

"Which makes the case against him perfectly irresistible," said Reuben, smiling; "and now don't you think, my dear aunt, we might throw a few ladies overboard with advantage?"

"Let them all go, if you please, my love," said Mrs. Mountjoy, "I don't give balls, only dinners; so a circle of men is what I want; you and Mr. Primrose, must go elsewhere for beauties and fortunes."

So it was arranged. Mrs. Mountjoy, in fact, gave Reuben a *carte blanche* to fill her rooms with men of intellectual renown and moral grandeur; but as such fruit grows not on every tree, he was forced to put up for some time with company not quite so distinguished. The first set consisted of Mr. Araby, a handsome young clergyman, the author of "Melancthon" in twenty books; Mr. Bavard, a talkative and parasitical doctor, who held the distinguished office of family physician in the household of the Earl of Powderham;—these were the nominees of Mr. Primrose. De Tabley brought his uncle, a veteran dandy and old clubbist, who represented at that time the borough of Breeches-Pocket. Winning contributed a couple of loquacious barristers, and there was a certain Captain Shunfield, of the Guards, who got in by some means or other, nobody well knew how.

When Reuben reviewed his troops, he felt almost as much ashamed of them as Falstaff was of his regiment, and could not but feel that he had turned out the Leadenhalls and Goldfinches without getting much better men in their place. The dinner days were Wednesdays and Saturdays. On Sundays Mrs. Mountjoy, Reuben, Primrose, and Winning excluded all the rest of the world. The remaining days were open, and for these Mrs. Mountjoy felt herself quite at liberty to accept agreeable invitations when she received them. Reuben used often, in his latter days, to relate the little incidents of his aunt's first entertainment in Burlington Gardens. One of these was the following:—Mrs. Mountjoy received a note from Winning in the morning, requesting permission to bring his friend, little Master Turner, with him to dinner. Reuben and Primrose were astonished and indignant at a request so monstrously unreasonable; Mrs. Mountjoy was very unhappy; but at length her good-nature and regard for Winning prevailed over other considerations, and she returned a civil answer, saying, that she would be happy to receive Mr. Winning and his young friend. When the dinner-hour came, old De Tabley was one of the earliest arrivals, and Mrs. Mountjoy commissioned his nephew to prepare him for what was to happen. The old gentleman, not over fond of children at any time, was scarcely able to conceal his annoyance, and fidgeted about the room until Mrs. Mountjoy almost feared he would leave the house. Reuben looked on like a philosopher, not a little annoyed by all the fuss that he saw made about the seemingly trivial occurrence of a little boy accidentally brought to a dinner-party. When Mr. Winning and Master Turner were announced, a comic painter could not have had a better subject than the company presented, particularly the figure of old Tabley, who stood in the centre of the room, perfectly rigid, his features puckered up with the acrimony of his feelings, and his eye-glass intently fixed upon the door.

The object of all this alarm proved the next moment to be a little master, indeed, but only a Master in Chancery.

"A pleasant opening," said Primrose aside to the widow, "of your London campaign." But the pleasantry all evaporated in that one trivial occurrence, and notwithstanding all the preparation for an agreeable dinner, it turned out one of the dullest that ever was given. For a long time nobody could talk for Mr. Bavard, which provoked no one so much as Mrs. Mountjoy, who was anxious that her nephhew should come forward, and had no notion of giving dinners for Mr. Bavard to shine at. Reuben would probably have spoiled the dinner himself, if it had not been done for him by the parasitical and prating doctor, who, by virtue of his longer experience, possessed the assurance and pertinacity which our "coming man" had yet to acquire.

At length, having exhausted all other topics, Doctor Bavard began to hold forth upon the art of conversation itself (in which he was such an adept), and said, among other things, that it was like Nature, and abhorred a vacuum, upon which Winning quickly and pointedly added that "it more resembled Commerce, for it abhorred monopoly."

"And Law," said Master Turner, following up the blow, "for it is averse to perpetuities."

"Attica and Laconia in close alliance," said Reuben, with some pomposity, "but war to the knife with Thebes."

And having thus got what the French call the "parole," he kept possession of it with a tenacity of purpose worthy of a better cause; beginning with Plutarch's Apothegms, and ending with the Facetiæ of Hierocles, not one of which would he probably have left untold, if he had not been suddenly cut short by a hint to pass the bottle, which had been standing stock still while his tongue had been running so volubly. The pause delighted everybody save Mrs. Mountjoy, whose admiration for Reuben was such that she could have heard him talk for ever with satisfaction.

"However, I agree with Mr. Bavard, that conversation is a mere art," said Captain Shunfield, filling his glass: "I have met with works on the subject."

'Have you found them practically useful?" said Primrose cruelly.

"Well," said the Captain, "I think I picked up some good hints."

"I'll tell you what the art of agreeable conversation consists in," continued Hyacinth, getting the start of Bavard, who was preparing to begin again; "it consists in being agreeable to the present at the expense of the absent."

"A good definition of tea-table talk," said Reuben.

"Apropos to that," said Bavard, but got no further.

"Does not a great deal depend upon the accompaniments, as in music?" said George De Tabley: "the accompaniment of a good dinner, for instance."

"Depend upon it there is," said Primrose. "Just for a moment imagine the dishes and wines before us swept away by magic, and the Barmecide's feast in its place, or Timon's last dinner to his summer friends."

"I remember an anecdote," said Bavard,——

"I should not undertake to be witty under such circumstances," said old De Tabley.

"Nor I, positively," said the guardsman.

"Apropos——," said Mr. Bavard, but was again cut short, for Reuben began to recollect his astrology, and observed that to make society perfect, Mercury ought to be in conjunction with Bacchus.

"Unfortunately there is no such planet," said Winning.

"There must be a planet Bacchus," said Primrose, "or I should blush for the Copernican system. It will be discovered one of these days."

"All very prettily observed," said Master Turner; "but perhaps I may venture to improve upon what has been said by recollecting the advantage which we now enjoy of a conjunction between Mercury and Bacchus in the house of another planet, and a fair one."

"They ought to be in trine," said Reuben.

"Why, I think your nephew is an astrologer," said old De Tabley, addressing Mrs. Mountjoy, and laughing heartily.

"I have read a little on the subject," said Reuben, slightly colouring.

Winning glanced at Primrose, as much as to say, What is there about which he has not read something?

With the exception of this little trifling conversation, which took place towards the end of the dinner, the day was a decided failure. As to Mr. Bavard, Reuben made an enemy of him for life, but he was compensated by the golden opinions he won from Master Turner, who extolled him highly to Mrs. Mountjoy; and having learned from her who he was, took Reuben aside just before he retired, and astonished him very much by saying, "I have not the pleasure of knowing your father, but I heard the Chancellor say, not long ago, that the best sermon he ever heard in his life, was one delivered by a Mr. Medlicott, in a country church near Chichester; if you are the son of that distinguished gentleman and eminent divine, allow me to congratulate you."

CHAPTER II.

NOT IMPORTANT, BUT NOT LONG.

PRIMROSE often breakfasted with Mrs. Mountjoy: he did so on the day after the dinner related in the last chapter. Reuben mentioned what Master Turner had said to him, and told the story of his grandfather's sermon, which diverted his aunt and his friend extremely.

"By the by," said Primrose, "where is the Dean at present?"

Reuben knew nothing about him.

Mrs. Mountjoy knew just as little. There was nothing extraordinary in this, for no man had so many whereabouts, between his ecclesiastical duties, his university connections, and his private affairs and speculations.

"But," said the widow, "it is so long now since I have heard of my father, that I begin to grow a little uneasy. I wonder where we would be most likely to hear something about him?"

"Well," said Primrose, "the Barsacs are connected with a house in the city—Barsac and Upjohn—perhaps by inquiring there we might pick up some information."

Reuben and Primrose walked towards the city, through as thick a fog as encompassed Æneas when he visited Carthage. When they had got as far as the Temple, the darkness was actually Cimmerian, so they abandoned their purpose, but thought they might as well call upon Winning.

"If it were not for the fog," said Winning, "I should say I was glad to *see* you."

"Suppose a bill payable at *sight* were dishonoured on a day like this, could an action be maintained?" asked Primrose.

"By the custom of London, I suppose it could;" said Winning, groping about in the obscurity for chairs to accommodate his friends. He then stirred up his fire, which made the geography of his chambers rather more distinguishable than before.

Winning, as we have stated, had all the qualities for the bar, on which Dean Wyndham had expatiated—the head, the lungs, the stomach—and Reuben and Primrose now had a proof, while they sat with him, that he possessed the element of bulldoggism also; for an attorney happened to call who had neglected to prepare some important proofs which had been advised by Winning, and the latter gave him such a rating that Reuben and Primrose concluded there must necessarily be an end to all professional connection between them.

"On the contrary," said Winning, "he will send me more business than ever. This is my way of entertaining the attorneys."

"Upon my word," said Reuben, "it costs much less than entertaining them at dinner."

"I reserve that for my private friends," said Winning; "you must both dine with me to-morrow at the Rainbow."

Primrose was prevented by an engagement. Reuben dined with Winning *tête-à-tête*.

"You heard me give a fellow a scolding the other day," said Winning during dinner.

"I never heard such abuse," said Reuben, "since you abused me for learning the flageolet. I suppose the case is a very heavy one."

"Who do you think is the defendant?" said Winning in a serious tone—"a near relative of yours."

Reuben was unable to guess.

"Your grandfather!"

The young barrister then told his friend in strict confidence more about his grandfather's private affairs than it was pleasant to hear. Winning was counsel for an architect who was bringing an action against the Dean, arising out of the contract for the new buildings and terraces at Hereford, of which the reader has heard something already. One item in the bill of particulars was five hundred pounds for the erection of the fountain, which Blanche Barsac had suggested for the ornament of the square bearing her maiden name. Reuben was shocked at this intelligence. He had been led to believe that the influence of Mrs. Wyndham had cured his grandfather of his unhappy mania, and now he found that his affairs were more embarrassed by it than ever, to the extent of even exposing to obloquy his character as a clergyman and dignitary of the Church, for the Dean was actually residing at Boulogne, to keep "the perilous narrow sea" between his sacred person and his creditors.

"However," added Winning, "I have the satisfaction to inform you that matters are not quite as bad as they look, for my private opinion is that the case will not go to trial; I have reason to think that your grandfather's friends have proposed an arrangement which will keep things quiet, at least for some little time.

"The Barsacs, I presume?" said Reuben.

"Yes," said Winning,—"I suppose you know that the Barsacs are in town."

"No,—Primrose and I were on a voyage of discovery to find their house in the City, when we were lost in the fog-bank off Temple Bar."

"I know nothing of their house in the City," said Winning, "but they have lately taken a splendid one in Portland Place, where they are beginning to live with their usual discreet extravagance, and calculating hospitality."

Mrs. Mountjoy no sooner heard of her father's difficulties, so far exceeding all she had ever imagined, than she was very unhappy; and instantly resolving not to be behind the Barsacs in contributing to his assistance, she commissioned Mr. Primrose to call on the merchant, without delay, and acquaint him with her wishes and instructions. Barsac, however, would hear of nothing of the kind; he treated the proceedings against "his very reverend relative" with the utmost contempt, said his liabilities were mere trifles, some paltry thousands or so, not worth mentioning; in short, he had taken the liberty to arrange the matter himself in a friendly way during "his very reverend relative's" temporary absence on the continent. Barsac avoided mentioning the particular spot chosen by the Dean for his foreign residence, which Mr. Primrose thought extremely discreet on the part of Mr. Barsac.

The Barsacs were delighted to find that Mrs. Mountjoy was in town, hoping through her interest to make their way in London society more rapidly than they had hitherto succeeded in doing; and they were highly gratified also at the opportunity of reviving their old acquaintance with Reuben and Primrose, but especially with Mr. De Tabley.

The Barsacs had not been long in London without discovering that they were not of the same significance there as they had been in a place like Hereford. At the same time, with a good income, the disposition to be gay, and a decided interest in gaiety, they had no great difficulty in surrounding their dinner-table with guests, and filling their house with well-dressed people. Their drawing-rooms held some two hundred people—a number far exceeding the utmost range of their London acquaintance. The parlours were hung with family portraits, which gave Barsac occasion for continually remarking that they were not *his* ancestors; from which you were of course to infer that some other mansion contained that interesting gallery of pictures. In short the house suited them perfectly, and they laid themselves out for enjoying themselves in it, blending pleasure and profit together, in the laudable spirit of Mrs. Gilpin. If Mrs. Mountjoy was dependent upon Reuben and his old schoolfellows for her success in Burlington Gardens, still more were the Barsacs upon the same allies for the execution of their designs in Portland-place. To Reuben and his aunt, as near connections, their house was thrown open as a matter of course, but De Tabley, Primrose, and Winning, were soon requested to consider themselves on the same familiar footing; and the next step in the progress of this hearty though interested hospitality, went very nearly the length of conveying the same intimation to all Mrs. Mountjoy's friends and acquaintance, old and new, not forgetting Mr. Leadenhall, Sir Finch Goldfinch, and Lord Greenwich.

"I must do the Barsacs the justice to say," said Primrose, "that they are not deficient in gratitude; we often did them the honour of supping with them at Hereford, and it is quite right they should return our civilities in dinners in London."

"But now, remember," said Mrs. Mountjoy, "I shall never sacrifice my Wednesdays and Saturdays to their ponderous fatiguing dinners."

"I have settled all that," said Primrose. "Let Mrs. Barsac attempt a dinner on a Wednesday or Saturday at her peril."

While they were speaking, two cards, each containing a rood of pasteboard arrived, with formal notifications of a dinner and ball at Portland-place; the dinner for a Tuesday, the ball on the following evening.

"That will do," said Primrose.

"Yes," said Mrs. Mountjoy, "the ball won't interfere with our dinner here."

"I don't think I shall go to the ball," said Reuben.

"Not go to the ball," cried Hyacinth. "I love a ball; a ball is a mob of youth and beauty. I love to see the fans fluttering, the ankles twinkling, the bouquets waving, the diamonds sparkling, and the eyes out-beaming them."

"There is no conversation at a ball," said Reuben.

"You would like to address the mob," said Hyacinth.

———•◆•———

CHAPTER III.

A SOCIAL REVOLUTION.

REUBEN grew enthusiastic about those dinners of his aunt's, and devoted himself, with all his energies, to make them perfect, and go off with *éclat*. He almost put himself to school under the Gunters and Soyers of the day, though no man was less of an epicure; and though only a toper in theory, and chiefly conversant with Chian and Falernian, he took up the subject of wines practically, bought works upon the vineyards, and (as Primrose said) went about with a lantern, like Diogenes, looking for that truly noble work of God, an honest wine-merchant. The same pains he took with every convivial arrangement; tried tables of all shapes and sizes, squares, rounds, and ovals; made experiments with all sorts of lamps and candles; actually invented a new kind of chair for dinner; suggested a decided improvement in corkscrews; almost broke his aunt in the beauties and novelties of glass and china; and threatened to dismiss footmen if the sound of a foot was heard on the carpet. Then he investigated profoundly the much-agitated and yet undecided question of the number of guests proper or necessary to make a banquet most successful; and alternately astonished and amused Mrs. Mountjoy by the incredible trouble he went to, lest the sexes should not be justly balanced—lest the slightest discordant element should find its way into the party; and even to guard against the possibility of the guests sitting down out of the prescribed and predetermined order.

No sooner had this active and volatile genius, with no little expense of thought and anxiety, with considerable physical as well as mental exertion and a very serious expense to his fair relative, brought all this social and convivial machinery as near perfection as perhaps it was practicable to bring it, than he suddenly threw it all up, discovering, or having it brought unto him in some dream or revelation, that regular dining was waste of time, and totally irreconcilable with vigour of mind and body. He begs to speak slightingly of claret and champagne, to disparage French cookery, cry up mutton chops, and magnify tea and coffee, and bread and butter.

"He is not even constant to his dinner," cried Primrose.

"The man who will not stick to that will stick to nothing," said Winning, not, however, in quite as serious a tone as Primrose's.

De Tabley said very little, but what he did say was solemn and bitter, with the air of a man who felt more than he had words to express.

"What most surprises me," resumed Winning, "is, that Medlicott should quarrel with the table, just as he was beginning to get a little character in London for conversation."

"He was beginning to talk a great deal too much," said Primrose, who had never before dealt hardly with Reuben's blemishes.

"He soliloquises, he lectures, he cannot be said to converse," said De Tabley; "however I could have forgiven that; I don't talk much myself at dinner."

Reuben had better have attempted any revolution than one in the dining-room.

Mrs. Mountjoy, amiable Mrs. Mountjoy, was only too complaisant, too accommodating, as usual; always ready to sacrifice her own enjoyments and plans to the pleasure and convenience of those she loved as she did her nephew. It was not, indeed, a case for tears, or even for sighs; but had it been such, Mrs. Mountjoy would have wept and sighed in secret.

If there was one man living less excusable than another for forgetting the maxim, that "there is a time for all things," that man was Mr. Medlicott, the lesson had been so diligently inculcated on him by his old schoolmistress, Mrs. Hopkins; but he was now either so oblivious or neglectful of it, that in the midst of the pleasures of London, and the guest of his aunt who laid herself out to introduce him into all its gaieties, nothing would serve him but to work within an inch of his life. The truant of Cambridge became a model student in Burlington Gardens, and good, easy Mrs. Mountjoy soon had business enough on her hands making arrangements for the indulgence of this new and most unseasonable freak. He sent to Cambridge for all his books, even the encyclopædia which Mr. Cox had made him a present of. His aunt assisted him with her own hands to arrange his library in his chamber; pitying, all the time, the poor head destined to be freighted with so huge a cargo of learning. Reuben attempted to make her understand his mother's doctrine of the boundless expansiveness of the human understanding, but to very little purpose. She had, however, so high an opinion of the severity of intellectual pursuits that she thought it indispensable to do all in her power to mitigate it by the most luxurious arrangements she could devise. She provided Reuben with the cosiest arm-chairs she could procure; he had two of them constructed upon different principles, one with an apparatus attached for supporting books, and even for writing, should the student feel inclined to compose in a recumbent or languishing posture. Beside the chairs, there was a soft spacious sofa, on which he might dispread himself, when it was his fancy to lie on his back, or his face, reading or writing. There was a superb library-table with a desk in the centre of the room, and a smaller moveable one besides, which he might moor by the fire-side when he was cold, or station near the window on a foggy morning. There was also a tall desk to read at standing, when the soft chairs and sofas were too hard for him. For his books he had a revolving receptacle with several sides to it, which he could wheel round with a touch of his finger, so as to enable him to change his studies in a twinkling—a device of his aunt's, which she must surely have introduced under the impression that Reuben was in danger of narrowing his mind by devoting himself too doggedly to some limited course of reading. Finally, she presented him with the most charming dressing-gown and slippers of black velvet, an appropriate morning toilette for a young man studying for holy orders. In short, she omitted nothing that ingenuity, quickened by affection, and softened by feminine delicacy, could suggest to assuage "the sorrows of a poor young man" condemned to the mines of theological learning.

"And now, my dear," she said, about to leave him to himself for the first time, after installing him in all this luxury, "is there anything more I can do to make your little study comfortable? I trust you will not hesitate to mention it, if anything occurs to you."

"My dear aunt, it is only too complete; if there is a fault, it is that my apartment is too comfortable. How Primrose will laugh to see me in this magnificent *robe-de-chambre*, probably as rich as was ever worn by a Cardinal."

"I hope and trust, my dear, you will find it warm;—but does the light of the room suit you? is it the proper colour? the blinds might be pink, or violet, or rose-colour, whatever tint in fact you please."

"All is *couleur-de-rose*," said Reuben gallantly, "in the society of my aunt Mountjoy."

She smiled, embraced him, and left him to his labours.

Going to her own room, she next rang for Agatha, her maid, informed her with the greatest solemnity of the nature and importance of Reuben's studies, and warned her to go up and down stairs with as light a step as possible during the early part of the day.

"Mr. Medlicott," she said, "will always study until four o'clock, except from two to half-past two, when he will take an early dinner. From four to six he will exercise; at six he will take coffee; and then he will resume his studies. I must insist upon there being no noise whatever in the house as long as he is in it."

"You had better, madam," said the maid, "speak to the landlady as well."

Mrs. Mountjoy took the hint, and down she went immediately to the landlady, and to her communicated also what the pursuits of her nephew were, and how momentous it was that silence, the most profound, should reign in the precincts of his bower.

This was a pleasant nephew to have for a gay widow in gay lodgings, with gay dispositions and designs! Fortunately, she had Mr. Primrose to take Reuben's place at her side in promenades and at balls and concerts, or she might have found the London season hang heavy on her hands. As to Hyacinth, he was probably pleased with the onerous duties that devolved upon him in consequence of his friend's perverseness, or he would have been more incensed at Reuben's entire conduct at this period than he appears to have been. The dinners, however, though not so frequent, were not entirely given up. Though Reuben was too intellectual to dine at seven o'clock with a pleasant party, other people were not. There was generally one dinner in the week, at least; and when Reuben condescended to appear Mrs. Mountjoy was in ecstacies, and loaded him with thanks, and even with more attention, and more devoted audience, than her invited guests.

Though Mrs. Mountjoy probably enjoyed Mr. Primrose's company more, she was prouder of Reuben's; and whenever he proposed to take her with him to the British Museum, to a lecture, a meeting of some learned or scientific society, or some ramble through the town to visit ancient nooks and corners, of which he was passionately fond, she was very unhappy when anything absolutely prevented her from accompanying him. Poor Mrs. Mountjoy! she got more than one cold in public libraries, while Reuben was making extracts from dusty volumes; and many a time did she visit the Elgin Marbles, and the Albemarle-street Institution, when she would have greatly preferred a stroll to the Soho Bazaar, or shopping in the Burlington Arcade.

In one of his excursions through London he met with a curious proof of the success of one of his own literary efforts, though he was not personally the gainer by it. He had taken his aunt with him into the city; shown her the courts where Doctor Johnson lodged: marched her through Clement's Inn and the Temple Gardens; then to Cock Lane, famed for the apparition; from thence to Crosby Hall and Christ's Hospital; concluding the antiquarian ramble with a peep into Doctors' Commons, and the Heralds' College, or Menagerie, on St. Bennet's Hill, where, in the little quadrangle of the latter quaint old institution (as remote from public view as from public utility), he happened to meet his old pupil Lord Appleby.

Lord Appleby said he had been calling to see a common friend of theirs—no less a personage than Blue Mantle, pursuivant.

Reuben had no notion he had the honour of knowing Blue Mantle.

"You may remember little Griffin," said his lordship.

"To be sure. Blue Mantle is just the appointment to suit him: a snug thing, I dare say."

"Five hundred a year, and little or no duty; owes it entirely to his own talents and exertions, poor fellow. Wrote a paper on dragons and lions rampant; attracted the attention of the Earl Marshal, who gave him the first thing he had to dispose of."

How indignant Mrs. Mountjoy was when Reuben informed her, after parting with Lord Appleby, of the real authorship of the article which had led to the advancement of the shabby and audacious little Mr. Griffin! Her only comfort was, that she supposed Reuben would not have accepted the office.

"No, not Blue Mantle," said Reuben; "Clarencieux, or Norroy, would be another matter;—as to Griffin, poor devil, I forgive him; I suppose he was very hungry."

Primrose was exceedingly pleasant with Wming on the idea

of Reuben holding the office of a pursuivant or herald, the business of such a post having been stated by a noble and learned lord to consist "in walking in processions and *holding one's tongue*," for the latter of which duties Mr. Medlicott was so eminently qualified.

There was, indeed no danger of his neglecting to cultivate the gift of speech, whether for private or other purposes. As to table talk, he was already far more proficient therein than was agreeable to such of his friends as were not content to subside into mere listeners, while Reuben recited, lectured, quoted, narrated, argued, expatiated, and harangued. He seemed ambitious of rivalling Mr. Bavard, instead of being instructed and warned by so bad an example. Those who "were very kind to his virtues," and more than "a little blind to his faults," admired him exceedingly. So did a considerable number of persons also who, being mutes themselves, thought everybody who could talk continuously for half-an-hour a prodigy of cleverness. But the judicious minority found Reuben a great deal more fluent than agreeable; even his dearest friends did not hesitate to say that he deliberately practised upon the guests at his aunt's table, to improve himself in confidence and loquacity.

But it was "the talking era," and why should not Reuben Medlicott, like others, talk himself into reputation? Seizing every occasion for speaking, he systematically neglected what Bishop Butler calls "the obvious occasions for silence," easy as they are to be distinguished by everybody, "namely, when a man has nothing to say, or nothing but what is better unsaid." He came into society with no design but display, and habitually entertained himself at the expense of the company, over whom he tyrannised like a Czar, or a President. It was the reverse of conversation, for it excluded all reciprocity. Reuben discoursed, and his idolising friends or enduring victims listened. He was the Protectionist of private society, often to the extent of imposing a prohibitory duty upon every colloquial commodity not of his own production, no matter how interesting and attractive to other people. As to the article he supplied himself, there was a good deal in it of what made Coleridge so remarkable; his talk was a sort of sparkling mist; the majority applauded but nobody understood. You knew what he was talking about, but never could tell exactly what he was saying about it. If there was a meaning, it was beyond the depth of the expertest divers; but for that very reason it was presumed to be a pearl. He was particularly given to illustration, and his similes, metaphors, quotations, and anecdotes (of which, as we have seen, he had a bank of his own, where his credit was unlimited), were very pleasing and pretty in themselves, but what they illustrated was a difficult thing to find out. In short, it was just the kind of eloquence to wrap all sorts of absurdities, paradoxes, and delusions in; it captivated visionaries, it delighted enthusiasts, it charmed mountebanks, it won the hearts of women especially. It was just the oratory for Exeter Hall, the Dublin Rotunda, or the Caledonian Chapel; it would never have answered for the bar, the House, or even for the pulpit of a quiet unfanatical parish.

Primrose called on Winning one morning, after a dinner at which Mr. Medlicott had been particularly disregardful of the rights of others, in his ambition to exhibit himself.

"Can anything be done?" he said, "to open our friend Reuben's eyes to the monstrous indiscretion and indecency of monopolizing conversation as he does. He eclipses Bavard. Nobody could get in a word yesterday. If he goes on this way he will be as great a bore as ——, or ——, or ——."

Winning agreed that it would be most desirable to make Medlicott sensible of the great mistake he was guilty of, but could not think of any means of doing it.

"It was occurring to me," said Primrose, "that *you* might, with propriety, give him a hint upon the subject."

"My dear fellow," said Winning, laughing, "do you remember the fable of the monkey and the roasted chesnuts? A hint from yourself would be as useful as from me. Suppose you try it."

"I never was good at giving advice," said Primrose.

"I was very great at it when I was a boy," said Winning. "I have long since learned that to tread on a friend's faults is nearly as dangerous as treading on his corns."

"I believe you are right," said Primrose, foiled in his ingenious attempt to make a cat's-paw of Winning.

Possibly Mr. Medlicott was of opinion himself that he had become sufficiently accomplished for all practical purposes, as a talker in private society; for he soon began to profit by the opportunities which London afforded him for qualifying himself to be equally ready and fluent upon public occasions.

His mother had frequently alluded, in her letters, to the professors of elocution, some of whom undertook to instruct young men in all its branches—the senate, the bar, the Church, and even for ranting at Exeter Hall, or spouting at public dinners.

"My dear," said Mrs. Mountjoy, one morning at breakfast, as her eye glanced at the advertisement of one of these great masters, in the columns of the *Times*, "if you think it would be of use to you to take lessons from this accomplished gentleman, only let me know. You cannot have a more favourable opportunity than the present for improving yourself in this way. It will be a great pleasure to me to incur that or any other expense, necessary for your success in life."

Mr. Medlicott owned that he felt strongly disposed to place himself for a while under the instruction of Professor Chatterton, and a day did not pass without a syllabus having been obtained of that distinguished gentleman's course of lectures.

CHAPTER IV.

THE SCHOOL OF RHETORIC.

THE general card or prospectus of Professor Chatterton (whose School of Elocution, as it was termed, was held in Leicester Square), announced the intended delivery of four courses of lectures during the London season, on the theory and practice of public speaking, in its several leading applications to the senate, the bar, the pulpit, and miscellaneous purposes, such as county meetings, public dinners, vestries, mobs, weddings, and demonstrations generally.

There was a particular syllabus for each course. That of the lectures on pulpit eloquence was as follows. The reader will please to imagine the enthusiastic Mr. Medlicott and the buxom Mrs. Mountjoy, reading it together at the tea-table, with all the gravity becoming the subject.

"*Lecture* 1. Importance of the Lungs, Throat, and Tongue to Public Speakers in general, and to Clergymen in particular, of all persuasions. — Oratory an art, especially Pulpit oratory — Encouragements to the study of it — Easy acquisition of, in twelve lessons. — Idea of a perfect sermon. — Professor will endeavour to embody it in a Specimen of his own Composition. — Strictures on Taylor, South, Barrow, and Tillotson — Their several defects criticised. The Lecture will conclude with a Speculation on the effect Demosthenes would have produced had he adopted the Profession of the Church.

"*Lecture* 2. General principles of Pronunciation — Special Rules for the reading-desk and Pulpit — Solemnity — Unction — Dignity — Action, Action, Action — Passion — Emotion — Sentiment. — Vital Importance of Earnestness — of Look — Voice — Manner. — Origin and Derivation of the word Pulpit — the Pulpit a stage. — the Preacher 'to hold the mirror up to nature.'

"*Lecture* 3. Rhetorical Artifices — Adaptation to Sacred purposes — Use of the Hands and Arms — the Eyes — the Eyebrows — Pauses — Starts — Points — Transitions — Tones, Intoning, and Intonation. — Distinctions to be observed in Churches, Cathedrals, Chapels, and Conventicles — Drawling, whining — a digression on nasal eloquence. Lecture will conclude with a rehearsal by the Professor of one of Mr. Irving's Sermons, in the course of which he will introduce some Criticisms on the Unknown Tongue, and Remarks on Jargon in general, in connexion with the study of Rhetoric.

"*Lecture* 4. Rules and directions of Particular and Critical Occasions — Preaching in the Chapel Royal — before Archbishops and Bishops — in the presence of the Lord Chancellor — Rhetorical Incense — Pleasing Personalities, &c.

"*Lecture* 5. Charity Sermons — the emotion of Pity — 'If you have tears, prepare to shed them now' — Charitable Statistics difficult to handle — how to reconcile Petticoats with Pathos, and extract eloquence from Slate-pencils. The Professor will illustrate his precepts by delivering a Speech of Mr. Hume's, in the character of a Minister of the Kirk.

"*Lecture* 6. Miscellaneous hints and suggestions — *In tenui gloria* — Coughing, its management — capable of being made effective in the Pulpit — Pulpit-lozenges, prepared by Professor Chatterton, and strongly recommended to the Clergy. — Remarks on the Snuff-box — Dissuasives from Snuff in general — Sneezing not as manageable as coughing, with a view to Oratorical effect. — Peroration, embodying all the previous principles, with the results of the Professor's experience, in a sermon on Peace and Good-will, supposed to be preached before the Bishops and Clergy of the Church of England, assembled in Convocation."

"Well, indeed," said Mrs. Mountjoy, "that does seem to be a very excellent and judicious course of lectures, and I cannot doubt but it must be highly improving to attend them."

"The Professor," said Reuben, "has certainly shown his judgment in the choice of the subject to preach on before Convocation. But we are not quite done with the bill of fare: here is an N. B. at the bottom, and a postscript after that again."

"A Supplementary Lecture will be given by Madame Chatterton, on the Dress and Address of a Clergyman. — The Looking-Glass, its importance — Canonical Drapery — the Hair — Wigs — Attention to the Teeth — Use of the Handkerchief in the Pulpit — Cambric — Cambrai — Archbishop Fénélon — Scents, Rings, &c. &c. Tickets Half-a-Guinea.

"P. S. Professor and Madame Chatterton will give Private Lessons on all the above topics adapted to the use of gentlemen of the Church of Rome, or disposed to embrace its Doctrines. The Professor having lately returned from the States of the Church, has had the honour of importing into England sundry interesting novelties in Theatrical Devotion, including several cases of Relics in admirable preservation, and undoubtedly genuine. He begs also to recommend his *Tract* on the all-important subject of Holy Histrionics, dedicated, with permission, to the Lord Bishop of ——.

" Surplices, Crucifixes, Rosaries, and Disciplines (the use of them), Gratis, during the Course.

Reuben was not surprised to find that Mr. Chatterton had some years previously been a player of some note, at several of the minor theatres. Of course, he was only the better qualified to teach what Mr. Medlicott wanted to learn—the artistic management of the voice, the play of the hands, the bearing of the body; in short, all the external part of oratory, which is, no doubt, in a great measure, an histrionic art—a truth which may help to account for the concurrent decline of eloquence and the drama of late years in England.

The Professor, who was attired in decent black, as became a teacher of the clergy, made no secret of his former calling, but on the contrary put it prominently forward among his qualifications; and in truth nobody but a player of considerable skill could have maintained not only his own gravity, but that of his disciples, through a course of instructions in which there was so much real and almost unavoidable imposture.

"Church, chapel, or conventicle ?"—with the bow of the old trade, and the solemn tone of the new one, was the Professor's first inquiry, when Mr. Medlicott intimated his wish to put himself under his tuition for the clerical portion of the lectures.

" The Established Church," was of course the reply.

"High or Low—Cambridge or Oxford ?" inquired the Professor.

Reuben answered with a smile, which led Professor Chatterton into an explanation of the necessity he was under of making separate classes of his pupils, from the two universities. Reuben was astounded: he had never before heard of the new school of divinity at Oxford, which was then, indeed, only in its infancy.

"Ah," said the Professor, "it is very little known as yet, but the world will hear enough of it by-and-by. My Oxford class is not numerous, but it is steadily increasing, and contains my most diligent and promising pupils. There is Mr. N——n, Mr. W——d, Mr. St. John Crozier, Mr. Cyprian Palmer, Lord Henry Holyrood,—very promising young men, all of them, I assure you."

"I am happy to hear there is likely to be such a harvest of eloquent preachers," said Reuben.

"Well," said the Professor, "my Oxford pupils don't attend to that so much as to—what shall I call it?—the—I don't like to use the word pantomimic; you know what I mean—the pageant—the drama—but perhaps you have seen my tract on 'Holy Histrionics,' dedicated by permission to the Lord Bishop of———?" Reuben was more and more amazed, and inquired the name of this new Oxonian sect.

"Tractarians," said the *ci-devant* comedian. "Perhaps I may flatter myself that the title of my little work, originally suggested the name." .

"It seems to bear a strong family likeness to Popery, all this," said Reuben. "I now see the meaning of some words in your prospectus which at first I did not understand—'*belonging to the Church of Rome, or disposed to embrace it.*'"

The Professor showed an anxiety to distinguish between the system of his Oxford pupils and flat Popery, but perceiving that he made no great impression on Reuben, he changed the subject, declaring that he made it a rule not to interfere with the doctrines of the gentlemen who honoured him with their attendance: he did not pretend to teach divinity—that, of course, had its importance—he was prepared to give lessons to gentlemen of all persuasions, without distinction; if a Mufti, or a dancing Dervish, came to his school, he would not refuse to give him the benefit of his instructions.

Mr. Medlicott thought the views of the Professor just and reasonable, and the lectures commenced the following day.

Mr. Chatterton filled up the outlines of his syllabus with great ingenuity and spirit. As might have been expected, he treated learning, argument, and things of that sort, as matters of secondary importance; and some of his hearers, Reuben among others, more than doubted whether his specimen of a perfect discourse was equal to a sermon of Barrow or Massillon. But he declaimed with energy, and laid down many rules which speakers in general would do well to observe, mixed with others which not one man in a hundred could possibly attempt to follow, without making himself supremely ridiculous. Reuben speedily discovered (particularly in the second and third lectures) the source of many of the affectations which he had seen practised in some of the metropolitan pulpits. Indeed, he remarked two young clergymen on the front benches,—one was Mr. Araby, the author of

Melancthon, in twenty books—who were already beginning to be talked of as eloquent preachers; and he did not fail to observe, also, that they redoubled their attention to the lecturer when he came to give his instructions for special occasions, such as preaching before a bishop, or in presence of the Lord Chancellor. Reuben, however, though the most disinterested of the class, was soon more intent than any one else upon the subject of the lectures, and made his enthusiasm so conspicuous that the Professor was excessively flattered, and at length invited him to occupy a chair in the most distinguished position in the room. This led to private conversations when the lecture was over, and one of these conversations ended in Reuben inviting the Professor to dinner in Burlington Gardens. Primrose, De Tabley, and Winning dined with the widow the same evening, and Reuben yielded the *pas* to the Professor, who, finding himself very comfortable, made himself very agreeable, and had the judgment to refrain from giving his model sermon, diverting the company nearly as well with admirable imitations of Dowton, Liston, and Matthews. As the wine produced its effects, Chatterton began to talk at large of his profession, and to disclose many of its arcana, about which Winning and Hyacinth were very curious, Winning being particularly anxious to find out what members of the bar frequented the school of oratory in Leicester-square. It soon appeared that the lectures were the smallest part of Mr. Chatterton's professional engagements; he gave private instructions, also, to clergymen, lawyers, senators, and even to simple squires, who, though not in parliament, were called on to second resolutions at county meetings, or propose healths at dinners.

"I should have thought," said Winning, "that the chief embarrassment of a squire would be to find the speech itself."

The Professor shrugged his shoulders, and intimated that he did a little occasionally himself in the speech-making line for the squirearchy.

"Eloquence is not to be had out of buckskin," said Winning, "any more than a silk purse—you know the saying."

"Bucksin," said the Professor, "cuts a wonderful figure whenever the church is supposed in danger, as some think it is just now. A squire's lungs are made of the same material as his breeches, and it's as easy to shout 'No Popery!' as to cry 'Tally-ho!' A dozen repetitions, at short intervals, of the phrase 'No Popery,' with any stuff you please to fill up the crevices, make a capital speech for a "fine old English gentleman" in the

Protestant interest; but the speech must always end with "a long pull, a strong pull, and a pull all together,"—recollect that, gentlemen, if a squire ever requests you to compose an oration for him. The last sentence is the only one, in fact, that is ever heard between the clatter the orator makes himself, with his boots and stick on the platform, and the uproar and rioting of the bold peasantry in the body of the court. Baronets in general make the best hits, as public speakers, in a constitutional crisis. The Baronets will have their day yet, take my word for it. Every dog has, sooner or later. The deuce of it is, that when one of your Sir Johns and Sir Rogers once gets to the 'long pull' without breaking down, and is complimented by the county paper for his 'manly eloquence,' he never gives a silent vote for the remainder of his life."

"I have met with a story," said Reuben, "of a certain devout orator of the class you allude to, who having sat down amidst deafening cheers, was overheard mumbling to himself, 'non nobis Domine,'—only for the Latin I should say he must have been a baronet, and one of your men in buckskin."

"Probably a man of Bucks," said Primrose.

"Have you any Irish pupils?" said Winning.

"They come to me," said Chatterton, "but they don't want me."

"Do they pay you?"—asked De Tabley.

"They will, I make no doubt," said the Professor, with comic gravity, "they will, when they get their own again. Their estates were all forfeited, you know, poor fellows. I have six Irish pupils at present, and they all confidently expect to come into parliament before long,—I have polite invitations at this moment, I assure you, to three castles on the banks of the Shannon, and positive promises of ever so many elegant situations at the disposal of the Lord-Lieutenant."

"You are not often required to write speeches for the Irishmen, I should think," said Winning.

"I only wish I could make speeches at the rate they do," said Mr. Chatterton; "but then Ireland is such a great manufacturing country, you know."

"Hold, Professor, I believe you are mistaken there," cried Winning.

"What does Ireland manufacture except butter and bacon?" asked Reuben.

"I know of nothing but oratory," said the Professor, "and it was oratory I meant, when I spoke of Irish manufactures. Dublin beats Manchester hollow for fustian. I don't mean to say that John Bull has not the talent also, for he has it in him as well as Paddy, and he is making rapid strides in eloquence of late years, but Paddy has more experience. Everything in Ireland is done with a speech and a shout, and the form of government the island is blessed with, favours the cultivation of my art extremely. '*Esto perpetua,*' I say,"

"You mean the castle?" said Winning.

"I do," said the Professor. "It may have its faults, but it has one great virtue, it gives the people something to talk at. The Viceroy is a target for the practice of oratory. If a man has the vein of panegyric, he has got something to address and flatter; if he is up to a philippic, he has always something to abuse. If he unites both gifts, he may throw flowers at his Excellency to-day, and fling thunderbolts at him to-morrow. At the very worst, the Lord Lieutenant keeps the tongues of the doctors and professors in constant exercise; for it is the duty of the king's representative to stand an amount of lecturing, a twentieth part of which would make his majesty himself abdicate his crown. '*Esto perpetua,*' say I."

I am disposed to say so too," said Medlicott, thoughtfully. "A form of government which promotes eloquence of all kinds so powerfully as you describe cannot be anything but a good one."

"The Irish, unfortunately, are not so partial to facts as to figures," said Winning.

"There," said Chatterton, "I am disposed to agree with them; I don't think facts make the best speeches; facts are dry; sentiments do better."

"I suppose your Irish pupils live very much together," asked Primrose.

"The men who are talking of coming into the house," said Chatterton, "chum together in Panton Square, where they practise franking at breakfast, paliamentary elequence at dinner, and have quiet little evening parties, with oysters, punch, Lalla Rookh, and Grattan's speeches."

"They have capital oysters in Ireland," said De Tabley.

"I should like to be present at one of their paliamentary dinners," said Primrose.

"So should I of all things," said Mrs. Mountjoy.

"And I can tell you, madam," said the Professor, "you

would be a very welcome guest; for much as they admire the Peris of Paradise, they admire the Peris of this life more;—but the great fun is at supper: they get up little imaginary squabbles and rows with one another, to accustom themselves to coughing members down, and calling to order."

"We shall see droll people in the house if the Emancipation Bill passes," said De Tabley.

"As long as there are droll people out of the house," said Winning, "there will be droll people in the house, and there ought to be."

"I own I long to see Ireland, and even Panton Square, fully and fairly represented," said Primrose, "and besides, to speak seriously, the best way I know to put an extinguisher upon folly and extravagance of all kinds, is to make a constituency of it, and give it a member, or members, in the House of Commons. They may be bores, to be sure, and do a great deal of mischief even there; but depend upon it, they would be ten times as troublesome and mischievous at the Corn Exchange, or the Crown and Anchor."

Mr. Medlicott, who had always sided with his grandfather upon the catholic question, was not to be convinced by this reasoning; but Winning coincided with Primrose, and was stating the grounds of his opinion, when De Tabley again returned to the subject of Irish oysters, and changed the conversation in good time, for Mrs. Mountjoy disliked politics; they puzzled her, and women don't like things that puzzle them, except conundrums and family secrets.

CHAPTER V.

THE PROFESSOR'S WIFE.

A FEW days later Mr. Primrose was walking in the Strand, when he was met and eagerly accosted by Professor Chatterton, who exclaimed—

"Why, your friend, Mr. Medlicott, is the most wonderful young man I ever met with in all my professional experience; he comes to my lectures when he is more fit to lecture himself. Talk of Irishmen—why, there's not one of them fit to hold a candle to him! He's a perfect orator, sir, this moment; such fluency I never heard in my life: such beautiful language, and such abundance of it. By the merest chance I made the discovery; I had no notion he was such a clever fellow—he never said a word about it."

Primrose said it surprised him that Mr. Chatterton's sagacity had not sooner detected his friend's genius. He then begged to know how the revelation took place.

It appeared that at a certain stage of the Professor's course, it was the custom for his pupils to give practical proof of the progress they had made under his tuition, by rehearsing some composition of their own, or the model sermon already mentioned. On the present occasion it occurred to Mr. Chatterton, to try what his disciples could do at an extempore discourse, and Temperance was the topic fixed on, as it would not have been reverent to discuss a religious subject. Two or three fair attempts were made; the majority were dull in the extreme; some broke down after the first sentence; but when it came to Reuben's turn: his facility, his copiousness, his endless variety of figures, images, metaphors, similes, allegories, illustrations, and quotations, astonished everybody present; until at length they cheered him as if he was haranguing at Exeter Hall, the effect of which was, that he quite forgot the nature of the occasion, and actually held forth so long, that at length, said the Professor, "I believe, some of the gentlemen present thought he would never stop."

"You were lucky that he did," said Primrose.

"He is nothing less than a prodigy," said the Professor. He will either be a bishop, or marry a duchess, before he is a year in the Church."

"Or purchase a chapel, and set up on his own account," said Haycinth.

Twenty voices, at least, were busy at the same moment trumpeting in different parts of the town Mr. Medlicott's extraordinary display in Leicester-square. It takes, however, more than the breath of twenty voices to make what is called fame. Detraction was of course very busy also. Envy began to nibble at his reputation, when it was yet green, by way of earnest of what she would do hereafter, when it should attain its full growth. Some of the men who applauded him at the lecture, revenged themselves with sneers as soon as it was over. One declared the speech was all verbiage and fustian; another, more malignant, said "it was pretty;" a third admitted it was cleverish, but denied that it was clever. Very just criticisms, all of them, most probably, but they were ot on that account the less narrow and ill-natured.

"He possesses talent," said Mr. Araby, the sacred poet, in conversation with Primrose, " but it's a talent I dont envy."

"Nobody envies another's talents," replied Haycinth; "the thing we envy is admiration, popularity, success. We envy a man his fortune—not his genius, and still less his virtues. Virtue was never envied."

"Well, I confess I envy his facility," said Winning, who spoke ably, but not fluently enough to satisfy himself.

Of course there was an end of lectures as a vehicle of instruction. Reuben's rhetorical education was finished. He bore his honours meekly—he wore his laurels gracefully; if he triumphed it was in private, when his aunt Mountjoy prophesied all human glories for him; still more when his mother, down in Sussex, echoed the praises that reached her from London, through her sister's letters and other authentic channels.

Nothing remained but to attend the supplementary lecture by Madame Chatterton. Her one lecture excited more curiosity than the whole course delivered by her husband. Reuben took tickets for himself, his aunt, and Primrose. The Professor positively refused payment for them.

The lady no sooner appeared than Reuben felt assured he had seen her before, though where or when he tried in vain to recall. She was very little French, except in name; but she was very handsome, very lively, very clever, fluent, and exceedingly entertaining. If the husband was convinced that the most important qualifications for the pulpit were histrionic, the wife was no less under the firm impression that they were more of a cosmetic nature. Chatterton relied on action and passion; Madame upon kalydor and cambric. She dwelt upon the beauty of the latter, as if it had been the beauty of holiness; mixing up the topics of Fénélon and fine linen with so much practical address, that she disposed of a few dozen French handkerchiefs, at half-a-guinea each, before she concluded her observations. Mrs. Mountjoy bought a box of them, embroidered with mitres, cherubs, and other ecclesiastical devices, half for herself and half for Reuben. From handkerchiefs Madame passed to the arrangement of the hair with a view to devotional effect, and began by lamenting that this was so little attended to by the majority of the clergy, and by some of them held almost in contempt. Apropos to that, she had a little anecdote to relate. She would not mention names, but what she was about to mention had actually occurred within her own experience, and would prove the utter indifference of even the highest dignitaries of the Church to the vital subject of *coiffure*. Before she had proceeded a sentence further, Reuben recognised in the Professors's wife the charming young Frenchwoman who had redressed the wrongs which he had sustained from his grandfather's scissors, the night before he went to school. That incident was the subject of her anecdote. After the lecture, he hastened to renew his acquaintance with her, and introduced her to his aunt, who thought her so amiable, as well as so pretty and clever, that she could not help purchasing several more little articles on her earnest recommendation; one of them was a carved ivory box, which, to Mrs. Mountjoy's horror, was found, upon examination in the evening, to contain three teeth of a Neapolitan saint, whose very name she had never before heard. This was, probably, the first box of relics introduced into England, in consequence of the stimulus given by the Tractarian movement to that important branch of our Italian commerce.

Previous to Mr. Medlicott's attendance on the Chatterton lectures, his chamber had been pretty well furnished with looking-glasses, as well as with most other objects of use, ornament, or luxury, by the attention of his fair relative; but Reuben now felt the want of a mirror of the largest size, and did not hesitate to intimate to his aunt how much he desired to have one in which he could see himself at full length, when he practised before it. The deficiency was no sooner mentioned than it was supplied. A new looking-glass, reaching from the floor to the ceiling, was immediately purchased and put up; standing before which, as it were in a pulpit, and recollecting all the lessons of the Professor, and the instructions of Madame, Reuben either theatrically recited some discourse he had committed to memory, or extemporised a sermon of his own from his exhaustless treasury of words and ready fund of all possible embellishments and amplifications of diction. Many a time did the curious and astonished Agatha witness his histrionic exercises through the keyhole; and sometimes the good landlady, passing the door on tip-toe, would pause, attracted by the volumes of sound, and, availing herself of the same convenient little orifice to gaze at the handsome young man, declaiming in his robe of black velvet, yield herself prematurely to the captivations of pulpit oratory.

BOOK THE SIXTH.

"Eloquence, like the fair sex, has too prevailing beauties in it to suffer itself ever to be spoken against. And it is in vain to find fault with those arts of deceiving wherein men find pleasure to be deceived."—*Locke's Essay on the Human Understanding.*

Socrates. "What if I bring you to a conference
With my own proper goddesses, the Clouds?"
Strepsiades. "'Tis what I wish devoutly."
Aristophanes.

ARGUMENT.

A GOODLY catalogue might be made of writers, ancient and modern, Greek and Roman, Italian, Spanish, English, nay even among the gallant French themselves, who, in learned treatises, or pleasant composures—in prose some, and in rhyme others—have inveighed against womankind, down from the fragile Eve, our general mother, to the lowliest slave of the mop and broom amongst her daughters; but what good has ever come of continually abusing and snubbing the female race, or what fruit is to be expected from it? For whether it be true, as one poet expresses it, that they are to be reckoned among the "fair defects of Nature," or ranked with her most exquisite pieces of porcelain, as another will have it, they cannot be denied to form one of the great estates of the world as it is, although fancy is free, of course, to choose any star in the firmament and people it

"With men, as angels, without feminine."

What sort of a place to live in such a planet would be, this is not the place to discuss; but from all we know of all the Utopias hitherto discovered, not excepting the terrestrial little paradise of O'Connorville itself, we have never felt a strong inclination to migrate to any one of them, and it is very doubtful if a world, one hundred and eighty degrees from Venus, would prove more attractive than the rest. To look at woman with the eye of philosophy is not easy, but if you can manage it, you must see at once that there is no use in quarrelling with her, any more than with any other "*fait accompli.*" As we take her individually from the hand of Sir Priest, "for better, for worse," as the rubric phrases it, so we must accept the entire sex, and accommodate ourselves to our lot as Socratically as possible. Nor would matters be quite as bad as they are, only that unfortunately the female element in the world is not confined to the precise limits of the fair sex, but largely intrudes itself into the masculine, in return perhaps for sundry small loans of their proper attributes, which the lords of the creation occasionally make to the ladies, as in the case of the Amazons, the Blue-stockings, and the Bloomers. Some writers insist that each gender is the better for a little alloy of the other; that a touch of the woman becomes the man, while a little of the man improves the woman, provided 'tis not from his chin the little is borrowed. Now, if we inquire for which of our gifts we are in all probability most indebted to Eve and her daughters, we suspect it will be found to be no other than the nimble and eager exercise of the tongue, which appears beyond controversy to be the womanly parcel of us, and is, possibly for that reason, so proverbially difficult to keep in order and subjection. The tongue is essentially of the feminine gender, let its possessor be of what sex he may; and if in form it is serpentine, in motion voluble, and in its employment often even double and venomous, its origin is only more clearly to be traced to the first beauty that charmed and the first rhetoric that seduced. This is the shrew that everybody is more or less cursed with, a virago in every man's mouth, which the wisest cannot at all hours tame like Petruchio. Homer, not less philosopher than poet, seems to have considered the teeth as a rampart or line of circumvallations, expressly designed by provident Nature to check the sallies of this termagant spouse of ours. And the same idea seems to have struck our own Shakspeare—

"Within my mouth you have engaoled my tongue,
Doubly portcullised with my teeth and lips."

It is further observable that Homer, to return to him, when his wise Ulysses speaks, describes his voice as issuing not so much from his mouth, the seat of the tongue, as out of his heart or mind—the profounder region of thought and feeling. It is a sorry thing when the tongue is vocal and the understanding mute; when the womanly organ is the only part of the machinery in full work, and "*loquax magis quam facundus*" is the motto of the age. Perhaps we are to blame the dentists for not looking better after our teeth, which certainly perform but indifferently, in many cases, the duty assigned them by Homer, and are not to be numbered among the defences of the nation. Why, do we not see men in our own days, as there were in Mr. Medlicott's, whose tongues scarce a triple row of elephants' tusks could effectually blockade, though kept in the best repair by all the art of dental surgery?—

"Men who at any time would hang
For th' opportunity t' harangue;
And still their tongues run on the less
Of weight they bear, with greater ease,
And with their everlasting clack
Set all men's ears upon the rack,
With volleys of eternal babble,
And clamour most unanswerable."

Such men, methinks, are as justly to be held women, by reason of this vicious excess of the female quality in them, as the king of Dahomey's regiments of guardswomen are to be counted men, notwithstanding the want of whiskers and beards. What correcter judgment, indeed, can we pronounce upon the remorseless race of talkers and speech-makers, this "thundering legion" by which the nation is overrun, who are rapidly becoming a distinct function and profession in the state, overpowering common sense, as Niagara drowns all ordinary voices, and threatening with ruin the public interests, especially the dignity and efficiency of parliament—what can we say of them more correctly than that they are all tongue, just as a glutton is all stomach; or as Milton describes the unfaithful shepherds of the Church, as mere "mouths,"—a word which would serve our turn as well, did we need it.

CHAPTER L.

A GLIMPSE OF GLORY.

A BARREL of gunpowder is as quiet as a barrel of oysters until a spark touches it; then it explodes, and blows the house out of the windows. While Reuben Medlicott was practising and accomplishing himself in the art of rhetoric in Burlington Gardens, expecting nothing less than an early opportunity for displaying his proficiency in it, a political movement was going on in Sussex, which no sooner reached his ears than it set his ambition on fire, and turned everything topsy-turvy.

A public meeting was on the point of being held at Chichester, in defence of the Protestant interest, which at that time was supposed to be in a very delicate and critical situation. At this meeting, when the news of it reached him, Mr. Medlicott, flushed with his recent honours in Leicester-square, determined to make his first experiment in public speaking. The opportunity seemed singularly favourable: the place was benign, the subject was propitious: hundreds of familiar faces would surround him on the platform. He anticipated and dutifully sympathised in his mother's raptures: even his grandfather himself would at least approve his zeal.

Was the Dean's approbation so very certain? Winning and Primrose no sooner heard of their friend's design, than they took a widely different view of the matter. They thought Reuben's intention to take an active part in the proposed meeting the height of imprudence; and we must be excused for devoting a few words to account for their being so decidedly of this opinion.

It was the period when a cabinet, which had hitherto ranged itself in determined resistance to the claims of the Roman Catholics, was understood to be wavering upon that long agitated point. Rumours were abroad that great concessions were on the eve of being made, though whether to reason or to clamour opinions were divided. There were many whispers also afloat affecting individuals. Some of the most eminent men in the nation, particularly in the Church, were beginning to be hinted at in the public journals, as being only too ready to wheel about with the government, not of course without weighty considerations, proportioned to the risks and sacrifices attendant upon all such evolutions. Among those who were most pointedly alluded to in this unpleasant way was the grandfather of our hero—for we may call him a hero with some propriety, now that the Protestant interest at Chichester is about to claim and use him as its champion. For several years, as we have had occasion already to state, Dean Wyndham's elevation to the bench had been spoken of as a probable event, not only on account of his learning and talents, but his strenuous employment of them in support of the policy of the government. Latterly, however, his friends had begun to despair of his promotion; and the unmitigated violence of his writings and sermons seemed to be rapidly diminishing his chances with a ministry which was growing milder and more tolerant every day. But now it was confidently stated that the Dean had caught the popular infection like others, and that the mitre, which had been denied him as the preacher of exclusion, was immediately to reward his conversion to the doctrines of liberality. All this was still mere rumour, but it was a rumour that was gaining ground; and whatever men like Winning might privately think of the purity of the Dean's conduct as a public man (should he have really made up his mind to put on a new suit of doctrines and principles in his old age), they were not the less clearly of opinion that Reuben Medlicott (on the eve of entering the Church) could not possibly choose a more unfortunate moment for the public display which he was now meditating.

Reuben, however, was most indignant at the imputations upon his grandfather, which the remonstrances of his friends assumed to be well founded. He had been brought up from the cradle in extreme veneration for the Dean; and as he advanced in years this feeling had increased in proportion to his capability of estimating his grandfather's talents and erudition: a doubt as to his sincerity upon any point (much less upon the great question to which he had for years chiefly devoted his powers as a conversationalist) had never crossed his mind, except as a profane idea which it was sinful for a moment to harbour. In short, had Doctor Wyndham been a man as well qualified to command his grandson's love as he was to excite his admiration, Reuben would have regarded him with an enthusiasm little short of what another Luther might have inspired. To Luther, indeed, his mother and he had frequently exercised and pleased themselves by comparing their distinguished relative. It will easily be believed that no alalogy with Melancthon was very likely to suggest itself to the most partial of the Dean's friends.

Reuben had never forgotten that glorious sermon, with which he had heard the Cathedral of Hereford, nave and choir, resound; the thunders of which had scared the rooks from their settlements in the square tower, and frighted from their propriety the neighbouring closes. That those eloquent denunciations of the vile doctrine of expediency, which had thrilled him when a schoolboy, were nothing but sound and vapour, he was not prepared to admit. He was determined to believe that there was still such a thing as principle in the world; or at least that among the apostates from it, the name of Wyndham would not be found.

"Well," said Primrose, at length, after a great deal of unavailing remonstrance, "don't make enemies for yourself among the bishops, at all events: avoid personal allusions. Though it is whispered that one or two of the right reverend bench are about to veer with the wind from Downing-street, you are under no necessity of adverting to them, or to anybody else about whom similar reports are current."

"On the contrary," said Reuben, ostentatiously, "my intention is to paint the character of an apostate Churchman in the most glowing colours: in fact, this will be absolutely necessary for the effect of my speech."

"Totally irrelevant, however," said Winning, calmly; "but *that*, I know, was considered a slight objection in the debates of our society at Cambridge. Besides, what right have you to set up yourself as the judge of any man's sincerity, or the impugner of any man's motives?"

"Will you allow Winning, or me, to see what you have prepared?" asked Primrose.

"Certainly," said Reuben.

He redeemed his pledge in a few days.

The character of the apostate Churchman was the portrait of

his grandfather, in everything but the details and personal features. His friends looked at one another in amazement; then pressed on him, as strongly as they could, that should the rumours of the Dean's change of opinions have any foundation in fact, the delivery of such a passage by his grandson could hardly fail to lead to an irreparable breach between them.

"But my grandfather is not about to apostatise—for it comes to that," replied Reuben, with confidence and displeasure; "so that your premises fall to the ground, and your conclusion tumbles along with them."

Winning perceived that argument was useless, and left the room before he lost his temper.

De Tabley came in almost the next instant. Primrose asked him what news he had; for De Tabley, through his uncle, who was in parliament, and closely connected with a member of the ministry, had often pretty good information of what was going on behind the scenes.

"Nothing talked of but desertions," he answered; "we shall witness startling events before a week is over. Medlicott will be more astounded than any of us by some of them."

"You hear," said Hyacinth to Reuben. "Depend upon it you will commit a monstrous imprudence if you persevere."

"Lay it hard on the bishops," said De Tabley, "as hard as you please; but take my advice, and don't meddle with the deans!"

Primrose and Winning now made another effort. They went together to his aunt, and after explaining to her the views they entertained of the step which her nephew was about to take, they strongly advised her to exert her influence with him, and dissuade him from doing what might possibly end in blasting his prospects for life. Poor Mrs. Mountjoy was greatly distressed and excited; she felt very little disposed to credit any of the reports that were going about her father's promotion, but she had already some vague notion that Reuben was about to do an unwise thing, in attending a political meeting of any kind, and she promised to do all in her power to bring him to reason.

Reuben was seated in one of his luxurious chairs, arrayed in his velvet robe-de-chambre and slippers, with his speech before him, to which he proposed to put some new touches before dinner (he was engaged that day to dine with Master Turner), when he heard a little timid tap at the door of his chamber.

It was his aunt's maid, to say that her mistress wished particularly to see him, if a visit from her would not be very inconvenient. The girl gazed almost idolatrously on Reuben; and no wonder, for, in his gorgeous gown, there was scarcely any dignity so high, that he might not well be supposed invested with it.

"Shall I go to her?" he inquired.

"She will come to you, sir," said Agatha, with profound deference: and presently in came the portly, beautiful, and amiable widow.

Reuben would have been very hard-hearted not to have been moved by the sweetness and earnestness with which his aunt repeated and reinforced the advice and remonstrances which his friends had in vain urged. But Reuben Medlicott was so far from having a hard heart, that, on the contrary, the softness and warmth of his nature made him, all through life, only too susceptible of the sort of influence which was now brought to bear upon him. The end of the interview was, that though he continued to treat the apprehensions of his aunt as utterly groundless, and little less than a libel on her own father, and though his frankness kept him from concealing the extent of the sacrifice he was called on to make, he nevertheless assured his fair relative that he was prepared to make it, if it was necessary to set her mind at ease.

Mrs. Mountjoy was now as overflowing with thanks, as if she had been petitioning for some mighty favour for herself, instead of merely deprecating an act of excessive imprudence on his part. Gazing admiringly on the manuscript which she recognized on the table, then tenderly taking it up, and turning over the pages with a mingled expression of curiosity and regret, she hoped he would permit her to read it. He could not deny the request, but assented with a sigh, which did not escape her ear, touchingly intimating, at the same time, that the speech was made to be spoken, not to be read.

The sigh of the young orator explained this distinction infinitely better to the fair widow's apprehension, than a long lecture on eloquence could have done. It made her more thoroughly sensible of the extent to which Reuben was sacrificing his own glory to her gratification, than if she had studied the treatise "De Claris Oratoribus." Such, indeed, was the effect of that sigh upon her, that it is possible the interview might have ended in Mrs. Mountjoy changing her mind altogether, and even imploring her nephew to do what she had just so earnestly dissuaded him from doing, had not her maid opportunely tapped at the door, to remind her that it was time to dress for dinner, and also to hand Mr. Medlicott a letter which had just been delivered by the postman.

"I'll leave you to read it, my dear," said his aunt, as she ran away.

That letter could not possibly have come at a more unlucky moment. It was from his mother, to acquaint him with the arrangements that had been made for the meeting at Chichester, and the intense excitement that prevailed in the neighbourhood about it, of which no small part, according to Mrs. Medlicott, was owing to Reuben's expected participation in its proceedings. Several bishops, whom she mentioned, had expressed their anxiety that the day should go off well. Flocks of clergymen were to attend it. Everybody deplored his dear grandfather's absence; but perhaps it was reserved for somebody, who was still dearer to her, to supply, and more than supply, the place which the Dean had been wont to fill so ably upon occasions of this nature. Such an opportunity for a young man to cover himself with glory might not occur again for a ages. The maternal solicitude about his preparations and his success, were visible even in the tremulousness of the handwriting. The letter was crossed and recrossed, yet, after all, the most urgent part of it was contained in the last of three postscripts, where his mother informed him that the committee to conduct the meeting was to dine at the Vicarage on the day preceding it, and his father was anxious to have his son's assistance to entertain them. The Earl of Stromness, she added, had sent a haunch of venison for the occasion, an earnest of the interest taken by him in the approaching demonstration.

Reuben had not been so agitated by a letter since the painful communications he had once received, when a schoolboy, from Mrs. Barsac and her daughter. He paced his chamber in a superb state of excitement, rendered still more tragic by his pompous dishabille, which swept the ground behind him like the robe of a heroine on the stage, or a lady's train at a drawing-room. He now felt that he had entered into an inconsiderate, and even improper engagement with his aunt; he had made a vow as rash as Jephtha's, not sufficiently weighing either the bitter disappointment his absence would occasion to his mother, or the mischiefs which might possibly result from deranging, at the eleventh hour, the arrangements for a great county meeting. In all probability it also crossed his mind, as he traversed his room, that the

Protestant interest itself might suffer some slight injury; for as the meeting was considered absolutely necessary for its support, even the least significant personage attending it must needs contribute something to its success and efficiency. What was the public voice, when it roared loudest, but the aggregate of the voices of individuals? Even those who only cheered and shouted were not altogether useless.

Then as to his grandfather's imputed change of views—the only argument his friends in London had to stand on—was not the letter in his hand a triumphant answer to it? All Sussex was deploring the Dean's absence from a demonstration so congenial to his principles. "Offended at my speaking on such an occasion!" cried Reuben, at the end of the soliloquy; "he is a thousand times more likely to bellow like a bull, if I desert my post, especially were he to suspect the reason."

He dressed with feverish precipitation, and, with his mother's letter in his hand, went in search of Mrs. Mountjoy.

CHAPTER II.

THOUGHTS THAT BREATHE AND WORDS THAT BURN.

It was no very difficult achievement. Mrs. Mountjoy released her nephew from his promise much more readily than she had prevailed on herself to extort it from him. She was a woman who had the humblest opinion of her own judgment, especially in comparison with her sister, whom she habitually regarded as a very superior person to herself; and, moreover, being of that more amiable than numerous order of beings to whom it is always extremely painful to allow their own gratification, or their own opinions and wishes, to interfere with the gratification of others for one moment, she felt it utterly impossible to oppose her nephew any longer, when she found herself so decidedly in opposition to his mother also.

The fact that the meeting was under the patronage of so many of the clergy, and even of several bishops, was not without its effect likewise. All Mrs. Mountjoy begged now was, that Reuben would in his speech avoid everything calculated to give offence to individuals, and make enemies for himself. Subject to this little stipulation, she consented to his leaving her the very next morning, which, indeed, was necessary, to enable him to be at home in time for the dinner to be given to the Committee. As Reuben dined out, he took leave of his aunt then, promising to send her a newspaper with the best report of his speech, and to return soon after the meeting and finish his visit. He dined, as we have said, with Master Turner, who amused him by repeating in the course of the evening, "The Chancellor told me, that the best sermon he ever heard in his life, was one which he heard your father preach in a little country-church near Chichester."

Mrs. Mountjoy dined alone, and thought she was doomed to pass the entire evening in solitude, which was not to her an agreeable prospect, when, to her great delight and surprise, while she sat at tea, who should arrive but Mrs. Wyndham? She had come from Boulogne that morning, had dined at Portland-place, and could not let the evening close "without paying *her daughter* a visit." Mrs. Mountjoy, on her part, was equally charmed to receive her fair young step-mother. This relationship was always a cause of pleasantry, though really Mrs. Mountjoy looked very little senior to Mrs. Wyndham.

Mrs. Wyndham had left the Dean behind her; perfectly well, but in a state of feverish excitement, owing to affairs in England, and, as his wife said, receiving letters and despatches every hour from members of parliament, ministers and public men in every situation. As to anything that might be in agitation affecting his personal interests, Mrs. Wyndham was very little better informed than Mrs. Mountjoy, the Dean had been of late so extremely reserved about politics and about himself; but it was impossible not to believe that something very extraordinary would happen before long.

Mrs. Mountjoy inquired whether he had been lately corresponding with her sister, Mrs. Medlicott, or her husband?

"He had a letter from Mr. Medlicott," said Mrs. Wyndham, "and I think it annoyed him more than any other communication he has had from home; he is excessively angry about some meeting or other they are going to hold at Chichester."

"You don't tell me so!" cried poor Mrs. Mountjoy, starting from her chair with an emotion that made Mrs. Wyndham start likewise.

Mrs. Mountjoy then related everything that had occurred relating to the meeting.

"Oh, my dear Mrs. Mountjoy," said Mrs. Wyndham, "why

were you not more confident in your own judgment, you judged so very correctly; it would absolutely ruin that dear clever nephew of yours in my husband's favour, if he were to take any part, much more a prominent one, in this Chichester meeting."

Mrs. Mountjoy was unable to speak, she was so distressed and excited.

"And just now it would be so particularly unfortunate," added Mrs. Wyndham, with still more earnestness, "when nobody knows what a day may bring forth—how soon the Dean may have it in his power to be of the greatest service to Reuben in his profession. Can nothing be done to prevent him from taking so very indiscreet a step?"

"Reuben dines out; he will not be at home until a late hour, and early to-morrow morning he has arranged to start for Chichester."

"You must either see him again before he goes," said Mrs. Wyndham, "or write him a very, very strong letter."

"One thing certainly might be done," said Mrs. Mountjoy, but she paused and immediately added, that it was too strong a measure for her to take.

Mrs. Wyndham insisted upon hearing what her idea was.

"His speech is lying in his room," replied Mrs. Mountjoy, laughing at herself for the absurd thought that had come into her head; "it just occurred to me to carry it off and burn it or hide it."

"Well, but that is a most capital notion," said Mrs. Wyndham, jumping up with the greatest animation, "let us go, my dear Mrs. Mountjoy, and put it into immediate execution. I am for burning the speech: I am against half measures."

"It will answer every purpose to lock it up," said the widow.

"Let us go to his room, at all events."

They went up together to Reuben's apartment. Blanche was not a little amused by the minute daintiness of the arrangements, which his solicitous and bountiful aunt had made for Reuben's accommodation. She was near forgetting the business in hand, in her admiration of the velvet dressing-gown and slippers especially.

"I see how it is," she said, laughing; "you do every thing to spoil your nephew: no wonder you find him so perverse and unmanageable;—you are quite as bad as any mother."

"Perhaps you will be a mother yourself, my dear, one of these days," said Mrs. Mountjoy, parrying the attack, in a laughing whisper.

"Ah, no!" said Blanche, with a sigh that was not very sorrowful; "I shall never be more than a grandmother and a stepmother, but that's dignity enough, I think, for a little woman like me."

The speech was lying just where Mrs. Mountjoy had seen it a few hours earlier in the evening; but now, when she took it up, she handled it even more lovingly than before; and again she repeated that there could be no advantage in destroying the papers—she would carry them away to her own bed-chamber, and hide them on some high shelf, or in some inaccessible nook or corner. Mrs. Wyndham was curious to look over the speech. Mrs. Mountjoy placed it in her hands, and just at the same moment Agatha came in, with a great fuss, to get some directions about Mr. Reuben's linen, as he was to leave town in the morning. Mrs. Mountjoy went with the maid into her nephew's dressing-room to settle this little business, which did not occupy five minutes. When she returned to where she had left Mrs. Wyndham, she found that resolute young lady standing near the fire, contemplating with firmness, though not, perhaps, without some little misgiving and scruples of conscience, the burning eloquence of Reuben Medlicott.

The affrighted widow knew at a glance, only too well, what it was that was curling and twisting in the flames, as if the papers themselves actually felt the pangs of martyrdom. Passionately clasping her hands, and regarding Mrs. Wyndham with looks which expressed at once astonishment, sorrow, and reproach, she uttered a series of the most piteous exclamations, ending with bitterly upbraiding herself for having been the first to suggest so barbarous a proceeding.

"My dear Mrs. Mountjoy," said Blanche, with the agitated manner of a woman who, having done an energetic thing, is inclined to fear she has been too vigorous, "it would never have done for you to have merely carried it off; your nephew would infallibly have got it from you."

Mrs. Mountjoy made no reply, but stood with her eyes riveted upon the burning papers, while over and over again her friend repeated, that what she had done she had done for the best, and she was confident Reuben himself would one day thank her for it. At length the flames devoured the last of their prey, and the two fair dames went down together, both a little more composed; Mrs. Mountjoy telling her friend that she could only regard her in the light of an executioner, and Mrs. Wyndham defending herself, by declaring in more explicit terms than she had used before, that she had a presentiment of a bishopric, and was bent upon having Reuben for her domestic chaplain.

CHAPTER III.

THE APOSTACY.

The events of the few succeeding days put Reuben Medlicott, his oratory, prospects, and all about him, quite out of remembrance, at least in the thoughts of his London friends. They had something far more exciting to think of, for rumour had told a true story, and Dean Wyndham returned from Boulogne, to give his adhesion to the Government, and receive the mitre, as the recompense of his sudden and suspicious adoption of a new set of political opinions. The career of this eccentric dignitary reminded the public of those hurricanes which occur in the Caribbean Seas, where the gale will often begin from the north or the south; then suddenly chop round, and blow with equal determination from the opposite point of the compass. And from the history of the same tempests might have been likewise borrowed an apt illustration of some of the effects of the Dean's conversion; for as it is found that the trees upon one side of an island, subjected to one of those abrupt and fierce visitations, are commonly blown down in one direction, while the trees on the opposite side are found prostrated in the reverse one, in like manner, before Dr. Wyndham's former opponents had ceased to reel beneath the tremendous buffets which he had dealt them in the pulpit and the press, his new antagonists were already staggering under the equally formidable blows which it was now their turn to receive.

The event affected people variously, according to their political views, their notions of public morality, their private interests, or their previous estimate of the Dean's probity. Those who were least surprised at his tergiversation were those who best knew him. Those who affected to be most indignant at his perfidy were those who would have been most ready themselves to receive a political traitor with open arms. He was loudly reviled for his hypocrisy, by men who never had better reason than his violence for believing him sincere while on the other hand he was now extolled for sincerity by many of his new associates, who had no other grounds for their opinion than his present adherence to their own standard. Many blushed for his infidelity to his party, but many more envied him for the prize he won by it. Some were ashamed of human nature; some were disposed to disbelieve in the existence of truth and virtue; some proclaimed that religion itself had received a mortal blow. There were persons who never would have thought it, and there were others who all along expected it. A great many people said it was not worth his while, at sixty-five, to barter his principles even for a bishopric; but men of the stamp of Lord Greenwich and Mr. De Tabley, who took a secular view of the matter, maintained that if he was only to enjoy his prosperity for five years, there was an amount of good living in five years of episcopacy, for which the price paid was far from unreasonable.

Those who took a metaphysical view of the case did not fail to recollect the ancient doctrine of the duplicity of the human mind. The Socratic philosophy, for instance, consisted in the retiring of a man within himself, to hold communion with the *alter ego* which Nature has assigned to each of us. When this communion is of an harmonious and amiable nature, the result is what we call singleness of mind or purpose; when it is controversial, it necessarily leads to the phenomenon of doublemindedness, of which the practical result is the line of conduct vulgarly called tergiversation. "According," says Lord Shaftesbury, "as the dual number is practically formed in us, we are supposed to advance in wisdom and moral perfection." The microcosm, in fact, or little world in our bosoms, is divided into two parties, and the more thorough the division is, the more metaphysically complete is our intellectual constitution. We are therefore always to understand a perfect, or (what is tantamount thereto) a double public character as speaking in only one of his persons at a time. Such a man has his Whig self and his Tory self; what are loosely called his inconsistencies, are in reality nothing but the discordant relations subsisting between the two parties in his breast. Two minds, like two heads, are obviously better than one; but what would be the use of two minds, if they were always to think the same thing, or always come to the same conclusion? Nature does nothing in vain, and it is well worthy of observation, as a beautiful analogy between our physical and our moral structure, that the cavity of the human thorax contains two lungs, or organs of breathing, for which no other moral use can be assigned but to enable a man to blow hot and cold with the same breath.

It was at Mrs. Barsac's ball, the day after the incidents of the last chapter, that the Dean's promotion was first announced authentically to his family. The ball far exceeded in splendour anything of the kind at Hereford, but in London it made no more sensation than a *réunion* at a spinster's tea-table at Islington or Hackney. There were three lords, however, wherever Mrs. Barsac had picked them up; but, to be sure, two were only in the Irish or Scotch peerage, and the third was Lord Greenwich, whom Barsac had met one day at Mrs. Mountjoy's, and toadied with so much industry and success, as to prevail on him to grace his wife's ball with his portly presence. Lord Greenwich, indeed, was more like an alderman than a nobleman, and he was as aldermanic in his tastes as in his personal appearance. But the star on his coat was the cynosure of many an eye notwithstanding, and it fascinated no eyes so much as Mrs. Barsac's, who had already conceived the idea of securing him for one of the remaining Sherries.

Mrs. Barsac was not much of a star-gazer, astronomically speaking; but of a star on the breast of nobility she was as sharp an observer as Sir John Herschel, and as diligent with her optic glass as Galileo himself. She took a baron's altitude with precision, noted the transit of a viscount across the floor to a second, and could tell how many digits an earl was eclipsed by a marquis, with a degree of accuracy that was quite scientific. In short Mrs. Barsac was a very clever practical astronomer in her way; and there was this always to comfort her in her attention to the phenomena of the peerage, that if she failed to win a husband for her daughters, she succeeded probably in gaining a customer for her husband.

Neither Primrose nor Henry Winning had seen Mrs. Mountjoy since the interview they both had with her upon the subject of Reuben's interests. They now formed a little group in a corner with the fair widow and Mrs. Wyndham, and it was then that Reuben's absence from the ball was first noticed by his friends. Winning was delighted at the burning of the speech, and applauded Mrs. Wyndham to the skies for her energy and decision. Primrose shook his head, and expressed his apprehensions that all was not quite safe yet: it depended entirely, he said, upon the question, whether his eloquent and wrong-headed young friend had committed his oration to memory or not.

Winning thought he had not, and Mrs. Mountjoy fortified his opinion by mentioning what her maid had related of Reuben's extreme vexation at missing the papers on the morning he left town.

"In all probability, however," said Winning, "we are attaching more importance to the matter than it merits, so that if Mrs. Wyndham feels disposed to dance, and would prefer me for her partner, to the gallant Captain Shunfield, who is advancing to solicit that honour, I am humbly at her command."

Mrs. Wyndham, as she looked that night at her mother's ball, was as charming a little duodecimo edition of woman-kind as you ever saw in the library of beauty. The milliner had bound her with extreme elegance; the jeweller had embellished her richly but simply; and if it would not be pushing the metaphor too far, it might be truly added that the contents of the volume were as pleasing as its exterior was attractive, every page being illustrated with good sense, and illuminated with good humour.

Mr. Primrose remained at the widow's side. She was not one of the youngest beauties in the room unquestionably, but she was probably the most agreeable woman, and, indeed, she was surprisingly handsome, considering the date of her charms, for though much younger than her sister, Mrs. Medlicott, she was still of the same generation. Hyacinth Primrose had a longer *tête-à-tête* with her upon this occasion than he had ever enjoyed before, and, no doubt, he made considerable progress in the course of it towards that distinguished position in her favour and confidence, in which it was his lot eventually to be placed.

Occasionally, however, they talked of little matters connected with the scene before their eyes and the people whirling about them.

Mrs. Mountjoy, for example, wanted to know—"Who was the important little man dancing with Miss Barsac?"

"My dry old friend Amontillado!" said Primrose. "But the man, let me see, I ought to know him,—why it's little Griffin, who purloined Reuben's paper on heraldry, and sold it for the place of Rouge-Dragon, or Blue-Mantle. In common justice, he ought to be dancing on the tread-mill at this moment."

"Now, is it possible such a wretch can be popular in society? I have heard of a set of men called diners-out. Surely, Mr. Griffin cannot be one of them."

"Griffin dines very seldom out," said Primrose, "when the

town is healthy; he gets an invitation now and then when influenza is going, or the cholera."

"Is he a doctor?"

Primrose laughed.

"No, no, he is not a doctor, but during epidemics people are constantly getting apologies; they must fill up their tables, and they ask people like my friend Blue-Mantle, of whom they never think except under such desperate circumstances."

"Very amusing," said Mrs. Mountjoy; "now who is the man dancing with Miss Jane Barsac?"

"A youth unknown to fame, at all events to me," said Primrose. "One is not bound to know people in a house like this, though as a general rule one ought to know everybody; in fact, to live in London, one should know two things, who's who, and what's what. I can't think of any other branch of knowledge that's absolutely necessary."

"What would Reuben say to that?" said Mrs. Mountjoy.

"But see!" said Hyacinth, "here is Mr. Barsac coming towards us, with some design, I fancy, upon you."

"To take me down to supper. How particularly great he is to-night; he reminds me of a nabob."

"Nabobbery itself," said Hyacinth; "that must be the Lord Mayor's chain he has to his watch, and observe the conservatory in his button-hole! He resembles Lombard-street and Covent-garden combined."

"He reminds me," said De Tabley, who was passing, "of one of his own magnums; I doubt if many of them have got such a bouquet."

Mr. Barsac led Mrs. Mountjoy to supper with great state and ceremony, talking of nothing under a coronet the whole of the way, and speaking much less to be heard by her than to produce an imposing effect upon his mob of guests, particularly Mr. Leadenhall and Sir Finch Goldfinch; and upon far the greater proportion of them he probably succeeded in producing the effect he desired. The merchant was immediately followed by corpulent Lord Greenwich, conducting Mrs. Barsac; next went Winning with Mrs. Wyndham. The order of the rest is of little consequence. As to Primrose, he slipped down alone, with a view to get near Mrs. Mountjoy again, and save her from being bored to death by Barsac's dull pomposity.

But the precaution was superfluous. Just as Mrs. Wyndham reached the door of the supper-room, a servant put a slip of paper carelessly folded and directed in a scarce legible scrawl, into her hands. The haste and agitation with which she opened and read it, dropping Winning's arm and her fan at the same moment, left no doubt upon the mind of any one who observed what took place that it was a dispatch from the Dean. He had just arrived in town, and, with his usual singularity, had gone to his daughter's lodgings in Burlington Gardens, instead of to his father-in-law's house in Portland Place. The note communicated in the driest and fewest terms possible, the fact of the writer's elevation to the bench, and commanded his wife's immediate attendance.

Mrs. Wyndham and Mrs. Mountjoy flew to him without a moment's delay, while the Barsacs hastened to disseminate among their company, in as easy and indifferent a tone as they could assume, the important fact that their son-in-law was Bishop of Shrewsbury.

Mrs. Mountjoy wrote Reuben a few lines that very night before she retired to rest, to apprise him of what had occurred. She flattered herself that, even if his speech had been destroyed to no purpose, her letter would arrive in time to prevent any thing unpleasant happening at Chichester. But that ill-advised young man, the victim at once of his own and his mother's vanity, had already taken the fatal step which rendered all the kind offices of his judicious friends totally unavailing.

CHAPTER IV.

THE TREMENDOUS DEMONSTRATION.

Mr. Primrose's conjecture hit the mark only too truly. Although Mr. Medlicott had been annoyed and embarrassed by the loss of his speech, the toil of composition, the collection of the flowers, the accumulation of images, the forging of the thunderbolts, the hammering, the moulding, the filing, and the polishing had sufficiently impressed the principal portions of that great effort on his memory; so that those daring incendiaries, his good aunt and his pretty grandmamma (though we must acquit them on the criminal charge), stand clearly convicted on the most serious part of the indictment, the count for a blunder.

The "great and important day" arrived; the mighty meeting, the "tremendous demonstration," was held at Chichester, and went off with only too much *éclat* for the most conspicuous personage who figured at it.

All "tremendous demonstrations" resemble one another very closely; an excited knot of noblemen and gentlemen on a platform, a tumultuous sea of heads on the floor, an agitated bevy of mothers, aunts, and sisters in a gallery, a little table for reporters, a peer in the chair, if a peer can be found to fill it; but never anything beneath the baronetage. On the present occasion, the platform was thronged with parsons and squires until it overflowed; and every now and then a vicar, or a pair of top-boots, came tumbling down among the smock-frocks, who united their shoulders to heave him up again. When this disaster befel a man of ordinary dimensions, he was reinstated on the platform with no great difficulty; but when it happened to public characters of more than average weight, the attempt to replace them sometimes proved as ineffectual as in the case of the celebrated Humpty Dumpty in the nursery rhyme. It was unquestionably "a tremendous demonstration" of the lungs of the men of Sussex. John Bull bellowed like a herd of his four-footed namesakes, and the Protestant lion roared his best, without the slightest respect to the nerves of the ladies. Bottom would have been greatly scandalised. Awful resolutions were proposed by peers, and seconded by commoners, but as to the eloquence, it was uniformly stifled by its own applause, and perished for ever in the premature raptures of the audience. It was proved, however, beyond a doubt, that there were two Curtii present, ready to jump into any chasm which the British soil might please to open beneath their feet; a Brutus in buckskin was equally prepared to sacrifice all the private affections to the public welfare; as to Sydneys, Hampdens, and Russells, they appeared that day in a force that reflected undying honour upon the patriotism of Englishmen. How often Popery was flatly negatived with the energy of Cromwell himself, is not to be told in figures; but three orators, at least, pledged their lives and fortunes to defend the throne and the altar; the same number of prophetic voices foretold the sunset of British liberty; and thrice three times was it powerfully urged upon the vast assembly to unite, heart and hand, in "a strong pull, a long pull, and a pull altogether."

In the front of the gallery assigned to the ladies, who came to brave the roaring of the lion aforesaid, sat Mrs. Medlicott, and

Hannah and Mary Hopkins. Their eyes were riveted on the platform, but it was not on the chairman they gazed, although he was the Earl of Stromness, nor on the Vicar, for he was lost in the crowd, nor on Mr. Pigwidgeon, ludicrous figure as he cut, for there was no novelty in that—you had only to watch the point where the three lines of female vision united, to convince yourself that they sought nothing, saw nothing, thought of nothing during that great day and demonstration, but the youngest of the patriot band, he who came to dedicate the first-fruits of his talents and his fame to the service of his creed and his country. Probably few of the ladies present had been unobservant of Reuben from an early period of the day, for he was conspicuous not only by his handsome person, but by his dress, which could scarcely have been gayer or more elaborate had he been going to be married, instead of only going to make a speech. His hair, artfully divided, shone like Apollo's, and flowed on his shoulders almost as wantonly as in his boyhood; a bouquet, nearly as large as Barsac's, bloomed in his button-hole; and the virgin whiteness of his gloves typified the maiden eloquence with which he was about to enchant the world. The foppery was not entirely his own; the gloves were due to his mother, the flowers had been insisted on and even arranged on his breast by the young Quakeress. Nor was it amiss that so much care had been bestowed on his toilette; for had he been confounded with the parsons and the squires, his rising would not have commanded the attention that it it did, and his oratory would probably have been lost, like that of the rest, in the incessant uproar of the meeting.

Everything, however, was propitious, but, perhaps, most of all, the emphatic and gracious manner in which the Earl of Stromness, a man of the highest courtesy, introduced him to the audience, as "the son of his respected friend, the Rev. Thomas Medlicott."

Instantly the chawbacons, hundreds of whom were the Earl's tenants, raised a shout that well nigh brought down the roof of the Court-house. The din was little in unison with the modesty and gentleness with which the palpitating Reuben took his place in the front of the platform. His rising was soft as the south wind; and you might have marked its effects in the female gallery, how the breeze fluttered the bonnets, rustled among the ribbons, and especially how it made the maternal stomacher rise and fall, like a sail when the wind is irresolute. He rose, he spoke, he triumphed. His was the only speech that was not only delivered, but of which a considerable portion was heard. A most excellent speech it was of the school of oratory it belonged to, though there were principles of eloquence by which it would have been cruel to have tried it. If, however, it had the defects of youth, it had its merits also; it was fresh, it was fiery, it was animated and courageous. There was not a Quintilian in the meeting to find fault with it. Tried by the test of success, not Demosthenes himself could have gained a completer victory. Up flew a cloud of hats before the exordium was over; the orator was actually invisible for a second. The same demonstration was repeated a score of times; upon one occasion Mr. Pigwidgeon (who was striking another stroke for a dinner) must throw up his beaver among the rest, and he never recovered it, for it fell among the mob, and was trampled to pieces in an instant. The hat was not worth sixpence, but he vowed it was a new one—a thing he had never been known to possess in his life. What signified Mr. Pigwidgeon's hat, or Mr. Pigwidgeon himself? Even Protestantism was forgotten in the excitement and enthusiasm occasioned by the flowers of Reuben's rhetoric, not unaided by the flowers in his coat. If one passage outshone another, where all was splendour, it was the dangerous topic of apostacy— the graphic picture of a renegade divine, which reached its climax, when the orator described the vain endeavours of such a fallen character to regain his lost position, and imagined the reception he would assuredly meet with from every honest man. Here he turned to good account the lines in Milton:—

> Think'st thou, revolted spirit, thy shape the same
> Or undiminished glory, as when once
> Thou stood'st erect in heav'n, erect and pure.

The air was darkened with waving hats again; the enthusiasm mounted to the galleries, the women waved their handkerchiefs wildly, and Mrs. Medlicott and the Quakeresses, who had taken off their bonnets in consequence of the heat, tossed them about fanatically, and almost forgot their sex in the violence of their transports.

In short, it was a relief to everybody when the last bolt was launched, and the last long-protracted peal of applause greeted the solemn and high-wrought peroration.

The Vicar himself, though not nearly so susceptible as his wife, was carried away by his son's eloquence almost as much as she was, although he forbore from expressing his feelings with equal energy, partly from his native reserve, partly out of regard for his hat. At the door of the court-house he was overwhelmed with congratulations. Old Matthew Cox, with a tear in his eyes, shook his hand, but said nothing. Mr. Broad was like a madman. The apothecary pretended that only for his exertions the mob would have insisted on carrying Reuben home on their shoulders. Lord Stromness came up to the Vicar in the kindest manner, and told him that his son had made one of the most effective speeches he had ever heard in his life. "That portrait of a turncoat," said the Earl, "was quite a masterpiece."

The next moment a servant handed Mr. Medlicott the letter from Mrs. Mountjoy, informing him, in substance, that the most conspicuous turncoat in England was his father-in-law.

"A pretty kettle of fish," said the Vicar, as, with visible agitation, he put the letter in his wife's hands. She almost shrieked when she came to the announcement of her father's promotion.

"A pretty kettle of fish," said the Vicar.

Reuben turned white when he received the news. His mother and he exchanged looks in silence. In his countenance there was nothing but pride and resentment; in hers were depicted the same feelings, but mixed with vexation and regret. The poor Quakeresses were quite at a loss to comprehend what was in the wind, seeing joy and triumph so soon turned into chagrin and disappointment; and they were still more at a loss to understand matters, when they learned that all arose from the announcement that Dean Wyndham was Bishop of Shrewsbury.

"I don't believe it yet," said Mrs. Medlicott, abruptly laying down her fork in the middle of the silent dinner; "I can't bring myself to believe it."

"At all events," said Reuben, "I shall never regret having told the truth."

"Thou never wilt have cause," said poor Mary Hopkins, enthusiastically.

"At the same time," said the Vicar, in a low and very serious key, "I hope the truth you have told will be confined pretty much to our own neighbourhood; I should not like it to travel up to London."

He had scarcely uttered the words, when in bustled Mr. Pigwidgeon to say that he had taken measures to secure a full report of Reuben's speech in the "Chichester Mercury," and some other provincial organ, with which he had some influence or connexion.

"Thank you very much for your kind offices," said the Vicar, drily, and biting his lip, "but my son is content with the reputation he has made among his friends here; he has no ambition to be a political character; in fact," he added, rising from the table, approaching the apothecary, and speaking in a lower but more earnest tone, "if you could induce the papers you mention to report us as concisely as possible, we should take it as a particular favour."

The fawning apothecary shook his head and said, "he feared that would be quite out of the question; Master Reuben's speech was the speech of the day, and a report of the meeting without it would be the play of Hamlet, with Hamlet's part omitted."

"That's very true," said Mrs. Medlicott, still unable to see her way clearly through Reuben's unlucky laurels.

"What does my eloquent friend say himself?" said Mr. Pigwidgeon.

Reuben replied, not without more vain-glory than quite became him, that he had thought it his duty to express his sentiments freely and boldly on the late occasion; but, that duty having been performed, he would leave it to others to decide whether it would be of service, or the contrary, to the cause he had advocated, that his speech should be circulated through the empire.

"Upon that there can be but one opinion," said the flattering, false Pigwidgeon.

"Possibly," said the Vicar, drawing him aside; "but I am averse to unnecessary publicity upon many accounts; in fact I am anxious on the point; go and use your influence to have the reports short, and come back and sup with us. There will be a venison hash and a roast pullet, and we will not sit down until you return, if you don't come back till midnight."

The apothecary had been aware that a present of a haunch from Lord Stromness had recently been received at the Vicarage, and that it had regaled the committee of management, which Mr. Medlicott had entertained on the preceding day; but he had given up all hopes of partaking of it in any form, so that when he heard of the hash, it sounded in his ears melodiously, then pleasantly affected his imagination, and finally made his lips water. As he drove to Chichester in his gig, he had time, however, for other thoughts, and among his various mental employments, he puzzled himself thinking what could possibly be the Vicar's reason for wishing to suppress his son's speech. While he was trying to solve this riddle, he saw a gentleman on horseback approaching him, who proved to be his patient, Mr. Oldport. Pigwidgeon asked if any news had arrived from London?

"News, indeed," said the Canon, "very agreeable news for me, and still more agreeable for your old acquaintance Medlicott,—the mitre has fallen on my friend Wyndham's head at last."

"You don't say so," said the apothecary in his gig.

"I have it under his own hand and seal," said the Canon. "Here's his letter for you to read:" and he fumbled in his pocket, drew forth the Dean's letter, and handed it to Pigwidgeon, who read it greedily.

"You see," said the Canon, "he is very angry with you all for getting up that meeting, and by the by, let me ask, what could have possessed Medlicott to allow his son to come out so strongly as I am told he did; why it was just the very thing to put his grandfather beside himself."

"Then he is ratting with the ministry?" said the apothecary.

"To be sure he is," said the Canon, "if ratting is the word. Do you think he got the bishopric on condition of opposing them?"

"I see," said Pigwidgeon.

The Canon ambled home, and the apothecary trotted into town, now in full possession of the Vicar's motives for desiring to cushion his son's oratory. After visiting the newspaper-offices, he trotted back again to the Vicarage, which he reached in reasonable time to enjoy the hash, the pullet, and a bottle of the Vicar's best wine. Of his mission he said very little, only shook his head, winked a great deal, protested he had done his best; what more could Pigwidgeon do? The Vicar loaded the apothecary's plate, replenished his glass often, and waited for the papers of the morning.

It then appeared, not that the apothecary had not used his best exertions, but that he did not possess as much influence as he boasted over the public press of Chichester. One newspaper, the Mercury, printed Reuben's oration at full length; the other published only an abstract of the greater part, but gave the objectionable passages in full, which of course had the effect of making them doubly conspicuous and doubly offensive.

So strong is the principle of maternal vanity, that Mrs. Medlicott was more pleased by seeing her Reuben's oratory in print, than distressed to think of the ill blood it was calculated to produce in the family, and the injury it was so likely to do the young man himself.

As to the latter personage, he had made up his mind to stand by his grandfather's cast-off opinions and principles at all risks. Nothing annoyed Reuben so much in the whole affair, as the blundering of the Mercury, which utterly destroyed his quotation from Milton, by giving "revolting spirit" instead of "revolted."

This alone would have suggested the expediency of presenting the public with a revised and authentic report of his speech, which he accordingly did before the expiration of a week, in the form of a pamphlet. Mary Hopkins copied it for the printers with her own hand. It was published at Chichester, and it was with no little difficulty the Vicar restrained his wife from getting an engraving prefixed to it from the picture which Blanche Barsac had made of Reuben when at school. The engraving was actually executed, and Mrs. Medlicott had already distributed many copies of it among her friends.

CHAPTER V.

A CHAPTER OF CONSEQUENCES.

At a wonderfully early hour on the morning succeeding that memorable ball, at which the Dean's conversion and its splendid reward had been first publicly announced, Mr. and Mrs. Barsac were actively engaged revolutionising all the arrangements of their household, to get a suite of apartments in readiness suitable to their notions of the rank and dignity of a bishop. Closets were turned into bedrooms; governesses rose in the world, not much to their comfort, as happens in many elevations; removing, shifting, exchanging, and packing, were the order of the day; in short, there was no amount of inconvenience to which the Barsacs were not prepared to submit in their own persons, and inflict upon everybody else (particularly upon their servants and dependents), for the sake of paying all due respect to the man whom the King had delighted to honour. But this was not all: the furniture of the bed-room designed for the right reverend Prelate was not thought new or rich enough for him, so Barsac went immediately to the shop of one of his Majesty's cabinet-makers and upholsterers, and bought a variety of superb articles, for which he paid a proportionally superb price. Among others was a gorgeous bed, which the upholsterer, as soon as he learned that it was intended to receive a bishop, proposed to hang with curtains of purple silk or velvet, which, with a fringe of gold lace, would, he conceived, be at once rich, chaste, and appropriate. Barsac was of the same opinion. Indeed, it was surprising he did not order the arms of the see of Shrewsbury, or at least a mitre, to be embroidered upon the drapery. However, the canopy of purple and gold satisfied the merchant's notions of what was "chaste and appropriate;" and so expeditiously were his orders executed, that before dusk the same evening the upholsterer's men were putting up the episcopal couch, surrounded by the Barsac fry and a bevy of curious maids, bereft of the faculties of speech by the spectacle of such magnificence.

But, unfortunately, the Bishop did not go to Portland Place at all, so that all these fine preparations were thrown away upon him. Burlington Gardens suited him better, and as there was room enough in the same house with Mrs. Mountjoy, he took up his quarters there for the present. The Barsacs were greatly mortified, and it would have increased their mortification not a little, if they could have heard the observations the Bishop made upon their vulgar folly, when his daughter told him of the trouble and expense they had gone to.

It was a hint to Mrs. Mountjoy. She recollected her own sumptuous arrangements for Reuben, and for fear of her father discovering them and making more of the same remarks, she took the prudent precaution of locking up her nephew's room.

The Bishop remained sequestered for some days, paid one or two official visits, received a few friends himself, but peremptorily declined to dine out, even with the Barsacs, who were most importunate, promising him nothing but quiet family parties, though, had he consented, they would have been capable of the perfidy of inviting one or two of their lordly acquaintance and customers—Lord Greenwich, at least—to meet him.

The Dean—we should say, the Bishop—never thought of Reuben, until he was reminded of him by a congratulatory visit from Mr. Primrose. Then he spoke of him kindly, but dismissed the subject in a moment, with his usual absorption in his own immediate concerns. Hyacinth he received most cordially, and though in conversation with him he never alluded to the sketch of himself which had appeared a couple of years ago, in the Cambridge Miscellany, the reception he now gave the writer showed how extremely agreeable had been the incense offered up to him upon that occasion. Indeed, he told his wife and daughter privately (and between them, it soon reached Mr. Primrose), that he considered himself in some measure indebted to that article for the professional advancement he had at length received.

Mrs. Mountjoy, who was beginning to reciprocate the tender sentiments with which she had long since inspired Mr. Primrose, and who had also known for some time a secret not yet imparted to the reader—namely, that Hyacinth (as unstable as Reuben, but more calculating) was now much more inclined to the Church than he had ever been to the bar,—Mrs. Mountjoy was gratified upon every account to see him standing so well in her father's estimation. At the same time being a lady, who not only had a heart, but whose heart was always in the right place, the chief object of her anxiety, at present, was her nephew; she was on the rack until she heard from Chichester, and when the news arrived of the occurrences there, it almost drove her distracted.

She was informed of what took place sooner than her father. He read the account of the meeting for the first time in a Tory London newspaper, which continued to advocate his cast-off opinions. The Bishop was at breakfast. His wife and daughter were all in a tremor, knowing what the paper contained, and furtively watched him with the most fidgety anxiety, as his eye roved from column to column, until at length it arrived at the report of the "tremendous demonstration," and was arrested by the name of Mr. Reuben Medlicott.

"What's here?" cried the Bishop, after grunting inarticulately for some time over the "Morning Post."

"What, sir?" faintly echoed the ladies, only too well knowing what it was that had caught his attention so strongly, and elicited the exclamation.

"What Reuben Medlicott is this?—it can't be Eleanor's son?" looking up at Mrs. Mountjoy from beneath the shaggy portcullis of the eye that was next her.

"I suppose you are reading about the meeting at Chichester, sir?" she replied evasively and nervously.

He read on for a few moments, knitting his bushy brows, and uttering strange sounds, alternately expressive of contempt and displeasure.

"My poor Reuben," said Mrs. Mountjoy, in a low tone to Mrs. Wyndham, but wishing to be heard by her father; "he had very little idea of what was to happen when he left town to attend that meeting."

"Impossible he could," said Mrs. Wyndham, in the same key.

"What business had he there at all?" growled the prelate, lowering the paper suddenly, and scowling over it at both of them.

To this there was no attempt at an answer. He then recommenced reading, every now and then repeating aloud, either in mockery or indignation, some phrase that particularly struck him, such as "public duty"—"political principles"—"Protestant constitution"—and so forth, until he came to the word "apostacy," which he muttered between his teeth with extreme bitterness; then flung the paper down, exclaiming—

"This is worse than burning my hay-ricks!" then he stopped, and commenced taking his coffee.

"Indeed, sir," said Mrs. Mountjoy. "Reuben never intended——"

The Bishop desired to have more sugar. His wife, as she sweetened his cup, threw in a tremulous word to sweeten his temper also, but instead of noticing what she said, he again mumbled the word "apostacy," in a tone of fierce derision, and, resuming the paper, proceeded with tolerable patience until he came to the quotation from Milton, when he flung it from him once more, and never spoke again the whole morning, except to observe that the words were "revolted spirit," not "revolting."

"The fellow could not even cite a hackneyed passage correctly."

Mrs. Mountjoy and Mrs. Wyndham, taking Mr. Primrose into consultation, agreed that to make any immediate effort to mollify the feelings of the Bishop towards Reuben would be injudicious. It was better to leave it to time, which would probably have soon set all to rights, had not the same newspaper the following day singled out the new Bishop of Shrewsbury for a violent personal attack, and pointedly applied to him Reuben's full-length picture of a clerical turncoat, adding with superfluous malignity that the eloquent speaker was nearly related to the prelate, which made the denunciation the more terrible and crushing.

It was ascertained long afterwards that this unjustifiable bit of personality was intended to injure Mr. Medlicott as much as to annoy his grandfather. The author of it was Mr. Bavard, who never forgave Reuben for having out-talked him one day at dinner, and being connected with the press took this honourable method of revenging it.

However, it was useless after this to plead for Reuben. Nobody dared to breathe his name in the Bishop's presence. The Vicar wrote to him in terms little short of abject. The letter was not answered. Mrs. Medlicott travelled to Shrewsbury to appease him, but he feigned illness and refused to see her.

BOOK THE SEVENTH.

"Hold your peace, Sancho," said the Knight, "and don't interrupt Mr Bachelor, whom I entreat to proceed; and let me know what more is said in this same history."
—*Don Quixote*, Part II., Book I.

ARGUMENT.

As it is the usage of certain authors to choose subjects for their books, more for the sake of something from which to digress, than as topics to pursue steadily, and themes always to keep in view; treating them, in fact, rather as a Station to depart from, than as a Terminus to arrive at, so it is with a great many who enter the learned professions; there is frequently observed between what they profess, and what they practise, that wide interval or discrepancy, which, when it takes place in politics or in private morals, we call inconsistency, or by a harsher name. How common is it not, for instance, to see the physician abandoning the cure of his patients, and betaking himself to quacking the body-politic; or the lawyer spurning the courts, as soon as he is qualified to plead, and turning speech-maker, play-wright, place hunter, or diner-out. If we desire to know what manner of men these loose and often odd fish of the several professions are—these camp-followers of the regular troops of law, physic, or divinity—we shall find them invariably consisting of your clever fellows; the clever young divine superior to the churching of women, and as high as the steeple above the catechising of children; the clever doctor, disgusted with the hospitals, or the versatile and voluble young barrister, infinitely too smart to wear his wig every day and mind his business. The Greeks called a genius of this volatile description Πολυπράγμων; the Romans had the word *ardelio* to express it; proof, if proof were wanting, that ancient Athens and Rome had their "coming men," or their Reuben Medlicotts, as well as modern Chichester and London. Attalus was our Reuben's parallel in Martial's days, even to the smattering of astrology.

> "Declamas bello; causas agis, Attale, belle.
>   Historias bellas, carmina bella facis.
> Componis belle mimos, epigrammata belle;
>   Bellus grammaticus, bellus es astrologus.
> Nil bene cum facias, facis attamen omnia belle.
>   Vis dicam quid sis? Magnus es *ardelio*."

These scatterlings of the church, the bar, and the faculty, may be said, indeed, collectively to form a sort of profession of their own, the profession of having no definite calling; and of all vocations it is the most vocal, for the men who have least to do have ever got the most to say. The greatest talkers of all are the *ardelios* of the bar. The law is a noisy profession when it is followed, but a noisier still when it is professed without being practised. Prolixity is a part of pleading which the young barrister is sure to master, though he may not pick up a grain of law, and when he lacks the legitimate sphere for its exercise, he bestows it on the public at large, with the liberality of Dogberry "bestowing all his tediousness" on Leonato. Iron turns not more instinctively to adamant than does this precocious garrulity seek its natural vent in politics. The platform is its magnetic pole. Thither, with one accord, or rather with one voice, or better still, with one bray, rushes the whole Arcadian herd, ambitious to unite their several wordy torrents to the mighty flood of speech and jargon by which the country is at once inundated and deafened; a Deluge and a Babel at the same time. Every one of these gentlemen is a Cicero, a Pericles, a Demosthenes, or an Æschines (at the lowest estimate) in some circle, club, society, or corporation of his own. Each "shakes" his little "arsenal," and fulminates over his shire, or his native borough, or some Musical Hall, or Tavern, at the very least. Is it so very true, after all, that no man is a hero to his valet, or a prophet in his own country? The truth seems rather to be, that in a general sense everyman has a valet to whom he is a hero, and a country where he enjoys prophetic honour and reputation. Every home has its hero; on every hearth-stone some little demigod is adored, nor did Egypt ever raise altars to more preposterous divinities than are to be found in the family-worship of many a house in this Christian land. We have seen in more than one an ape receiving divine honours; in another a parrot canonized; what sacrifices have we not seen made to a puppy, what incense offered to the "asinus communis" of these islands? Mothers especially have a hankering after strange gods, bowing the knee to the dolls and idols of their own making; the least blind and most orthodox of women will take her donkey for a zebra, and adore him as a saint, if she does not absolutely worship him as a deity.

CHAPTER I.

MR. MEDLICOTT QUARRELS WITH THE CHURCH.

ALTHOUGH Mr. Medlicott quarrelled with his grandfather, it was by no means incumbent on him to quarrel with the Church, but he was not of that opinion. He declared himself disgusted with a career where the roads to eminence were so foul and crooked.

It was to no purpose that his father and others represented the injustice of drawing so sweeping a conclusion from a solitary case, and pointed to men on the bench of bishops who were not less distinguished by their genius and learning than by their consistency and honour; reason was against Reuben, and Reuben was therefore against reason.

It was a pity that talking was not a profession. Mr. Medlicott would have embraced it with ardour and soon obtained the degree of a doctor. But a man must talk with some authority, or he will not long have an audience to hearken to him; in fact, he must procure a license to talk from one of the learned professions; or, if he desires to talk in Parliament, he must obtain a warrant from some portion of the public, which in Reuben's time was as purchaseable as a horse or a debenture; nor, are we yet grown so desperately virtuous as not to buy and sell the same desirable privilege occasionally.

The first person to put the senate into Mr. Medlicott's head was not his mother, to do her justice; it was Mr. Broad, the cutler, who, being a rapturous admirer of eloquence, as well as an arrant Protestant, had formed such an exalted opinion of Reuben's powers since his speech at the " tremendous demonstration," that he rambled about Chichester all day long, lamenting to everybody he met that such an extraordinary and highly gifted young man was not in the proper place for him, and when people either did not know, or pretended not to know what he meant, then Mr. Broad would twitch up the long skirts of his swallow-tailed blue coat, throw back his head and cry—" Why the House, sir, to be sure, where else? That's the only place for such an extraordinary and highly gifted young man. It's nonsense to talk, but we must get him into Parliament by hook or by crook. I'll subscribe a hundred pounds myself to purchase a borough, if it can be managed in no other way. It's a public duty, sir, and England expects every man to do his duty."

Mr. Broad was indeed so eloquent in extolling Mr. Medlicott's qualifications for the senate, that people used sometimes to laugh and advise him to go into the house himself.

Keep your hundred pounds for your own return, Broad,—if it's talking we want in Parliament, you are just the man that will do it as well as Mr. Medlicott, or any man alive," said Alderman Codd, a member of the corporation of Chichester.

" I never saw that much good came of talking in Parliament, or anywhere else," said Mr. Bliss, another burgess.

" Talking does very well," said a third, " when the man what talks is a squire with ten thousand a year, or when he is a lord or a marquis."

"When squires and lords do talk," replied Mr. Broad, "they talk for themselves and not for us; but how do they talk, sir? We had a specimen of their abilities the other day at our great meeting. Did anybody think the squires and lords worth listening to? Did anybody hear a syllable anybody said, or care sixpence to hear it, until my young friend, (if it is not too great a freedom to call him so,) until young Mr. Medlicott rose and showed us what talking was. I never knew what talking was until that day. As I hope to be saved, I thought my friend the alderman there the greatest orator living, ho, ho, ho; but I don't think so now, for which I hope he wont be very angry, ho, ho, ho."

The alderman was so far from being angry that he laughed as loud as Mr. Broad, modestly admitted the immense superiority of our hero as a public speaker, and promised to subscribe fifty pounds whenever a fair occasion should arise for procuring a seat for the eloquent Mr. Medlicott.

"We'll soon have a handsome fund, I make no doubt," said the zealous cutler; "England expects every man to do his duty."

The thing went not much further, however, at that time. Reuben himself affected to ridicule the proposition.

"You must not only get me into the house," he observed, somewhat ostentatiously, "but maintain me in it; for what am I, but the son of a poor country clergyman—with my bread to make, and nothing to depend on but my own exertions?"

It was full time, indeed, to think of that, and think seriously. He was in his five-and-twentieth year, with immense reputation for cleverness of all kinds; but beyond the speech, and the rupture with his grandfather, just when his friendship would have been most valuable, Reuben Medlicott had done absolutely nothing.

There still remained law and physic. To the latter profession Reuben had entertained, since he was a child, a singular aversion, resulting from its association in his mind with Mr. Pigwidgeon; a similar distaste to that which Sir Samuel Romilly early in life had for the law, occasioned by the intimacy of his family with a particularly disagreeable attorney. In fact, if Romilly had not conquered that juvenile repugnance, he would have lived and died a poor goldsmith like his father, instead of becoming one of the foremost men of his age and country.

Few of Reuben's friends harboured a doubt of his brilliant success in whichever of the two professions he should select; but the most ambitious of them advocated the law, as leading to the highest distinctions, both political and social, besides being the natural theatre for the talents of which he had lately given such extraordinary and decided proofs. Mr. Broad, who thought the bar a very good plan as a subsidiary to the senate, declared, from his experience in the jury-box, that no jury could possibly resist the appeals of such an orator as Master Reuben.

"Jurors are only men, sir: I have sat upon juries for five-and-twenty years, and I know what juries are made of. He would twist them round his finger, sir, as easy as his watch-chain; make them believe anything he pleased, or nothing at all, if he liked it. I promise him verdicts as plenty as blackberries, at least in this city and county. What juryman, sir, would listen to a prossy old judge, after hearing a spirit-stirring address from an eloquent and handsome young lawyer? If he chooses the law, sir, he will make a fortune as sure as he earns a guinea; in the mean time, he comes into the house, as a matter of course--there's where the country wants him; the next step makes him his Majesty's Attorney or Solicitor General; and from that it's only a hop, step, and jump, to the bench, sir, and the House of Lords."

Mrs. Medlicott took much the same sober view of the case; but the Vicar, and the more obstinate and wrong-headed of his son's friends, had much less confidence than Mr. Broad both in Reuben's oratorical talents and the susceptibilities of Sussex juries. These considerations, with the obvious pecuniary ones, led them to favour medicine; and thus his friends were divided into two parties, with a little detachment of waverers, as usual, including Mrs. Mountjoy and Mrs. Wyndham, whose ambition sometimes inclined them to side with his mother in behalf of the law; but at other times, when they recollected Reuben's agreeable person, and sweet and engaging manners, and imagined him stepping out of a handsome chariot, in full-dress suit of black, to visit a duchess, as the celebrated Doctor Medlicott, they felt that this was a proud career also, and were very much disposed to concur with the Vicar.

Physic, however, would not have suited Mr. Medlicott. The medical profession is a grave and silent one—too saturnine for men of mercurial gifts, more is done by wise looks than by fine speeches; the physician, in short, has many more opportunities of seeing the tongues of others, than of exercising and displaying his own.

How the balance of argument really inclined it is of little use to inquire: it probably was against the law, since that was the course which Mrs. Medlicott approved, and upon which her son ultimately decided. And now, once more, his friends vied with one another to send him on his course with a fair wind in his sails, and a handsome outfit to trade on. Mrs. Mountjoy insisted on paying the rent of his chambers in King's Bench Walk, Mr. Cox presented him with a hundred pounds for the foundation of a library, and Mr. Broad, not to be behind others, travelled up to London expressly, and bought him a set of massive book-cases of richly-carved oak, which had to be cut down considerably to make them suit the chambers, and even then they were not to be got in, except by a machinery of ropes and pulleys, through the windows.

His usual fortune attended him to the Temple. His fame had gone before him like a morning star, and soon he gathered about him another little circle of worshippers, who, captivated by his specious and showy talents, granted him the honours of a triumph on credit, without giving him the trouble of fighting any battle, or winning any victory. Throughout his life it was his fortune to be thought capable of achieving anything, while, in fact, he was achieving nothing but that unsolid praise which is so easily silenced by the simple question, "What has he done?" He was certainly much injured by injudicious friends, but when he had a man of experience and sound judgment to consult, he seldom profited by his advice, when to follow it required a steady course of discipline or distasteful labour. There was something in Mr. Medlicott's nature that was always in revolt against the practical. He had always some views of his own, which wore an imposing and philosophical aspect, while leading to conclusions utterly irreconcileable with common sense. But perhaps his greatest fault of all, was, that he invariably soared too high, when, by attempting a less ambitious flight, he might have risen higher, and sustained himself longer on the wing.

The men who knew him best predicted his failure at his new profession from the beginning; some expressed their conviction that he would never be called to the bar. The same ample, imposing, *chiaroscuro* discourse, which made fools gape, and think him a prodigy of parts, was the very thing that made his judicious friends despair of him. As to Winning, nothing terrified him so much as Reuben's " broad views," for which shallow people were continually extolling him, until at length he thought himself called on to support a character for " broad views," and take a " broad view" of every question presented to him. He consulted Winning as to the particular line he should take in his legal studies. "I have given him," said Winning, afterwards, "the best advice in my power, and now I leave him—to neglect it, as I am certain he will do."

There was something in the mind of our "coming man" more French than English in its character. He had the Frenchman's national passion for abstract ideas, that passion, which (as Sir James Stephen has truly remarked) animates not the books of the French only, but their discourses in the senate, their speeches at the bar, their conversations in their clubs and salons. Reuben had acquired the habit of making abstractions as other men do the habit of rhyming or joking. He could be transcendental, at a moment's notice, upon anything, or upon nothing at all. His mind, like a distempered stomach, rejected everything solid and substantial. Facts would never lie on it for a moment. It lived upon intellectual trifle and whip't cream, upon half-meanings and no-meanings, with the appetite of a chameleon for air, or the devotion of the comic Socrates to the clouds. In short it was a petticoated mind, floating in muslins, swimming in gauzes, and fluttering with gay ribbons, an admirable mind to bustle and rustle through life with, if life were a conversazione, or the world a mere Debating Society.

CHAPTER II.

MR. MEDLICOTT IS CALLED TO THE BAR.

IN one respect, however, Mr. Medlicott did not fulfil the predictions of those who best knew him, for he was called to the bar in due season, after three years spent in many pursuits very loosely connected with the law, and some far enough removed from it. There was a place at the profession for him, in which, with very little knowledge, his peculiar talents might have been brought into play with effect and profit.

Those only who understand the secrets of the craft are able to form an idea with how small a pittance of legal learning the very highest honours of the bar are attainable, and frequently attained by men of ordinary acuteness, shrewd enough to hide their ignorance, and confident enough to make the best use of the little information they possess. At Nisi Prius especially, with plenty of tongue for the jury, and a few points of aw for the court, or rather to impose on the attorneys, some men manage to turn their brass into gold rapidly. The "progress of a lawyer" would be admirable matter for a satiric poem. A very useful essay, also, might be written upon the various causes both of success and failure in the profession, upon its high-ways and byeways, its blanks and its prizes, the marvellous fortunes of a few, and the rocks that many split on. As to Mr. Medlicott, he split not upon one rock, but on several—he went to pieces on a reef.

In the first place he took one of his excessively broad views, and aimed at being a constitutional lawyer, and a jurist forsooth. He filled his superb book-cases with the State Trials and Rhymer's Fœdera, with Montesquieu and Bentham, Vattel and Grotius. He had heard of the study of the English law narrowing the mind, and being determined that his own at least should not be narrowed by it, he paid considerable attention to the law of nations, and the Code Napoléon. Nor was he content with thus expanding his faculties in the privacy of his chambers; he made all his acquaintance fully aware of the range of his researches; the Pandects were his table-talk; he harangued upon the *casus belli*, until he got the nickname of Puffendorf; and just about the time that he bought his wig and formally presented himself to the public as a practising barrister, he not only published a big pamphlet on Codification, but talked at large wherever he went of a design of editing Vattel.

Should the reader, unacquainted with such matters, be at a loss to understand the propriety of these studies, undertakings, and proceedings, considering Mr. Medlicott's declared professional views, it will assist his perceptions to imagine the Duke of Wellington in the peninsular war devoting himself to the geology of Spain, or Professor Airy, during a transit of Venus, engrossed with the last new novel.

The pamphlet on Codification, however, brought its author into connexion with a law-bookseller, named Trevor, who was mightily taken with Mr. Medlicott, and did all in his power to serve him.

Mr. Trevor had a box at Hampstead, where Reuben soon became a regular guest on Sundays, when there was always a social little audience, partly literary, partly legal, assembled round a comfortable dinner to listen to his dissertations on the "casus belli." Between two of the *habitués* of this house, a proctor named

Fox, and an attorney of the name of Reynard, Mr. Medlicott was somewhat in the position of Lucian in his dream, with art and literature pulling him in opposite directions. The proctor wanted to entice him into the Arches Court, and urged him to take a doctor's degree ; the attorney was equally bent upon "marking him for his own," and securing him exclusively for Nisi Prius.

Sometimes Mr. Fox would get him all to himself, and almost persuade him to enter the lists with Lushington ; again the attorney would have the advantage, in the other's absence, and Reuben would persevere in his design of disputing the palm with Scarlett. Mr. Reynard, however, it was observable (being a man of more prudence than sincerity), though he put down some thousands as a moderate calculation of Mr. Medlicott's probable income in a few years, allowed term after term to pass, without sending him a single guinea from his own office.

In one respect, it must be admitted, Mr. Medlicott's acquaintance with Mr. Trevor was a humiliating one. Instead of bringing him celebrity, it brought him nothing but sordid money. Mr. Trevor not only dissuaded him from his edition of Vattel, which would have been a pure addition to his fame, but he threw some humdrum business in his way, which was not merely profitable, but calculated to advance him in the vulgar and plodding track of the profession. The first job put a hundred guineas in his purse, the second and third still larger sums ; between the three he netted upwards of five hundred pounds, which Mr. Trevor thought a very good thing for a briefless barrister, particularly as the employment was of that kind which tended to attract briefs, instead of repelling them.

But Mr. Medlicott himself was inexpressibly disgusted at such success. Doing well, indeed, but in what a paltry and obscure way ! No applause, no distinction—a name like his on the title-page of a book of practice ; he felt his mind growing narrow already ; his five hundred gave him no satisfaction ; it weighed down his spirits while it weighed down his pockets ; in fine, he magnanimously determined (encouraged most probably in his noble resolution, not only by his mother's letters, but by his aunt's remittances) that he would go through no more of such base, servile drudgery, for any pecuniary consideration. The earnestness of this declaration was soon tested. Trevor made another offer, and still more favourable than the preceding ones. Mr. Medlicott declined it, and Trevor never troubled him again with propositions of the kind. Dining the same day at the Temple, Mr. Medlicott vaingloriously related his refusal to work any more for the law-booksellers; several of his friends applauded him loudly, some shook their heads dubiously, and one plain-spoken man, more good-humouredly than politely, told him he was a fool. The next morning, one of the friends who had been foremost in commending him for scorning to be a bookseller's hack, called on him in his chambers, and begged an introduction to Mr. Trevor, confessing that he was a poor fellow, under the necessity of putting his pride in his pocket, and prepared to do so, if the publisher would employ him, even for a much smaller sum than had been offered Medlicott. Reuben was now in the proud position of a patron of industry, and very frankly and generously did he perform the duties of that office, flattering himself with the notion that he was not less industrious, but only more ambitious, than the honest poor fellow who stepped into his shoes.

In the same elevated frame of mind, he disdained to cultivate the attorneys. Mr. Trevor, who continued to wish him well, gave him more than one hint to take his friend Reynard down to Greenwich in the white-bait season, but Mr. Medlicott not only neglected the suggestion, but actually went out of his way to entertain the Proctor, which was the most superfluous hospitality in the world.

He made, however, some useful acquaintances, without courting them: he met a few attorneys here and there, in the chambers of his friends, or up and down the world, and stole the hearts of one or two of them, without the least deliberate intention of committing such petty larceny. Thus the guineas did, in process of time, begin to flow in—not in an actual Pactolus, certainly, but in a pretty little sparkling streamlet, very agreeable to contemplate, and wonderfully interesting for a season even to the young lawyer himself, though Mammon had never a much less devoted servant.

When the rumour that he was making money crept into the provinces, and got as far as Chichester, it made a prodigious sensation among his relatives and friends there, gratified even his mother (wondrous to tell), but pleased nobody more than Mr. Broad, who multiplied every guinea in his imagination by ten, and even by larger multipliers, until he began already to fancy Reuben very near the top of the ladder, and a dangerous rival to the chiefs of the bar.

Mr. Medlicott's fee-book showed that he received fifty guineas in his first year of practice, nearly twice that amount in the second, and the third year he realised a sum which, with some money that remained over from his transactions with Trevor, amounted to about a thousand pounds, which, acting on the advice of Mr. Trevor, he invested in certain Brazilian mines, considered at that time an eligible speculation.

This was palpable success, and the more remarkable as the success of a man who seemed to be prospering in spite of himself; for he considered the business which came to his share as a junior rather derogatory to him than otherwise—spoke of it with supreme contempt, and went through it with an air of superciliousness, as if he scorned to be employed except in weighty causes. A little avarice mixed with Reuben's ambition would have made a better working metal of it; but he cared much too little for money, particularly for money obscurely earned in King's Bench Walk, without reputation, and without even newspaper notoriety. The fastidiousness with which he accepted business was enough of itself to prevent its rapid accumulation. The attorneys were not over-anxious to employ a man who was ostentatiously indifferent whether he was employed or not; and he that disdains his work, or takes it in hand squeamishly or languidly, is not likely to execute it either with care or punctuality. Reuben lost one attorney by not keeping time; another by not keeping to his instructions; a third by not keeping to himself the contempt he entertained for the formalities and prolixities of the profession. The most perverse of all his complaints was his objection to prolixity, which he was only averse to when it was in the way of his vocation, and tended to put money in his purse.

CHAPTER III.

A RIVAL ORATOR.

But his forensic career was distinguished by something more whimsical still than even his perverse dislike for that prolixity which was in his day as much the soul of law, as brevity has been said to be the soul of wit. There was one short, very short, period of Mr. Medlicott's life, in which (extraordinary to relate) he conceived an actual aversion to the exercises of that faculty which, in him, predominated over all other endowments ;—a parenthesis of his existence when a spirit of silence obtained temporary mastery over him, which, if it had kept its ground, might have degraded him into a common-place sensible man, and a mere useful working member of society. Most whimsically did it happen that this quarrel with his tongue, as it were, occurred while he was at the bar, which is not usually the profession that leads men to talk less than they are disposed to talk by nature. A circumstance, however, happened, which for a time thoroughly disgusted Reuben with rhetorical exhibitions. He had attended Professor Chatterton's course of lectures on pulpit oratory, and with such satisfactory results, as he believed, that he now resolved to give himself the benefit of that gentleman's instructions to lawyers, and for that purpose returned to the school of eloquence in Leicester Square, and enrolled himself again among its pupils. Having attended the public course, and still fancying himself not quite perfect in some points of importance in addressing juries, Mr. Medlicott continued to avail himself privately of the Professor's services for some time longer. One day, arriving before his appointed hour, he was under the necessity of waiting in an anteroom, while Mr. Chatterton was concluding a lesson which he was giving to another pupil in the adjoining apartment. The declamation was loud enough to be distinctly heard through walls and doors twice as thick as those which separated the chambers. Not many moments elapsed before Reuben's ear caught the name of Coriolanus. He smiled to recollect his own juvenile effort on that theme, and listened with some curiosity to the harangue on the same subject which the unseen orator was vociferating with most stentorian lungs, occasionally interrupted by the Professor's remarks and repetitions. Soon a sublime figure of rhetoric occurred, which was decidedly "his own thunder." Presently he recognised a second gem filched from his casket. Then a third, his own property, if he had a right to anything. Before he had been listening for five minutes, he discovered that it was actually his own old speech, image for image, and word for word, which was shaking the house to its foundations. This diverted, surprised, and puzzled him extremely. Who could the orator be, and how could anybody have got possession of the speech? Reuben knew the very press in his mother's room at Underwood, and the very shelf, where the only existing copy of it was deposited, among many other such literary treasures. While still he wondered, the storm of elocution suddenly ceased, the lecture was over, and the thunderer having retired by the usual private passage, Professor Chatterton entered the room where Reuben was waiting to take his turn.

Reuben congratulated him upon the proficiency of his pupil who had just departed.

"Ah, that is a prodigy," said the professor. "Excepting yourself, sir, he promises to do me more credit than any gentleman I ever had the honour of instructing."

"Is he intended for the church, or the bar?" asked M. Medlicott.

"Neither," said Chatterton; "he is cultivating eloquence purely for its own sake. He possesses the talent, and he has the laudable ambition to improve it. Indeed, he is in a profession where it cannot be of much practical use to him,—he is a doctor."

"I suppose his name is a secret—I wouldn't ask you to reveal it for the world."

"Well," quoth the Professor, "as a general rule, I am as secret as the Inquisition, but in this case I feel myself free, especially with you,—it's a droll name enough—Doctor Pigwidgeon."

So diametrically opposed to one another were the ideas of Pigwidgeon and oratory, that Reuben would never have thought of him, of all the doctors in England, although it was now so easy to understand how he had come by the speech on Coriolanus. A few days later he met the Professor in the street, and was invited to go with him in the evening to attend a meeting of the Cicero Club, of which the eloquent doctor was a member, and where upon that night he was expected to make a grand display of his powers, upon one of the exciting questions of the hour. Reuben's curiosity induced him to consent, provided he could maintain a strict incognito, which Chatterton satisfied him would be easily managed, the arrangements of the place being favourable to it. Accordingly, enveloped in an ample cloak, and with his hat pulled sufficiently down over his eyes, Reuben accompanied Mr. Chatterton to the Cicero at the proper hour, and further to elude observation, took his seat on the bench behind the Professor, in the gallery set apart for strangers. Long before Doctor Pigwidgeon spoke, it was obvious that he was the orator *par excellence* of the society. He looked the leader, every inch; and swaggered about the room, like O'Connell at the Corn Exchange, or Henry Hunt in Covent Garden. There was bluster in his face, even when he was not speaking; he laughed, cheered, coughed, and even listened like a bully. Proud was the Professor to see with his own eyes how great his pupil was among the Ciceronians; but when he rose to speak, he astonished Reuben himself by his prodigious command of words, and the ceaseless torrent with which he poured them forth. The abundance was so overwhelming, that several minutes elapsed before the severest auditor could have discovered the almost total absence of all rational drift in the discourse. There was in Pigwidgeon's oratory none of that false show of argument, none of those pretty deceptive half-meanings, none of that radiant mist of language (in itself elegant and pleasing to both the ear and the fancy), which made Mr. Medlicott's eloquence pass current even with many persons of superior education. The Doctor was literally "vox et preterea nihil;" there was the mist without the least sparkle in it; the merest bray that was ever mistaken for rhetoric, for in fact (as Reuben well knew) the fellow had neither common sense, knowledge, or imagination, notwithstanding all that had been done for his mental development. Yet, without one of these qualities, he made the foremost figure in his club; the close of every period, no matter how barren of all appreciable signification, was received with the most painful explosions of applause, to such a degree that Tully himself could not possibly have been more admired, if indeed the true orator could have escaped being coughed down by the audience that extolled Doctor Pigwidgeon. All this disgusted Reuben beyond conception; particularly when he observed how carefully the Doctor availed himself of the Professor's instructions, and with what delight and triumph that great master of elocution witnessed the successful application of his precepts to practice. So elated was Chatterton, that at the end of the speech he attracted the Doctor's notice by the extravagance of his complimentary demonstrations. In a moment the pupil was in the Professor's arms; and the reader must only imagine Demosthenes, after one of his mightiest victories, in the embraces of Isæus, or Isocrates, whichever had the honour of instructing him, that point being undecided. For Reuben now to escape recognition was impossible, despite of all his precautions. Chatterton was as much delighted as surprised to find that the two pupils he was most proud of were old acquaintances and friends, for indeed the Doctor could not have testified more rapture at meeting Reuben, had they been brothers. A difficult thing it was to bestow the commendation upon that speech which the young doctor expected, and the young lawyer could not decently withhold. Reuben did his best under the circumstances, but it was done so hesitatingly, and with such manifest repugnance, as naturally enough to suggest the idea that he grudged Pigwidgeon the laurels with which he was compelled to wreath his brow, or, in other words, that the wonderful effort he had witnessed had excited in his breast the passion of envy. Whether Chatterton suspected this, or not, he thought of nothing now but closing the night with a festivity worthy of its commencement, and for this purpose he invited his pupils to a supper at a celebrated tavern in the neighbourhood. Pigwidgeon embraced the offer as warmly as he had embraced Reuben, but to the taste of the latter, the notion of supping with the Doctor was even more revolting than the necessity of complimenting his rhetoric; so, declining the invitation with an abruptness and haughtiness of manner well calculated to offend both Chatterton and Pigwidgeon, he folded himself again in his mantle, and, with an ill-timed display of dignity, stalked out of the gallery.

The Cicero club was just the hospital to cure the worst case of the *cacoethes loquendi* that ever existed, on the principle which Lycurgus adopted when he made the Helots tipsy to instil the love of sobriety into the youth of Sparta; and the warning might possibly have been effective, if Mr. Medlicott's vanity had permitted him to weigh himself in the same scale with Pigwidgeon even for a moment; so as to perceive what was really in common between them, namely, the enormous preponderance of sound over sense in the eloquence of both. As it was, however, the gift of speech fell for some time in Reuben's estimation, in consequence of what has been related; and while this fit was on him, nobody inveighed so copiously as he did in private society upon the misrule of the tongue, often talking against talking until nobody was left to talk to at the table.

However, there can be no doubt that with respect to Dr. Pigwidgeon, Mr. Medlicott had not acted handsomely, or with the magnanimity which became his pretensions to superior abilities. Had the Doctor been a more complete and accomplished booby than nature and art had combined to make him, Reuben ought not to have objected to meet him at supper, particularly as he was his townsman, and owed his intellectual development, such as it was, to the identical source of his own genius. Are we never to eat oysters and broiled kidneys save with men of our own intellectual stature or calibre, measured, too, by the private rule which each of us carries in his pocket? A pleasant society it would be to live in, if it were to be torn to pieces with intellectual distinctions, as well as with political and religious ones; if knowledge and ignorance were to refuse to associate, and talent and dulness were not to tolerate one another, even over a flask of wine. Dunce, however, as Dr. Pigwidgeon was, he was a star in his own sphere, and not one of the third magnitude. He told the Professor his simple story that night, over the broiled kidneys. From the day that he read Reuben's speech on Coriolanus aloud from the fork of the pear-tree in the garden of Underwood, an ambition to become an orator had possessed him; but for a considerable length of time, as Milton said of Cromwell, "he nursed his great spirit in silence," feeding it principally with the incessant study of Reuben's orations, which he borrowed from Mrs. Medlicott, and, to fasten them on his memory, copied out repeatedly, with the same ardour for self-improvement which led Demosthenes to pay the writings of Thucydides a similar honour. Then, although he had no natural defect of utterance, he commenced a course of pebbles on a solitary part of the beach; but he did not continue the system long, for, as he told Mr. Chatterton, the pebbles hurt his teeth, and rather impeded his pronunciation than assisted it.

"Perhaps," said the Professor, "the pebbles you tried were too large for your mouth."

"Possibly they were," said the Doctor; "but at all events they did not answer. I found more benefit from fancying the cabbages in our garden an audience, and addressing them as loud as I could shout!"

"Trees would have been better," said the Professor; "I always recommend trees, or if trees are not convenient, hollyhocks, or artichokes. However, you don't want that sort of thing now."

"No," said Pigwidgeon; "but let me tell you what I did next. I got my sisters, and cousins, and their school-fellows, a dozen of them or so, into a room at the top of the house—sometimes into a hay-loft, and I placed them all in a row, or in two rows; then I mounted a chair opposite to them, and went on just as you heard me to-night, only not so fluent, for I was only beginning, you know."

"Rome was not built in a day," said Chatterton.

"You may well say that," said the Doctor; "but it was a very good idea, I think, and I improved it afterwards by teaching them to cry 'hear,' and 'spoke, spoke;' sometimes they had cough.; and I often gave them full permission to try to put me down in every possible way, but they never were able to do it."

"Capital practice for the House," said the Professor.

"I used often to repeat the speech of young Norval," added the Doctor,—"'My name is Norval on the Grampian hills,' you know."

The Professor suggested the propriety of making a pause at the Norval, and told him the story of the actor in Dublin who adopted the Doctor's reading, whereupon a wag in the galleries called out, "And what the deuce is your name in Patrick Street?"

The Doctor laughed very long and loud, and after taking a note of the improved reading, said,

"I'll tell you a very odd thing,—my grandmother was an Irish woman, one of the Beamishes of Cork—if she wasn't a Beamish, she was a Murphy."

"You will be coming in for an Irish borough one of these days," said the master of rhetoric.

The Doctor heaved a profound sigh, pleaded guilty to a hankering after senatorial honours, and alluded pathetically to the closeness of a rich old father he had, which had always stood in the way of his advancement. But he was not without hopes, he added, that the old fellow might be induced to come down with a few thousands for a borough at the next general election, which he understood was not very far off.

Mr. Medlicott lost this and much more of the like curious discourse, by not accepting the Professor's invitation to supper. What followed would, of course, not have met his ear,—probably would not have passed at all.

The Professor asked Pigwidgeon what his private opinion of Reuben was, as he had known him so long, and was so intimate with him.

"Well, he is a deuced clever fellow, I won't deny," replied the Doctor. "though he is not such a prodigy as his family take him for; they think he is the greatest genius that this country ever produced; I am told they talk of him as 'the coming man,' whatever they mean by that."

"Always coming, but never comes," said the Professor, hitting off happily enough the contrast between Mr. Medlicott's promise and performance in every stage of his career.

"Don't you think him a coxcomb?" said the Doctor.

"A confounded coxcomb," said Chatterton.

The conversation ended in Pigwidgeon asking the Professor what he sincerely thought of Mr. Medlicott's style of eloquence.

"I'll tell you candidly," said Chatterton; "he is not fit to hold a candle to you, and if ever you are both in the House of Commons together, and pitted against one another, which is not an unlikely event in these stirring times, you will beat him to stock-fish, if you only mind my instructions."

CHAPTER IV.

MR. MEDLICOTT SYMPATHISES WITH THE POLES, AND IS NATURALLY LED FROM ONE SYMPATHY TO ANOTHER.

In consequence chiefly of the brief revolution in taste mentioned in the last chapter, Mr Medlicott was actually in some little danger at this period of being confounded with the common herd of working lawyers, to whom Chancery Lane is the world, and a bigger wig the summit of human ambition. A few friends stuck to him through thick and thin, and the horrors of professional success were almost beginning to stare him in the face, when he was opportunely seized with another of his paroxysms of genius, in the form of a violent sympathy with the cause of Poland.

We have been rather neglectful of Mr. Medlicott's social existence and experiences for some time back, hoping the reader would kindly presume that dinners and balls went on as usual, and that a respectable list of good houses in the proper streets and squares were ambitious of the honour of receiving the coming man, if not always successful in securing him as their guest. Let it not be supposed that he persisted obstinately in that hostility to the practice of dining, which had formerly distressed some of his best friends, particularly the convivial Mr. De Tabley. Mr. Medlicott resumed the knife and fork soon after he joined the bar, and not only frequented those tables where he was duly appreciated, but gave a dinner now and then in his own chambers, or invited a select party of agreeable listeners to Lovegrove's, or the Star and Garter. His chambers were furnished only too handsomely for a man of his means and standing. Mrs. Mountjoy had insisted on transferring to them all the articles of luxury which she had accumulated for his use in her lodgings in Burlington Gardens, the cosy chairs, the comfortable sofas, and even the spacious looking-glass in which Goliath of Gath might have surveyed himself from top to toe, had his giantship lived in the age of mirrors, or had mirrors existed in the days of giants. The Barsacs had frowned on him, ever since his grandfather did so, but this littleness of theirs Reuben was so far from stooping to resent, that meeting the consequential merchant one day in Fleet Street, he carelessly extended him a finger, and asked him to dine the following day, to meet Lord Appleby. Barsac would have bristled like a porcupine at such an informal invitation, prrticularly from such a quarter, if the name of the peer had not effectually stifled every unchristian feeling within him. To meet Lord Appleby, however, was a most agreeable prospect, and having had that privilege, it was incumbent on him to return Mr. Medlicott's dinner, which he did shortly after. Mr. Medlicott went to Portland Place, and met a distinguished company, among whom was Lord Maudlin, a nobleman, conspicuous at that time (as more eminent nobleman have been since) for his zeal in behalf of the Poles, and patron of a society for sympathising with that suffering nation. Barsac had invited the secretary of the society on the same day, as a delicate compliment, no doubt, to my Lord Maudlin; and the secretary (a gentleman with a black moustache, and a name ending with "inski"), having had the good fortune to be placed beside Mr. Medlicott at dinner, an acquaintanceship commenced between them, which grew first into intimacy, and afterwards ripened into sympathy before long. Mr. Barsac himself sympathised with the Poles, that is to say, he invited the secretary to dinner, whenever Lord Maudlin honoured him; but the merchant was not so devoted to Poland as to sacrifice to her cause either his time or much of his money. Mr. Medlicott was not long without setting him an example of sympathising with spirit. He introduced the secretary to many of his friends, and among others to Trevor, the bookseller, who enlisted him occasionally for his Sunday parties at Hampstead. Mr. Medlicott walked into town, one fine evening, with the representative of Poland, and discoursed himself into a fever upon her history, and her wrongs. The Pole, a man of business and a capital secretary, determined to strike while the iron was hot, as the saying is; so, pulling out of his pocket a list of recent subscriptions, he excited Reuben's indignation by showing him the names of two such wealthy men as Mr. Barsac and Mr. Leadenhall, who were the paltry contributors of no more than a few guineas each. Mr. Medlicott, with one of Professor Chatterton's electric starts, seized the paper, and by the light of a lamp at the corner of Tottenham Court Road, where it meets the New Road, he wrote his name down for fifty pounds; and before he reached Holborn he suffered himself, after some little coy resistance, to be persuaded to move a resolution at the next public meeting, which was very soon to be held.

Fifty pounds was a munificent subscription. It deserved a conspicuous announcement, and it received it. The newspapers complimented Mr. Medlicott upon his well-timed liberality, and mentioned him among the noblemen and gentlemen who had promised to honour with their presence, and adorn with their eloquence, the approaching meeting at the Freemasons' Tavern.

A general impression prevailed in the neighbourhood of Chichester, particularly in the parish of Underwood, as soon as these announcements arrived there, that Mr. Medlicott was about to compel Russia and Austria to disgorge their several shares of the plunder of Poland, and that nothing short of the restoration of that country to a glorious place among the independent states of Europe would be the result of the philippic that was now in preparation. Mr. Broad resolved to go up to town to hear it, and meanwhile ran about the streets in just such a state of excitement as you may fancy a cutler of Athens, exhibiting on the eve of an oration of Demosthenes, to be followed by instant war with Macedon.

"He will make the despots of the continent look about them, sir; he will make the tyrants tremble."

"Much the despots of the continent will trouble themselves about a speech at the Freemasons' Tavern, if it was made by Brougham himself," said the Alderman.

"I'm not of your way of thinking, Alderman Codd," said the cutler; "though making swords is my business, and though it will be a bad day for me when swords go out of fashion, I have a higher opinion of eloquence, sir, than of the best sword that ever was manufactured. The tryants hate eloquence, sir, as a certain personage hates holy-water. Did you ever hear of an orator at St. Petersburg, or in the Austrian dominions?—answer me that, Alderman Codd."

"Well, then, I never did, to be candid with you," said the Alderman.

"And now, Alderman, let me crave your subscription to the cause of Poland, for I want to have something handsome to hand in at the meeting to do credit to our city and our distinguished townsman."

The Alderman shook his head, laughed, and buttoned up his pockets.

"Come, Alderman, you won't have it said, I hope," said Mr. Broad, insinuatingly, "that you are in the Russian interest; you would not like people to say that?"

"I should not like that," said Alderman Codd, and ended by handing the cutler a couple of guineas, which was all he could afford the Polish cause without doing his family injustice.

Matthew Cox, who was always generous when the interests of freedom or of humanity were to be promoted, subscribed handsomely, Mr. Oldport and Mrs. Winning did so likewise; so that Mr. Broad had a very respectable tribute to bring up with him from Chichester, which had never before distinguished itself in behalf of Poland. Even Mr. Pigwidgeon put his name down for a guinea, but he never paid it—an economical way of sympathising practised by many as well as Mr. Pigwidgeon.

Meanwhile, Reuben's London friends were equally on the *qui vive*. Mr. Trevor and his family were in the highest state of excitement; so were the Proctor, the Attorney—in short, everybody who either knew Mr. Medlicott, or had heard the whistling of his name. The Polish Secretary gave a breakfast in Golden Square on the morning of this second great demonstration. Mr. Medlicott was to have been present, but on the previous evening he was surprised, and to a certain extent embarrassed and disconcerted, by the arrival of a large party from Chichester, consisting of his mother and the two Quakeresses, under the escort of Mr. Broad. The Vicar was strongly against this expedition, and still more displeased at the absurd munificence of his son. He wanted to know what Reuben had to do with the Poles. Mrs. Medlicott said he might as well ask what he had to do with the Protestants. The Vicar shrugged his shoulders, and wished, with considerable bitterness, Reuben would let both Poles and Protestants alone, and attend to his profession.

Mr. Broad conducted his little band of enthusiasts to the old Black Lion, in Whitefriars, the inn which he patronised whenever he travelled to town, and where everything, he said, was always tidy, and the landlady did her best to make her guests snug and comfortable. It may have been so; but the Black Lion was nevertheless an odd house to bring Mrs. Medlicott to—a quaint old curiosity of a place, with one of the last of the wooden galleries running round the yard, and altogether as queer as Mr. Broad himself.

Reuben gently reproached his mother for putting herself to the trouble of such a journey for such an object, and under such a singular convoy as the cutler. And so old a woman as Hannah Hopkins, too,—to think of her incurring such fatigue, and such expense, merely to hear him " offer a few remarks at a public meeting "—for so Mr. Medlicott always modestly expressed himself, when he was about to make some particularly elaborate oratorical display. His mother had nothing to say in her own defence, except that she would not have missed the opportunity for all the world, as Mr. Broad was so good as to offer to take care of her. With respect to the Quakeresses, Mr. Cox, as usual, was to pay their little expenses. It appeared that their ardour for the expedition had been uncontrollable; the idea of it had even cured old Hannah of a fit of the rheumatism. It was more, however, as a great philanthropist she idolised Reuben than for his eloquence; Mary Hopkins, on the contrary, though philanthropic also, was more anxious about the oratory than about the cause. It was to gratify her, chiefly, that Mr. Cox had offered to take upon himself the cost of the journey.

"That poor girl's passion for eloquence, my dear," said Mrs. Medlicott, "is something very extraordinary."

She little dreamed that the fair Mary's breast was, and had for some time been, the seat of another passion, also; one that had possessed her ever since the meeting at Chichester, and might have been traced back to the tour in Wales; nay, probably to the still earlier days when she and Reuben were schoolfellows and playmates. But nobody could have helped remarking that a great change had taken place in Mary Hopkins. She was neither so fat as she had been formerly, nor so merry either. The girlish laughter for which she had been noted wherever she went, had subsided into a quieter expression of delight. But if she was neither so gay nor so plump, she atoned for it by being decidedly handsomer; a more delicate intellectual charm had taken the place of her former mere rustic attractions; she seemed also to have gained something in stature by the decreased roundness of her person. In short, when she came from her room to receive Reuben, she scarcely appeared to be his old friend Mary Hopkins at all; he was greatly struck by the improved style of her beauty, but still more by the grave, thoughtful, reserved manner, with even something of melancholy in it, which had usurped the place of her former exuberant spirits. Reuben ascribed the change altogether to the development of her excellent faculties, the general cultivation of her mind, and especially to her passion for eloquence. He thought, upon the whole, that she was altered in every respect to her advantage, except, perhaps, in the point of reserve; her manner towards him was not wanting in affection and even tenderness, but it was not altogether as sisterly as formerly—that he could not help perceiving and feeling.

Reuben entertained them all at breakfast the following day, and knowing what a tenderness the Quakeresses had for flowers, he took care to be provided with several of the finest bouquets Covent Garden could produce, which would delight them the more as they little dreamed of seeing such things in the heart of London. That morning, as he made his toilette with unusual care (not forgetting a single one of Madame Chatterton's precepts), a withered bunch of what had once been flowers tumbled out of one of his drawers. It was the faded relic of the bouquet which he had worn at the Chichester meeting, and which Mary's tremulous fingers had fixed in his coat. He wondered what chance had preserved it, but felt glad, he scarcely knew why, that it had escaped destruction, to form a sort of poetical link between his first and his second display in public.

As things repeat themselves in this world, there would have been nothing very surprising in the fair quakeress again offering to perform the same graceful little ceremony upon the present occasion; but Mr. Medlicott would have gone without a rose in his breast, or been reduced to stick one there himself, if it had not been for Mr. Broad, who, with twenty diverting bows and scrapes, declined the bouquet that was offered him, adding, that it would look infinitely better in Mr. Reuben's own button-hole, particularly if a fair young maiden could be found to place it there. Thus appealed to, Mary Hopkins could not but take the flowers, and decorate the orator with them, though in doing so her cheek grew damask as the roses themselves, and she pricked her finger with a pin which she employed to fix them. But nobody noticed such minute things, while the thunder was preparing to burst on the head of the Czar.

Having given an account of one public demonstration, the details of another would be as wearisome as was the actual thing itself to the must judicious of the persons present. Sub.titute town for country, and numbers of meagre and moustached foreigners, with their vociferous sympathisers, for the black-coats, top-boots, and smock-frocks, which composed the meeting in the country—put Poland for Protestantism, partition for Popery, and fraternity and sympathy for loyalty and orthodoxy—and the scene in the country town was only acted over again on the London boards. Mr. Medlicott was again the great gun of the day, but a much greater gun than at the Protestant meeting, chiefly in consequence of his donation, which led many people to fancy that he was a gentleman of ample fortune, as well as splendid abilities, a notion that did not abate the respect of the assembly for him a jot, or the raptures with which he was received.

Mr. Broad made himself almost as conspicuous as if he had been on the platform. He potently believed that the fortunes of Poland, nay, of Russia itself, were involved in the issue of the meeting, and, of course, that his "illustrious townsman," as he called him, was arbitrating that day the fate of empires. Mrs. Medlicott herself was several times obliged to restrain his enthusiasm, or it would have actually disturbed the proceedings.

"Let the Czar answer that, if he can!" he cried, at the end of one passage, in which Reuben had put the European despots in a logical difficulty. Mrs. Medlicott laid her hand on his arm to keep him quiet. Then there was a superb flight, in which the orator stated a long list of grievances and oppressions, concluding by demanding "whether all this was to be borne?" Mr. Broad jumped up on the form, waved his hat, and shouted aloud that he, for one, was determined not to bear it. The Chairman mildly but firmly requested silence. Mr. Broad sat down, but he was not long seated before he was on his legs again, cheering uproariously a sublime image of unhappy Poland, figured by a giant prostrate and chained, with the Russian and Austrian eagles preying on his vitals. However, that sublime image set everybody else mad also, so that Mr. Broad was not very remarkable; but he soon misbehaved himself again, for Mr. Medlicott, after criticising with some severity the course taken by the friends of Poland in Parliament, went on to inform his audience what course he would take himself, "if he were in the House of Commons," —"And you ought to be there, and we'll send you there!" screamed the little cutler, suddenly springing on his seat again, and drawing the eyes of the whole assemblage upon him.

"I must entreat that zealous gentleman to resume his seat

and preserve silence," said the Chairman, again obliged to interfere, which he did with a smile, provoked by the oddity of Mr. Broad's appearance, which was doubly comical when he was in a state of excitement.

"Now do, Mr. Broad," added Mrs. Medlicott, imploringly, "and we shall hear Reuben the better."

That last argument prevailed, and Mr. Broad conducted himself pretty well until the conclusion of the speech (which was, of course, the shriek of Freedom at the fall of Kosciusko), when, there being no longer any rule of propriety to restrain him, he went through such an amount of physical exertion, cheering, waving his hat, beating and thumping the seats, the floor, and everything within his reach, that he had scarcely strength left to hand in his subscriptions, and pronounce the names of the little band of sympathisers of whom he was the representative and envoy.

"Now," said Mr. Broad, when the meeting was over, and Reuben had been embraced and congratulated by all his relations and friends, until he was almost drunk with applause,—"Mr. Medlicott has entertained us at the Freemasons' Tavern, and entertained us royally; the least we can do, I think, is to entertain him in our own humble way at the Black Lion, where I have ordered an early supper; and the more of his friends he brings with him, the more we shall feel honoured and obliged."

The orator not only accepted the invitation for himself, but for Mr. Trevor, the Secretary of the Polish Association, and his professional friends, the Attorney and Proctor, who wrangled the whole of the way to the Black Lion on the question, whether Mr. Medlicott's eloquence was more suitable to the King's Bench or to Doctor's Commons. The Proctor said it stood to reason that the speaker who could give the Czar such a tremendous dressing, and draw so affecting a picture of an oppressed country, was just the man to show up a tyrannical husband in the proper colours, and contrast his odious conduct with that of his beautiful and ill-used wife. The Attorney argued that there were abundant opportunities in the Courts of Law for abusing husbands and extolling wives, or *vice versâ;* but what he most relied on was, that such eloquence as they had just heard was much too good to be thrown away upon any mere judge—it deserved both judge and jury; and as it was one of the gross defects of the Ecclesiastical Courts to want juries, he thought the reason was hollow upon his side of the question. This dispute might have lasted longer, if Mr. Trevor had not raised another, by venturing an opinion that Mr. Medlicott was too universal a genius to prosecute any branch of his profession very steadily.

"I doubt, very much," said Trevor, "if that style of speaking is the thing for the bar at all. It might do very well ———"

"In the House," interrupted the Proctor.

"In the pulpit," said the Attorney.

"What do you know about the pulpit?" said the Proctor.

"As much as you do about the House," said the Attorney.

The question was not settled until they reached the Black Lion, when Mr. Broad's hearty entertainment brought it to an abrupt and agreeable termination. The old inn had not been so jovial for many a day. Everybody was in the humour of applauding and sympathising with everything: the supper was the best that was spread on a table; the Poles the greatest nation that ever existed in the world; the speech transcending every effort in ancient or modern times. Mr. Medlicott was literally smothered with praises and flatteries, for an injudicious display that virtually ended his career at the bar, and threw him again adrift upon the world.

There was no louder panegyrist of his eloquence than Mr. Reynard, the Attorney; but he sent the orator no brief the next day; and one or two other solicitors, who had already given him business, ceased to do so, after his demonstration in behalf of the Poles.

CHAPTER V.

HOW MR. MEDLICOTT FELL AMONG THE QUAKERS.

ORDINARY men are wont to marry, when they have succeeded in their professions; but Mr. Medlicott, being an extraordinary man, married just at the moment when his failure began to be a subject of general remark. We must observe, however, that his failure at the bar was so far from shaking either the faith of his sanguine friends, or his own confidence in his powers, that it confirmed both one and the other, wonderfully; some imputed the result to the gross stupidity of the public; others were of opinion that the defeats of genius in inferior employments were to be regarded in the light of triumphs; they said, in short (and Mr.

Medlicott himself, probably, supplied them with the image), that he failed with the distaff, only because his hands were made to wield the club.

Still, it was an odd time to choose for marrying; but as he had already put the cart before the horse, in cultivating oratory in preference to law, he was only repeating the same brilliant mistake in taking a wife first, and making a fortune afterwards.

It all came of sympathy. We have seen that the pretty Quakeress had long been sympathising in secret with Reuben; and the time was now arrived for Reuben to sympathise with her, which he very soon did as strongly and as publicly as he had lately sympathised with the Poles.

But let us not travel too fast. Mrs. Medlicott, after taking advantage of her presence in London to visit all the literary and scientific institutions, and attend as many lectures as she could thrust into a week, returned to Chichester with the cutler, who proved charming company; for he talked of nothing, the whole journey, but the parliamentary glories that were in store for her son. The Quakeresses remained behind in town, partly because the yearly meeting was at hand, and partly because the fatigue of travelling, with the excitement of Reuben's exploits, followed by Mr. Broad's gaieties at the Black Lion, had proved too much for Old Hannah Hopkins; and an interval of repose was necessary to enable her to take the road again. They remained for a few days at the Black Lion, but the old woman continuing weak, Reuben took lodgings for them in Grace-church Street, that they might be near their friend and relation, Mr. Harvey, the bookseller. But although the Harveys were the kindest people, and omitted no attention that their aged relative required, Mr. Medlicott was so far from neglecting his own duty to his friends, that he spent almost every evening in Gracechurch Street, and took care that his old schoolmistress should want nothing that money could procure for her. There was, indeed, a charitable rivalry between him and friend Harvey, who should do most to make Hannah's last days as comfortable as possible; for the doctors who saw her were of opinion that it was most unlikely she would ever return to Chichester. This announcement touched Reuben exceedingly, when he thought of the occasion which had brought the good woman up to London; and he was the more constant in his attendance, because he could not but perceive that Mary was much more pleased to receive his attentions than those of her relation, who was a prodigiously fussy man, and somewhat ostentatious of his friendly services.

Had Mr. Medlicott's judgment been as solid as his heart was sound, he would have made few mistakes in his career. He had numerous acquaintances in London, and was never more in request among them than since his display at the Freemasons' Tavern. Even those who censured him for wandering from his proper course, admired the brilliancy of his aberrations, and caressed him for his graceful accomplishments, while they lamented his deficiency in the sterner stuff of which ambition ought to be made. Master Turner made a party expressly for him; so did the nobleman who filled the chair at the Polish demonstration; but Mr. Medlicott excused himself to both, though no man valued such flattering attentions more than he did ; nor was this all, he also did what was very unnecessary and highly imprudent; he declined business, and even returned fees, preferring to take his way every evening, and at other times of the day not unfrequently, into the far city, to share the fatigues and anxieties of those obscure lodgings where Hannah Hopkins seemed destined to close her days. Those numerous visits brought him closer to Mary than he had ever been in the greatest familiarity of childhood. He would have been welcome to her for his friendship merely, but the pride she took in his attentions made them doubly acceptable. Reuben, upon his part, would have been attracted to her side by her distress, without any stronger magnet ; but everything now contributed to draw him towards her, her affliction, her beauty, and that most potent of all fascinations, the feeling that he was valued for those qualities which he most valued in himself.

There was a lapse of several weeks, with the usual fluctuations between hope and despondency. Notwithstanding the closeness of Mary's attendance on her mother, Reuben had many opportunities of various discourse with the fair Quakeress; he discoursed—of what did he not discourse ?—of poetry and eloquence, of poets and orators, on a thousand interesting questions of art and literature; sometimes even entering into abstruser subjects ; and always, when Friend Harvey was present, discussing some one or other of the hundred enlightened or humane projects in which he was interested or engaged, for in Harvey's company it was impossible to talk for many minutes upon anything but enlightenment and philanthropy.

In the natural course of things, the guardianship of poor Mary Hopkins, after her mother's decease, ought to have devolved upon this Mr. Harvey, who was her nearest relative, and of her own religious persuasion; but whether it was that the old woman's understanding was slightly impaired by her bodily suffering, or that her long knowledge and enthusiastic admiration of Mr. Medlicott (lately excited to the highest pitch), led her to place greater confidence in him than in any other human being, and imagine that he alone possessed the requisite amount of benevolence for the discharge of such a trust, she took the extraordinary step, when she imagined her last moments were at hand, of calling him to her bed-side, and, with the utmost solemnity, confiding her disconsolate daughter to his special protection, enjoining her to be guided in all her actions by his advice and to seek his assistance and support in all her trials and tribulations. Mr. Medlicott was so much affected by the scene, that he was not as much surprised as he would otherwise have been by a proceeding so extraordinary, and indeed unwarrantable. When the old lady even went the length of placing the weeping Mary's hand in his, to impress the solemn nature of the trust more emphatically upon him, Reuben melted into tears also, and in the tender passion of the moment, not only kissed the hand confided to him, but committed himself by language more impassioned than was discreet or necessary.

Notwithstanding all this melancholy preparation, the hour of Hannah Hopkins was not yet come. There was a time for all things under the sun, but the time for Hannah's sun to set was much more distant than either her friends or her physicians supposed. It is useless to speculate how Mr. Medlicott would have acted if Mrs. Hopkins had ended her days then, when everybody thought she had made up her mind to do so; but whatever chance of escape he might have had in that event was utterly destroyed by her recovery, which, being a tedious process, led to such a combination of tender little occurrences, and wove such a web of sentiment and sympathy about him, that had he been a stronger fly than he was, it would have been scarcely possible for him to have disentangled himself, or burst through it.

Friend Harvey was not, perhaps, an intentional match-maker; but if he did not actually lay himself out for it, he was probably only the more successful for that very reason. Having a small family and a large house, he began by inducing the Hopkinses to remove to it, as soon as old Hannah was equal to the effort; and not long afterwards, the accident of a fire in the building having made it necessary for Mr. Medlicott to leave his chambers in the Temple on the shortest possible notice, Mr. Harvey offered to accommodate him too with a temporary asylum, and was so warm and pressing, that Reuben at length accepted his proposition, and thus came into closer contact and more perilous proximity than ever with the sweet enthusiastic Mary.

Friend Harvey, as we have intimated, was the most indefatigably busy, and the most fervently zealous creature in the wide world. At the same time no man was shrewder in his trade, had a sharper eye to the main chance, or better knew how to make a friend of the Mammon of Unrighteousness. He was either an acting or a corresponding member of every society, institution, and committee in England, for suppressing slavery, abolishing capital punishments, putting down human chimney-sweeping, and war, and pestilence, and gin-palaces, and gin itself, everything in short that was not perfectly blameless, and after the strictest and purest pattern of Quakerly morality. But as he aspired to be pre-eminently a philanthropic and Quaker bookseller, this extensive concern in humane projects and undertakings was so far from injuring him in his trade, that it served him extremely, making his shop the principal one in London for the publication and sale of benevolent works and fanatical tracts, essays, treatises, and discourses, of all descriptions, sizes, and pretensions. In domestic life he was the same active, lively, and excitable personage that he was in his projects and his trade. When Harvey once said that his friend must dine with him, spend a month with him, or do anything else he wanted him to do, there was no help for it; the thing must be done, even when it was not as agreeable to the friend as it was to Harvey himself. You must either give him his way or offend him, and who would willingly offend a man who never offended anybody except by being too friendly and hospitable. It was thus that he almost forced Reuben to take a room in his house in Gracechurch-street, or rather a suite of rooms, for he was only too proud and happy to give him the best of everything he had to give. Mr. Bread himself did not entertain a more exaggerated notion of Mr. Medlicott's capabilities than did Mr. Harvey, before he had been a fortnight acquainted with him. Not only did Reuben completely impose upon the Quaker by his copious flood of elocution, which Harvey considered the very overflowing of the fountains of wisdom, but Reuben had been gradually growing warm upon some of the subjects which kept the mind of the bookseller in a perpetual fever, particularly on the questions of capital punishments and peace, over the latter of which Mr. Medlicott had been already brooding to an extent that was truly formidable. On the subject of capital punishments he had once made a speech when he was at college; his mother had given it, with others, to the Quakeresses to read; and the subject being broached one day at Harvey's table, Reuben's speech was not only remembered, but Mary Hopkins, to his great surprise, and perhaps his equal gratification, produced a copy of it, in her own neat hand, which it is not too much to say that the philanthropic bookseller actually devoured.

"Thee must permit me to print it," said Friend Harvey.

Reuben smiled as if the notion was ridiculous, but before a week expired, the speech was published, and might have been seen in Harvey's shop-windows, and announced in huge letters on one of the many boards which hung at the door. What is more, this puerile rhapsody had a wonderful run among the Abolitionists, and Harvey did not relish its eloquence the less because his pocket was benefited by it in common with the cause, for it may be supposed that Mr. Medlicott declined receiving any share of the profits. After this substantial proof of our hero's value, it was curious to observe how he rose in the Quaker's estimation, high as he had stood there before. Friend Harvey would stand gazing on Mr. Medlicott with an eager expression in his eye, and an appetizing movement and watering of his lips, just as if Reuben had been a turtle and his talents all green fat; so much did he hope to make of him, partly, no doubt, in the way of his business, but in a great measure, also, it is only just to say, as an instrument for advancing his multifarious schemes for the benefit of the human species. Harvey's two sons, likewise, who were in his shop, would also stand gaping at the same intellectual prodigy, as if they were equally disposed to eat him; or as if he had actually been the author of the Book of the Proverbs. Jonas and Samuel were twins, lank-haired, smooth-faced, brown-coated youths, who had been brought up to think it ill-manners to speak except when the were spoken to; it was not easy to distinguish them, they were so like one another, but Jonas was kind enough to keep his mouth generally wide open, which helped people to discriminate between them.

But an incident in which his grandfather had a share, tended more than anything else to tighten the bonds between Mr. Medlicott and the Society of Friends, an alliance which was destined to exercise such a powerful influence on his future life and fortunes.

We have lost sight of the Bishop for some time; indeed a little too long, for the fact that Mrs. Wyndham had astonished the world by presenting the venerable prelate with a son, was important enough to have deserved an earlier notice. It engrossed his lordship's thoughts, and swelled his pride and importance more than if he had been appointed to an additional see. At home, or abroad, this marvellous infant was seldom out of the paternal sight for a moment, his extravagant anxieties making poor Blanche almost appear in the light of a step-mother to her baby. It was to be seen puling opposite to the Bishop in his coach as he drove to the House of Lords. It had already accompanied him to a visitation; and frequently, when clergymen waited on him in his library to transact ecclesiastical business, their ears were saluted with little squeakings out of a corner, proceeding from the cot or the cradle where little Tom Wyndham was deposited.

We are more concerned, however, at present with another child of his Lordship's old age, which made its appearance at the same time, and made some noise in the world also. This was his long-threatened onslaught upon the doctrines and principles of the Quakers, a tract which was composed with all the force and virulence which had formerly distinguished his writings against the Roman Catholics. It had already gone through three editions, without attracting much notice in Gracechurch Street; but the announcement of a fourth, with a considerable flourish of trumpets by the Bishop's publisher, was more than Harvey could stand; and accordingly he came bustling in, one morning, to breakfast, with the tract in his hand, declaring that it must be answered immediately.

Reuben took it up, and read it aloud, with a running commentary as he proceeded, taking part very decidedly against his grandfather, sometimes reprobating the violence of his language, sometimes the unfairness of his statements, and often even the correctness of his facts, absolutely astonishing the Quakers by appearing to know twice as much as they did themselves about William Penn and their other celebrities. Many a remark which he made was all Greek to the Hopkinses and Harveys, but this only impressed them the more with his amazing wisdom and erudition.

"That's a flat *petitio principii*—there again, more begging of the question—not the fact—against all the authorities on the subject—adroitly put, but admitting of the simplest possible reply—very true, my Lord Bishop and most respectable grandsire, but quite irrelevant,—another sophism: what we used to call at college *ignoratio elenchi*—another—see what it is when a writer suffers his passion to run away with his reason—words, words, words, nothing but words for several pages.—I am sorry to find such mere babble in the production of a man who was once such a profound thinker, but do you know, Mr. Harvey, I am afraid there are signs of the garrulity of age in this pamphlet of my grandfather's? It admits of the easiest and the most triumphant answer."

" And thou wilt do us that service thyself," said Friend Harvey.

Reuben smiled, shook his head, and gently ridiculed the notion of a lawyer entering the lists of controversial divinity with a bishop, not to speak of the oddity of a member of the Established Church taking up the cudgels for a body of Dissenters.

" Thou knowest we may not take up the cudgels for ourselves, friend Reuben," said Harvey, with an oily smile.

" You may wield the pen," said Mr. Medlicott; " and all the more freely, as it is the only weapon you have to defend yourselves."

" But we have not thy learning, or thy beautiful diction, or thy knowledge of our antagonist," urged Harvey.

" Thou wouldest not be long about it," said his wife, a quiet, dove-coloured Quakeress, whose voice was seldom heard in the house or anywhere else, and who seldom entered ostensibly into any of her husband's projects, either sentimental or mercantile.

Hannah Hopkins took her breakfast in her room, but Mary was present, catching every word that fell from Mr. Medlicott's lips, as if it had been a jewel of Golconda, and tenderly interested in Friend Harvey's object, though only her animated looks and attitude of eager attention showed it.

Reuben now commenced his breakfast, but soon discontinued it; and throwing himself back in his chair, began to apologise for the Society of Friends, and demolish his grandfather's positions in his amplest and most variegated style of *extempore* declamation. Harvey, though a great eater, suspended his knife and fork, though his lips still moved as we have before described, and the tip of his tongue might be seen going in and out with a liquorish volubility, no otherwise than if Reuben's sentences had tickled his palate as well as enchanted his ear. His sons Jonas and Samuel (whose time for breakfast was limited), made a shift to swallow the bread and butter, and the galimatias at the same time; while friend Wilson, a tall, prim, drab, and ultra-broad-brimmed Quaker from the opposite side of the street, who dropped in while the torrent was flowing, sat near the door with his hands clasped over his breast, as he was wont to do upon First day at the Meeting.

After thus improvising a pamphlet, it was idle to decide writing one; but, Mr. Medlicott continuing coy, friend Harvey, who was not to be foiled when he set his heart upon an object, appealed to Mary Hopkins for her support, alluding in no very delicate manner to the influence he suspected she possessed over Reuben.

The allusion set her cheek on fire, and would have utterly defeated Mr. Harvey's purpose, if it had been necessary for Mary to have made a speech upon the occasion in presence of the assembled company; but it happened opportunely that Harvey was called away just at the instant; whereupon everybody rose, and in a few moments, before Mary's cheek had ceased to glow, she and Mr. Medlicott were the only occupiers of the apartment.

It was the beginning of summer, and one of those days of rare occurrence when the sky was actually blue and the sun shone visibly over Gracechurch Street. Reuben and Mary had never yet walked together in London without other company. Mary had never visited the British Museum. Reuben proposed to take her to see it. She hesitated, blushed again, smiled, and said she would much like to go, but would first mention it to her mother and obtain her consent, That proved no difficult point. Mary returned, wearing her bonnet of silver-grey, her First-day robe of the same hue, and her shawl as white as the driven snow. They set out on their expedition, and many an eye that day in the London streets, and many an eye in the great national institution over which they ranged together, was attracted by the pretty Quakeress, under convoy of the handsome young man, clothed in the fashions of this wicked world. That day was pregnant with a great deal, but its first and immediate result was Reuben's consent to defend the fair Mary's religious opinions, and the character of her sect, against his grandfather's libellous strictures.

Harvey's glee was indescribable when he found at dinner that his point was carried; he jumped about, rubbed his hands as if he was washing them, and talked of nothing for half-an-hour but pica and long primer.

"Thy response shall be published on fifth day next," he said to Reuben, "and thou wilt put thy name on the title-page, or not, as thee pleases. If thou wilt take my advice, thou wilt avow thyself the author, and make thy name known to the world."

The vanity of Mr. Medlicott would have led him to acquiesce

in this suggestion, rash as it was, but the strong sense of Mary Hopkins saved him from so false a step; she perceived how imprudent it would be to make his grandfather still more his enemy than he was already, and by a quiet little hint to that effect in the course of the evening, determined him to pull down his vizor, and enter the lists of controversy anonymously.

Fifth day came and the pamphlet with it, shining, smooth, and hot-pressed. Its appearance made old Hannah young again; Mary read it aloud to her mother twice, but how often she perused it in secret was known to herself alone.

Reuben had no mean opinion of this work of his, but Harvey could find no language to praise it sufficiently. He crammed his windows with it, placarded it in letters a foot long, sent copies to all the Meetings in the three kingdoms, and presented a copy to every customer that entered his shop. He might well boast, as he did, every day at breakfast and dinner, of its wonderful circulation, though probably the copies actually sold did not amount to a dozen. The following little dialogue took place in the shop every ten minutes:—

"Hast thou seen this? It is worth thy reading!" pointing to the pamphlet, then rubbing his hands.

"Excellent, no doubt, but it is not in my way," the customer would reply.

"Permit me to present thee with a copy."

On the third day of the publication, however, a customer came who actually bought the work. A large family coach, with mitres on the panels, and servants in dark purple liveries, drove up the street and stopped at Harvey's. A tall, robust old gentleman, wearing a shovel-hat and an apron, handed a great chubby infant to a comely woman who sat opposite to him, and alighting with very little assistance from the footman, pushed his way into the shop.

"You have published an attack upon me, I want to see it."

"What is thy name, friend?"

"The Bishop of Shrewsbury—Doctor Wyndham," was the reply, given very drily and impatiently.

"This is the work thou alludest to, friend Wyndham; but thou must permit me to observe, that the book is not an attack upon thee, but a reply to thy attack upon us."

"Who is the writer?"

"Thou mayest not be informed, friend."

"I put *my* name to *my* tract."

"Thou wert free to publish thy observations with thy name, or without thy name, at thy pleasure, friend."

"You took a long time to answer my observations."

"Peradventure, friend Wyndham, thou wilt take a longer time to answer ours."

The Bishop put down his shilling, disdaining to bandy more words with the bookseller, and, returning to the coach, drove off with the nurse and Tom, the latter trying to possess himself of Reuben's pamphlet for a plaything, and tearing off the title-page in the attempt.

The bookseller flew up to his wife and his guests, to tell them who had been in his shop, and what he had said to my Lord Bishop, which evidently pleased himself vastly. But Reuben and Mary had witnessed all that passed through a glass door which separated the shop from Mr. Harvey's private office, and the scene recalled to their memories the evening at Underwood, mentioned early in this history, when Dr. Wyndham had first menaced the Quakers with his wrath, and when Mary and her mother, scared by his termagant demeanor, had fled from the Vicarage, leaving their tea and their flowers behind them.

"How you laughed, Mary," said Reuben, "when he fished his hat out of the well, and shook it, and sprinkled us all round with the water."

"I was only a foolish, giddy girl at that time, Reuben."

"You certainly laughed a great deal more then than you ever do now," said Mr. Medlicott, looking tenderly at her.

She blushed and tried to repair the fault which he noticed, but the effort to laugh ended in a sigh.

Reuben took her hand, and in the softest of all possible tones, attuning his voice to the utmost sweetness, whispered the first words which directly intimated to Mary the existence of a feeling in his breast answering to that which had long agitated hers. The words were few, and their hands were scarcely joined before they were parted, for Jonas and Samuel were inconveniently near, only separated by the glass door. Harvey, too, was hurrying down stairs again, looking everywhere for his beloved pamphleteer, whom he met coming out from his office, followed by the fair Mary, who (if we may divine what was passing under her white muslin kerchief) was never so truly a Quakeress at heart as at that moment.

Mary had heard Reuben's oratory in the Court-House of Chichester, his eloquence in London at the Polish demonstration, and his conversational rhetoric a thousand times; but those few brief words were to her the most magical and thrilling that ever fell from his lips. For once he had made a laconic speech, and probably it was as effective a speech as he ever delivered. It was not, however, the last of the kind; in a few days he made her another, more studied, more formal,—in fact sufficiently declaratory not only of his sentiments, but his intentions.

The chief difficulty he experienced was from the maiden herself, whose feelings towards him had long been those of Helena for the unworthy Bertram; she felt that

> "In his bright radiance and collateral light
> Must she be comforted, not in his sphere."

she naturally feared that he mistook generosity for love; and it was not until after a siege of some duration, during which he gave every proof of the most ardent attachment, that she at length yielded to his solemn declaration that her consent was necessary to his happiness.

As to the difficulties on the part of his parents, who concurred in thinking him nothing short of a madman, it is hard to explain how he overcame them, except by obstinately following his own inclinations.

His mother especially was mortified and enraged, at what she considered a *mésalliance* for a man of Reuben's promise, and the result of an abominable conspiracy among the Hopkinses and Harveys; nor was her resentment in the least diminished, when Mr. Cox settled an annuity of two hundred a year and a pretty cottage on poor Mary, which made the prospects of the marriage less dismal than at first they seemed.

But Mrs. Medlicott's indignation was not very unreasonable after all, considering the hopes she had cherished. She had dreamed of brilliant nuptials for her son, alliances with ministers sustained in office by his eloquence, with chancellors happy to connect themselves with the rising talent of the bar, or with millionaires only too well off to exchange a daughter with a hundred thousand pounds for a handsome young orator and a volume of speeches. All these bubbles of love and vanity were burst, when Reuben flung down his gage to fortune, and became the daring husband of the fair and fortuneless Mary Hopkins. In truth, however, Mary renounced more for him than he did for her, for she left not only her mother but the Meeting, when she became his wife; whereas Reuben, far from giving up the world, was not two years married before he began to play a more prominent part in it.

During those two years he became the father of two children, and living entirely in London, increased his reputation and popularity among the Quakers enormously; to such a degree, indeed, that his fame crossed the Atlantic to New York, and a deputation of American friends actually came to England, to invite him to visit and enlighten the new world. He was busily engaged in preparing a course of lectures, upon the elastic subject of popular education, when his plans were altered by domestic events, which led him to neglect the Americans for some years, and devote himself to his own countrymen.

BOOK THE EIGHTH.

"If Alma, whilst the man was young,
Slipp'd up so soon into his tongue,
Pleased with his own fantastic skill,
He lets that weapon ne'er lie still.
But one may speak with Tully's tongue,
Yet all the while be in the wrong;
And 'tis remarkable that they
Talk most who have the least to say."—*Prior.*

ARGUMENT.

"Now entertain conjecture of a time
When general clamour and election fuss
Fills the wide circle of the commonwealth.
From camp to camp, through borough, town, and shire,
The cry of either party shrilly sounds;
Tongue answers tongue, and through their flaming prints
Each faction sees the other's brazen face.
Whig threatens Tory, in defiant strains
Dinning the public ear; and on each side
The Coppocks and committees, for the knights,
In flys and wagons bringing voters up,
Give dreadful note of preparation.
Now thrive th' attorneys; and election tricks
Reign solely in the thoughts of ever man.
They sell the manor now to buy the seat.
The candidates do treat, th' electors drink
Till the third hour of drowsy morning comes.
And now sits expectation in the air,
And holds a bag, stuff'd to the very mouth
With sovereigns, guineas, and with five-pound notes,
Promised to voters and their families.
A largess universal, like the sun,
The millionaire doth give to every one
Securing his return. Oh, do but think
You stand upon the hustings, and behold
An orator to th' inconstant rabble bawling.
So swift a pace hath thought, that even now

You may imagine him at Westminster,
With fatal mouth gaping on crowded benches
Till all do fly before him. Still be kind,
And eke out our performance with your mind."

CHAPTER I.

THE TOBACCONIST OF CHICHESTER.

It was the close of a splendid day, about midsummer; and the fatigued shopkeepers of the city of Chichester, like people of their class in a thousand other places, were beginning to think of shutting their long opened windows, and betaking themselves to refreshment or repose. A street of business, like a rookery, is most noisy at the hour in question, for though the shops that vend muslins and calicos, or such commodities as sugar and figs, usually close quietly enough, the goods being removable from the doors and windows without a clatter, it is otherwise with the houses that deal in iron-mongery, or crockery, for it is the nature of such wares to ring and rattle abominably when the articles come into contact; not to speak of the loud objurgations of the shopkeepers, and the shriller scoldings of their wives, when some awkward 'prentice drops a resounding fish-kettle or a clanging set of fire-irons from his overloaded hands; or when some still more unfortunate wight lets fall a pile of plates, or teacups, and destroys more in a second than his employer has probably sold in the course of the day. The finer the weather, the greater is generally the hurry-scurry and the din accompanying these operations, for there is yet light enough for a good ramble in the fields, or time to bathe, or to fish, or play at leap-frog, or pop at the sparrows; and the youths who have been chained to the counter from the rising of the sun are naturally over-eager now to relax and amuse themselves, and think they can never scamper off fast enough with the goods, or sweep away too many things at a time.

Evening is not so poetical a season in many respects when it falls on the streets of a town, as when its shades gather round a village in the country; but it is a time of rest and recreation in all places—a kind of little daily Sabbath, uniting those whom the labours of the day have parted, gathering friends and relations in their accustomed groups again, bringing forth the social flask, the economised pleasantry, the suppressed affection, and the hoarded jest. In these respects it is not to be questioned that "the hour when daylight dies" is equally dear to shopkeeper and shepherd, and as charming in the tradesman's contracted and Kidderminstered parlour, as in the rosiest thatched cottage, or the picturesque abode of the Vicar of Underwood. It is the time of the unwrinkling of brows, the washing of hands, and the unbending of sinews of both mind and body; it is especially the time for the replenishing of that vacuum which the nature of man most devoutly abhors, and happy are they who have wherewithal to replenish it. We are not, however, going to relate how the inhabitants of Chichester were off for provisions at this period of our story, nor what cause any of them may have had to grumble. We are simply mentioning what these innocent country shopkeepers were doing on this particular summer evening; how the curriers, jumping out of their skins, were beginning to remember that there is something better in the world even than leather; how the weary tailors, nine to the complete man, were standing up to repose themselves; how the baker was breaking the bread which his hands had kneaded in the morning; how, in short, men of all trades were trying, with more or less means of success, to make themselves comfortable; but as pretty much the same things were doing, at pretty much the same time of day, in every city, town, and village in the kingdom, we may safely leave it to the reader's imagination to complete the picture.

As it were expressly to make the evening more delightful, there fell a slight shower in the midst of these various doings, just enough to sprinkle and lay the dust (that troublesome incident of fine weather), and freshen the verdure of the neighbouring fields and woods, whose leaves were scarcely stirred by the sparkling drops, so gently and graciously did they fall upon them. The shower was but an affair of a few moments. When it passed away, it left the sky as blue as before; and the anxiety of the townspeople who meditated little excursions into the suburbs, was heightened in proportion to the improvement of the evening's fascinations.

One of the shops earliest shut on the evening in question, and also one of those which closed with the least bustle, was that of a tobacconist, situated in one of the chief streets, but nearer to the skirts of the town than to its centre, and at the corner of a lane which a quarter of a century since was still almost a green one, through which, in a wonderfully short time, you found your way into the region of fields and gardens, if you preferred the smell of the new-mown hay to the municipal perfumes, and the song of thrushes and blackbirds to the music of hurdy-gurdies.

It was a good old house, in the construction of which timber and red brick seemed to have been employed in proportions about equal. An antique in good preservation, it looked as if it was mouldering, and yet as if it would take a long time to moulder quite away at the rate decay was travelling. It looked, too, as if in its old age it was cherished and well looked after: nothing was out of repair, not a tile was deficient or broken on its steep roof; the windows were scrupulously bright; and the painting of all the woodwork, though excessively grave, as became the exterior of a house of its years, was at the same time perfectly fresh and clean. Upon the whole, it had an air of not only decency and respectability, but it might almost be said of goodness; for it cannot but have been often observed that houses have their physiognomies as well as their inhabitants; though, no doubt, in most cases it is the character of the man that impresses itself upon the dwelling, which looks cheerful or dismal, hospitable or the reverse, according as it is tenanted by people like Matthew Cox or men like Mr. Pigwidgeon.

The shop itself was utterly devoid of decoration—plate-glass had not come into general use, and the tradespeople of that day never dreamed of the twentieth part of the embellishments with which, now-a-days, they lure customers to their counters. However, even in his own day, our tobacconist's shop was the plainest and homeliest shop in the town; not a bit of brass was to be seen nor an inch of gilding; and the doors and windows were painted some sort of snuff-colour, which, if not gay, was unquestionably appropriate. Nor was there any sign or symbol of the business vsible outside; no wooden Highlander stood sneezing everlastingly over the door; nor were even the leaves of the Virginian weed depicted upon the posts. The words "Cox, Tobacconist," in dull pale yellow on a dusky board, were almost the only outward indication of the traffic carried on within, if we except a few old canisters which stood in the windows, for the proprietor confined himself strictly to the sale of snuff, and had no notion of the exhibition of boxes, with varnished portraits of kings and queens, groups of shepherds and shepherdesses, or those grotesque faces with mutually convertible chins and noses; nothing, in short, that makes the shop of a snuffman of the present day scarcely distinguishable from the studio of a Cheapside miniature-painter.

The house had two doors; one was the entrance to the shop, and at the angle formed by the street and the lane; the other was private, situated in the lane, about forty or fifty feet from the corner, facing an old garden-wall, over which some laburnums were hanging, now almost past their bloom, forming a canopy over that wooden bench upon which the Vicar found Mr. Broad, the worthy little cutler, seated, in the beginning of this narrative.

The bench was now occupied by three personages. About two of them there can be no mistake. One was Mr. Broad himself, in the white hat and nankeen shorts which he always wore in the summer season; the second was unmistakably our shabby acquaintance the apothecary; and the third was the good-humoured Alderman Codd, who was always so ready to place his subscriptions and sympathies at Mr. Broad's disposal. They were eagerly confabulating together upon many matters, but chiefly on the prospects of an approaching general election, and formed a striking little group of provincial politicians, sitting there that fine evening, with the fading flowers of the laburnums dangling to the crowns of their hats, and now and then a pearly drop of the late shower falling on their knees, or coat-sleeves, after having gently trickled from leaf to leaf, down from the uppermost bough. Among other things, they chatted, as was natural, about the proprietor of the shop opposite to them. Mr. Broad expatiated on his public and private virtues, and pronounced him the best man in Chichester, doubting whether there was a better man in all England.

"He is one of the richest, at all events," said Mr. Pigwidgeon.

"He is an honest man, let him be ever so rich," said the Alderman.

"If he was as rich as he is good," said the cutler, "he would be as rich as King Crœsus."

"You know more about him than I do," said the apothecary.

"Nobody knows anything about him but what's to his honour and credit," replied Mr. Broad.

"He knew how to make the money, at all events," said Mr. Pigwidgeon.

"He made it honestly, and he spends it generously," said Mr. Broad; "can any body say to the contrary?"

"His snuff was always snuff," said the Alderman.

Just at this moment the opposite door opened, and a fine old man made his appearance, whose countenance was sufficient to identify him with the subject of Mr. Broad's enthusiastic praises.

He was an old man, whose knees had not yet begun to totter, nor his shoulders to stoop; and his dress and entire exterior denoted the thriving tradesman and influential and worshipful burgess. His hat, which now he carried in his hand, was broad-brimmed and black, with something of the form and cock of the hats worn by ecclesiastics. The rest of his attire was of corresponding gravity; it consisted of a plain brown suit, with abundance of good broad-cloth in it; the collar of his coat was single, and the quaint pig-tail nodded over it; the waistcoat reached half way down his thigh; his roomy smallclothes were furnished with silver buckles at the knees; and hose of light grey, with a stout pair of shoes, well blacked, but not shining, and also provided with massive buckles of silver, completed his respectable attire. Such was old Matthew Cox, the opulent tobacconist of Chichester, the friend of the Medlicotts, the creditor of Bishop Wyndham, and the kind benefactor, as well as relative, by marriage, of the Hopkinses, which led him, of course, to take a deeper interest in Reuben than he had ever felt before, though always his admirer and benefactor. Matthew had been in his youth a very handsome man; and he was handsome still in his green and flourishing old age. His hair had been black as the raven's wing, but now that glory was departed, and his head being uncovered, you perceived that time had strewn his temple with silver, while it filled his coffers with gold; yet even the silver was not as abundant as it once had been.

No sooner did he appear, than Mr. Broad and the Alderman rose, and saluted him with equal respect, but each after his fashion; while the apothecary kept his seat, making a gruff and ungracious return to the civil nod of recognition with which the ancient burgess honoured him.

"Good evening to you, Mr. Broad," said the old man, who was first to speak, "and to you too, worthy Alderman, and you, Mr. Pigwidgeon; a very good evening to you all three."

The Alderman made another civil obeisance, and the apothecary repeated his ungracious little nod. Mr. Broad, always ready to be the spokesman on such occasions, returned Mr. Cox the compliments of the evening, adding——

"And a beauteous evening it is, sir, after that refreshing shower."

"It fell opportunely for us," said Mr. Cox; "my wife and I are going to sup, and probably sleep, at the garden which I took lately, between this and Underwood. We expect our good friends, the Vicar and his wife, to meet us there; and if you three will walk with us and join the party, I promise you all a warm welcome and a hot supper."

The apothecary, contrary to his usage, returned an ambiguous and surly answer to this hospitable invitation, saying that he had still business to transact in town, and did not know to how late an hour he might be detained by it; but Mr. Broad and the Alderman embraced the old man's proposal with alacrity.

"And we accept it the more gladly," said the former, "as the Alderman and I were waiting here expressly to see and consult with you, sir, on a subject of the greatest importance to a common friend of ours, and indeed, I may add, to the public at large at this eventful crisis."

"That you may well call it," said the Alderman.

"Perhaps I guess what you both allude to," said Mr. Cox.

"It's an eventful crisis, sir," said Mr. Broad; "that's all I'll say on the subject at this present moment."

"It is an eventful crisis," said the old man: "I quite agree with you."

"Eventful crisis!" muttered Mr. Pigwidgeon, rising and moving towards the town; "there has been an eventful crisis once a-year, at least, as long as my memory serves me. I see nothing in this crisis more eventful than in any other, except that there will probably be more bribing, and treating, and corruption of every sort, at the impending election, than ever there was before in this city and county; but, but for my part, I wash my hands of it."

"The first time I ever knew Pigwidgeon object to treating," said the Alderman.

"To be treated, you mean," said Mr. Cox: "but here comes my wife, after keeping her old man standing for half-an-hour at the door."

As soon as Mrs. Cox appeared, she dropped a civil curtsey to Mr. Broad and the Alderman, the former of whom saluted her in his most antic manner, with one hand making his hat perform a curvet in the air, with the other twitching up one of his long coat-tails, while with his feet he kicked up a little cloud of dust, in the enthusiasm of his politeness.

There was something decidedly Quakerish about Mrs. Cox's exterior; her brown silk dress and her gray silk bonnet might have passed in the Meeting; indeed it was only from the minor details, and the use of the plural pronoun when she spoke, that you discovered she did not actually belong to the Society of Friends. She had, however, been a Quakeress in her time, and was come of worthy and excellent people, the Hopkinses and Penroses of Devonshire, a race not more distinguished by their mercantile enterprise and success than by their indefatigable exertions in the cause of humanity and civilization all over the globe. The Romillies and the Clarkson's knew them well; but though their history is worth writing, it cannot be given here. The evening advances rapidly, and the old man is impatient to proceed. His wife took his arm conjugally, as if she had a right to it, and a right she was proud to exercise. Then the order to march was given, and the married couple led the way to the garden, followed by the Alderman and the cutler, the latter talking indefatigably on the subject of the election, and thanking Providence at every third step that Mr. Medlicott had not set out on his projected lecturing tour in the United States.

CHAPTER II.

A SUMMER EVENING'S WALK.

The way to the garden consisted almost entirely of a crooked series of green lanes, winding through orchards and meadows; sometimes passing a nest or a row of cottages, sometimes conducting to a substantial farm or a villa of some pretension. At a short distance from town stood three extremely neat little houses covered with roses, two of them joining one another, the third separated by a paddock, but at a neighbourly distance. From the lane they were divided by small enclosures, full of flowers, particularly the detached one, which was so very full that you could scarce see the smallest patch of the earth which yielded them. This row of cottages had been built by Doctor Wyndham, and had lately come into Mr. Cox's possession, together with other property (including the more imposing structures at Hereford), in satisfaction of the pecuniary obligation under which the Bishop stood to the wealthy tobacconist, as has been recorded in the beginning of these memoirs. No landlord was ever more particular about the character of his tenants than old Matthew; but in him this arose far less from anxiety about his rents, than from his desire to be connected in every relation of life with respectable and worthy people. As to those cottages, he would sooner have pulled them down than have let them to anybody whom he did not believe deserving of a settlement in so pretty a colony; and one of them had actually been untenanted for some months, because the proprietor had not yet met with an offer from a quarter he approved. The insulated cottage was called Maryland, in compliment to Mary Medlicott; for Mr. Cox had virtually settled it upon her on her marriage, not so much, however, in the hopes of Reuben ever making so humble a spot his permanent residence, as to provide a comfortable retreat and asylum near her friends for the venerable Quaker-mother during the remnant of her days. Mrs. Hopkins was established there already, and though her daughter was with her husband in London, the old woman neither complained of her solitude, nor, indeed, found it irksome,—her flowers were such agreeable company, and she was so proud to reflect that she was mother-in-law to the most promising man of the age.

What was now in agitation among Mr. Medlicott's friends at Chichester was to procure him a seat in Parliament, and, if possible, for that city. Mr. Cox, Mr. Broad, and the Alderman, talked of nothing else during their walk, Mr. Broad being of the three the most energetic and enthusiastic on the subject, the idea having originated in his ardent mind, which gave him a kind of parental interest in the scheme. He had almost brought himself to think that the very existence of the renowned British empire depended upon Reuben's introduction into the House; and, such is the contagion of honest zeal, not a day passed without his making some new convert to that opinion, extravagant as we must admit that it was. Mr. Cox had been brought round, not without some difficulty, and even now, although he concurred in the design, it was with more moderate expectations than Mr. Broad cherished, and not without some doubt on his mind that Parliament was a hazardous enterprise for a man like Mr. Medlicott, without a square inch of patrimony, and with little more than the name of a profession. Mr. Cox, however, saw clearly that Reuben was not destined ever to be a working lawyer, and he was, therefore, the more easily persuaded to assist in placing him in a new sphere, and giving his talents another trial. Although politically opposed to the objects of that memorable demonstration at Chichester, where Reuben had delivered his maiden speech, old Matthew had attended the meeting expressly to hear his young friend's oratory, had heard it with extreme delight, and fallen, with many other people, into the serious mistake of conceiving platform success to be proof of parliamentary ability. A complete change of parties had taken place since that time. The question of reform had brought Reuben and Mr. Cox into harmony again, so that there was no inconsistency in the part which the latter was now taking; on the contrary, it was a juncture when opulent and influential men of Mr. Cox's class were everywhere on the look-out for rising talents and promising abilities,—for "coming men," in short, to wield the new powers with which the democracy was now invested, and turn the improved representation of the people to immediate practical account. Every one, of course, had his own favorite question, or questions. Mr. Cox, for example, having, with his naturally strong and shrewd understanding, early in life, grasped the great principle of free trade, was, perhaps, more anxious upon that subject than any other; but he was also led by his family connections with the sect of Quakers to take a lively interest in the abolition of slavery in the West Indies, prison reform, and some other questions of the same philanthropic character. Mr. Broad was more bent upon reforming the Church, and restoring Poland to independence, in which objects he was followed most obsequiously by Alderman Codd, who; however, entertained a private opinion (which he sometimes took occasion to broach), that the grand measure to look forward to, in the Reformed Parliament, was the paying off the National Debt.

"There is plenty of work to be done," said Mr. Cox, as they moved along, enjoying the fragrance of the fields, and the evening song of the thrushes and the blackbirds: "we only want the men to do it."

"The men will not be wanting, sir," said the Alderman, "I'll answer for it."

"You'll answer for it," repeated the little cutler, mockingly; "it's easy to say that: but when a man is to be found equal to the work, will you put your hand in your pocket, and come down with the dust?"

"I was never backward to come forward, when I once saw my way clear before me, and nobody knows that better than you, Mr. Broad. Didn't I sympathise with the Poles, when you asked me? Didn't I sign the petition to expel the bishops from the House of Lords? And now let me tell you, if a hundred pounds, or so, is wanting to bring Mr. Reuben Medlicott in for this city, or any place else, on the popular interest, there is not a man in Chichester will give it more cheerfully than I will; only I hope Mr. Medlicott will be prepared to answer a question I shall feel it my duty to ask him on the subject of the National Debt."

"Ask him what questions you like," said Mr. Broad, "and I warrant you will get your answer. I have heard my distinguished friend talk for an hour on that very subject, and about the currency, sir, and the sinking-fund, and the one-pound notes."

"I doubt, Alderman," said old Matthew, "if the question of the National Debt is as pressing just now as some others I could mention."

"The Church, sir, and the dangerous power of Russia," said Mr. Broad eagerly.

Old Matthew smiled, and the cutler perceiving it drew in his horns, and proceeded to candidly admit that the Corn Laws and Negro Emancipation were also very proper objects to engage the attention of Parliament.

"In my opinion," said the Alderman, "we ought to pledge our representatives to everything."

"Pledge them to nothing, I say," said Mr. Cox; "let us look for the honestest and ablest men we can get, agreeing as nearly as possible with ourselves in the general principles of liberal policy, and then let us leave their discretion absolutely unfettered,—that seems to me to be the wisest course, and the most constitutional."

"It stands to reason, sir," said Mr. Broad.

"Well," said the Alderman, "I think there are two pledges, at least, that ought to be required from every member of Parliament."

Mr. Cox asked him what pledges he meant.

"Never to be absent from the house while the Speaker is in the chair, and to speak upon every interesting and important question."

Mr. Cox shook his head and laughed.

"I am afraid," he said, "there would be more talking than doing, Alderman, if your principle was carried out."

"My principle is," said the Alderman, "that the Government is for doing, and the Parliament for talking;—that's my idea of the British Constitution, which I once heard Mr. Medlicott himself say was 'the envy of surrounding nations and the wonder of the world.'"

"And it was an original and eloquent observation, sir," said Mr. Broad,—"it's eloquence we want, sir, and eloquence we must have. The House of Commons is not a Quaker's meeting-house, humbly begging Mrs. Cox's pardon for the remark, which I make with no disrespect for the Quakers,—a sect which nobody honours more than I do." Here he drew up to make one of his ludicrous bows, and again kicked up a cloud of dust with his too active politeness.

"You were treading on dangerous ground," said old Matthew, smiling, "but you have brought yourself off very cleverly, we must confess, and I dare say my wife will forgive you this time."

"I doubt if I shall," said Mrs. Cox, "for Mr. Broad speaks as if there was no such thing as an eloquent Quaker; and I can assure him I have heard in my time, not only eloquent Quakers, but eloquent Quakeresses,—what does he say to that?"

"Eloquence is a strong word, Rachael," said her husband, shaking his head.

"When I said eloquent, Matthew," she answered, "I meant Friends who could hold forth for a long time together, and talk very loud, though we did not always perfectly understand what they said, and sometimes, I am afraid, it came in at one ear and went out at the other."

"Long, loud, and incomprehensible; there, gentlemen, is my wife's notion of eloquence for you," said Mr. Cox, laughing.

"Well, indeed," said Mrs. Cox, "I never could understand poor Hannah Hopkins, although I did my best, and she was very large in the ministry and considered very eloquent. Some people thought she did not always understand herself."

"I heard her preach once," said Matthew; "it was all about Daniel in the den of lions, and I very well remember how she ended her sermon.—'I don't know, she said, whether you understand me. It is very likely you don't; but I know myself what I mean.'"

Apropos to Hannah Hopkins, the pedestrians were now very near her cottage, and a little consultation took place whether she should be invited or not to join the party. It was decided in the negative, no doubt for sufficient reasons, and Mr. Cox was anxious to pass by without being observed by the Quaker-mother; but that was out of the question, for she was sitting at her door knitting and enjoying the wilderness of sweets in her little garden. Mr. Cox, no longer holding his wife's arm, was now leading the way, with his hands clasped behind his back, as his manner was, and looking straight before him in the most determined manner.

"Matthew Cox, Matthew Cox, dost thou hear me, friend Matthew?"

He was defeated, and there was nothing for it but to surrender at discretion, which he and his worthy wife did with the best grace, and all their natural cordiality, desiring Hannah to put her things on at once, and accompany them to Virginia to supper.

"And Mr. Broad and the Alderman will see thee safe at home again, Hannah," said Matthew, "if thou wilt trust thyself with such gay fellows."

"Thank thee kindly, friend Broad,—friend Codd, thou art always kind and obliging."

Mr. Cox offered her his arm, but she declined the attention, to keep her hands free for her needles, which, had they been worked by machinery, could not have been plied more unintermittingly.

"I'll walk by thy side, Matthew," she said, "and enjoy and profit by thy conversation."

The wild flowers, however, were continually seducing her from the path of rectitude. At last she nettled her hand in grasping a dog-rose, and Matthew had to gather dock-leaves to cure her, promising her, at the same time, abundance of flowers from his garden, and bidding her trouble herself no more about the weeds in the hedges. This quieted her, but she carefully stuck the dock-leaves into her nosegay, and soon forgot all other subjects of interest in talking of Reuben and Mary, from both of whom she had a pocketful of letters, which she would have stopped to read on the roadside if Mr. Cox had encouraged her. She gratified Mr. Broad, however, by letting him see Reuben's handwriting, which he happened never to have seen before, and now pronounced to be decidedly the hand of a man of genius. "The hand of a statesman, sir; not of a writing-master"—and Alderman Codd was compelled to agree, though he had certainly never seen the hand of a statesman before.

CHAPTER III.

PLEASURE BEFORE BUSINESS.

VIRGINIA, or the snuff-box, as the wits of Chichester used to call it, was a mere garden, covering about an acre of ground, with a neat lodge or cottage in the middle of it. From the road, or lane, it was separated by a high wooden paling, in which there was a small gate, or rather door, provided with a bell, hung in the most beautiful belfry you can imagine, among the boughs of a magnificent horse-chestnut, now covered with its fine hyacinth-ine flowers in all their summer glory. Mr. Cox pulled the cord, or wire, and the first answer he received was the deep bark of his great dog Constable, a terror not only to the evil-doers of all the country round, but also to many who were not evil-doers, especially the Quakers, who always shuddered at his voice, and were miserable until they were assured that he was chained up in the securest manner.

"He is not the most amiable dog in the world, I must own," said Matthew, "but he defends the cucumbers and the strawberries: we must give him credit, Hannah, for that."

"A good public officer, though a bad family-dog," said a familiar voice on the other side of the door, which was instantly opened by our old friend the Vicar, who had already arrived at the hospitable rendezvous.

"I hope you are not alone," said Mr. Cox, shaking the Vicar's hand heartily.

"Very far from it," said his reverence; "there are more of us than I believe you bargained for; but a couple of friends gave us an agreeable surprise this morning at breakfast, and we ventured to bring them with us, hoping to give you an equally agreeable surprise this evening at supper."

The next moment produced Mrs. Medlicott from behind a screen of bushes, accompanied by Hyacinth, Mr. Primrose, and Dr. Page.

The visit of the latter to Chichester was merely in performance of his long-standing promise to spend a few days with his friend, the Vicar; but it proved exceedingly opportune for Reuben, for his greatest enemy was a man with whom nobody was so fit to grapple as the Doctor; and, moreover, it required all the influence of so old a friend and crony as Page to overcome the Vicar's repugnance to the new rig (as he called it), which his son was about to run, instead of working steadily at something or another to provide for his wife and children.

The Doctor was the same pleasant, confident, hearty, energetic, ready fellow, in the same flagrantly unmedical costume as when we last saw him on the Welch mountains; but there was a decided change visible in Hyacinth, and the Vicar had noticed it the moment he saw him; it was not in his figure, for a few years had not much increased his portliness, nor in his face, for that wore its habitual agreeable air of "genteel comedy," nor in his manners, for they were airy and mercurial as ever; it was almost entirely in his dress, which was a complete suit of black, although he was not in mourning. In fact, Mr. Primrose was on the point of taking orders, and we may add (although it was then still a secret from the world), on the point of taking a wife also; it having been arranged that he was to espouse the Church and widow at the same time,—a species of bigamy which the bishop was so far from disapproving, that he had already promised him his domestic chaplaincy and the first vacant living: so much better than Reuben did Hyacinth understand the art of thriving by his versatility.

Primrose, however, while about to take that comfortable place in the favour of fortune which Mr. Medlicott spurned, felt it the more his duty to interest himself in his friend's success in the more hazardous enterprise he was now engaged in. If he had been rich, he would have spent his money freely in Reuben's cause; as he was not, he did all that was in his power to do, by promptly and zealously complying with Mrs. Mountjoy's request, that he would hasten to Chichester, and take care that her nephew's promotion in the world should not be stopped for the want of a few hundred pounds.

While daylight lasted, which was not very long, the party rambled about the garden, sometimes pairing off, sometimes meeting in knots where the alleys crossed, and eagerly confabulating all together. Dr. Page was pleased with Dr. Cox; Mr. Primrose was enchanted with Mr. Broad; Mrs. Medlicott found a patient listener in the Alderman; the Vicar and Mrs. Cox had long been the best friends in the world. Everybody, in short, was charmed with everybody, which is not always the case in more distinguished assemblies. In truth it was an election-committee, and nothing else, so much did the election and Reuben's prospects engross the conversation, until at length Mrs. Medlicott (who looked on the party in that light only) became so excited, and talked so volubly and so wildly about this borough and that borough, the subscriptions to be raised, the speeches to be made, the agents to be employed, what she was resolved to do herself, and what she thought everybody else ought to do, that it ended in her vehemence and prolixity completely bothering and disgusting the men of the party, especially her husband, who protested, as soon as supper was announced, against hearing any more on the subject, appealing to Hannah Hopkins whether there was not " a time for all things."

Mrs. Medlicott was most indignant at this appeal to the Quakeress, towards whom she still entertained a grudge, for her share in Reuben's marriage. Her eyes flashed green fire at poor Mrs. Hopkins; at least it looked green, through the medium of her spectacles; but in truth Mrs. Hopkins was as little tired of the discussion as herself: only the good old woman knew no more about elections and boroughs than the man in the moon.

The supper was a good specimen of the domestic arrangements of the Coxes, of which extreme neatness and simplicity were the sensible and agreeable characteristics. Matthews's Quaker marriage had been a source of great comfort and rational enjoyment to him all through life; it brought the best members of that excellent sect about him, and it gave him what mere wealth would not have given, the cheap luxuries of order and cleanliness in perfection. Cleanlines is as inherent in the Quakers as a sect, as it is in the Dutch as a nation. Rachel Cox was not excelled in this respect by the most exemplary housewife in all Holland. The only dust in her house was the snuff in her husband's canisters, and the very sight of her table lent a zest and piquancy to the plainest food that was laid upon it.

It was comparatively easy to avoid talking of election matters, but absolutely impossible to avoid talking of Reuben, when so many of his devoted admirers were present, and when his very absence, as usual, made him only the more thought of. Mr. Primrose had never heard Reuben speak in public. Mr. Broad gave him a delicious account of the speech at the Freemasons' Tavern, and this set every tongue going upon the tiresome cause of Poland, until the Vicar was as much bored by this new topic as he before had been by the general election. He was meditating how to effect a division without offending anybody, when his end was answered by old Mrs. Hopkins, who, being always fond of hearing learned discussions, was now suddenly seized with a desire to hear the opinions of the company on the nature of sympathy: "for," said she, "my Mary and I have puzzled our brains many and many a time about it, and we were never the wiser for our pains. What dost thou think, friend Primrose?"

Primrose was almost too much amused to answer; but at length he said, "that sympathy was one pole of an animal-magnet; antipathy was the other."

The question was then passed to Mrs. Medlicott, who had been disagreeably silent on ceasing to be disagreeably loquacious; but now, being under the necessity of speaking and maintaining her philosophical reputation, she assumed her most didactic tone, and replied, "that it was a very abstruse subject, more abstruse than probably Mrs. Hopkins had any notion of;—there was a great deal about it in Kant's philosophy; more, indeed, than she was disposed herself to concur in; she hardly hoped to be perfectly understood; but the view she was disposed to take was, that sympathy was that which formed the species, while it absorbed, or, in a transcendental sense, annihilated the individual."

"There, Madam, I must make bold to differ from you," cried the Alderman, "for when I, as an humble individual, sympathised with the Poles, at the urgent request of my friend beside me, I was certainly not annihilated, for here I am to say so."

"But you were absorbed, sir, were you not?" said Primrose, with a side-glance at Mrs. Medlicott, as if he fully participated in the contempt which her countenance already showed she entertained for the simple Alderman.

"Yes, you were absorbed, Alderman,—I must do you the justice to say you were absorbed," said Mr. Broad.

The Alderman "owned the soft impeachment;" and now it came to poor Mrs. Cox's turn, who soon gave the riddle up, with a despairing sigh, which made everybody laugh; the Vicar, however, maintained that it was a capital practical definition.

"What dost thou say thyself, friend Thomas?"

"Well, Hannah," replied the Vicar, laying down his knife and fork, and looking as metaphysical as he could;—"Well,

Hannah, let us see—What is sympathy? Now suppose I was just now to feel an inclination for a glass of this old port, and that you were to feel at the same time, or that I were to inspire you with a wish to have a glass too—I should be strongly disposed to say that was sympathy."

Mr. Cox filled the Qakeress's glass to the brim.

"Our host's port, Hannah, is better than my philosophy," said the Vicar, drinking to her, and laying down his glass.

"I like friend Matthew's port, and I like thy philosophy," said the old woman, growing mellow rapidly;—"dost thou remember the fable of the shepherd and the philosopher? My Mary would be happy to repeat it for thee, if she was here."

Mrs. Cox was so good-natured to Mrs. Hopkins, or so cruel to her company, as to express a hope that Hannah would favour the company with the fable herself, in her daughter's absence; and beyond a doubt the hope would have been indulged, had not Mrs. Medlicott (who was in no very equable temper after the dry rub her husband had given her before supper) risen from the table abruptly, and with a most unconvivial allusion to the progress of time, put an end to the merry meeting.

"We have spent a very pleasant evening," said the Vicar, putting on his hat.

"A little business, in my opinion, might have been mixed with the pleasure, at a moment like this," said Mrs. Medlicott bitterly, and putting on her bonnet.

"Morning is the time for business," said her husband.

"I agree with his reverence," said old Matthew.

The Doctor, as a medical man, was of the same opinion. Mr. Broad agreed with the Doctor, and the Alderman, as a matter of course, concurred entirely with Mr. Broad. The result of this general concurrence was an arrangement to meet for the dispatch of business at breakfast the following morning, at the Vicarage. It was not, however, understood that either Mrs. Hopkins or Mrs. Cox should attend the committee; and the Vicar would not have been displeased if his wife could have been included in the same understanding.

CHAPTER IV.

FRIENDS IN COUNCIL.

THE Vicar was quite right. Evening is the time for pleasure, and morning is the time for affairs. Reuben's little committee of friends got through more business round the breakfast-table in a couple of hours, than they could have transacted at supper in twice the space of time; nor did any of the party sincerely regret that Mrs. Medlicott was prevented from appearing in consequence of an attack of rheumatism, brought on by walking home from supper in the night air.

"Let us begin with the finances," said Mr. Cox. "It is not the fault of us, reformers, if elections are not to be conducted without money. As things are, however, it is out of the question. Bribery will never be encouraged, or sanctioned by me, either in Chichester or elsewhere; but an election, under existing circumstances, involves other expenses of no inconsiderable amount, and for those we must provide in the first instance. Supposing a contest to take place, what sum, Broad, do you think we shall have occasion for—to meet the legitimate expenses?"

Mr. Broad thought a thousand pounds would bring his illustrious friend into Parliament for his native city.

The Alderman sensibly remarked, that legitimate expense was a very indefinite thing; he should not like to engage in a contest, unless there was at least a couple of thousand in the purse.

The Vicar was afraid that so large a sum might be a temptation to cross the boundary between the legitimate expenses and the illegitimate.

"That can be provided against," continued the Alderman, "by placing the purse in the hands of somebody of such rigid probity as to remove all fear upon that score."

"If Mr. Cox will be treasurer," said the Vicar, "I waive my objection."

Mr. Primrose here sagaciously interposed, observing that it would be unfair to impose such a heavy duty on Mr. Cox, and suggesting that Mr. Broad should carry the bag.

The little cutler jumped up, then sat down, fidgeted in his chair, thanked Mr. Primrose, and was manifestly pleased at being nominated to the office.

"But," said he, "the responsibility will be too much for the shoulders of an humble man like me; I hope, gentlemen, you will give me a colleague."

"I am sure," said Hyacinth, "my friend Dr. Page won't object to be named along with you."

"On the contrary, I shall be most happy," said the confident Doctor; and as nobody, of course, had any objection to make, Mr. Primrose had the satisfaction of seeing the financial arrangements placed in the hands of two of Reuben's most enthusiastic and least scrupulous friends. The Vicar and Mr. Cox were completely hoodwinked; and, indeed, neither the cutler nor the Doctor had a notion of what Hyacinth's drift was in making them joint-treasurers; but Hyacinth knew who was who, and what was what, better than anybody at the table.

"Now, to raise the money," said the Alderman.

Primrose took out his pocket-book, and held his pencil in readiness to enter the subscriptions.

"Put down three hundred for me," said Mr. Cox.

The Vicar rose from the table to conceal his emotion at old Matthew's liberality, which he knew had its source in the strength of his private affections. He then left the room to acquaint his wife with Mr. Cox's munificence. While he was absent, Mr. Broad subscribed two hundred, the Alderman one; and then Mr. Cox, putting his hand into his pocket with solemnity, produced two letters he had received that very morning. One was from a Quaker bookseller in London, no other than our friend Harvey, who had levied contributions to the extent of six hundred pounds from members of the Society of Friends in the metropolis, interested in the cause of universal philanthropy, and anxious to have it eloquently represented in Parliament. The other was a communication from Mrs. Winning, of Sunbury, subscribing a hundred.

"We have one thousand, three hundred already," said Primrose, entering the sums; "and I am authorised by another London bookseller, Mr. Trevor, to put down his name for any sum not exceeding a hundred. Master Turner will give the same, and Lord Maudlin will go as far as three, if we want it."

"Who the deuce is Lord Maudlin?" cried Dr. Page.

If you had but seen Mr. Broad's looks and gesticulations at such a question!

"Lord Maudlin, sir," he replied, with ludicrous energy, "is it possible, sir, you don't know who Lord Viscount Maudlin is?

"Why. sir, it was his lordship who took the chair at that great meeting in London on behalf of unfortunate Poland, where Mr. Reuben Medlicott made that famous speech, which I had the pleasure and honour of hearing. Why, sir, he spoke upon that grand occasion for two mortal hours and a half without ever drawing his breath."

"Quiet, Broad, quiet now," said Mr. Cox, gently tapping him on the shoulder; "keep to the point, or we shall never get through business. How much have we now, Mr. Primrose?"

"One thousand, eight hundred," said Hyacinth, totting his entries.

"Which I am ready to make the square two thousand," said Dr. Page. He had scarcely spoken when a servant came in and presented Mr. Medlicott with a letter. It was from the Earl of Stromness, and assured the Vicar that if the contest for Chichester took the turn it threatened to take at that moment, he would be very happy to support his son, and would willingly bear a reasonable share of the expense of his election.

"We shall have too much money," said the Vicar.

"No harm in a little surplus," said the Doctor.

"The only man who ever finds a surplus troublesome is the Chancellor of the Exchequer," said Primrose.

So little was he perplexed himself by the superabundance of resources, that it made him very comfortable to think he had Mrs. Mountjoy's contribution quietly in reserve. He said nothing about it for fear of alarming the Vicar still more, but determined to put it privately into the Doctor's hands, having little doubt a necessity would practically arise for relaxing the strict rules of morality for which, in theory (he flattered himself), he entertained as profound a respect as any man.

"Now," said Mr. Cox, addressing Mr. Broad, "now I give you your freedom; if you have anything to say on the subject of our friend Reuben's qualifications for Parliament, we are ready to hear you." He laid a gentle emphasis on the word "'qualification" in this sentence.

"He has every possible qualification," cried the zealous cutler. "Let any man get up and say what qualification he wants."

Primrose shook his head.

"I am afraid," said he, "I must respectfully differ from Mr. Broad, though I entertain so high an opinion of my friend's abilities; but I have a letter from himself upon the subject; you shall all hear what he says."

"The modesty, sir, that always accompanies distinguished merit," said Mr. Broad.

Primrose smiled, and read Reuben's letter to the company, which soon enlightened Mr. Broad as to the nature of the qualification that was now in question.

The Vicar disliked evading the law, although an unreasonable and absurd one.

Mr. Primrose suggested that a successful evasion of the law could never be a wrong proceeding, for it could only succeed by being beyond impeachment; and if unimpeachable by law, it was permissible by law, and therefore legal in the strictest sense of the word.

Mr. Broad applauded this reasoning highly; but Matthew Cox looked sceptical, and smiled, adding, however, that a way had occurred to him by which Reuben could be provided with a bonâ-fide property qualification, though he was unable to say more on the subject at that moment. Perhaps the gentlemen would refer that subject altogether to him. With the advice of his lawyer, he trusted to settle it satisfactorily.

This matter having been disposed of, it seemed as if everything had been done that could be done at present, when it suddenly occurred to Mr. Primrose that Reuben's consent had not yet been formally asked to stand for Chichester.

"We must write to him to come down at once," said Mr. Cox.

"Pardon me," said Primrose; "in my opinion, instead of asking him to come down to you, some of you ought to go up to him."

"Hear Mr. Primrose," cried Broad, lustily.

"Hear, hear," re-echoed the Alderman.

"Hear, hear," cried another and a strange voice, at some little distance. It was Sirach the raven, who had just hopped in through an open window, and who had never forgotten the cry since he first learned it, when Dr. Pigwidgeon delivered Reuben's speech from the pear-tree.

"My advice is a deputation," said Mr. Broad; and the general opinion being in favour of that measure (the Vicar alone dissentient), a deputation was then and there resolved on, to consist of Mr. Broad, the Alderman, and another influential citizen, whose co-operation might be relied on. Mr. Broad was for setting out that very evening, but the following morning was ultimately fixed on; and it was also agreed to keep the entire affair as quiet as possible for the present. Mr. Cox and Primrose pressed this strongly.

"Especially from Mr. Pigwidgeon," said Doctor Page.

"From Mr. Pigwidgeon above all men," said Mr. Cox.

"Mum's the word," said Mr. Broad; but before the sun went down upon Chichester, nobody in that city, who was in a position to know anything of such matters, was ignorant of what Mr. Medlicott's friends were about, or of the important embassy that was going up to London.

———•••———

CHAPTER V.

SIRACH, THE RAVEN.

"A FINE old bird, that raven of yours, Mr. Medlicott," said Primrose, as they sat under the walnut-tree, after sunset, that same evening; "a fine old bird; what may his age be?"

"Unknown," said the Vicar; "I had him from my predecessor in this living, who told me he received him from his predecessor, who told him the same story. When I came first to Underwood, there was an ancient gravedigger here—his own grave has since been dug—from whom I learned that he remembered Sirach as long as he remembered anything connected with the parish; and when he first knew the bird, one of his phrases was Old Noll—he used to cry Old Noll—from which I infer that Sirach could tell us something about the Commonwealth if he was disposed to be communicative. I sometimes say to my wife, that it is not impossible he may have seen 'the Good Parson.'"

"I should say he certainly has, sir," said Primrose.

"Sees him every day," said Dr. Page.

The Vicar acknowledged the compliments of his guests with a bow and a smile, while Primrose began to speculate upon the notion of the raven writing his memoirs.

"What an historian he would make, with his old experience, if he would only pluck a quill from his own wing and give us his personal reminiscences."

"The annals of a single vicarage," said Mr. Medlicott, "would doubtless be a valuable supplement to general ecclesiastical history, as well as an acceptable addition to our knowledge of domestic life and manners. I wish we could induce Sirach to undertake it."

"Is he conscientious?" asked Primrose.

"For a raven," said the Vicar; "but I fear a comparison with other fowl would not be much in his favour; in fact, were he to apply himself to literature with his present habits, I should be apprehensive of his being detected in a plagiarism now and then."

"I dare say," said the Doctor, laughing already at the remark he was about to make, "he has not lived so long among Churchmen without having learned how to feather his nest."

"Take care of yourself, Doctor," said Hyacinth, "take care what you say of the Church; we are three to one on the present occasion, for I reckon Sirach an ecclesiastic."

"He may know how to feather his nest," said the Vicar, "and he does know how; but he has only one to feather; he is no pluralist, let me tell you, any more than myself; nor was he ever proceeded against by the Ordinary for non-residence. He passes his life pretty much as his master does, between this garden and that consecrated ground yonder, behind those yews, where he spends much of his time of late, particularly towards the dusk, hopping and croaking among the graves; probably communing with those who sleep there, and informing them, out of his prophetic spirit, how soon it will be my lot to join them, and his to be raven to a new incumbent."

"*Huc omnes cogimur*," said Primrose, with a sigh that responded to that with which the Vicar had ended his speech.

"The house that lasts till doomsday," said the Doctor.

The Vicar then related how Sirach had first learned to cry "here, here," like a parliament man.

"A taste for eloquence in a raven," said Primrose, "is not more surprising than a taste for poetry in an ass. Ammonius, a philosopher of the Greek empire, had an ass who had such a love of poetry, that he would forbear eating his provender rather than withdraw his attention from a poem read to him. The story is told by Photius."

"For the edification of the marines, I presume," said the Doctor.

Here the party was joined by Mrs. Medlicott, which, as usual, put an end to all rational conversation. She dashed at once into the controversy between reason and instinct, uttering such a farrago of hard words, and odds and ends of metaphysical disquisitions, bringing in Malebranche head and ears, and even going the unfeminine length of talking of " æsthetics," which was her husband's horror, that it was a general relief to her audience when the bells of Chichester, tolling the hour of nine, and distinctly audible in the stillness of a summer evening, interrupted the lecture.

The delighted Vicar held up his finger, inviting attention, while the clock of St. Martin's commenced the concert, with a voice of profound solemnity. St. Mary's followed with a plaintive sweetness, like a snatch of psalmody, as if its bells were of silver. Before she was quite done, St. Olave took up the tale; but ere it was half told, St. Peter the Great came chiming in so sonorously that St. Olave might just as well have remained mute. At this point the humble clock of Underwood struck modestly in, only louder than its brazen brotherhood, because it was so near at hand. After this there was one moment's intense silence; and then spoke out St. Andrew, sending his nine piercing notes into the sky so very hastily, that you fancied he was trying to overtake the others, or that he had suddenly awoke, and was impatient to have done with his task and go to sleep again. He was the last of the ecclesiastical clocks; and as to the civilians, they were scarcely worth sitting to listen to, with the exception of an old cuckoo in the Vicar's kitchen, which sang out the usual hour of supper so sweetly and naturally, that you could scarcely have heard it at any season of the year without thinking it was the warm month of June, and, in truth, it was generally sultry weather in the place where that cuckoo's note came from.

CHAPTER VI.

IN WHICH A DISCOVERY IS MADE THAT SURPRISES EVERYBODY.

Mr. Hyacinth Primrose and Dr. Page were now such good friends, with such a mutual relish for one another, that they were pleased to find there was a door between their bed-rooms, which they had only to open of a morning, to converse together while they were dressing. The windows of both apartments opened upon a sort of balcony, about which a luxuriant vine clambered, and over which the thatch projected pretty far. To throw these windows open, and admit the fragrant air, occasionally even popping out on the balcony, and taking a view of the garden and the picturesque church-yard fast by it, was a very agreeable mitigation of the troubles of the toilette, a business which, with Mr. Primrose particularly, was always a tedious and grave one. On the third day of their visit to Underwood, the Doctor and Hyacinth were dressing as usual, availing themselves of the social advantages of their quarters, and discussing Mr. Medlicott's chances and prospects, when Hyacinth, who had stepped out for a moment into the open air, suddenly drew back, and with the utmost surprise, delight, and curiosity depicted in his countenance, ran into the Doctor's room, exclaiming,

"Good Heavens, Page! come here,— see this! Such an animal!—I had no notion there existed such a creature in the whole animal kingdom."

Page concluded from the hue and cry that some rhinoceros, or ourang-outang, must have escaped from a menagerie in the neighbourhood. Hyacinth led him out on the balcony, and through the tangled branches of the vine, pointed with his finger to an object in the garden, nearly opposite them, which the moment the Doctor got a distinct view of, he recognised without the least difficulty as his old acquaintance, and the object of his everlasting aversion—the apothecary.

"He is more like an exaggerated father-long-legs, than anything else," said Primrose. "Medlicott often tried to describe him for me, but in vain; he beggars description."

"You don't much admire his exterior," said the Doctor.

"The most ungainly, the ugliest I ever set my eyes on," said Primrose.

"There is something uglier, nevertheless," said the Doctor.

"What can that be?" said Hyacinth.

"His interior," said the Doctor, and then he made Primrose acquainted with all that he knew of Pigdwigeon's antecedents, after which Primrose told him of his juvenile performance, entitled "The Country Apothecary," founded entirely upon the account he had received from Reuben, and which had appeared with other literary freaks and follies, in the MS. periodical of which they had been joint-editors at school.

"Has the rogue any local influence in Chichester?" inquired Page, adjusting his green silk carvat, which made a lively contrast with his red waistcoat.

"I fancy he has some," replied Primrose; "I believe he has some interest or share in the 'Chichester Mercury;' I have heard something to that effect,—a sleeping partner probably."

"I am sorry to hear it," said the Doctor, "and I only wish he was asleep in reality, just at the present moment, for if he has the means of mischief in his power, he is not the man to let them lie idle; however, if he is disposed to be troublesome, I'll prepare a composing draught for him, that will keep him quiet enough."

"We shall have him at breakfast, I presume," said Primrose.

"N doubt," said the Doctor, "but my company won't improve his appetite, I promise you."

They went down together, and found Mr. and Mrs. Medlicott and the apothecary in the parlour. Whatever business Mr. Pigwidgeon had with the Vicar had been deferred until after breakfast; a postponement proposed by the latter, to which the former had made no objection. His visit had surprised Mr. Medlicott not a little, for there had been a coolness between him and the apothecary for several years, in fact ever since the public meeting at Chichester, when the Vicar had good reason to suspect Mr. Pigwidgeon had played him false, respecting the publication of Reuben's speech.

"Mr. Pigwidgeon—Dr. Page," said the Vicar, shrewdly observing, as he spoke, the effect of the introduction upon the former. It was comic enough, but obviously not the comedy of "The Agreeable Surprise" to one of the parties, although the apothecary did not cower before the Doctor to the degree that the latter had led Primrose to expect.

"Mr. Pigwidgeon and Dr. Page are already acquainted, I believe," said Mrs. Medlicott.

"I have the pleasure of knowing Dr. Page," muttered the apothecary, in a low, dogged tone of voice.

The Doctor repeated the same formula, only substituting "honour" for "pleasure," with a dry emphasis on the word.

Mr. Pigwidgeon's appetite, too, was in much better order than Page had predicted, and the Doctor himself had practical proof of it, for a cold round of beef stood before him, to which the apothecary paid marked attention, utterly regardless of the trouble which he gave the carver, upon whom he made repeated calls, with the utmost coolness and effrontery. In fact Mr. Pigwidgeon made such a hearty breakfast, that Mr. Primrose began to suspect the Doctor had grossly exaggerated the flaws in his moral character, if there was any reliance to be placed upon Bishop Wyndham's theory of the connection between a good appetite and a clear conscience.

The Doctor at length, having thrice helped the apothecary to the beef, and being apprehensive of another demand, bethought him of a little stratagem to save himself from further trouble, and in pursuance of his scheme began to talk about medical reform, maliciously stating that he had heard and believed it was the intention of Government to issue a commission to inquire into the management of infirmaries and dispensaries.

"And Mr. Pigwidgeon will be glad to hear," added Page, "that the inquiry is to be retrospective and most searching, probing everything to the bottom, sparing nobody, and followed by prosecutions in every case of jobbing brought to light."

"I'll try another slice of that capital round," said the apothecary.

The Doctor was obliged to drop his own knife and fork, which he had just commenced using, and again minister to the wants of the imperturbable Mr. Pigwidgeon.

"I rejoice," said the Vicar, "to hear of the surgeons being cut up, and the doctors getting a pill."

"The inquiry will be no joke to some people, you may depend upon it," resumed Page, returning to his own plate.

"I'll trouble you for the mustard, Doctor," said Mr. Pigwidgeon again, with inimitable *sang froid*.

The Doctor, finding his adversary impregnable, either by dint of his impudence or through the vigour of his appetite, said no more, but, as the best way of concealing his discomfiture, transferred his personalities to the round of beef, while Mrs. Medlicott began to talk to the apothecary about his son.

"It was a long time," she said, "since she had had the pleasure of seeing him—she hoped he was attentive to his profession."

"Well, I can't say that he is more attentive than other people," replied the apothecary, very disagreeably.

"Humph," said the Vicar, perceiving the hit at his own son.

"But I hope he is not idle," continued Mrs. Medlicott, not as sharp as her husband with all her mental superiority.

"I suppose if he is not doing one thing he is doing another," said the apothecary in the same unpleasant and somewhat mysterious manner.

"I hope and trust so," said the lady; "I take a great interest in your son, indeed I do, Mr. Pigwidgeon; and you know I always said he had talent—it only wanted awakening." She touched her forehead as she spoke, to show that she was still as great a phrenologist as ever, and knew the precise longitude and latitude of all the provinces of the understanding delineated upon the globe of the skull.

"It is only justice to say, ma'am, that you always did; and time will tell," answered Mr. Pigwidgeon.

"At all events," said Mrs. Medlicott, still further to prove the interest she continued to take in Dr. Pigwidgeon, "he has friends to do something for him,—who knows, for instance, but Reuben himself may have it in his power to be of use to him one of these days?"

The apothecary was as proud as he was shabby, and it is hard to describe how this most injudicious speech galled him. He tried to reply, but his voice stuck in his throat, with the irritation of his feelings. The Vicar, however, who was equally displeased for different reasons, came to his relief with a sharp rebuke to his wife's arrogance, telling her that Reuben was just as likely to want Dr. Pigwidgeon's services as Dr. Pigwidgeon to want Reuben's. Mrs. Medlicott was forced, in common politeness, to admit that this was true; but in doing so, she committed herself again by broadly alluding to Reuben's parliamentary intentions—the subject, of all others, which she should not have touched upon in the presence of the apothecary, the most notorious gossip in the whole county of Sussex. The Vicar tried to give her a little admonitory kick under the table, but he was on the opposite side, and his legs were too short to reach her.

Perhaps Mr. Pigwidgeon did not comprehend the allusion, broad as it was; but whether he did or not, a dry cough was the only notice he took of Mrs. Medlicott's last observation, accompanying it with a request for a final cup of tea.

The conversation would now have ceased, if it had not suddenly occurred to Mr. Primrose that he had seen the name of a Dr. Pigwidgeon lately mentioned in one of the London newspapers in connection with a celebrated Irish borough. He immediately asked the apothecary whether *his* Dr. Pigwidgeon was identical with the gentleman who was "up for Blarney." Never did Mrs. Medlicott lay her spectacles down with such nervous haste, as she did when the apothecary, glowing with paternal pride, and at the same time all shaking with excitement, answered,

"I have the honour, sir, to be father to that gentleman."

The revelation very naturally surprised everybody.

"I trust the news is true," said the Vicar, frankly and good-naturedly.

"It's true, and it's not true," said the apothecary.

"That's an enigma we must beg of you to explain," said the Vicar.

"Excuse me," said Mr. Pigwidgeon.

"I was never so amazed in all my life," said Mrs. Medlicott. Everything she said that morning was *mal-à-propos* as possible.

"I see nothing so amazing in my son coming into Parliament, Madam," said the apothecary, regarding her bitterly and speaking in a sort of slow growl.

"Nothing whatever," said the Vicar, heartily; "your son is a very eloquent man, we all know, and I don't see why he should bury his talent more than anybody else."

Mrs. Medlicott hastened to say something to the same effect (for, in truth, she had still some sparks left of her old intellectual *tendresse* for Theodore, and was pleased as well as astonished at what she had heard), but it was too late; the apothecary rose from the table, and after taking a profusion of snuff, followed the Vicar into his study to discuss the business, whatever it was, that brought him to the Vicarage that morning.

Page proposed a cigar to Primrose under the walnut-tree, and the proposition was gladly accepted, particularly as a mode of escape from Mrs. Medlicott, who, if she had ceased twaddling about politics, would have infallibly commenced twaddling about something else.

"Well, what do you think of Mr. Pigwidgeon?" said the Doctor, lighting his Havana.

"He is a man," said Mr. Primrose, "take him for all in all, I trust I shall never see his like again. Can it be possible he is rich, he looks such a miserably poor devil?"

"A devil, but anything but a poor one," said Page.

"What puts borough-mongering in the head of such a man as that?" said Hyacinth; "I thought it was too high a species of jobbing for so low a fellow."

"I'll tell you," said the Doctor; "it is the only description of knavery he has not yet practised, and he wants to be perfect in every branch of the art."

It was a short colloquy, for it ended here. Before the half of their cigars was turned into smoke and ashes, they saw the apothecary sneaking off through a door in the hedge; and the Vicar rejoined them, puffing and blowing. Short as his interview had been with his visitor, it was evident something had occurred at once surprising and vexatious, and his friends were not long in ignorance of the truth.

"A pretty kettle of fish," quoth the Vicar, panting. It may have been remarked that this was a favourite phrase of his.

"What's the matter?" asked the Doctor.

"Why, that booby of a son of his is not going to stand for Blarney, after all," replied the Vicar, still out of breath.

"What is that to you, or to me?" said Page.

"But he is going to stand for Chichester—for Chichester against Reuben," said the Vicar, almost in a scream, and staring at the Doctor energetically.

"No!"—cried Page—"you don't say so!—that's too good."

"He came to solicit my vote and interest—he came to canvass me, sir."

"In earnest?"—cried Page.

"Perfectly in earnest, and they are in the field before us, let me tell you; here's Dr. Pigwidgeon's address to the electors, actually in print," and he pulled out of his pocket as he spoke, a printed hand-bill, with which the apothecary had just presented him.

"And Parliament was dissolved yesterday, and the writ will be down before you can say Jack Robinson," continued Mr. Medlicott, recollecting by degrees all he had heard.

Doctor Page now jumped up, uttering a variety of exclamations, mingled with a few oaths of no very profane character, but mostly appeals to "Jove and Jingo," "Lord Harry," and "All that's lovely;" ending by vigorously buttoning his coat, and heartily abusing the Vicar, Mr. Primrose, himself, and everybody, for passing their time lounging in the garden, smoking cigars, and chatting about a worthless old raven, when so much was to be done, and there was so little time to do it in.

"My wife was right, after all," said the Vicar, looking a little ashamed of himself.

"By the Lord Harry, she was, sir," said the Doctor.

"Here comes the lady herself," said Primrose.

"That's always the case with my wife," said the Vicar, "the moment she is mentioned she is sure to appear."

The news struck Mrs. Medlicott like a thunderbolt, and after inveighing against the ingratitude and presumption of her old pupil, in the strongest terms permissible to a woman's lips, she vented all the indignation she had remaining upon her husband, and by implication upon his friends, for being so remiss while the foe was so active.

"Well, Madam, we shall do better in future," said the Doctor.

"Indeed I hope so, Dr. Page," said Mrs. Medlicott, rather imperiously, "there is work for everybody—I was at mine early this morning. Here is an address which I have written for Reuben;—you never thought of this, I venture to say, Mr. Medlicott."

The Vicar stood aghast at the woman's presumption, while the Doctor and Mr. Primrose furtively exchanged looks of nearly equal alarm, well justified by the very bulk of the papers Mrs. Medlicott held in her hand, big enough, in fact, to be the manuscript of a pamphlet.

It was hard to know what to say, or what to do. The Vicar shrugged his shoulders, said the address was the most ticklish thing of all, and thought it ought to be left to Reuben himself, who would probably arrive in the course of the evening. Fortunately he got into an altercation with his wife upon this point, which enabled the Doctor and Mr. Primrose to consult together aside, as to the best course to take in the emergency, when they wisely resolved to accept the lady's composition, with as many compliments to its excellence as they could bestow, and having thus got it into their hands for instant publication, to slash it and hash it at their discretion, throwing all the blame upon somebody or another with sufficiently broad shoulders, Mr. Cox, for example, whose munificent subscription might seem to entitle him to take a liberty of the kind.

This course was, accordingly, adopted; Mr. Primrose took upon him the task of eulogising the address, which he did with no economy of flattering expressions; after which, the three men of the party got into the Doctor's little open carriage (the same old machine that had made the tour of Wales), and, at a rapid, electioneering pace, drove into the city.

CHAPTER VII.

MR. MEDLICOTT RECEIVES THE DEPUTATION.

THERE was never perhaps a queerer embassy than that which the liberal and enlightened electors of Chichester sent up to London, to overcome the modest reluctance of Mr. Reuben Medlicott to represent them in the British Parliament. With Mr. Broad, the head and front of the embassy, we are well acquainted already. Alderman Codd was almost as fat as he was facile, and Alderman Gosling, the third, was considered a droll fellow in his corporation, a character which he sustained chiefly by puns and jokes upon his own not inappropriate name. This last worthy was accompanied by his son, a lad of some twelve years' pith, one of Mr. Medlicott's numerous godsons, and a Reuben into the bargain. The Alderman thought the present opportunity a good one to introduce this hopeful youth to the notice of his illustrious sponsor, and, to make him worthy to appear in such a presence, he had clothed him from head to foot in a new suit of sky-blue, which, decorated with a profusion of conical silver buttons, formed a very imposing holiday costume.

Mr. Medlicott had no fixed residence in the metropolis at this period, but led a sort of oscillating life, as became a man of genius, and suited a man of his circumstances, occasionally taking advantage of Lord Maudlin's house when he was out of town, but generally moving back and forwards between Mr. Trevor's convenient box at Hampstead and Friend Harvey's accommodating house in Gracechurch-street. Fortunately for the dignity of the present occasion, he happened to be quartered at Maudlin House in Cavendish-square, when Mr. Broad and his colleagues arrived to lay the representation of Chichester at his feet.

Poor Mary Medlicott, anxious as she was about what was going on, was in no condition at the time to take a very active part in the preparations to receive the embassy. There were palpable grounds for believing that she would soon present her husband with a third pledge of their mutual affection; a male it was devoutly hoped, to inherit the father's talents, and perpetuate his name and blood.

But Reuben was in no want of friends far more competent than his wife to lend him the sort of assistance he wanted in the present circumstances. He was now living on terms more intimate than was perfectly discreet, with his old acquaintance Adolphe, and his charming and clever sister, Mrs. Chatterton. The former had long since given up all his mechanical and mercantile speculations, and the latter had been for some time separated from her husband, the Professor. Brother and sister now went by the name of Monsieur and Madame Beauvoisin, and were proposing a great many ingenious plans for the future, the favourite one being to establish a Musical Academy at Chichester, under the patronage of Mr. Medlicott, which naturally made them take the liveliest interest in all that was now going forward.

It was Madame Beauvoisin who arranged the largest of the drawing-rooms for the present occasion. A gilt chair was placed for Reuben at the top of the room, flanked with sofas and couches for the members of his family and such of his friends as might wish to be present; in the middle space was a table strewed with blue books brought up from my Lord's library, and supporting also a plate of oranges for the speakers, while beneath the table were set three chairs for the gentlemen composing the deputation.

Mr. Medlicott, always attentive to dress, as well as address, took his usual pains on that important day to appear as captivating as possible in the sight of his townsmen and acquaintance. It was about this period of his life he adopted the particular costume from which he rarely deviated afterwards, except for the short interval of his total amalgamation with the Quakers, hereafter to be recorded. This was a light-brown body-coat, with gilt buttons, white waistcoat, light drab or pearl-coloured trousers, and a blue silk cravat; all rather flowing and ample, as if his taste for looseness and prolixity had extended from his mind to his apparel. A gold watch-chain with a bunch of seals hung from his fob; and a superb cluster of flowers, such as were then in season, completed as usual the decoration of his person.

Thus armed at all points for civil conquest, burnished like a mirror, perfumed like a garden, radiant with satisfaction, and a little swollen with importance, he decended from his dressing-room about half-an-hour before the time appointed; turned over his private collections of similes and metaphors, selecting a few for the occasion, and then taking his flageolet (which had been much in request since his marriage), he threw himself with "artless heed" on a pile of cushions, and surrounded by the fair Louise, as useful as she was charming, his adoring wife, and his crowing progeny, tricked out with enormous blue sashes, he regaled them with a succession of the old melodies which he had learned under the shadow of the great square tower of Hereford Cathedral. In the interval between two tunes, Madame Beauvoisin, not quite approving of the disposition of his hair, produced a little ivory comb from her pocket, and improved its arrangement with a coquettish touch or two of her old art, while his wife inquired if the interview with the deputies would occupy much time.

"I should say very little, my dear," replied Reuben, "if people will only abstain from speechifying. The deputation has only to ask me a simple question. I have only to return a plain answer,—perhaps make a remark. Including the collation, I cannot conceive the whole affair occupying more than one hour."

"Then we shall have our drive round the Regent's Park before dinner," said Mary.

"By all means," replied her husband, and, resuming the instrument, he was playing another lively air, in the attitude of a shepherd on a bank, in a picture of the "learned Poussin's," when the door was thrown open and a servant announced Mr. Trevor, the law-bookseller, Mr. Fox, the proctor, Mr. Reynard, the attorney, and these were soon followed by Mrs. Mountjoy with several of the old *habitués* of Burlington Gardens, including Mr. Bavard and Captain Shunfield.

You may fancy how the pompous arrangement of so fine an apartment, the display of the blue books, such a charming group of lovely women and rosy children, and the showy figure of the rising statesman in the centre of it, like a diamond surrounded with rubies, must have affected the imaginations and dazzled the eyes of the beholders. The proctor, when he was able to speak, made a clumsy attempt to compliment Mr. Medlicott upon his combination of graceful accomplishments with talents of the highest order.

"Ah," replied Reuben, quickly availing himself of one of his cut-and-dry classical allusions, "I am, unhappily, a contrast to Themistocles; I can fiddle, which he could not, but I cannot make a small town a great city, as he could." He handed, as he spoke, the flageolet to his wife's maid to lay it aside, and the air with which he performed this little action was well calculated to throw considerable doubt upon the sincerity of the disclaimer.

"Pardon me, sir, but you are the very man to do both,"

returned the proctor, "I am sure if you had only practised in Doctors' Commons——"

"I am reminded," said Mr. Bavard, who came to the meeting in a spirit of malicious curiosity, among other improper motives, "of a remark of Bacon's on the subject in question; there are many, he says, who can fiddle well enough, but are so far from being able to make a small town a great one, that their gift lies the other way, to bring a great town to ruin. I don't mean, of course, to insinuate that Mr. Medlicott possesses that description of talent; but to be sure nobody knows what any man can do until he is tried. I remember an anecdote."——

But an influx of Quakers just at the moment took the parable out of Mr. Bavard's mouth before he could utter another syllable. Friend Harvey led the way, or rather came rushing in, as brown as a berry, all but his hat, and as brisk as any bee, his smooth oval face glowing with enthusiasm, one hand employed pulling out his watch, the other full of tracts and pamphlets, which proved to be all copies of Reuben's speech on capital punishment, and his eloquent defence of the Meeting. Harvey was followed by Friend Wilson, his opposite neighbour, and the solemnest of his sect, at whose heels came Jonas and Samuel Harvey, the former with his mouth wider open than ever, but both looking like malefactors, they were so amazed by all that they saw. Then there was Isaac Hopkins, a Smyrna merchant, in full fig; Joshua Hopkins, his brother, a brewer of Bermondsey; and two or three exceedingly drab and dreary Quakeresses, whose harsh and forbidding countenances showed that they had not yet in their hearts forgiven our poor Mary for deserting the Meeting, though outwardly reconciled to her, in gratitude for her husband's services, and probably with hopes of further advantages from his genius.

Friend Harvey had not been in the room for five minutes before his extraordinary zeal and indefatigable activity gave him a kind of ascendancy over the rest of the company. Mr. Trevor had intended to be the most prominent of Reuben's supporters; Mr. Reynard, the attorney, had also contemplated taking the lead, and so had the secretary of the Polish Association, who considered himself quite at home in Lord Maudlin's house; but nothing could stand before the restless energy of Harvey; he constituted himself secretary, had a string of resolutions ready prepared, cut up the oranges, sprinkled all the room over with his tracts, elbowed Mr. Bavard without the least ceremony, told

Friend Trevor, his brother bookseller, to make himself useful, and stationed his two gaping sons at a window to proclaim the arrival of the deputation at the hall-door.

The Quakers, being all pinks of punctuality, kept looking at their watches incessantly, and, indeed, the moment was almost come for Mr. Broad and his colleagues to make their appearance. There was very little occasion for alarm on that score. Mr. Broad had his heart and soul in the business of the day as much as Friend Harvey himself; he had the old "Black Lion" in a ferment the whole morning about a respectable coach for the occasion, and after holding forth on the dignity and importance of his mission, to the vast astonishment of the coffee-room, he sallied forth to have his hair dressed and powdered by a London hair-cutter, and insisted upon the two Aldermen having their wise noddles dressed also,—nay, while the operator had him in hand, the excited little cutler could not refrain from going over the whole story again of his business in town, which made the hair-dresser feel that he was exercising his talents on the head of a personage of no little weight in the political world.

"Broad," said Alderman Codd, as they left the shop, to step into the coach, which had been brought to the door for them, "Broad, you have out-talked the barber."

"You won't have a word in you, when the talk is wanted," said Alderman Gosling.

"You must take my place, Alderman," said Broad.

Here the coachman inquired where he was to drive their worships, for having heard the word alderman, he concluded they were all personages of the same municipal rank and dignity.

"To the Right Honourable Lord Viscount Maudlin's," said Mr. Broad, "with whom my illustrious townsman Mr. Medlicott is on a visit."

"Where does his Lordship live, please your worships?"

"You ought to be ashamed to ask such a question," replied Mr. Broad; "in Cavendish square, to be sure, sir."

"Your worship doesn't happen to know the number of the house?"

"House, sir!—it's not a house, it's a mansion;—drive us to Cavendish-square; I don't suppose there will be much difficulty in finding the mansion of the Right Honourable Lord Viscount Maudlin."

"You are going to the house of a Viscount, think of that,

boy," said Alderman Codd to Master Reuben Gosling, the youth in the sky-blue suit.

"Is godfather a Viscount?" said the boy.

"Not quite so great as all that," said his sire.

"Your godfather, boy, is a statesman and an orator," said Mr. Broad, "which is much greater than any Viscount. Wait till you hear your godfather talk."

"He talked for you when you could not talk for yourself," said Alderman Gosling, chucking his son under the chin, and laughing at his own wit.

There was no difficulty in finding Lord Maudlin's house. Directly the coach drove up to the door, the young Quaker booksellers announced the event with a simultaneous shout.

"Friends will be so kind as to take their places," cried Harvey himself; and not content with making this request, which indeed was in the tone of a command, he actually forced several people to sit down who were disposed to remain standing. Among those on whom he exercised this compulsion was the gallant Captain Shunfield, and so little did Harvey care where the Captain sat, provided he was seated, that he wedged him in between the two grim and sour old Quakeresses upon a sofa, who were scandalised beyond measure by finding themselves in actual contact with a dragoon, little dreaming that he was in truth as peaceful a personage as any in the room. The Captain on his part looked grim enough also, and twisted his moustache with considerable ferocity; but like everybody else he succumbed to Friend Harvey, and kept his uncomfortable seat most submissively to the close of the proceedings.

Hard it is to say which sight was better worth seeing, Mr. Medlicott when he took the gilt chair at the top of the table with the oranges and blue books, or Mr. Broad when he marched in with his fidgetty strut (something between the magpie and the peacock), and suddenly found himself in the presence of a larger assembly than he had reckoned on, including so many ladies, to make his situation the more embarrassing. There was not much room for the ludicrous evolutions with which he usually made his bows; but he turned the space he had to the best account, and diverted exceedingly everybody who had the least eye for the ridiculous. Ushered by Friend Harvey, he took the middle place at the bottom of the table; the Aldermen supported him on each side, staring like stuck pigs, as the vulgar saying is, and no chair being provided for Master Reuben Gosling, Harvey soon disposed of that young gentleman, by assigning him a place on the same chair with Mr Bavard, who soon assigned him to a seat on the ground almost at Mr. Medlicott's feet.

These arrangements having been made, Friend Harvey approached the table, and standing bolt upright, and addressing Reuben, in tones to which his nose contributed more than was pleasant to the ear, said—

"Friend Medlicott, it now becomes my duty to acquaint thee that a deputation of thy most distinguished townsmen (here Mr. Broad bowed) has the honour of waiting upon thee, for objects and purposes which they will explain with far more circumlocution than it would become me to do; they will address thee one after the other, and from all I have heard, I think the lovers of eloquence and friends of humanity will have a rare treat."

This most unauthorised programme made the three deputies twice as nervous and fidgetty as they were already disposed to be; a mutual elbowing, whispering, nodding, and winking took place, which ended in the Aldermen joining to push Mr Broad forward, as it had all along been settled that he should be spokesman.

Considering that everybody present perfectly well knew what Mr. Broad had got to say, before he opened his lips, the speech that he made answered its purpose to admiration. Had the object of his mission not been previously understood, it is very questionable if his speech would have thrown much light upon it; for never having addressed a dozen people before, and being almost completely overwhelmed by the combined effect of the splendid mansion, the presence of the fair sex, and more than all by the premature compliments paid to his eloquence, he lost his voice almost completely, and the train of his thoughts, such as they were, along with it. In short, after stammering for five minutes, the only audible words being "reform," "Poland," "Chichester," and "my eloquent and distinguished townsman," the poor little cutler sat down, with no great reason to be pleased with his performance, except that it called forth as loud plaudits as if it had been made by the best speaker of the day.

"*Vox faucibus hæsit,*" said the Proctor, aside, to Mr. Bavard. It was a scrap of Latin he had probably picked up from Dr. Lushington.

"The beginning of the line is equally applicable," said Bavard, "*steteruntque comæ,*" and truly so it was, for Mr. Broad's well-powdered hair, which he always wore brushed up to the shape of a cone, being now fresh from the hands of the hair-cutter, stood straight up on his head like nothing so much as a sharp alpine peak, to which we compared it on a former occasion.

Friend Harvey worked hard to get speeches from Alderman Codd and Gosling. The former, indeed, got on his legs, but it was only to say that "he endorsed Mr. Broad's bill;" a short speech, but an energetic one, particularly as he closed it (by way of peroration) with a thump on the table which nearly broke it, and sent the oranges rolling about the floor; at the same time he resumed his chair with so heavy a plump that it went nearly to pieces under him, being one of French manufacture, and ill-suited to the weight of an English Alderman. No one but Friend Harvey was much displeased by these little interruptions, which were rather of a pleasant nature. To one person present they were even propitious, for the son of Alderman Gosling, having been very active in picking up the oranges, attracted Mr. Medlicott's attention, and had the honour of having his head patted and being asked at the same time what was his name. The boy was ready enough to answer, and not only told his name, but the sort of moral relationship in which he stood to his eminent namesake.

"I believe," said Mr. Medlicott, most graciously smiling, "I have a great many young namesakes in and about Chichester."

"Two Reuben Medlicotts and three plain Reubens," answered the youth as glibly as possible.

Mr. Medlicott again patted his head, and told him he would not forget him.

"That boy's bread is baked," said Mr. Broad, aside, to the elder Gosling, who had been most anxiously watching what passed.

At the same moment the other Alderman was provided with a stouter chair, and Mr. Medlicott, with one hand on his breast, and the other upon one of the blue books, the very picture of the dawning statesman, rose to make "a few observations."

CHAPTER VIII.

MR. MEDLICOTT GIVES HIS FRIENDS A TREAT.

"Will you stand for Chichester, Mr. Medlicott?" was the plain question put to him, and a "yes," or a "no," would have been, to all intents and purposes, a sufficient answer to it. But his zealous and admiring friends had not assembled in such force, to be put off with a monosyllabic oration; and the Quakers especially (albeit a sect whose communications are yea and nay), would have been offended by an affectation of brevity upon the present occasion. In fact everybody present, except Mr. Bavard, came expressly for what friend Harvey called "a treat;" and as neither the speech of Mr. Broad, nor that of the Alderman, could well be considered in that light, it became the more incumbent upon Mr. Medlicott to satisfy the cravings of the little meeting. It was not two o'clock when he commenced his palaver, and it was past four when he had done: nor will it be thought in the least surprising that he spoke at such great length, when the number of topics is considered which he was either expected, or thought it his duty, to handle; embracing most questions of foreign and domestic policy, the vast circle of human interests, and every project of reform that ever was broached. We hope to be pardoned for declining to give the speech *in extenso*. There is some danger of even an abstract being voted tiresome; but as it seems indispensable to give the reader a specimen of Mr. Medlicott's mode of proceeding, when he rose to offer a simple remark, or make a few short observations, we must run the risk, great as it is. He commenced with a broad view (an exceedingly broad one) of the British constitution; then he discussed the onerous duties and awful responsibilities of a member of parliament; from which he proceeded to the serious inquiry whether he possessed the proper intellectual, moral, and physical qualifications for a trust of such magnitude and importance, seeming at first to be of opinion that it was far beyond his strength and abilities, but eventually comforting his friends by coming round to the conclusion that, under all the circumstances of the case, even his poor talents might be acceptable to his country. Sometimes he shrank from the task he was called on to perform; but then again, was it for him to set up his weak judgment against the public, if the public thought fit to command his services? *Vox populi vox*

Dei, he continued, looking at Alderman Gosling, who nodded as if he understood what that meant; and having delivered this oracular sentence, he thought it his duty to state, very briefly of course, his opinions and sentiments on all the leading questions of the day. It was unnecessary to assure his friend, Mr. Broad, that he was unalterably attached to the cause of Poland, and eternally hostile to the power of Russia. He felt honoured and gratified by the cordial cheer with which that worthy gentleman bore witness to the strength and sincerity of his feelings upon that subject: in fact, he could only do perfect justice to those feelings by protesting that his hatred of the Czar amounted to a personal animosity. But he could not consent to confine his views to Muscovy; he begged to be allowed to spread his mind over the whole terraqueous globe—

"Let Observation, with extended view,
Survey the world from India to Peru."

He was sure his excellent friend Mr. Harvey would not quarrel with him for that, nor his friends, the Messrs. Hopkins, whose enterprising benevolence was known and felt wherever the name of England had penetrated,—

"Whatever clime the sun's bright circle warms."

Were they not all profoundly interested in the politics of our Indian empire? who was unconcerned in the welfare of the great Australian continent? who did not love the Kaffir as his kinsman? who did not yearn to the New Zealander as his brother? He knew how his words touched all their hearts; he saw how they particularly touched his fair hearers (meaning the grim old Quakeresses to whom he had especially directed them). What course, then, ought a public man to take? What, in fact, did "foreign politics" mean? He would answer in one word, and that word was sympathy! He had touched another chord of the harp of feeling, another string of that divine instrument, the human heart, which heaven itself had tuned, 'more musical than is Apollo's lute;"—alas, that he was not a Wilberforce, or a Burke, to touch it worthily, to bring forth all its sweetness,

"Untwisting all the chords that tie
The hidden soul of harmony."

While Mr. Medlicott was making these happy and beautiful allusions to melody (most of them extracted that morning from his common-place book), his wife had found it extremely difficult to keep the yearling in her arms as quiet and mute as the gravity of the occasion required. The child (fortunately a good-humoured and deserving little creature) was continually stretching out its arms, as if to catch Reuben's as they winnowed the air, at the same time crowing as if it actually desired to concur in the compliments which the deputies and the Quakers paid to almost every sentence. Mary was at length about to retire with her infant, when the felicitous idea occurred to Reuben to take it out of her hands, and continue his speech with the child in his arms, which he did with such a mixture of parental tenderness and statesman-like dignity, that it drew forth louder plaudits than he had yet been honoured with. Of course, he had now only one hand at liberty, but he sawed the air with that sufficiently, and now began to roam through a wilderness of topics, where, if we were to attempt to follow him, we should infallibly lose our way, as he did himself more than once during his rambles. Probably it was of little consequence in what order the topics were disposed; but Mr. Medlicott was never much of a martinet in the point of logical discipline called method, and the remainder of his address was literally nothing but a mob of circumlocutions about the various questions which he knew were uppermost in the thoughts of his friends. He knew Mr. Trevor was anxious about the law of copyright; he expatiated accordingly for ten minutes on that subject. To please Isaac Hopkins he was prolix on temperance for a quarter of an hour. To gratify the Proctor he went to an unnecessary length into the abuses of the common law, and then to compensate the Attorney, he held forth with equal superfluity upon the reform of the ecclesiastical courts, after all which he unluckily caught the fanatical eye of Friend Wilson who was the president of a Peace Society; and his ideas rushing forthwith into that new train, off he went at a tangent, dashing into the Horse Guards, demolishing the army estimates, and inveighing against iron and saltpetre, very much in the belligerent strain of Mr. Cobden at the present day, and nothing daunted by the presence of Captain Shunfield, who, to do him justice, took the assault upon the profession of arms in the utmost good humour, though the old Quakeresses were afraid that he would draw his sword every instant.

14*

The speech came to an end at last,—all things do, all things must, and the law must be an inexorable one, or the genius of Reuben Medlicott would not have submitted to it. The moment he ceased, Alderman Codd jumped up to ask a question about the National Debt, but Mr. Broad pulled him down, and for so doing well deserved the thanks of the meeting. The other Alderman, however, Mr. Gosling, managed to get in a word, and a very sensible one it was.

"He begged to know whether Mr. Medlicott did or did not accept the invitation; for though he had paid his eloquent speech the greatest attention, he had heard nothing distinct upon that which was the main point."

"I must say," said Mr. Bavard, maliciously supporting the Alderman, "I never heard a more admirable speech than my eloquent friend has made upon every subject in the world except the question at issue."

Mr. Broad was furious at this, and exclaimed that he had never heard anything more explicit than the language of his distinguished townsman. Friend Harvey was also most indignant. Friend Wilson concurred with Alderman Gosling. The Proctor and the Attorney differed as usual. All spoke at once, while Mr. Medlicott, piqued at the nature of the dispute, (involving as it did an unpleasant criticism upon his display,) preserved a dignified and sarcastic silence. At length, after a little tumult for five minutes, Mr. Trevor made the shrewd suggestion that one word from the learned gentleman himself would settle the question.

"Yes, or no," he said, addressing Mr. Medlicott.

"Yea, or nay," said Friend Wilson, with a deep, hollow voice, as if it issued from the jaws of a sepulchre.

Reuben looked at neither of the speakers, but rising again with much state, addressed himself to Mr. Broad, and said, "he thought he had explained himself sufficiently; if he had not, he was sorry for it; but he begged now to assure that gentleman that he wanted words to thank his friends at Chichester for the honour they had done him, and he would take the earliest opportunity of waiting on the electors and canvassing them in person."

"Now, Alderman, *I* hope you are satisfied," said Mr. Broad, accosting his colleague triumphantly.

"You ought to have held your tongue, brother," said the other Alderman, "if it was only for your son's sake."

"I believe I was a goose," said Gosling.

A collation followed, and Mr. Medlicott appearing to be exhausted by his effort, one of the old Quakeresses addressed him and said—

"Friend Reuben, thou needest the refreshment of repose more than thy victuals; if thou wilt take my advice thou wilt go to thy chamber and take a lay."

His wife explained to him afterwards that "taking a lay" meant, in Quaker phraseology, stretching one's-self on the bed without undressing, the common practice of the Society of Friends at their great anniversaries, in the intervals between their morning and afternoon Meetings; the Jacobs and Obadiahs, moved by the spirit of drowsiness, retiring to one side of the corridor, and the Rachels and Hannahs seceding to the other.

Mr. Medlicott, however, remained to do the honours of his feast, which was extremely acceptable to everybody after so much speaking. A very industrious hour was spent over the viands, and it was nearly six o'clock before the majority of the guests dispersed. The deputies lingered after the rest, and so did Friend Harvey, Mr. Trevor and Mr. Reynard. They lingered, however, for practical objects, although the bottle went round while they were discussing them. One of the objects was secured by the obliging and handsome manner in which Mr. Reynard undertook to conduct the election, in the capacity of Mr. Medlicott's law agent. This, however, it is to be observed, to the credit of the solicitor's sagacity, he did not do until he was informed by Mr. Broad that upwards of three thousand pounds had been raised, and was actually forthcoming, if necessary, to secure the return.

Reuben said, he knew nothing of the expenses of elections; but since the subject had been mentioned, he might as well take that opportunity of stating most distinctly, that he intended to represent the city of Chichester, and not his own, or any other man's pocket. He begged the deputies to take a note of what he said;—there must be no bribery—no treating—and no intimidation. He would only stand upon these three conditions.

"In regard to bribery," said Reynard, addressing Reuben, "you may be perfectly satisfied, sir, if I have the management of the election, there will be nothing of that sort. The name of Reynard is, I hope and trust, security enough in itself that everything done under his direction will be done honourably and above-board."

"If I might presume to advise thee, friend Reuben," said Harvey, "I would say thou shouldst start for Chichester thyself, at thy earliest convenience."

"By all means," said Reynard, "the sooner the better. Manage a public entry, if you can, in an open carriage. Address the mob from the box, and leave everything else to Mr. Broad and me."

Mr. Broad said he was entirely at Mr. Reynard's disposal, and he would say the same for his colleagues, the Aldermen.

"The Aldermen ought to go down, this very night," said Reynard, "to convey Mr. Medlicott's determination to the constituency, and order the flags, music, and all that sort of thing."

The Aldermen looked at one another, and seemed disconcerted.

"The fact is," said Alderman Codd, "my brother and I are invited to-morrow to a grand feast at Fishmongers' Hall, to meet the Lord Mayor of London."

"That," said Mr. Reynard, "may be done by proxy."

The Aldermen evidently disliked the notion of dining with the Fishmongers by proxy, and Mr. Medlicott, observing their perplexity, said he should be extremely sorry if his worthy friends were put to any inconvenience upon his account.

"By the bye," he added, addressing Alderman Gosling, "I am greatly taken with that fine boy of yours. Judging from his answers to some questions I put to him, I should say he has a decided talent for social statistics. Make him mind his arithmetic. I may yet be in a position to serve him."

This well-timed hit made Gosling his own for ever. He cheerfully sacrificed turtle and venison, setting a bright example to his brother Alderman, which the latter did not fail to follow; and after drinking a final bumper to the toast of Medlicott and universal philanthropy, the municipal dignitaries took leave of their host, and hurried away to be in time for the mail.

The rest of the company soon dispersed. The solicitor and Mr. Broad walked away arm-in-arm. The former was anxious to collect from the latter as much information about local politics as he could procure, and he was further desirous of having some portion of the three thousand pounds lodged in his own hands with the least possible delay.

"I must have a few hundreds this evening, or very early to-morrow," said Reynard.

"We had better go to friend Harvey's," said the cutler. "The Quakers (to their credit be it spoken) are greatly interested in the election, and have undertaken to advance a large sum, should money be wanting."

"Money will be wanting, let me tell you," said Mr. Reynard.

"Five or six hundred pounds will cover everything, won't it?" said the other.

"The Quakers you say," said Reynard, instead of directly answering the question, "are interested in Mr. Medlicott's election?"

"Interested, sir—to be sure they are—everybody is interested! Did you ever see such an important meeting? Did you ever hear such a wonderful speech? Why, sir, it will be a great era in English history, Mr. Medlicott coming into Parliament. It will change the face of the world."

"The thing must be done, cost what it may," said Reynard.

"Cost what it may, sir," said Broad, energetically; "at all sacrifices and risks."

"Nobody has a greater respect for purity, or a livelier horror of corruption in every shape, than the man who is now talking to you," said Reynard; "but I'll tell you a maxim of mine, ever since I began to practise this branch of my profession. If a man is going to dine with a friend, and if there's no way to his house but through a dirty lane, he takes the dirty lane."

"He does, sir," said Broad, "of course he does."

"Or he would lose his dinner," added the Attorney.

"Nobody likes that," said Broad.

"I have no reason to think Chichester a particularly dirty place," said Reynard, "but I don't know as much about it as you do."

"It is not a particularly dirty place, I'll say that for it," replied the cutler, "but there are dirty people in Chichester, let me tell you, and dirty people that have votes, sir."

"The votes of dirty people count for as much as the votes of clean people at an election," said Mr. Reynard.

"That's a just observation," said Mr. Broad.

"And the upshot is, that we must have the money, Broad, or we can't make sure of returning our man. We must have the money, and we must spend the money; when a great object is to be carried, it won't do to be squeamish."

"I'll tell you what it is, Mr. Reynard," said Broad, speaking very confidentially, but at the same time very eagerly; "I'll be frank with you;—I hate foul play of every sort, and I trust we will not have much of it; but I would strain a point or two, that I would, sir, to secure the return of my eloquent and distinguished townsman."

"The feeling does you infinite credit," said Reynard, "let us go and call upon Mr. Harvey."

They found Harvey and Friend Wilson confabulating together over a cup of tea. The spirit of Jesuitry is not confined to the Jesuits. There was not a pair of more arrant Jesuits, after a fashion of their own, in all England, than Friends Harvey and Wilson; that is to say, the value they set upon an object made them shamefully indifferent as to the choice of the means of accomplishing it. Had you talked to either of them of any species of corruption in connexion with some movement which did not concern them, you would have found them as pure as any men need be; but when they believed that the interests of their sect were involved, when the advancement of their thousand philanthropic schemes and speculations was in question; when, in short, the dirty lane had such "a treat" at the end of it as the genius and services of a man like Mr. Medlicott, the muck and the mire must have been very thick indeed that would have deterred either of those worthy Quakers from tramping through it. Mr. Wilson, indeed, was beginning to put one or two very natural questions to Mr. Reynard, as to the employment of the gold he required, when he was checked by Harvey, who said—

"Thou art not a man of the law, Friend Wilson, any more than myself. Neither thou nor I understandest these matters; sufficient to every man is the knowledge that appertaineth to his own trade and calling. Friend Reynard will take care that everything is done that ought to be done, and that nothing is done that ought not to be done. If thou requirest three hundred pounds, Friend Reynard, thou shalt have it,—in what shape wouldest thou like the money?"

"A bag of sovereigns," said Reynard.

"If thou callest on me at ten o'clock in the morning, thou shalt have the bag."

Reynard pondered a moment, and then said, it would be impossible for him to call himself, but he would send a trusty person to Mr. Harvey at the hour appointed.

"As thou pleasest, Friend," said Harvey.

"Better still," said Reynard, "you will hand the bag over to Mr. Wilson, who will hand it over to my messenger."

"Thou hast good reasons, Friend, I have no doubt," said Harvey, "for thy circumbendibus everything shall be done agreeable to thy wishes."

Mr. Broad asked the attorney, as they left the Quaker's shop, what his reasons were for passing the bag of gold through so many hands.

"Oh," said Reynard, "it would not be necessary only for the number of mean suspicious rogues there are in the world, particularly on election committees. You have no idea how prevalent a spirit of low curiosity is among a certain class of honorable gentlemen, particularly where money is concerned. We can't be too cautious, let us be ever so honest, take my word for it."

CHAPTER IX.

WHEELS WITHIN WHEELS.

On the day of the meeting at Lord Maudlin's, Dr. Pigwidgeon had no more notion of standing for Chichester than he had of contesting the West Riding of Yorkshire; nor did Mr. Medlicott dream of meeting any opposition in that city, except upon purely public grounds. We have now to relate a little morsel of secret history, to explain how it came to pass that the movements of Reuben's friends became prematurely known in quarters most hostile to him, how the breast of the Doctor became fired with the same ambition that inflamed greater men, and who encouraged and supported him in his daring undertaking.

Mr. Bavard, who had started in life as a medical man, and acted as family physician to some of the ailing nobility, having given up for some years that line of practice, tried his hand successively at several other things, and settled down at last into a sort of professional toad-eating and sycophancy, which agreed well enough with his social talents, and raised instead of lowering his position in the world.

At this time it happened to be an *habitué* of the Barsacs, to whom he was both useful and agreeable, fetching and carrying gossip from great houses to which he had or pretended to have access; nosing out bargains of pictures for the merchant who had become a connoisseur in painting; doing the talk at their massive dinners, and a variety of little services of the like honourable nature. Among other things, he had managed to get the portrait of brown Sherry into the Book of

Beauty, without which, there was reason to think, she would not have completed the conquest of Mr. Leadenhall, the old East India director, to whom she had now been about a year married.

At Barsac's table Mr. Bavard had some opportunities (not many, for he was not often asked to first-class parties), of meeting the Bishop of Shrewsbury. The Bishop had treated him with as much contempt and neglect as it was possible for one man to show to another; he silenced him without mercy when he attempted to be anecdotic; but Bavard was not the man to be easily repulsed by any amount of snubbing and oversight. The more the Bishop overlooked him, the more intently he fixed his regards on the Bishop, and at length he discovered the true road and short cut to his heart, which consisted in bedaubing his works with the grossest flattery, and abusing everybody whom he knew his Lordship disliked. He very soon ascertained that to hear anything to his grandson's disadvantage was music to the old man's ears. How it became known beyond the Society of Friends that Reuben was the writer of the defence of Quakerism was by no means certain; probably his own vanity led him to boast of that production in places where it was imprudent to do so; but, however it happened, the truth oozed out, as all truth will sooner or later, and at length coming to Mr. Bavard's ear in London, it was not long in making the journey from thence to the palace at Shrewsbury. The rage of the Bishop was far greater upon this occasion than it had been before, even when he was attacked for deserting his principles, and denounced as an apostate. In fact, Reuben's pamphlet was, upon some points, (where the Bishop's passions had betrayed his judgment,) really a triumphant answer; and a man who piqued himself chiefly on his controversial powers could bear anything better than that. The Bishop was in London shortly after, met his informant at Portland-place, and for the first time noticed and smiled on him. Nothing passed, however, on the subject of Bavard's revelation, but the conversation turning after dinner upon the House of Commons and the rising talent of the day, somebody mentioned Mr. Medlicott's name with applause, adding that his friends were determined to procure him a seat in Parliament by hook or crook.

The Bishop instantly broke out into the stormiest abuse of his relation, greatly to the distress of Mrs. Wyndham, who was present. As usual, there was a great deal of truth mingled with the violence of his invectives. He never once mentioned his grandson's name, but assailed him with equal effect as one of a class of talking adventurers, who were springing up everywhere like mushrooms, and becoming the pest of the community. Men who failed at every thing else, for want of knowledge, or industry, or the commonest abilities, aspired to be statesmen, and thought themselves perfectly qualified to legislate for the kingdom; the offcasts of all the professions—doctors without patients, lawyers without briefs, fellows without an idea in their heads, or a guinea in their pockets, were talking themselves into notoriety, and there were plenty of fools to listen to them. The next Parliament would be a Parliament of quacks and coxcombs, of asses and parrots. The only fortunate circumstance was, that the same ignorance and emptiness which made such people politicians, usually made them paupers also: elections cost money, and he was glad of it. A few thousand pounds could not possibly be better laid out, than in defeating the impudent attempts of those worthless adventurers, to thrust themselves into the legislature.

Bavard lingered at the table that evening until he was alone with Mr. Barsac, whose slavish readiness to humour every whim or passion of the Bishop was perfectly well known to all his acquaintance. They conversed together in private for half an hour, and the result was, that Barsac commissioned the other to keep a sharp watch on Mr. Medlicott's proceedings, to discover what place he aimed at representing, "for," said the merchant, a littl· warmed with his own wine, "it's a public duty to try to keep such a man as that out of Parliament, and if it costs some thousands to do it, the money shall be forthcoming."

Bavard had now just the sort of occupation that suited his delicate moral tastes; and he had resorted to a variety of shabby tricks before he attended the meeting of Mr. Medlicott's friends in Cavendish-square. From that meeting he proceeded straight to Portland-place; but on his way he met little Griffin, the pursuivant, than whom Reuben had not a more malignant enemy in the world, ever since Griffin stole his paper on heraldry, and got himself made Blue Mantle on the strength of it. To this gentleman, accordingly, Bavard related everything; what Mr. Medlicott was about to do, and what steps Mr. Barsac was bent upon taking to counteract him. Griffin was not slow to propose himself as the rival candidate, but Bavard satisfied him that nobody would answer who was not to some extent locally connected with Chichester.

"Then I know a man," said Griffin, "who will answer your purpose to a nicety, my intimate friend, Mr. Pigwidgeon. He is coqueting at this moment with the Irish borough of Blarney, but he will only be too happy to give that up, and stand for his native city, if Mr. Barsac will come down with the necessary funds."

"What sort of a fellow is he?" inquired Bavard.

"I need hardly tell you he's an orator," said the other, "or the people of Blarney would never have looked at him; he is the best speaker, beyond all comparison, I ever heard in my life. He is the 'coming man,' in my opinion. A noble, high-minded fellow, full of heart as he is of talent. He is just the man, let me tell you, who won't forget a service done him when he is in a situation to repay it."

This speech, particularly the last sentence of it, decided Mr. Bavard's course. He saw Mr. Barsac, and then Griffin again, that same evening; went with him to Mr. Pigwidgeon's, and then they all went together to Portland-place, where everything was arranged before midnight to the satisfaction of all parties. Mr. Pigwidgeon, having already prevailed on his father to advance a thousand pounds towards the purchase of the Irish borough, was perfectly content with Barsac's promise to advance another thousand; the latter reckoned on the Bishop paying the money himself, to gratify his spite against his grandson. Griffin engaged himself to write the squibs for the election, at the rate of five guineas a piece; and Mr. Bavard was gratified with an assurance of Mr. Pigwidgeon's future patronage, and the honour of his friendship in the mean time.

CHAPTER X.

HOW THE CONTEST WAS CONDUCTED.

A CONTESTED election splits the society of county or county town, no matter how united previously, just as a thunderbolt splits a forest-tree, let the wood be of ever so tough a fibre. Forty-eight hours before the public announcement of the candidates, not a dozen inhabitants of the place (beyond the circle of his immediate relatives and friends) were troubling their heads about Mr. Medlicott, and not half the number cared a groat whether his opponent was on this side or that of the Stygian ferry ; yet no sooner was the announcement made, no sooner did the recognised leaders of the local parties formally recommend those gentlemen to the notice of their friends and followers respectively, than the whole city divided itself in twain with a celerity that was quite astonishing ; every man you met was either a Reubenite or a Pigwidgeonite ; you would have supposed that the very existence of Chichester depended upon the relative merits of the Vicar's son and the apothecary's ; a disruption took place of the oldest social ties ; ancient friendships were suspended ; candour was banished by universal consent ; decency was sent off in the same ship ; in short, to express the moral change that took place in the inflated language, which Mr Medlicott would probably have used himself, Truth and Honesty flew back to Heaven, and the spirits of Falsehood and Corruption ascended from the bottomless pit, to reign for a season in their stead.

The head-quarters of Mr. Medlicott's friends was an inn called the Parrot. His opponents established themselves at the Magpie, and each interest made itself excessively merry with the other's bird, and pronounced it most appropriate and happily emblematic. In a few days the names of the birds began to pass current for those of the parties ; Reuben's friends going by the name of the Parrots, while Mr. Pigwidgeon's were called the Magpies. The actual bribery went on at neither of the inns, but in two modest and retiring places which had long enjoyed the appellations of Guinea Lane and Yellow Row ; no doubt given to them in consequence of the virtuous practices for which they were notorious. The particular houses in those lanes, where the business was carried on, were well-known to all persons connected with the city, with the curious exception of every one who had ever represented, or sought to represent it in Parliament, some of whom were even strangely ignorant that such places as Yellow Row and Guinea Lane existed.

The electric telegraph had not been discovered, yet the rapidity with which the facts were known that Mr. Reynard was agent for Mr. Medlicott, that there was an ample capital to draw on, and that a bag of three hundred sovereigns had actually been placed in the attorney's hands, was such as to justify a suspicion that some agency of extraordinary, if not magical, character had been employed to convey the interesting intelligence. Reynard's very name had the chink of ready money to the ear of the corruptibles. A physiognomist acquainted with the sordid lines which the paltry vice of covetousness delves in the human countenance, might have distinguished a certain class of voters as he walked the streets. The hope of a five-pound note brought the glorious privileges of the British constitution home to the hearts and bosoms of a band of electors, not, perhaps, the majority of the constituents, but sufficiently numerous to reduce the suffrages of the honest portion to practical insignificance. The coolest members of the community, at a moment of such general excitement, were those who had come to the determination of putting themselves up for sale, and knocking themselves down to the highest bidder. No personal affections or animosities warped them; no political passions inflamed them; no enthusiasm for reform or philanthropy betrayed them into extravagance, or for a moment diverted their minds from the simple calculation of the market-value of their votes. To them it was nothing whether Medlicott or Pigwidgeon was the greater orator, or whether this cause or that cause was likely to be advanced or prejudiced by the triumph of the one or the other. To these single-minded men, the only questions were, which of the candidates had the most to spend, and which of them was most disposed to spend it. They were to be seen walking about the town with their left hands thrust ostentatiously into their breeches pockets, a sign agreed upon among them, and perfectly well understood to be a public advertisement of their resolution to sell their country.

There was another fraction of the constituency which had intellectual tastes, political feelings, and moral principles; but being exposed to various foul influences, and deficient in moral courage, ardently desired to follow the dictates of their consciences, but were more likely, in the event of a fierce struggle, to obey the commands of their customers, acquiesce in the pleasure of their landlords, or yield to the intimidation of the rabble. Of this unfortunate class (to whom the possession of the franchise was nothing but a misfortune) some preserved a stubborn silence on the subject of the coming election; some openly and justly complained of the constitution that gave them a privilege without protecting them in the use of it; while others, ashamed of the tyranny to which they succumbed, affected approbation of the course to which they foresaw they would ultimately be driven by it. Practically and virtually, these unfortunate people were only the proxies of others, who really possessed the influence which the voters nominally wielded; in many cases they were the proxies of persons to whom the law had positively refused the right of suffrage, disqualifying them to vote themselves, while it most preposterously enabled them to dictate and control the votes of others.

The Vicar and his friend Mr. Cox had hitherto been opposed to secret voting, but being particularly interested in this contest, and consequently paying more attention to its details than they had ever paid to an election before, they could never afterwards understand how any man, sincerely desirous to diminish the evils of bribery and intimidation, could object to the system of the ballot. Old Mr. Medlicott had the evils of terrorism brought under his own eyes in a very distinct and curious manner. He discovered that his own wife had been guilty of threatening to withdraw her paltry little custom from bakers, and butchers, and other tradesmen, should they presume to vote against her son. You may suppose how angry this made an honest little man like him. He gave the lady a hearty rating for her unconstitutional practices, desired to have no more such foul doings, and going round to every one of the little shops that had been threatened, disclaimed in the most explicit terms all participation or approval of Mrs. Medlicott's most improper conduct.

But when the struggle began in earnest, there was corruption enough of every kind, which was utterly beyond the control of Reuben's friends, or the conscientious portion of them. Before either of the rivals appeared on the stage, Mr. Primrose saw enough to make him regret that he had taken any part in the business at all, and placing Mrs. Mountjoy's purse in Dr. Page's hands, he made a precipitate retreat to London.

In every battle somebody, of course, must fire the first shot. The first shot upon this occasion was fired by the enemy in the form of a monstrous libel upon Mr. Medlicott, from the pen of his friend Mr. Griffin.

Mrs. Medlicott was in despair, and went about the house wringing her hands, and complaining in the itterest terms of the falsehood of the article.

"One would think that you wished it was all true," said the Vicar. "The falsehood is just the thing you ought to be glad of. We must see about answering it, or getting it retracted."

Dr. Page swore he would make them eat their words, and taking a cudgel in his hand, which he had probably bought with an eye to such uses, he strolled into the village.

The libel was evidently the production of a master of the art. After stating a good deal that was reasonable enough about the desultory life Reuben had led, and treating his pretensions, upon public grounds, with a contempt and ridicule to which no fair objection could be made, the article suddenly assumed the highest moral tone, laid down the broad principle that public virtue was incompatible with private vices, and deplored the imperious necessity which sometimes compelled a writer to discuss subjects at once the most delicate and the most repulsive. But duty (as usual in all such cases) was the paramount consideration; and he would, therefore, give the electors of Chichester a plain, unvarnished history of the man who had the incomparable insolence to solicit the suffrages of that ancient and venerable city. Then followed a series of statements, many of them sheer fictions, others founded upon little facts in Reuben's early career, which we have already imparted to our readers without lowering him much in their good opinion. The writer trembled, as he said, to approach that particular era of Mr. Medlicott's life, when he was the favoured inmate of his grandfather's house in Herefordshire, and, after disgracing the hospitable mansion of that great and good man, with debaucheries for which even the hot blood of youth was no apology, set one wing of it on fire, to destroy the records of his orgies, and to some extent actually effected his profligate purpose. He willingly passed over in silence many a year spent in low conviviality, in habits of daily intimacy with the scum of society; but he would like to know whether the pot-companions of glaziers and carpenters, the bosom friend of shoe-makers and tailors, the Lothario of dairy-maids, and the Orpheus of the ale-house was a proper person to represent the capital of Sussex? Would he dare to confess to the world the nature of his well-known connection with a gang of French adventurers, who commenced their career at Hereford, who travelled from thence to Cambridge, shoemakers in one place, booksellers in another, and hairdressers (he believed) at this present moment in London? Mr. Medlicott was impregnable, indeed upon one point; he was safe on the subject of his intrigues with the fair sex; but he was safe only because they were too scandalous to be alluded to by any writer of common decency. What would the virtuous inhabitants of that virtuous city think of a man, of whom it was stated (and, alas, upon too solid grounds), that he had gone the horrible and incredible length of attempting to seduce the affections of his own grandmother; but, to the eternal

honour of her sex, that paragon of female purity had repelled
his insulting addresses, and had only been prevented by motives
easily understood from publicly exposing and denouncing her
shameless assailant.

With this libel in his pocket, Dr. Page walked into the
apothecary's shop. Mr. Pigwidgeon was not at home; he had
gone to town to meet his son, who was expected to arrive that
evening from London. The Doctor hired a horse at the inn,
rode into Chichester, and went straight to the office of the newspaper. He first asked for the editor, who was not to be seen;
then he inquired if by any chance his friend Mr. Pigwidgeon
was on the premises, putting the question with all possible sua-
vity, so as to disarm any suspicion of a hostile intention, which,
indeed, his whiskers and the cudgel were well calculated to
awaken. The stratagem succeeded. The Doctor was introduced
the next moment into a small room, full of desks and papers,
where he found the apothecary seated with another gentleman,
from whose countenance he concluded, at the first glance, he was
the person who wrote the libel, no matter who was responsible
for its publication. Griffin was the very incarnation of the spirit
of the cowardly, base, and malignant libeller. The cowardice
was in his complexion, the malignity in his eye, the baseness
everywhere. There never was a quicker operation of the mind
than that by which both he and Mr. Pigwidgeon connected the
cudgel with the attack on Reuben the moment the Doctor entered the room.

The latter being a man of very few words, came to the subject of his visit with the shortest possible preamble; said he took
the liberty of waiting on Mr. Pigwidgeon, in consequence of
some compliments that had been lately paid to Mr. Reuben Medlicott in print, and begged to know whether the apothecary or his
friend was the author, as, upon such occasions, he was always
particular about punishing the proper person.

Mr. Pigwidgeon replied, with a visible quivering all over,
that he knew nothing about what the Doctor alluded to, and
that, at all events, the editor was the only responsible person for
whatever appeared in the paper. Mr. Griffin had only just arrived in Chichester, and what could he know of any such matter?

"Gentlemen," said Page, planting himself pugnaciously opposite to them both, "if I had the editor here, I should probably
address myself to him alone, but as, fortunately for himself, he
is elsewhere, I mean to hold you two severally and jointly re-

sponsible for the ruffianly libel upon my absent friend, and there is but one condition that shall save you from my immediate vengeance; you must promise to insert the amplest retraction, and most abject apology, in the next number of your publication."

Griffin looked furtively round the room, to see if there was any window to escape by, while the apothecary mumbled a protest against unnecessary violence, and said he was sure his friend the editor would be glad to qualify any observations he might have made, in the heat of a moment, calculated to hurt the feelings of anybody in the world.

"Qualification won't do," said the Doctor; "retraction is the word; and to save you the trouble of additional composition, I'll dictate the terms of it. Take the pen in your hand, Mr. Griffin, and write what I bid you."

Griffin hesitated and murmured, but the club hanging over him like a comet, overcame all other considerations. The following was the Doctor's prescription, word for word:—

"The undersigned hereby acknowledges that the article relating to the character of Mr. Rer—n Medlicott, published in the 'Chichester Mercury' of the — inst., was written by him, and that the statements in it to the prejudice of that gentleman are utterly false and unfounded; that he had no ground whatsoever for imputing any immoral or dishonourable conduct to Mr. Medlicott at any period of his life; on the contrary, he believes and knows him to be no less distinguished by the spotlessness of his reputation, than by the variety of his accomplishments, and the splendour of his talents."

"Now read it over for me," said Page, "till I see if it runs smooth."

With this request, also, Mr. Griffin complied, and only muttered an objection to the statement respecting Mr. Medlicott's talents and accomplishments, of which, he said, he knew nothing.

"If you are ever called in question for that part of it, give me as your authority," said the Doctor; "and now your signature, sir, if you please."

"This is very hard," grumbled the caitiff, in the humour of Pistol swallowing the leek.

"I dare say" said Page, "this is not the first document of the kind you have put your name to, in your time."

He then took the paper, handed it to Mr. Pigwidgeon, told him he would hold him responsible for its publication, and went his way, much prouder of his exploit than he had reason to be.

for the result proved that such violent men as the Doctor are not the best friends to have at one's back in a contested election, any more than other critical situations in life.

CHAPTER XI.

THE CONQUERING HERO COMES.

"PIGWIDGEON for ever! Hurrah for Pigwidgeon!" No sooner had Dr. Page stepped into the street, than his ears were saluted with the foregoing animated cries, proceeding from a little mob collected round a stage-coach which had just that moment stopped at the Magpie Inn, which was situated in South-street, nearly opposite the principal front of Matthew Cox's house. Dr. Page hastened to the tobacconist's, where he found the Vicar, his wife, and old Hannah Hopkins, just arrived, in a state of great excitement, a letter having been received from Reuben which led them to expect his appearance every moment. Mrs. Medlicott and Mrs. Hopkins were conducted by Mr. Cox to an upper apartment, which commanded a view of the streets in several directions, and where several buxom matrons and fair maidens of Chichester and the neighbourhood were already assembled, admirers of Reuben every one of them, and all palpitating with anxiety to witness his public entry. Mrs. Winning, of Sunbury, a fine old lady, and an ardent politician, was there among the rest. Some of the mothers had brought their sons with them to stimulate their talents and virtues by Mr Medlicott's splendid example, and three of these hopeful boys were his godchildren and namesakes, Reuben Gosling, Reuben Bliss, and Reuben Medlicott Robinson. Little Gosling took great airs on himself, as having been one of the deputation to London; but young Robinson gave him to understand he considered himself quite as important a personage, inasmuch as he was a Medlicott as well as a Reuben.

The Doctor having tied up his horse under the laburnums in the lane, stationed himself with the Vicar and Mr. Cox at the shop-door, whence they all had the satisfaction of hearing the first speech of the new candidate, who was haranguing from the top of the Wonder, brandishing a stick almost as large as Page's, and as white as a miller with the dust of the road.

"Pigwidgeon for ever! Hurrah for Pigwidgeon! Hurrah, hurrah—hear him, hear him!"

When we say that Mr. Cox and his friends heard the speech, we only mean that they heard the noise or the wind of it, quite enough to satisfy them that the orator had an unrivalled case of lungs in his chest, but not sufficient to warrant any conclusion as to the brains in his head, if upon that point they had not been satisfied already. His action, however, was tremendous. The air never got such a buffeting; and how the boxes and trunks which served for a rostrum held together under all the stamping, was truly miraculous. The windows had already flown up all along the street, and were soon filled with clusters of excited faces; the young tag-rag and bob-tail of the town climbed the lamp-posts like monkeys, and everybody who could clamber upon a waggon, a van, or a donkey-cart, did so.

"He has words at will, at all events," said the Doctor.

"Wonders will never cease," said the Vicar. "I remember when everybody considered that fellow the greatest booby in Chichester, and now he is standing for the city, and will be returned for all that I know."

"Never, sir," said the Doctor energetically, and striking the floor with the end of the stick, as if that was the force that was to carry the election.

Mr. Cox shrugged his shoulders, as much as to say he had seen more marvellous things in his time.

Presently it was evident that the tobacconist's house was the object of the orator's attention.

"He is, no doubt, honouring me with his abuse," said old Matthew, who was standing in the back-ground; "I thank him for it, sincerely, and only hope he will never take to praising me."

At the same moment, a varlet from a lamp-post, who had once been sent by Mr. Cox to the House of Correction, proposed a groan for him, which was partially responded to by the rest of the tag-rag and bob-tail. But Page happening to draw to one side at the instant, this accidental movement brought the venerable old citizen into view, whereupon a very different demonstration took place; somebody from a window in Mr. Broad's house, called for a cheer in reply to the groan, and the call was so promptly, lustily, and heartily answered, that Mr. Cox could not but acknowledge 't, which he did with a courteous and dignified bow, directed to the window where the cheer commenced.

The orator, never a whit abashed, very adroitly took off his hat, and with a prodigious flourish began most respectfully to salute the object of his late scurrility, and probably began to laud him at the same time in an equally disgusting strain—the one gift, as well as the other, having come to Mr. Pigwidgeon by descent from his grandmother, who (it may be remembered) was "a Beamish, or at all events a Murphy." Presently he had an opportunity of making a still better hit, and, much as people might despise his abilities, he did not fail to turn it to advantage. A donkey, under a cart which stood not far off, began to bray as if the end of the world was at hand. There was no use in anyone else trying to be heard while the donkey held forth. Somebody vowed vengeance on the animal, and called "Silence!" as if it had been an ass of the human species, upon which the orator exclaimed—"Gentlemen, hear Mr. Medlicott—I entreat you to hear Mr. Medlicott—fair play, gentlemen." It was great fun to the crowd, and brought down thunders of applause from the lamp-posts and some of the windows, as far as the joke reached; but it made Mrs. Medlicott wild, and all the god-sons frantic. The Vicar, however, was much amused, and so was Mr. Cox; both more than the Doctor, who said it was an old electioneering joke, as long as he remembered anything of elections.

"I have observed," said the Vicar, "that jokes have their periodic times like the planets. They come round again as infallibly as the most regular of the heavenly bodies. Some return at Christmas, others at Easter, others come in with the grouse or the partridge. The Budget is sure to bring a budget of stale jests along with it. Did you ever know a session to close without a lament over the dropped bills, and a facetious allusion to the massacre of the innocents? A general election itself is only a septennial farce."

"Yet a dissolution is no joke to some people," said old Matthew.

"The turnip-tops are beginning to fly," said the Doctor, as several of those vegetables missiles now shot through the air in different directions. One of them, evidently aimed at the orator, struck him on the cheek, and he raised his hand to it.

"I wonder what's good for that?" said the Vicar.

"This work is beginning too soon," said Mr. Cox.

The general attention, however, was immediately engaged by a new cause of excitement. Distant shouts were heard, and presently an opposition coach, called the Triumph, came thun dering along, in a cloud of dust, and followed, like the other, with a running corps of ragamuffins, whose whoops and hurrahs, mingled with the blasts of the guard's horn, the barking of the curs, the bawling of Mr. Pigwidgeon, and the continued braying of his brother under the cart, made a din little short of fiendish. The women began to be frightened, just at the moment when they expected most to enjoy themselves, but the reflection that they were in a magistrate's house tended to reassure them.

"I should not wonder if Reuben is come down by the Triumph," said the Vicar, less composed now than he would have liked to admit.

The Doctor hoped Reuben would make his entry in a more imposing manner.

It was impossible as yet to distinguish anybody in the cloud of dust, but as the coach drew near, the cry of "Medlicott for ever! hurrah for Medlicott!" was heard distinctly.

The shouts of the two parties now began to mingle.

"Hurrah for Medlicott, the friend of the world!"

"Hurrah for Pigwidgeon, the friend of the people!"

"Medlicott for ever! Down with Pigwidgeon!"

"Pigwidgeon for ever! hurrah for Pigwidgeon! Down with Medlicott!"

"Medlicott and Reform!"

"Medlicott and Sympathy!"

"Pigwidgeon and Purity of Election!"

"Down with Pigwidgeon!"

"No Medlicotts!"

"No Pigwidgeons!"

Dr. Page began to forget himself in the general excitement and flourish his stick and bawl like the rest, until Mr. Cox called him to order, and showed him the absolute necessity of controlling his feelings, and setting a good example.

The Triumph, on its way to the Parrot, stopped within a few yards of the Wonder, for the very good reason that the throng prevented it from getting a step further; but the moment the dust subsided, it was plain that Mr. Medlicott was not among the passengers. The Doctor rubbed his hands with glee It would never have answered for Reuben to have entered the town on the top of a stage coach like his plebeian rival. Mr. Broad, however, was there, as his harbinger and precursor, and his appearance answered nearly as well for the purpose of increasing the hubbub. Mr. Reynard was along with our friend the cutler, but kept himself quiet: and the only other outside passenger seemed to be a foreigner, though, to judge by his vivacity, and the vehemence of his gesticulations, he appeared to be as deeply interested in all that was going forward, as if he had been an elector of the borough.

"Just look at Mr. Broad," said Mr. Cox to the Vicar. "He must make a fool of himself because other people are doing so. I remember when we could not get him to move a man out of the chair at the vestry, and now he promises to be as good an orator as the best of them."

"He is at it, by all that's lovely," said the Doctor.

Mr. Broad had now got on the box, beside the coachman, and if he was not making a speech, he was certainly going through all the dumb show of one, moving his lips volubly, and shaking both his head and his hand, either at the people on the roof of the Wonder, or the faces in the windows of the Magpie. The foreigner had jumped up behind him on the luggage; his weapon was an old cotton umbrella, which he flourished by way of reply to Mr. Pigwidgeon's stick, while he roared as loud as the best Englishman of them all—

"I am for Monsieur Medlicott!—*à bas* Peegviggin."

"That fool of a Frenchman had better hold his tongue," said Mr. Cox, knowing the feelings of the English rabble towards their next-door neighbours of the Continent, and how apt they are, under any circumstances, to quarrel with and abuse them. But Monsieur persisted in his violent exclamations and antics; defying the enemy with the *parapluie*, and crying—"*A bas* Peegviggin! Medlicott for ever!" Even the coachman of the Triumph endeavoured to make him sit down, but to no purpose; his enthusiasm was not to be controlled, until at length he excited the feelings of which Mr. Cox was apprehensive, and a rush was made by some of the Pigwidgeonites to pull him off the box. This attempt he resisted furiously, keeping his place for some time with great courage and resolution, and making savage use of his umbrella, the spike at the end of which made it a formidable instrument. His assailants, however, were too many for him, and at last they succeeded in dragging him down into the street, where he would infallibly have been sadly maltreated, if Mr. Cox, followed by Dr. Page with his cudgel, had not promptly rushed to the spot, and rescued him almost as soon as he was in danger. Old Matthew collared the infuriated Frenchman, dragged him into his shop, and locked him up in a little private office he had, while the Doctor had enough to do to defend Mr. Broad and Mr. Reynard, which he accomplished, however, though not without some hard knocks, and getting one sleeve nearly torn off his singular green coat.

"A good beginning," said the Doctor.

"Now, if I only had a little oak box of mine safe," said the man of the law, with considerable anxiety, as if the value of the box was considerable.

The Doctor now sallied forth again to fetch Mr. Reynard's property, but that was not so easily done. It was as much as a man could do to lift it, and while the Doctor was in the act of receiving it from the hands of the guard, he dropped his stick, and some rogue in the crowd hustling him at the same moment, he dropped the box also, which fell on the pavement with a loud ringing sound, as if it had been all metal, and being at the same time partially broken by the concussion, out flew half a dozen broken sovereigns and rolled about the street. The sight of the gold literally maddened the knaves who were near the spot and witnessed this untimely outpouring of the wealth of the Reubenites. A ferocious scramble instantly took place for the few coins that had escaped; and if Page had not been a man of powerful frame, he could not have saved the box itself from the hands of the rabble, as he succeeded in doing. After depositing the treasure behind Mr. Cox's counter, he missed his stick, and to recover that he had to make a third *sortie*, in the course of which he came into collision with Dr. Pigwidgeon himself, with whom he had a furious war of words, ending in actual fisticuffs.

Dr. Page charged Dr. Pigwidgeon with leading a band of ruffians and marauders. Dr. Pigwidgeon rejoined with the accusation of open and shameless corruption, well warranted, certainly, by the exposure of the box of gold. Page demanded whether the election was to be carried by terror and intimidation. Pigwidgeon retorted by asking if it was to be carried by barefaced bribery. After a few words more, Page struck the other, who instantly returned the blow, and it is hard to say how long the pugilistic contest might have lasted, if at length an uproar (much exceeding any that had yet been heard) had not announced the arrival of Mr. Medlicott himself.

He had made the greater part of the journey from the metropolis in the Triumph, but had quitted that conveyance at an inn about ten miles from Chichester, where an open carriage with four horses had been ordered by the Alderman to be in readiness for him. Mrs. Mountjoy would have been one of the party, only that she dreaded the Bishop's displeasure; and his wife, though she came down to the country with him, was not in a situation to face an excited mob, so that he would have wanted a lady to grace his side, if he had not fortunately been attended by Mrs. Chatterton, who, having come down from London with him, was delighted as well as proud to exchange the dust and obscurity of a stage-coach for the comfort and distinction of the seat in the four-in-hand. As in addition to being strikingly handsome, she was all energy and vivacity, and very gaily dressed, her substitution for simple Mary Medlicott suited the occasion extremely well. The mob took her for Reuben's wife, and the more readily as she held his eldest little girl on her lap, and looked personally flattered and gratified by every demonstration of popular affection and respect. To his parents and friends, however, the appearance of a strange lady in his company caused the utmost surprise, and not a little displeasure mixed with it. Neither the Vicar nor his wife recollected Mademoiselle Louise, but Mrs. Winning, with whom she had formerly lived as lady's maid, recalled her features as soon as she came sufficiently near, and was seriously offended with Reuben for what she considered a gross violation of propriety on his part, which indeed it was, though it was his vanity more than his gallantry led him to commit it.

The superior pomp and circumstance of Mr. Medlicott's entry, the equestrian display, the postillions with enormous pink cockades, his rosy children, and the gay lady who represented their mother, told powerfully in his favour, as Dr. Page had anticipated. The halt upon the road, too, had afforded him the opportunity of shaking off the dust, and changing his travelling dress for a fresh suit, in which he now shone as brilliant as a bridegroom—a complete contrast to the state in which his rival presented himself to the public. The consequence of all these circumstances was, that the uproar was redoubled. The shouts for "Medlicott and Reform!" and "Medlicott, the World's Friend!" became absolutely stunning. It soon became evident that the Pigwidgeonites were comparatively a small faction of the populace, and Mr. Cox, seeing the apothecary in the crowd, beckoned to him, and strongly pointed out the prudence of his son retiring into his inn, and suffering his opponent and his friends to proceed peaceably to the Parrot, which was their head-quarters.

Mr. Broad seconded this suggestion, but when Mr. Cox offered to engage that Reuben should not address the mob if his progress was not impeded, the cutler flatly refused to be a party to any such stipulation; and the hostile candidates being now within a hundred yards of each other, all things seemed to promise extremely fair for a general riot, and it was probably a shrewd idea of the Vicar's that prevented its occurrence. Mr. Cox, at his suggestion, made his way through the rabble to Reuben's carriage, and getting into it, commanded the postillions to advance. A prodigious shout was raised by the multitude as the order was obeyed. The crowd receded on both sides before the popular old citizen and venerable magistrate; they respected his hoary head as if it had been literally the crown to which a sacred writer beautifully compares such a head as his, and gave way to the expression of his will, with the submissiveness such as no other man in Chichester would have expected or could have enforced.

The progress of the carriage was necessarily slow, but so much the better for the display which Reuben and his friends were desirous to make. The Triumph and some other vehicles followed, and formed a sort of procession. They met with no molestation of the slightest consequence; not a missile was thrown of any kind; in fact anybody who had been rash enough to fling an egg or a turnip-top at Mr. Cox, would have run a serious risk of being torn to pieces by the mob. In front of the tobacconist's house, the only clamour audible was that of Reuben's own partisans. There the line of carriages paused for a few minutes, and the waving of handkerchiefs was such as for some time to prevent Mr. Medlicott from distinguishing his fair friends in the windows. The uproar was deafening, but decidedly propitious.

Mr. Pigwidgeon, still on the same perch, was entirely put out of countenance by his opponent's success, and assumed the air of a man too gallant and high-minded, to assail a rival who had placed himself under the triple protection of beauty, infancy, and old age. He kept bowing ostentatiously, now to Mr. Cox, now to Mrs. Chatterton, who, however, had pulled down her veil, to avoid being recognized by him. In doing so she had placed the little girl in the old man's arms. The child was as gay and fearless as if it had been "born to the manner" of a contested election, and as Matthew held it aloft, streaming with ribbons, and not unlike a banner, the effect upon the spectators was astonishing, particularly upon the female portion of them. Mr. Cox was again cheered vociferously, after which the hurrahs for Mr. Medlicott were renewed, and the opportunity seemed a fair one for making a short speech. Mr. Cox was against it, but yielded on condition that the speech was not to occupy more than ten minutes. Reuben sprang upon the seat of the carriage. His reported speech was probably the shortest on record. It consisted of but one word, which was "Fellow-citizens." The Pigwidgeonites were influential enough to prevent another syllable being heard, and they exerted their influence most successfully. In fact the storm was rapidly rising again, when Mr. Cox, pretending that the time was expired, made a sign to the postillions to move forward as quickly as they could; and in something less than half an hour, Mr. Medlicott arrived at the Parrot, where he amply compensated both himself and his friends, by making a speech which lasted until the sun went down, and would have lasted until the moon rose, if his own father had not put a slip of paper in his hand, adjuring him, by all the ties of affection and duty, to recollect that the custom of dining had not yet been laid aside at Underwood.

CHAPTER XII.

A CHAPTER OF OUTRAGES ON ALL SIDES.

Mr. Medlicott offended all his discreet friends, by making his public entry as he did, in company with a lady in Madame Beauvoisin's position, which, though not disreputable, was certainly ambiguous. Mrs. Winning ceased, in consequence, to take an active interest in his success. The good little parson, however, relented only too soon, upon his son's assurance that Louise was not only a married woman, but the correctest, as she was the cleverest, of her sex; and being satisfied upon this, which was the main point, he accosted the lady in his most cordial manner, and offered her both a dinner and a bed that night at the Vicarage. Mrs. Medlicott looked daggers at him; but having a kindly feeling for the pretty Frenchwoman *au fond*, from recollection of her service in former days, she too laid by her scruples before long, though she seconded but coldly her husband's invitations. Madame, however, was so uneasy about her brother, that she did not know whether to accept or refuse; and Reuben, also, was at a loss to think what had become of Adolphe, who had come down, he knew, from London in the same coach with himself.

"If it is a Frenchman you are all looking for," said Mr. Cox, "I think I can accommodate you; for I have got a gentleman of that country safe under lock and key below in my office."

"My poor Adolphe a prisoner!" cried Reuben with surprise; "Pray, worthy Magistrate, for what crime has he forfeited his freedom!"

"Oh, he is innocent: he is innocent!" cried his sister, springing forward, and astonishing the old man by falling on her knees at his feet, and raising her clasped hands in the theatrical manner of imploring mercy.

"Be comforted, Madame," said Mr. Cox, smiling, and courteously raising her; "we only locked the gentleman up for his own protection; there is no charge against him, and he shall be released this moment."

"You will give him his liberty," said the Vicar, "and I will give him his dinner:—liberty, and a dinner—two of the best gifts that man can bestow upon his fellow."

"Thank you, sir," said Reuben in his father's ear; "and the more as my friend in duresse has every talent in the world except that of providing a dinner for himself."

"What is he?" asked the Vicar.

"What is he not, sir!" replied Reuben in the same undertone; "he was first my shoemaker; then my music teacher; next my bookseller; after that my cigar-merchant; now he is— I really hardly know what."

"Your gentleman at large," said the Vicar; for Mr. Cox having liberated M. Beauvoisin, returned with him just at that moment, and then there was another impassioned scene between brother and sister, as if the former had been released from actual chains and a dungeon.

It is hardly necessary to say that they were both charmed at finding themselves comfortably provided for at the Vicarage, instead of paying for very inferior entertainment at an hotel. They found their quarters, indeed, so agreeable, that they showed no inclination to change them during the ferment; and being grateful for the father's hospitality, as well as sincerely anxious for the son's success, they made themselves useful while they remained, Louise by making a variety of tasteful banners and flags, Adolphe by a number of little attentions and activities, which kept him busy from morning till night. Adolphe, indeed, as it soon turned out, was a great deal too energetic; and so was Dr. Page, from whom a sounder discretion might have been expected. The latter, instead of returning quietly to his sober bottle of port at Underwood, lingered in town by way of transacting electioneering business; and before the evening was over, having most probably exceeded that temperate allowance, got into a fresh personal conflict with Mr. Pigwidgeon, which ended in their both being bound over by Mr. Cox to keep the peace, not only towards each other, but all the rest of his Majesty's subjects. Dr. Pigwidgeon made no objection to enter into these recognisances, but Page vehemently remonstrated, and begged with amusing earnestness to have his obligations limited to his particular antagonist, being anxious (though he did not own it at the time) to keep himself free to redeem the engagements he had entered into in the morning, with the apothecary and Mr. Griffin. Mr. Cox, however, was inexorable; and the two doctors were manacled together in a figurative way, as tight as the law could bind them.

"By Jove!" said Page to the old magistrate, when the coast was clear, "you little know the mischief you have done by your untimely interference. You may be a justice of the peace, but you have served the interests of peace better than those of justice. I heartily wish I had paid those libellous scoundrels in ready money, instead of passing my note to them for a thrashing."

"Never mind," said Reynard, taking him by the arm; "if they abuse us, we'll abuse them; that's my system, and I know something about conducting a contested election."

Reynard had brought down a little corps of libellers with him, quite as expert and unscrupulous in that respectable line of business; and it was not without the greatest difficulty that Mr. Medlicott (who had no taste for such tactics) succeeded in preventing his partisans from retaliating upon the other party with the same abominable system of warfare, calumny for calumny, and lie for lie. Mr. Pigwidgeon, however, met with contumely enough in all conscience; in fact, he was abused and disparaged by Mr. Medlicott's friends more than was consistent with a prudent regard to their own interests. Running a man down unjustly or excessively is a certain way to give him a lift in the general estimation. He rises in opinion much as a ball does, which, by rolling down one inclined plane, acquires a momentum that carries it to some extent up another. So it was with Mr. Pigwidgeon. He was nothing, in fact, but an empty, vapouring blockhead, not for a moment to be compared to his educated and accomplished opponent (allowing for all Mr. Medlicott's faults and deficiencies); but Pigwidgeon was set up a little by the violence with which he was decried; and Reuben himself felt this so much, that whenever he mentioned Mr. Pigwidgeon, he carefully refrained from adopting the tone which his party generally employed in speaking of him.

And here let us do Mr. Medlicott the justice and the honour of saying, that one admirable and remarkable quality distinguished him as a public speaker: he never loved to indulge in coarse or scurrilous language; his diction was generally refined and gentlemanlike, more tending to the extreme of too much delicacy, than too much force. His flowers of speech, as he would have expressed it himself, were often exotics, but they were never unsavoury weeds. From Billingsgate he shrunk with instinctive horror. When he assailed an adversary, it was not with the mire from the pool, but the shining pebble from the brook; much the most effective, as well as the most creditable, mode of levelling either a dwarf or a giant.

On the part of the Magpies, however, there was no restraint of either tongue or pen. Dr. Page's anticipations were perfectly correct. The fear of his cudgel being removed from the eyes of the slanderers, not only was the retractation dictated by Page flung into the fire, but the assault was renewed and continued, with the most malignant aggravations and embellishments, to the end of the contest. Upon one occasion only was personal retribution exacted. Though the apothecary escaped the cudgel, he was not so fortunate as to elude another corrector of the press, in the still more irregular shape of an umbrella. A crowd of Reuben's friends were standing one morning at an open window in the Parrot, reading the last and most scandalous production of the enemy, containing the broadest and vilest allusions to the Beauvoisins, and their domestic relations with Mr. Medlicott.

"It ought to be calmly answered," said Mr. Cox.

"And rigorously prosecuted," added somebody else.

"Answered and prosecuted!" cried the Doctor; "there is only one way of prosecuting an article like that; if my hands were not tied, I know the answer it would receive from me.

This comes of binding a man over to keep the peace towards all the rascals in England, at a great constitutional crisis like this. I'll never forgive you for it, Mr. Cox."

Mr. Broad and the Frenchman (the latter very naturally) were also among the indignants; the latter venting his wrath with all the grotesque action and in all the odd imprecations of his country. Presently some one near a window called out—"There goes the scoundrel himself, the leader of the gang!" The apothecary was sneaking past the Parrot on his way to his son's committee at the Magpie. Everybody ran to the window to hiss and groan him; but the Frenchman (after a single look to make certain of Mr. Pigwidgeon's person) rushed down stairs, out into the street, shouting that *he* was not bound to keep de peace towards Monsieur Pigviggin," and the next moment was seen banging the unfortunate apothecary about the head, and everywhere else, with his umbrella, kicking him at the same time in the most ignominious manner; and in return to all demands on the part of the kickee to know the reason for such outrage, simply replying, "You are Pigviggin, dat is de reason! you are Pigviggin, dat is reason enough, sare!" still banging him until the umbrella almost went to pieces, and the bystanders at length interposed on behalf of order and humanity.

"Seize him and hold him!" shouted Mr. Cox, hastening to arrest the assailant, and calling on the Aldermen to support him; but the mob in the neigbourhood of the Parrot, encouraged by the cheers of Dr. Page and others from the window, were only too ready to take the part of the foreigner on an occasion of this kind; so that before the magistrate could reach the scene of action, the perpetrator of the outrage had got clean off. The apothecary was sadly bemauled, and slunk away to the Magpie to stimulate his friends to revenge his affronts, which, in the finest spirit of even-handed justice, they did in the course of the day, by bemauling an apothecary of the Reubenite party, a most inoffensive man, who took no active part in the contest, and had never molested anybody in his life.

With this exception, Mr. Medlicott succeeded in keeping not only the pens, but the hands of his friends tolerably quiet, wishing to owe his return to moral superiority alone. It was not, however, so easy to prevent unlawful practices of another kind. Perhaps no man ever set his affections upon a seat in the House of Commons with a stronger aversion to every profligate art by which that distinguished and desirable object is too frequently obtained, or a sincerer desire to win it by honourable means only. He was certainly an exception to the general rule; and though he knew there existed such iniquitous dens as Guinea Lane and Yellow Row, he had no more notion of the deeds that were done upon his behalf in the former of those dark corners, than he had of the transactions in the Georgium Sidus. Perhaps he ought to have watched the proceedings of his friends more narrowly; but a man cannot have the aid of friends without implicitly confiding in them; and besides, his opponents, and not his supporters, were surely the proper objects of his suspicion. As to his own committee, nothing but honour and probity was ever talked of there—when he was present. The house in Guinea Lane was treated as an audacious fiction of the enemy, though nobody entertained a shadow of a doubt of the reality of the rival establishment in Yellow Row. When Mr. Medlicott repeated, as he did every hour in the day, that he stood for the city only on the three conditions of there being no bribery, no intimidation, and no treating, he was always lustily cheered, and by none so loud as by his attorney, who had organized as perfect a system of corruption in all its branches, as ever was recorded in a blue book. Not even Mr. Broad and Dr. Page were cognizant of all the lengths to which Reynard went; but as to Mr. Medlicott, he was completely blinded by being led round the town to canvass, in due form, the identical knaves who had their bribes already in their pockets, for this was a ceremony with which that astute and experienced agent never dispensed. As to the treating, it was going on merrily all the time in at least twenty public-houses and places of entertainment, but nowhere so profusely as at the Parrot, under Mr. Medlicott's very nose; which naturally made many think that he must have had a cold during the contest, as he never smelt the roast beef or the gin, though the former was turning on a dozen spits, and the latter flowing in rivers and torrents.

The worst of all this was, that in truth it was a superfluity of naughtiness. It was a waste of that commodity which Mr. Jonathan Wild, in his philosophy of knavery, considered too good a thing to be thrown away—a waste of roguery and mischief. The Parrots greatly over-estimated the strength and resources of the Magpies, who, having little or nothing but bribery to depend on, and not so much cash in their bank as their opponents, had already renounced all hopes of success, and only kept their candidate in the field to harass and worry Mr. Medlicott and enhance the market-price of votes. Mr. Pigwidgeon himself acted very discreetly; he freely and handsomely expended Mr. Barsac's money, but took heed not to encroach on his own funds, so as to have the fair borough of Blarney always to fall back upon in the last resort. In fact, before the election took place, all doubt as to Mr. Medlicott's return was at an end. All that remained was to go through the riotous farce at the hustings, the usual dumb-show of addressing the electors, the perils of chairing, and the dangers of the dinner.

CHAPTER XIII.

A POLITICAL VICTORY FOLLOWED BY A DOMESTIC TRIUMPH.

The election was a cross between a farce and a riot; it is scarcely possible to describe it more accurately. Fortunately, however, Mr. Pigwidgeon was not able to keep the poll open for more than a single day, so that the scene of hubbub and folly proved a short one. The candidates were proposed and seconded in dumb-show. A forest of hands were raised for Mr. Medlicott, but a considerable grove also were displayed in Dr. Pigwidgeon's favour. Which were the dirtier was very uncertain; and the same doubt existed as to the comparative sweetness of the voices that shouted for the rival interests. No other voices, of course, were audible, not even those of the candidates, except a few words at intervals, through the enormous tumult of the day. Mr. Pigwidgeon addressed the electors first, amidst terrific cries of "No Pigwidgeons!" "Go back to Blarney!" "No quacks!" "Who sent for you?" "You are only fit for Ireland!" "You sha'n't doctor us!" "He is only an apothecary's boy; go back to the mortar!" One of the Parrots, a fellow of stentorian lungs, proposed a groan for the apothecary.

"I am not ashamed of my father!"—roared the orator, directly the groaning ceased.

"More shame for you!" cried a free-born British cobbler in his green apron, standing at the speaker's elbow.

"I will say this for my father,"—continued the candidate.

"The less you say about him the better!" re-bellowed the cobbler.

"Say something for yourself!" bawled another, who looked very like a tinker.

"Hear me, then!" cried the doctor.

"No, we won't!" from the tinker, who had just before adjured him to speak.

"Hear Pigwidgeon!"

"Hear Medlicott!"

"*A bas*, Pigviggin!"

A rush was made at the Frenchman by a flight of the Magpies, but a flock of the Parrots came to his aid, and there was a wild engagement for some minutes, during which the umbrella again did conspicuous duty on the side of the Reubenites. When the fray was over, Mr. Pigwidgeon attempted once more to get a hearing. At the same moment, the restless Adolphe, assisted by Mr. Broad's foreman, displayed a blue silk banner of enormous size, upon which the fingers of Louise had embroidered, in huge scarlet letters, the words—

"Hurrah for Medlicott, the World's Friend!"

Scarcely was it unfolded before it was torn to a hundred shreds by the excited Magpies; but another flag was in readiness, inscribed—

"Medlicott, and Universal Sympathy!"

"Universal humbug!" screamed a dozen Pigwidgeonites; and the second flag met the fate of the first, after a somewhat longer scramble, during which some heads were broken, if any faith was to be placed in sounds.

The orator made a final effort after this last episode, and was proceeding to tell the constituency what good things he would give them in return for their votes. If they liked cheap bread, he was the man to provide it for them. If they liked cheap sugar, he would give it to them also. If they fancied cheap tea and coffee—"

"Perhaps you would fancy a cheap egg," cried a fellow, lying in ambush in a corner with a basket of them, and flinging, as he spoke, one of those highly constitutional missiles with aim so fair that it struck the candidate right on his breast, and instantly delivering its liquid contents, provided him with a buff waistcoat, to the infinite satisfaction of the Parrots, and the amusement of not a few of the Magpies themselves. But this was a game at which two parties could play. There was an opposition egg-store in another corner of the court-house. A battle of eggs ensued. Eggs flew like the fowl they were designed by nature to bring into the world, unless we suppose that the uses of a contested election were among those which Providence expressly contemplated in ordaining the generation of birds. Eggs darkened the air. Eggs flew like shot in a battle, or rather like shells, only that they were not charged with such deadly ingredients. Sometimes in the tug of war a Magpie's egg met a Parrot's egg, and the momentum of each being instantly destroyed by the other, the united yolks and albumens fell, in a torrent of whits and yellow, upon the head of some unlucky pot-walloper in the crowd. Several burgesses looked as if they had bay wigs; others as if their hats had fallen into basins of batter for pancakes. Some more unfortunate wights received the discharge in a more direct and unpleasant fashion; indeed, on all parts of their persons, even their noses and mouths, which disgusted them beyond measure with such practical joking, and made them perceive, in a twinkling, how grossly indecent pranks of the kind were on the solemn occasion of an election. It was well for Reuben that the storm of eggs was subsided, and the elements of it spent, before his turn came to take his place in front of the hustings. But if he was not so bespattered with one kind of nastiness as his opponent, he got even more of another. He was assailed with a thousand opprobrious imputations, supplied by Mr. Griffin's articles.

"Who burned his grandfather's house?"

"Are you a parson, or a lawyer? What are you?"

"He's a Quaker,—you won't do for us, friend Reuben!"

"He's a Jack-of-all-trades!"

"What are you now, Mr. Medlicott?"

"Play us a tune on the fiddle!"

"Who ran away with his grandmother?"

"Have you her love-letters about you?"

"Gentlemen!"—cried Reuben imploringly, "one word—hear me speak—"

"That's all you can do: it's not speeches we want!"

"One word, in common justice."—

"No Parrots for us!" shouted the political tinker.

"No Magpies!" roared the free-born cobbler.

"Gentlemen! if you send me into the House"—

"But we won't!"

"Yes we will! we will! Three cheers for Mr. Medlicott. Mr. Medlicott, the friend of the world!" vociferated Dr. Page, with a voice that put all other voices down, and triumphed, for a moment, completely over the general din.

Reuben now thought his time was come for a hearing, but in vain; for the other party must cheer their candidate also, and in cheering him they displayed a banner with the motto, "Pigwidgeon, and Purity of Election!" which so exasperated the Medlicott faction that they made a furious onset to get possession of the flag; stones were flung on both sides, and a fray commenced which soon became so serious that a body of special constables were hastily sworn in, and the court-house was cleared by order of the magistrates.

Mr. Medlicott was so well surrounded and stoutly guarded, by a troop of his friends, that he suffered little more in the tumult than the loss of his bouquet and the derangement of his hair; but Mr. Broad had his coat torn to ribbons; Dr. Page was reduced literally to rags; and poor Mr. Beauvoisin was nearly in the same condition, besides losing his umbrella, which had performed such exploits. Upon the other side, Mr. Pigwidgeon thought himself well off to escape with a black eye; while as to his immediate satellites, there was scarcely a whole coat, or an integral pair of inexpressibles, among them all.

In this condition of affairs the candidates went to the poll, the result of which has been already intimated. Mr. Pigwidgeon had scarcely fifty votes, after all his expenditure of breath and money. He pretended, of course, that the electors who had promised him were either corrupted or intimidated by Mr. Medlicott; and formally protesting against all the proceedings, made a precipitate and prudent retreat from the town.

His disappearance restored comparative peace and order; his party, wanting a leader, shrunk into instant insignificance; they seemed even to have lost the power of shouting, for when Mr. Medlicott, reaching the goal of his ambition, was declared by the Sheriff the successful candidate, and one of the sitting members for Chichester, the speech which he made to return thanks was not only patiently heard, but enthusiastically received and applauded by an immense concourse of the citizens.

So tranquil was the meeting, that his mother, wife, and mother-in-law, accompanied by the radiant Madame Beauvoisin, were conducted by Mr. Cox to the self-same seats in the gallery of the court-house which they had occupied many years before to witness Reuben's first oratorical display. There was not a more joyful mother in England at that instant than the elder Mrs. Medlicott. She recollected in this hour of justifiable exultation the flattering parallel which Mr. Primrose had once drawn between herself and a celebrated Roman mother; and though there was nothing particularly pathetic in any part of the speech which her son made upon that occasion, it nevertheless brought tears into the eyes of our English Cornelia; nor were hers the only moist ones of the party; it was observable that Reuben's tender and teeming little wife pulled down her veil more than once while he was speaking, probably moved by similar feelings of pride and rapture, and affected in the same natural manner.

But the blisses and triumphs of the matrons, great as they were, were destined to be still greater in the course of that memorable evening. Not many hours elapsed after the chairing (which was a peaceful, though a noisy ceremony), before Mary Medlicott made the heart of every human being under the Vicar's roof, and many a heart under other roofs besides, tingle and leap with joy, by selecting that auspicious day to bring a son into the world. The church bells had scarcely done ringing for Reuben's political victory, when they were set agoing again in acknowledgment of his domestic achievements.

"Sure such a day as this was never seen," said the benevolent and jolly Mr. Oldport, who made all the haste in his power, considering his corns and his corpulency, to congratulate his friend upon the accumulation of blessings in his family.

"This day, Oh! Mr. Doodle, is a day indeed," replied the Vicar; "let us have a magnum of my oldest port to celebrate it. Come, Mr. Cox, come, Doctor, come all our sympathising friends; and you, Reuben, lay aside your senatorial dignity, and set the round table and glasses under the walnut-tree. Your mother shall bring us the new citizen of Chichester, and we will drink his health and safe arrival in a bumper."

Mrs. Medlicott, as usual, appeared the moment she was talked of, carrying in her arms the illustrious little stranger, of whom she was as vain as if she had borne him herself, and in whose forehead she had already discovered all the protuberances indicative of the most brilliant talents.

The child was enthusiastically admired, and his father was overwhelmed with applause.

The Canon held his glass so awkwardly while he contemplated the infant prodigy, that some drops of the rosy liquor overflowed and fell on the child's face.

"A jolly christening," said Mr. Cox to Reuben, "your son, sir, is baptised with port." There was great laughing at the incident.

BOOK THE NINTH..

"Now, the melancholy god protest thee; and the tailor make thy doublet of particoloured taffeta, for thy mind is a very opal. I would have men of such constancy put to sea, that their business might be everything, and their intent everywhere; for that's it that makes a good voyage of nothing."—*Twelfth Night.*

ARGUMENT.

"The fancy the vulgar have for men of showy abilities, whose sparkling often proceeds from the intrinsic shallowness of their parts, is not unlike the taste which may be observed to prevail of a shining night among the spectators of the heavens for dancing meteors, shooting stars, and all sorts of flickering vapoury splendours, while the great and permanent features of the firmament shine unnoticed,—neither honoured for their grandeur nor admired for their beauty. You shall find the superb planets the true and old-established nobility of the sky—mighty Saturn, with his wondrous rings; belted Jove, with his brilliant staff of satellites; loveliest Venus, sister to the Moon, with the warrior Mars, in his brazen panoply:—you shall find them all slighted and overlooked, while the herd of star-gazers are intent upon some skipping exhalation, or some *parvenu* of a comet with the beard of a Jew, or the tail of a baboon. The vulgar notion of genius is something meteoric, and, above all things, vagrant in its habits,—sparkling, rather than shining,—shooting in all directions, rather than advancing in any,—more of a squib than a star, or, at most, a star without a pole or an orbit.

"Such are the luminaries the multitude gaze at, and applaud, while the genuine lights of the world—condescending to have spheres, and to keep them, and pursuing their respective paths, whether of high studies or serious duties—are neglected for the very fixity of their purposes and steadiness of their flame. In fact, there is no such plodder as talent of the higher order; no drudge like genius, whether it works in the mines of truth, to extend the boundaries of science; labours with the soldier in the field, to protect the frontiers of the kingdom; or toils in the cabinet or the senate, in the still more arduous cares of legislation and government.

"True ambition, inseparable from great powers, is content with magnificent results, and never impatient with the homely and undistinguished steps that lead to them. The quality of patience enters largely into the idea of genius. The man of genius imitates the operations of nature, which are not grander in their issues than slow, and generally minute, in their processes. Perseverance not only 'keeps honour bright,' but is an essential qualification for the winning of the brightest honours; Ambition has this in common with his illegitimate brother Avarice; the former, like the latter, prospers in his designs more frequently by gradual increments and advances, than by sudden enterprises and surprising strokes. More men reach the summits of the world by climbing than by flying. It is possible, even, to creep into renown. *Ars longa*, as Hippocrates laid it down—Hippocrates, whose life my friend Primrose has not yet had time to write. The gate of the Temple of Fame turns upon two hinges—Virtue and labour. The wise poet put this lesson into the mouth of his wise as well as pious hero—

"'Disce puer virtutem ex me, verumque laborem.'"

"Iulus had a sager father than Icarus.

"'Why, what a peevish fool was he of Crete,
That taught his son the office of a fowl,
And yet, for all his wings, the fowl was drowned.'

"But in Dædalus, the legendary artist immortalised by the labours of science, we may recognise, if we please, the type of honour legitimately won by patient intellectual toil; in which case the only fool will be he who disdains the same humble track to glory, and plunged into the Icarian sea, expressly to point our moral. There are architects of their own fortunes, and there are architects, also, of their own misfortunes. Who reckons on the stability of a house run up in a night? Faery palaces are only durable in song. The song itself owes its vitality to the common source of all great works and great reputations."—*A fragment from the Essays, Moral, Economical, Political, and Miscellaneous, of the late Mr. Reuben Medlicott.*

CHAPTER I.

THE ASCENT OF A SKY-ROCKET.

There is a certain time in the lives of all men, who start in the world with fervent hopes and ambitious aspirations, when they are apt to look round about them, and measure their successes or their failures by the positions of their friends and contemporaries. If they do not themselves institute such comparisons, there are people enough ready to do it for them. In the case of Mr. Medlicott, how now did the matter stand? The men who may be said to have entered the race along with him, and to have been in some measure his competitors, were Henry

Winning, Primrose, and De Tabley. Of Vigors, his only other intimate friend at Hereford, he had entirely lost sight from the time of his leaving school. Henry Winning was now an eminent lawyer, making a large income, talked of as a likely man to be the next solicitor-general, and looking out for an introduction to parliament, not as a mere freak or speculation, but as a step indispensably necessary to be taken at the brilliant point he had now reached in his professional career. De Tabley had also prospered. Combining intellectual with convivial tastes—and, fortunately for the cause of polite hilarity, they enter into combination extremely well—he had early fixed his desires upon the possession of some permanent and well-appointed office under the crown; and, through the interest of his friends, he had found, in the Comptrollership of the Navy-Victualling Department, just the snug and appropriate berth he coveted. With the fortune of Mr. Primrose the reader is already acquainted. He entered the Church soon after the events related in the previous book, and became the bishop's chaplain and son-in-law immediately afterwards, with all the fair emoluments, and fairer prospects, appertaining to the two situations. Reuben, on the other hand, was in the position of a man who had successively embraced and abandoned two professions; he had quarrelled with his best friends; he had no property but a few shares in some Brazilian mines, and no income but what he derived from the poor little wife whom he had so daringly married, and who had already made him the father of three children, including little Chichester, who had such a merry christening, and now promised to be a formidable rival to his distinguished relative, the right wonderful Tom Wyndham.

To balance all this, however, he was no longer the "coming Man." The Man was come. He had now only to fulfil his promises—only to realise the expectations of that portion of the public in whose eyes he filled a space so considerable. He was a member of parliament, invested with one six-hundred-and-fifty-eighth of its importance, and wielding the same fraction of its vaunted omnipotence. He franked letters, made laws, put questions to Cabinet ministers, and taxed his fellow-subjects. Brave privileges these! but he would have enjoyed them more comfortably and securely, had he been indebted for them to something more solid than the repute of a silver tongue. He entered the House of Commons, not merely as an adventurer, but an adventurer who had failed in several enterprises before he tried statesmanship and speculated on the senate. It is easier to talk of independence under such circumstances than to get credit for it, and easier to commend Andrew Marvel than follow his example. Mr. Medlicott, however, started with only too rigid notions of purity; for he not merely resolved to seek nothing for himself, but to ask nothing for anybody else; which latter determination was by no means as acceptable as the former to many of his friends and acquaintances, particularly in the place which had sent him to parliament.

Before parliament met, Mr. Medlicott took a house in London, or rather Mr. and Mrs. Primrose took one for him, and laughing enough they had about it.

In London there are many very great streets which contain very small houses, so as to enable people of small incomes to live in the closest neighbourhood with people of the largest fortunes. For instance, in Piccadilly, wedged in amongst the palaces of princes and mansions of peers, as it were to fill up a crevice and keep the street steady, there stood at the period we speak of, and probably is still standing, a dwelling so diminutive as to suggest the idea, that after the completion of the stately houses adjacent, some half-dozen bricks and a couple of rafters had remained over, which the architect, that nothing might be lost, and to demonstrate the universality of his genius, had combined, with the aid of a hod of mortar and a few twopenny tacks, into a residence for some dapper little bachelor weary of wife-hunting, or a Lilliputian spinster desperate of a husband. It was just the sort of thing that General Tom Thumb might take for the season; but still it had most of the usual members and appurtenances of an ordinary London house. A hall in which you might conceive Flibbertigibbet waiting with Oberon's great coat, a parlour where a dozen knights of faery-land might be comfortable enough round a table as large as a cheese, a drawing-room in which her Majesty Queen Titania might give a children's ball, a couple of bed-chambers to match, dressing-rooms to correspond, an attic in proportion, while subterraneously the baby-house had a kitchen where a very small cook might manage to dress a very small dinner, with a cellar in which pint bottles ranked as magnums, just as in the kitchen Devonshire chickens claimed the consideration of Norfolk turkeys.

In short it was the smallest mansion in London, but then it was neat as it was small. You might have fancied that it had come from Holland in a case of Dutch toys; the bricks looked as if they were rouged daily; the wonder was how it ever stood all the mopping and twigging, the brushing and brooming, to which it was plain it must have been incessantly subject.

Such was 144½, Piccadilly. Mr. Primrose said it ought to have been 144¼, for it would certainly have taken four such houses to make one of the houses in Pall Mall, such a house, for instance, as he was lodging in himself at the time, next door to his father-in-law.

"They will not be apt to break themselves in pictures, at all events," said Mrs. Primrose, "except in miniatures."

"Nor in books, except in diamond editions," said the Chaplain.

"I think the house would do very well," said De Tabley, who was with them, "only for the parlour; I don't see where we are to dine. Six will be a formidable party here."

"We shall converse the more agreeably," said Hyacinth; "the only difficulty I see is where to put the Bishop, if ever Reuben is reconciled to him."

Mary Medlicott was enchanted with her baby-house, as it was very properly called, both by reason of its size, and the ages of the majority of its inhabitants. So far was she from thinking it too small, that before the Easter recess there was a rumour in the family that an increase of the infant population was an event likely to happen at no very distant period. The honourable member's chief difficulty was to find room for his books, which were already a numerous collection, for he had been accumulating ever since he left school, and had now amassed something near two or three thousand volumes. However, by availing himself of every nook and corner in every room of the house, and even upon the stairs and landing-places, he managed to find space enough for his immediate wants. He now, for the first time, found use for the box of tools which he had been presented with when a boy by the workmen at Westbury; for he was able to put up a variety of neat little shelves with his own hands, which spared him not only the annoyance, but the expense of bringing carpenters into the house.

He was thus employed on the day before the House first met for the dispatch of business, the little Elinor and Hannah toddling after him, looking sharp after the chips, which were their perquisites, when a deputation from the Peace Society waited upon him to place a petition in his hands, and solicit his attendance at their next general meeting.

Reuben received and addressed them with the hammer in his hand; and illustrated by that instrument ingeniously enough the great secret of efficient political agitation, which consisted, he said, in a constant succession of blows, every blow driving the question a step further, a noisy and a monotonous process undoubtedly, but the only practicable mode of hammering a new principle or a broad view into the public understanding.

"Now," said Mr. Medlicott, tapping his library table repeatedly with the tool he was talking of, "this is what we all ought to do with every great popular question of the day; never stop hammering in the House and out of the House, battling in season and out of season, until we succeed in carrying our points."

"Thou wilt be always sure to hit the nail on the head," said Friend Harvey.

"Thou hast hit the nail on the head already," said Friend Wilson, using his nose, as usual, as an organ of speech, "when thou speakest of battling in season and out of season. He that regardeth the winds will not sow, saith Solomon. If our Peace Society will follow thy excellent advice, it is strongly borne in upon my mind that thou wilt live to sit under the olive-tree thou hast been instrumental in planting; and peradventure we shall see the day when there will not be iron enough in England to make a cannon-ball."

"We must keep a little for our sledges," said Reuben, with a bland smile, and bowed the deputation out so cleverly that he must either have taken a lesson on that head from Madame Beauvoisin, or studied Mr. Taylor's royal road to statesmanship very profoundly. We have mentioned this interview with the Peace Society only to show with what notions and intentions Mr. Medlicott entered Parliament, how deliberately he paved the way for his own failure, and adopted the very system most calculated of all others to ensure it.

Reuben's idea of working questions, and his mechanical elucidation of it, were regarded by his own clique, and by his friends the Quakers especially, as prodigies of wisdom and wit. A careful report of what he said to the deputation appeared in the newspapers, and caused a good deal of amusement, not unmixed with alarm in many quarters. The men of business were frightened at the prospect before them. Ministers, whose characters depended upon forcing a certain amount of legislation through the House before Easter, read of Mr. Medlicott and his hammer with feelings the most uncomfortable.

"Awful threatenings these," said one secretary to another, walking down St. James's Street.

"These talking men," said his colleague, "are like the dog in the manger; they neither do any business themselves, nor permit us to do it."

"Who is this Mr. Medlicott, do you know?"

"Here is a man who will tell us,—eh, De Tabley, who is this formidable Mr. Medlicott?"

De Tabley gave a substantially correct, but a good-natured account of his friend. The ministers, however, cared very little to hear of Reuben's amiable private qualities, having had long experience of the truth, that a man may have every domestic virtue, and yet be a bore of the first magnitude in the relations of public life.

"The hammer," said the Bishop, reading about it, just at the same moment, at breakfast, in his lodgings in Pall Mall, "everything is to be done by hammering in future,—let me tell him the hammer is a tool not so easy to use as he imagines; I know that by experience. I remember one day at Westbury I thought I could hit the nail on the head as well as any carpenter; I certainly hit the nail but it was my thumb-nail; that was what I paid for my hammering. I never took a hammer in my hand since; but wise men learn by experience, which fools never do."

Still Mr. Medlicott did not fail in the first instance. He spoke on the Address, an occasion eminently favourable to his peculiar powers, from the multiplicity of topics through which it is not only permissible, but necessary to ramble, in following the miscellaneous subjects introduced into the Royal speech. When he rose, there was that sort of buzz which is at once flattering and exciting to a speaker. There was, however, mingled with it the slightest possible tittering here and there, through the unusually crowded House, perhaps occasioned by the indiscreet zeal with which his friends had blown the trumpet before him, but more probably provoked by the elaborateness of his toilette, particulary the foppish arrangement of his hair, his white waistcoat, and a pair of canary-coloured gloves, which at once recalled to the memory of Winning and De Tabley, seated under the gallery, the gloves that Barsac was in the habit of wearing at his suppers when he carved the ducks. But this slight disposition to laugh, whatever was the cause of it, ceased almost as soon as it showed itself; and Mr. Medlicott delivered himself with *éclat* of the only speech of equal length which it was ever his lot to make in the Senate without the most painful and systematic interruptions. Experienced parliament-men saw clearly enough that his style of speaking would never suit that assembly; but, nevertheless, as a first speech, it was listened to with polite attention, and generally well received; everybody was surprised at the profusion of flowers, illustrations, anecdotes and quotations scattered through it; men of taste and judgment were offended, of course; but with a considerable number it passed for a superb effort, and their cheers at the time, and their congratulations afterwards, left a strong impression to the same effect upon the mind of the young member himself.

Probably the few months that succeeded this his first and only successful effort, were the most flourishing and satisfactory of his whole career in public. He had now, although he knew it not, like Wolsey,

"Touched the highest point of all his greatness."

The rocket had gone off, exceedingly brilliant in its ascent, and "the observed of all observers;" but it was short-lived as it was brilliant, and no sooner did it shoot to its full height than it began to fall, much diminished in lustre, and only emitted fitful sparks at intervals, before it went out altogether and completed its destiny. An event, too, that occurred at Chichester during this period, made a substantial addition to its prosperity, although in itself as melancholy as it was sudden and unexpected. This was the decease of the good Mr. Broad, the most zealous and devoted of all Mr. Medlicott's friends, and who, in retiring from the world, gave an irrefragable proof of the sincerity of his friendship, by leaving him property to the amount of upwards of ten thousand pounds, a most important reinforcement of his slender means. It was also during this smiling period that, at the solicitation of many of his admirers, he sat to an eminent portrait-painter for his full-length picture, which was duly exhibited at Somerset House, among the other works of the modern British pencil. It attracted particular notice on account of the interesting situation in which Mr. Medlicott was represented. He was painted in his library, habited in the same sort of robe which his aunt had formerly presented him with, and diverting himself with his children. The table at his side was covered with drafts of bills, the floor was strewn with blue-books, upon a pile of which in the back-ground his wife was seated, intently poring over the Mirror of Parliament, no doubt perusing her husband's speech. To do Mr. Medlicott justice, this egregious piece of absurdity was not of his own devising; it was the doing of Friend Harvey principally, who, having once conceived this mode of treating the subject, never rested until he persuaded everybody about him that there was no other way of doing it justice.

The Primroses particularly lamented indiscretions of this kind, and so did the worthy Mrs. Wyndham (always a warm and steadfast friend), because they tended greatly to increase the difficulty of bringing about a reconciliation between Reuben and his grandfather, which it was their desire of all things to accomplish. There was a portrait of the Bishop in the same exhibition, and by mere accident the two pictures chanced to be placed side by side, when the gallery was first opened to the public. At this the Bishop was so angry that he wrote to the Society of Artists, and requested them to place his portrait anywhere else in the room, or if that was not possible, to remove it altogether. The picture was actually removed to gratify his caprice, which was the less excusable, as he had himself entertained a serious design of having the portrait of little Tom executed on the same canvass with his own, and had only been diverted from it by the sensible remonstrances of his wife and daughter.

We must, however, do the Bishop justice to state that he did not contribute one farthing to the fund for resisting Mr. Medlicott's return to parliament. What he might have done, if Reuben's enemies had been more fortunate in their choice of a rival candidate, is matter of speculation; but he had no notion of spending his money to bring in such a person as Mr. Pigwidgeon; that was a length the Bishop's personal resentment did not transport him to, and accordingly he left Mr. Barsac to bear the whole expense of the contest, a just punishment for that gentleman's mean and malignant conduct in the transaction.

CHAPTER II.

AIRS AND AFFECTATIONS—DISCORDS AND RECONCILEMENTS.

It may seem surprising that several months should have elapsed without a second speech from Mr. Medlicott, particularly after a first effort which might fairly have been considered a triumph.

In fact it was not his fault that he did not make many orations in the same period; he came down to the House at least a dozen times, fully prepared to address it, an intention of which his toilette was always the most palpable evidence; but between the difficulty of catching the Speaker's eye, the countings out, and now and then the failure to make a House (which was sometimes more a personal matter than he suspected), his preparations were as often thrown away, his intentions baffled, and more than once parties of his friends disappointed, who had flocked to the strangers' gallery to hear him. As to his preparations, indeed, it is not correct to say that they were thrown away absolutely, for it was one of the advantages of his manner of treating most questions, that a speech of his never suffered much by postponement; if he failed to make it in one debate, he made it in another; and when the worst came to the worst, there was always the Freemasons' Tavern, or Exeter Hall, where there was no doubt of its making a hit.

Upon the whole, however, he had time enough on his hands for other employments than speech-making, and he divided it in fair proportions between preparing drafts of various bills, to immortalise his name as a law-giver, and defending his seat, (which he did successfully,) against the petition of Dr. Pigwidgeon.

This was one of the dining eras of Mr. Medlicott's variegated life. He brushed up his practical knowledge of gastronomy, revived the admirable corkscrew he had formerly invented, spared no expense with his banquets to have them *recherché*, and might have generally succeeded in making pleasant parties if he had been less parliamentary and loquacious at the head of his table, and if his inordinate vanity and desire to be in everybody's good graces had not led him to bring people together in the strangest possible groups, utterly incapable of amalgamation.

When the company was chosen from the list of his old friends and his near relatives and connections, all was well; and in like manner when the Harveys and Trevors came to a little social meeting at 144½, nothing could be more successful of its kind; but Mr. Medlicott made a great mistake in trying to fuse his fussy Quakers and dreary Quakeresses, his French adventurers, and his Chichester Aldermen, with the men of wit, fashion, and parliamentary distinction, whom he was in the habit of inviting to his Saturday dinners. Indeed he was too fond of inviting people merely because they were personages or celebrities. While they honoured his little table, they proportionally fluttered his little wife, poor Mary, with her simple Quakerly habits and inexperience of all stars and ribbons, save the stars in the sky, and the plain ribbons in her semi-Quakerly bonnet. Reuben was greatly attached and devoted to her; but, nevertheless, he would occasionally invite* the pompous Lord Greenwich, or a French Marquis with a formidable moustache, or a turbaned *attaché* of the Turkish embassy with a beard and a scimetar, to dine with him on a day when perhaps the rest of the company were all Obadiahs and Rachaels. Mary dreaded a moustache exceedingly, having never seen one at meeting, and having early associated everything hirsute with ideas of wars and tumults. Captain Shunfield was the only hairy man she felt easy in company with, but nobody feared the innocent Captain Shunfield. By-the-bye, he had learned to sing since we met him last; but, as he never sang war-songs, but was more given to serenades and lullabies, his voice rather mitigated than increased the effect of his whiskers.

Pleasant days, however, were spent in 144½, Piccadilly. It was the fault of the M. P. himself if there were not more of them, and if they were not always as pleasant as they certainly sometimes were.

The dinners were little, of course, because the kitchen and the dining-room were, as we have seen, on the smallest scale. On one occasion, when Mrs. Medlicott apologised to her friends for having only shrimp sauce with the fish, Mr. Primrose amused them by observing that no excuse was called for, as the house was too small for lobsters. Sometimes, indeed, the dinners, if not too small for the house, were too small for the society. It occasionally happened that a few of the Chichester people would come up to London, either with a petition, or smelling after a place or a job. In the lobby of the House one day, Mr. Medlicott met the two Aldermen, who had supported him so strenuously, and he thought it his duty to entertain them. Perhaps it was ; but it was still more clearly his duty, having invited them, to make proper provision for their animal wants. Just think of the dinner he set before Aldermen Codd and Gosling, and at nine o'clock, when their appetites called for barons of beef. A potage with a fine name, which they took to be chicken-broth ; a mackerel *à-la-maitre-d'hôtel*, absolutely Greek to their worships ; a Devonshire chicken *aux-truffes*—why, he might as well have served up a canary ; a *plat* of *rognons*, which he did not even acquaint them were only Frenchified kidneys ;—in short, a

Spanish ham on the sideboard was the only dish in the room that was not either above their understanding, or beneath their notice, and even of that they could only get a Vauxhall slice or two. What was it to them that they were attended by a gentleman in a white waistcoat, a powdered footman, and a black boy? They found themselves much in the situation of reynard at the stork's feast, and retired as soon as they decently could to get something substantial in a tavern; but it was already Sunday morning, and not a tavern was open, or would open their doors for love or for money.

The nine o'clock dinner was itself a piece of affectation. Ministers dined at eight. There was no reason in the world why Mr. Medlicott should not have dined at seven. The Bishop's hour was six, and whenever he heard of his grandson's invitations for nine o'clock, he was most indignant at his airs and assumption, and wondered how any sensible man would dine with the coxcomb. When the Primroses dined in Piccadilly, they did so almost by stealth, generally when the Bishop dined out himself, and always pretending that it was only to tea they were going. The Medlicotts more frequently dined with the Primroses in those days, than the Primroses with the Medlicotts. Hyacinth stood in great awe of his master, and never dared to be absent from his side, or at least out of his reach, for many hours at a time. Besides, another advantage of the dinners in Pall-Mall was that Mrs. Wyndham could now and then manage to come to them.

The favourite nights were those when the House of Lords happened to be sitting, for then poor Blanche would be rash or unnatural enough to confide her son to his regular nurses, and dine with her next-door neighbours, or even accompany them to the opera or a play. It was always, however, with fear and trembling, lest the debate should prematurely close, and the Bishop come thundering home at an irregularly early hour. More than once such surprises happened, and the apprehension of them kept Blanche in a state of nervousness that spoiled half her enjoyment. Upon one occasion, in the middle of a pleasant supper, she was suddenly electrified by the coachman's well-known knock at the door of her own lodgings; she ran from the table with only a shawl over her head, and by her agility and good fortune got into the house before her husband, who, finding her at her post, never dreamed she had been a deserter from her maternal duties.

Reuben was most sincerely anxious to be restored to his grandfather's good graces, but it was a ticklish subject to approach, and he was always doing something, often, no doubt, unavoidably, to increase the difficulties of it. If he could have given up the practice of attending all sorts of fanatical meetings and spouting at them, the Bishop might have been more placable; but Reuben was no longer entirely his own master in this respect. He had become almost a slavish instrument in the hands of the Quakers, in Harvey's especially. With all the appearance of following and idolising, they in reality commanded him; in fact they had found what is vulgarly called his "blind side," and turned the discovery to account most shrewdly and systematically.

The proceedings of the Peace Society were, of all others, the most offensive to Dr. Wyndham, as might have been expected from the muscular common-sense that distinguished him. He could have forgiven Reuben more easily for joining any other association than this; he could have pardoned his coquetting with the Temperance movement, and even his incipient hankerings after the Vegetarians; but the stark-staring nonsense of Friend Wilson, and the *soi-disant* apostles of Peace, made him so furious, that he sometimes was betrayed into speaking of war with less horror and disgust than was quite becoming in a Christian prelate.

If it had not been for Mrs. Wyndham's strong friendship for Reuben, and her perfect understanding of the best way of managing her husband, it is questionable if the reconciliation, so desirable on all accounts, would ever have taken place.

Reuben and the Bishop met occasionally; sometimes in one or other of the Houses of Parliament, sometimes in the streets; but the Bishop always affected not to see or recognise him, while the sudden aversion of his eyes, or sharp contraction of his brows, accompanied perhaps by a short, dry, little contemptuous cough, showed plainly enough that he knew him perfectly well.

Reuben used often to stand at a window with his aunt and Hyacinth, observing his grandfather getting into his carriage, accompanied by Mrs. Wyndham, the nurse, and the prodigy.

"I think," he said, one day, "I am provided with as curious a set of relations as any man living; only think of that pretty young woman being my grandmother; and my old schoolfellow here, and that brat yonder, being my uncles—uncle Hyacinth and uncle Tom."

Mrs. Primrose fell back on her chair laughing.

His friends then informed Reuben that his grandfather had been incensed beyond measure at his giving his son the ostentatious name of Chichester. He might as well, he said, have called him Sussex. Suppose *he* had christened his son Salisbury, what would the world have said? It reminded him of the blockhead Barsac wanting him to sleep in a bed with mitres on the curtains. The Bishop repeated the name of Chichester ten times a day to express his contempt for it; but sometimes he pretended to forget it, and called the child Dorchester and Porchester, and even Gatton upon one occasion.

His lordship was to dine that day with the Prime Minister. Reuben proposed that the Primroses should dine with him, and perhaps they might prevail upon Mrs. Wyndham to accompany them. His aunt shook her head once for the first proposition, and twice, still more distinctly, for the second. Hyacinth, however, took a sudden fit of independence, and promised for himself and his wife intrepidly. As to Blanche, the question, as usual, was whether she would venture to quit her post beside uncle Tom's cot for a few hours. Mrs. Primrose first thought she would, then again she thought she wouldn't; the chaplain's mind alternated the other way. They promised, however, to bring Blanche with them, if possible, and the issue was that Blanche was courageous too, and saw no reason why she should not for once take a quiet dinner with her grandson and old admirer. No doubt she was influenced considerably by her womanly curiosity to see the interior of Mr. Medlicott's little *ménage*, of which she had heard so much; but she was also beginning to feel strongly that the Bishop's aversion to Reuben was not to be overcome by yielding to it so tamely as his friends had hitherto done. She never dreamed, however, of dining at Piccadilly that day, without acquainting her husband with her intentions; but when she was dressed, and proceeded to his study or dressing-room (for the one chamber with him generally served both purposes), he was just stepping into the coach, and he drove away while she was running down stairs to speak to him before he went out.

The ministerial dinner was punctual. Mr. Medlicott's was needlessly and wantonly the reverse. One of his absurd and provoking social tricks (for they deserve no more indulgent name) was to keep his company waiting, and be the last to enter his own drawing-room, feigning to be more overwhelmed with state affairs than cabinet-ministers. It was half-past nine that day before he offered his arm to Mrs. Wyndham to conduct her to dinner. It was past midnight before she got back to her lodgings. The Bishop was half-way to bed, and there was such a fracas as had never before occurred between them. Blanche, though somewhat vexed with herself, was prepared for the scene, and comported herself spiritedly and dexterously through it. The Bishop, who had put on his night-cap, but had only partially disembarrassed himself of his clothes, cut the oddest possible figure during the altercation. He threw all his controversial energy and virulence into the abuse with which he deluged her. He attacked her in his low harsh tones, as a woman, a wife, and a mother; he called her a rake, reminded her of her marriage vows, and desired to know whether she had made up her mind to neglect for the future all her maternal duties. Mrs. Wyndham never interrupted him, until at length he insinuated that she had probably often gone about gadding to dinners and elsewhere, when his back was turned. This charge she at once denied in a few quiet emphatic words. He did not repeat it. Then she took up the other accusations, one after the other, and disposed of them successively. As to raking, she had never before dined out without him; and she had not been at a ball the whole season, even at Portland Place. With respect to her conjugal duties, she could only say that she had done her best, but she hoped his next wife would discharge them more efficiently. Finally, as to her motherly offices, she affirmed very decidedly that she was the best judge whether they were or were not incompatible with her dining now and then at a friend's house, particularly when that friend was his own grandson. Blanche knew very well the effect this was likely to produce.

"Don't call him grandson of mine," the Bishop growled, as he plucked off his apron; "I have long ago renounced him, and you know it."

"Not with justice, sir," said Mrs. Wyndham, with decision.

The Bishop was white with rage, and ran through a catalogue of Reuben's offences.

"He commenced by burning my haggard."

Blanche congratulated her old husband upon the vigour of his memory and the minuteness of his recollections.

"He assailed me in public; he had the spirit to slander a clergyman, and the decency to abuse his grandfather."

"He never did abuse you, sir."

"What, not abuse me! did he not denounce me a renegade, or an apostate?"

"No, sir, he did not." She paused, and slily added, "He did not know you had apostatised, sir, when he made the speech you allude to."

"Apostatised!—you, too, madam!" he rejoined, with uncontrolled amazement at her confidence, and pulling off his cravat while he spoke.

"You changed your mind, sir. Reuben did not know you had changed it. I did not know it myself, although I was your wife at the time."

"Probably not; I am not in the habit of communicating my political opinions to my wives."

"At all events," pursued Blanche, "whatever he did or said so long ago, it might very properly be forgotten now; he never intentionally offended you, and he has long sincerely regretted that he did so without intending it."

The Bishop was silent for several minutes, saving the strange abnormal sounds which he was in the habit of uttering involuntarily.

"How comes it, my dear," he said at length, in an altered and subdued tone, "how comes it that he has got, of a sudden, such a zealous advocate in you?"

"Mr. Medlicott was an old flame of mine, you know, sir, that's one of my reasons for taking his part," she replied, with the utmost gravity, while she picked up his cravat and other things which he had strewn on the floor.

"Any other?" he continued, now speaking in the manner of a man who really wished to hear the entire of what his opponent had to urge.

"For your own sake, sir, just as much as for his," replied his wife; "nay, more for your own sake a great deal."

"An old flame of yours," murmured the Bishop; "how many flames had you, I should like to know?"

"I am not in the habit," said Blanche, parodying the odd expression the Bishop had used a little before, "of communicating my love secrets to my husbands. However, I have no great objection to make you my confidant,—upon one condition."

He desired her to name it.

"You must retract all your abuse of me awhile ago—you called me a rake—now am I a rake?"

"It was too strong a word," said the Bishop.

"And a careless wife?"

"I don't think I said that."

"And you said I was an unnatural mother,—is that true?"

"Polemical habits," said the Bishop, giving way now to his fair opponent right, left, and centre, "lead men sometimes to overcharge their statements."

"Well, sir, I'll now tell you all my love-secrets,—I never had but one flame in my life; unfortunately for myself he was shockingly given to the habits you speak of."

"He must try to correct them," said the Bishop, kissing her.

"Naughty habits for a divine, are they not?" said Blanche, radiant with her amiable triumph.

"Even divines are human," said her husband.

"You will be a good Bishop in future."

"I'll try."

"And a good grandfather."

"I'll endeavour."

"Dr Wyndham was never so foiled in debate from the day that he first entered the lists of controversy. Blanche was far too discreet to push her victory farther at the time. She said nothing more of Mr. Medlicott, but encouraged her husband to talk of his dinner at the Minister's, which he did until he fell asleep.

CHAPTER III.

A SCENE IN KENSINGTON GARDENS.

It was an important point gained, bringing Mr. Medlicott back into amicable relations with the old Prelate, whose virtues, as well as his faults, were thumpers, and who, with his fame, rank, and force of character, made a powerful and splendid centre to the now rapidly extending family circle. The house was no longer divided against itself, and the amiable Blanche had earned the blessing of the peace-makers.

The next morning, at breakfast, to the vast astonishment of the Primroses, the Bishop was talking of Reuben as if he had never been estranged from him, and calmly discussing with his chaplain the *pros* and *cons* of his grandson's parliamentary success. Hyacinth was hopeful, as became a friend. The Bishop, more sagacious, argued nothing but failure from Mr. Medlicott's unfortunate mental habits, and particularly his morlid craving after applause and popularity. He spoke kindly however upon these points, and even referred with temper to Reuben's dangerous associations with the noisiest and most fanatical busy-bodies of the day. Mrs. Wyndham secretely cherished a hope, that her experienced and strong-minded husband would soon begin to exert a useful influence in this respect over his descendant, and possibly succeed in withdrawing him from some of the most objectionable connections in which he was involved: but this was a vain expectation. The Bishop was too old a man now to engage in the task of reclaiming anybody whatever; he was prepared to lay aside, and he did lay aside, every vestige of angry feeling, with the magnanimity that became him; but in the same philosophical spirit, he deliberately laid himself out to observe the rest of his grandson's career, as the mere working out of a sort of problem in the science of life;—given, as it were, a certain redundancy of the faculty of speech, certain considerable powers of memory, a known amount of self-conceit, a certain marked deficiency in resolution and perseverance, a wife and children, a seat in Parliament, and no stake in the country,—to determine what a man's place in the world will be at the expiration of a term of years.

The first meeting between the reconciled parties took place accidentally in Kensington Gardens. The Bishop was fond of taking a stately walk there now and then, attended by his suit, consisting of his wife, the Primroses, the nurse, and Uncle Tom, as the infant Wyndham was now generally called in the family. The Barsacs were always anxious to meet him there, but they were seldom successful, as the Bishop's times for doing any particular thing, or going any particular place, were not the most regular. It happened one day, however, that the Barsacs and Wyndhams met on the promenade, and formed a most imposing procession, marching in two lines, four abreast, the stout old Prelate slightly in advance of everybody, On his right, in the first line, was the nurse with Tom in her arms; on his left was Mr. Primrose, about whom there was now a good deal of clerichl foppery, more than the Bishop likèd. The Barsacs were in the rear, but as close to their right reverend son-in-law as they well could have been without treading on his heels. While they proceeded at the proper dignified pace, much noticed by the other promenaders, Mr. Barsac, to make himself as agreeable as possible, began to talk of Parliament with his usual pomposity, and soon fell into his usual way of making dull hits at Reuben.

"Eloquence won't do in the House of Commons now-a-days," said Barsac,—"if ever I go into Parliament"—

"You will avoid that fault," said the Bishop drily, taking Tom out of the nurse's arms as he spoke, and paying him much more respect than he paid his father-in-law.

"But, in fact," persisted the merchant, "that sort of thing is not oratory at all—that's what I mean to say, my lord."

"What sort of thing?" asked the Bishop over his shoulder.

"You know, my lord, we were talking of Mr. Medlicott's style of speaking; you don't call that eloquence?"

"But I do, sir," replied the Prelate, stiffly.

Mr. Barsac was meditating how to back out of his unlucky criticisms, when Mrs. Wyndham exclaimed—

"Oh, I protest there is Mrs. Medlicott and her baby under the trees yonder!"

"Where? which is Mrs. Medlicott?" asked the Bishop, with anxiety, turning round to his wife.

Mrs. Wyndham pointed her out.

"I'll go to her and make her acquaintance," said the Bishop, —" Do you hold Tom,"—and forgetting that the nurse was at his elbow, as well as his chaplain (who, indeed, often performed the duty of a *bonne d'enfans*), he placed Tom in the arms of the astonished Barsac, whose regard for his waistcoat and his nosegay made him always entertain the liveliest horror of infants of that age. Little cared the Bishop how Tom treated the merchant's gay bunch of exotics; he advanced to poor Mary Medlicott with a vigorous cordiality that charmed his wife and daughter, to whom this was a moment of the deepest interest. Mary, always timid before grandees, and apt to be alarmed by big wigs, was no sooner fluttered by the unexpectedness of this rencontre, than she was calmed and encouraged by the frankness and heartiness of the old man's voice and manner. He shook her by the hand, said he was to blame for not having known her before, but it was better late than never, and then he asked for her husband and her children with all the kindness of his softest hours.

"Mr. Medlicott is not far off," said Mary, still tremulous, but more with pleasure than awe; "he left me only this instant, to show Chichester the swans."

"And how is the little Chichester? I have heard a great

deal of him. Tom and he must be friends," said the Bishop, taking a seat that was vacant beside Mrs. Medlicott.

Before he was seated there a minute, he had fixed an early day for her and her husband to dine with him. Mr. Medlicott himself joined them in a few moments, and great was his amazement, as he approached, when he saw the Bishop seated by the side of his wife. The old man rose, and received his grandson with a happy mixture of the freedom belonging to his advanced years and venerable relationship, and the deference due to a man of Reuben's ripe age and eminent position. It was altogether an interesting and striking incident of domestic life. The bewilderment of the Barsacs, who had looked upon the breach as incurable, and had treated the Medlicotts as ill as possible, to make themselves agreeable to the Bishop, was a curious part of the scene; but the most curious of all was the mutual introduction of the infant prodigies. The Bishop himself put Tom's little red fist into Chichester's still smaller and redder one. Tom had his other hand full of the remains of Barsac's bouquet, which he shared most good-humouredly with his new acquaintance.

"Generous little fellow," cried Mrs. Barsac.

"*Haud sine diis animosus infans*," said Reuben, addressing himself to the Bishop, whom the quotation greatly pleased.

"To whom should he be generous, if not to his grand-nephew?" said the chaplain.

"Very true," said the old man, "that never occurred to me before; that is the relationship between the urchins."

The laughter was, in Homeric phrase, "inextinguishable." The Bishop leaned on Reuben's arm all the way back to his carriage. Mr. Barsac was as attentive to Mrs. Medlicott as if she had been a countess; and that very night a card of invitation to a distant dinner at Portland Place was delivered at the modest little house in Piccadilly.

They were now in the Easter recess.

"The talking period of the session is happily over," said Mr. Medlicott to the Bishop on the day he dined with him, "we shall now, I hope, get some little business done; I have several irons in the fire myself."

"Keep the hammer going," replied his grandfather, poking him slily under the midriff.

"That's the true plan, sir," said Reuben, "'constant strokes fell great oaks,' as poor Richard says."

"We shall meet you and Mrs. Medlicott at my father's, I hope," said Mrs. Wyndham.

Reuben shook his head, and informed Blanche of a resolution he had made not to dine out again for the remainder of the session.

He went down for a day or two to Chichester before the House re-assembled, and was *fêted* by his constituents. It was in his speech upon that occasion (after his health had been drunk with all the honours) that he made use of Sir Edward Coke's curious zoological illustration, in his Institutes, of the talents and virtues indispensable to a member of Parliament.

"I agree, sir," he said, addressing Mr. Cox, who was in the chair, "I agree with that illustrious lawyer, Sir Edward Coke, (with whose works my forensic studies necessarily made me intimately acquainted), that every member of the House of Commons ought to have certain properties of that noble animal, the elephant. As the elephant, in the first place, has no gall, so should the representative of the people divest himself of all personal animosities, of malice, and envy, and all uncharitableness. Secondly, he should resemble the elephant in the quality of inflexibility, upon which you will all remember what Shakspeare says, speaking of the same generous quadruped, that 'he has joints, but not for courtesy; his legs are legs for necessity, not for flexure.' Sir, I trust that mine will never deserve any other character. I shall use them to stand upon in the House, not for bowing at the levee, or cringing at the Treasury; it would ill become me, sir, to commend my own legs, but I may be permitted to say this much of them, that they are legs for necessity, not for flexure. I wish I could arrogate to myself with equal truth the third elephantine attribute noticed by the great authority I am quoting, that of a ripe and perfect memory, so necessary in the public councils, to prevent dangers to come by the remembrances of the perils that are past. He tells us, further, that the elephant is gregarious and sociable, going in companies and parties. I trust you will always find me an elephant in this respect also; only I trust I shall be oftener found, gentlemen, at such tables as this, meeting my constituents in the spirit of independent and constitutional conviviality, than a banqueter at ministerial white-bait dinners, or a guest at the royal table. But, sir, I have not yet done; or, rather, sir, Edward Coke is not yet done; he reserves to the last (and I shall imitate him) that particular virtue of this noble and exemplary quadruped, which distinguishes him from all the brute creation, and exalts him to a level with man himself. Sir, the elephant is the philanthropist of the animal kingdom. *Homini erranti viam ostendit.* This property, concludes Coke, and I think you will conclude with him, every Parliament man ought to have. Sir, I beg to propose the health of the elephants in the House of Commons, and I wish they were a larger party than I fear they are."

This elephant speech made a great noise, as will be easily credited, and increased the speaker's notoriety vastly. Unfortunately it was not equally effective in disposing the House to receive him with increased respect or gravity. Never did such mountains of promise bring forth such mice of performance. Never did a man more industriously prepare the way for his own ridicule, discomfiture, and downfall.

It seems hard to complain of a legislator for legislating, but law-making may be overdone like everything else, from the cooking of a mutton-chop upwards; and it was surely the height of imprudence in Mr. Medlicott, on the strength of his one speech (which was not, after all, of the best parliamentary promise), to move for leave to bring in seven bills at one sitting, as he did upon the first meeting of the House. There was a speech, too, upon each bill; seven bills and seven speeches. When the Speaker called on him a third time, there was a laugh; and the laugh grew louder and louder in consequence of his unhappily making repeated use of the phrase, "while he was on his legs;" for this put everybody in mind of his speech at Chichester, which had appeared that morning in the London papers.

"His legs seem inflexible, indeed," said one of the secretaries to his neighbour on the Treasury bench, "I think he will never sit down."

The laughing and coughing increased every moment, and made Mr. Medlicott so indignant, that instead of immediately condensing his observations, in wise submission to the manifest feeling of the House, he actually expanded them in order to punish the men who interrupted him. The consequence was, that when he rose for the seventh time, there was a general outcry; a number of members rushed out into the lobby, while those who remained, with their united clamours, effectually drowned the voice of the speaker, and compelled him to do at last what a man of common sense would have done an hour before.

The next day two caricatures of the member for Chichester appeared in all the print-shops. In one he was represented as an elephant, with a castle on his back containing the seven bills. In the other he was portrayed as Thor with his tremendous sledge, thumping the table of the House, and scaring the Treasury benches from their propriety.

It would be absurd to suppose that these things did not seriously annoy him. They increased his notoriety, however, and that was always a source of comfort to Mr. Medlicott. His friends certainly felt more acutely than he did, not only now, but upon many similar occasions afterwards, the "distressful strokes" which his public character suffered at this period from the journalists, caricaturists, and epigrammatists of the day. But there was another explanation of the calmness with which he bore himself through the laugh of the House and the ridicule that followed it out of doors. He had the platform always to fall back on, to retrieve himself in his own esteem; there he was certain to wield his hammer with success, there he never failed to be received and admired not only as an elephant, but as a lion of the first magnitude. Accordingly, every repulse he experienced in St. Stephen's chapel involved him still deeper with the various agitators and enthusiasts he was leagued with; and as he naturally availed himself of his benign audiences to revenge himself upon those that were unpropitious, by imputing the treatment he met with to personal motives, he always returned to the House with diminished chances of being heard with attention.

In short, during the three sessions that Mr. Medlicott represented his native town in Parliament, he literally did nothing but present monster petitions, move for masses of papers (destined to be printed, but never read), and delay the business of legislation by repeated abortive attempts to speak. His obstinacy was extraordinary; he might often have been listened to, if he had not been studiously prolix, or if he had been contented to rise between seven and ten o'clock, when many a speech is received with patience, that nobody would brook at a later and busier hour; but Mr. Medlicott disdained to subject his genius to any law or restraint whatsoever, and soon began to incline his ear to the melodious flatterers who told him that he failed in Parliament as he had failed in divinity, and failed at the bar, expressly because his talents were too various and too splendid.

According to these judges, the world did not contain an arena sufficiently spacious, or a stage sufficiently conspicuous, for the exercise and display of Mr. Medlicott's powers.

His parliamentary break-down was the more remarkable in the eyes of his friends, when they contrasted it with the comparative success of the member for Blarney. Doctor Pigwidgeon showed more wit in the senate than he had ever shown out of it, for, finding that he could amuse the house for twenty minutes with a species of buffoonery he possessed, he aimed at nothing further, and made it a rule to sit down on the first hint that he had said enough. Besides, he soon discovered that much as his constituents loved eloquence, they loved places more, and having also fixed his own eye on a good appointment abroad, he was much more anxious on all occasions to be present at the division than to shine in the debate.

CHAPTER IV.

MR. MEDLICOTT VISITS THE NEW WORLD.

Towards the close of the third year of Mr. Medlicott's parliamentary life, still confident in himself, and enjoying the undiminished idolatry of his mother and his aunt, his admirers in Chichester, and his Quaker followers in London, after making an oratorical tour of England (during which the House of Commons and the newspapers were abused most unsparingly) he suddenly announced his intention to visit the United States (an old design of his), and left it to his constituents to decide whether they would or would not require the surrender of his seat. There was a stormy discussion at Chichester on the subject, resulting in the adoption, by a considerable majority of electors, of an address, highly complimentary in its language, but ending in an unambiguous expression of opinion in favour of his resignation. In fact, he had satisfied neither his honest friends nor his interested supporters: the former he had displeased by showing too little parliamentary talent; the latter offended by displaying too much parliamentary virtue. At the same time, that gentleness of manners and amiableness of disposition, which distinguished him through life, inclined those who took the sternest view of the case to deal as tenderly with him as possible; and, to soften the rigour of the sentence, they voted him a superb piece of plate, and begged to have his bust, in marble or bronze, to adorn the town-hall.

His parents, particularly his mother, were deeply afflicted at his resolution to expatriate himself, even for a season; and they prevailed on the Bishop to exert whatever influence he possessed over him to detain him at home, and induce him either to return to the bar, or strike out some other path to fame and fortune. The Bishop, growing still mellower as his years multiplied, undertook this task, though his heart was not much in it; but to no purpose: Reuben persisted in his intention to cross the ocean, and make what he called a general survey of transatlantic civilization. His Quaker friends were probably the secret instigators of this step, reckoning with the utmost assurance upon his popularity and success in the United States, and the probability of his returning to England with such an accession of reputation and self-reliance as would bear down all envy and overwhelm all opposition.

It was a serious question whether he should, or should not, take his wife and children with him upon this wild-goose chase after fame in America; but after mature deliberation it was decided to leave them behind; and Matthew Cox gave them his snug country-house for a residence, the cottage occupied by old Hannah Hopkins being now much too small for a family so large as Reuben's. By this arrangement, also, the brood of little Medlicotts would be within a convenient distance of their grandmother, the Vicar's wife, who would be sure to keep poor Mary's vulgar common-sense in proper subjection, and look with becoming anxiety to the awakening of their faculties and development of their organs.

We shall not accompany Mr. Medlicott upon this romantic expedition, but will tell the reader who the squires of his body were. Monsieur Beauvoisin attended him in the capacity of private secretary; and his godson, Reuben Gosling, having paid attention to his arithmetic and education generally, was selected to fill another office about his person, something between a clerk and a valet. Mr. Medlicott was now in about his eight-and-thirtieth year, but looked younger, owing to the colour of his hair, the freshness of his complexion, and the elasticity and erectness of his carriage, from which you could not have inferred that he had miscarried so lamentably in one of the most conspicuous positions in life. There is the less reason for giving an account of his wanderings in the New World, as he published two ponderous octavo volumes (substantially blue-books) about them on his return; which, if the work is not out of print, the reader may consult if he pleases. It is quite enough to relate here, that he not only talked prodigiously in all the private houses to which he had introductions or invitations, but delivered elaborate lectures wherever he went upon the comparative merits of English and American institutions, civil and religious, and their moral and intellectual results. The lecture that made most noise was one upon the eloquence of the two nations, in the course of which he introduced some severe strictures upon the modern taste for oratory at Westminster, which he supported and defended by quoting his own speeches, and relating how totally they had failed. On the other hand, he applauded, and did so most conscientiously, the then prevailing style of the majority of the public speakers at Washington ; for his voyage was antecedent to the adoption in Congress of the celebrated one-hour rule, which imposed such heavy restraint upon the tongues of free-born citizens. That rule was just beginning to be talked about at this period, and Mr. Medlicott thought it his duty to leave behind him, in every state and city he visited, the important protest of a man of his great experience against its justice and wisdom.

Another subject upon which he said a prodigious deal in rooms of all sizes, and before audiences of every variety, was the abolition of slavery, upon which he may be said to have had a special commission to hold forth, from his broad-brimmed friends at home. He discoursed largely on this exciting topic all through the New England States, and finally announced his intention to make a little excursion into Virginia and the Carolinas, to put the question in its true light to the southerns themselves, feeling that the planters had probably never had the opportunity of hearing it properly stated and discussed. This design he executed so far as actually to cross the Virginian frontier, and he was on the point of commencing his proceedings at a place called New Argos, or Mycenæ, when he was waited on by a deputation of tobacco-growers, with immense sombreros and cart-whips of proportionate size, who, in a few energetic words, completely changed his purpose, and convinced him of the prudence of making a rapid retreat over the border. When he returned to Philadelphia, he addressed an earnest letter to the slave-holding states in general, in which he complained that the rights of free discussion had been invaded in his person, and counselled them to emancipate their negroes without delay, as he was firmly resolved never to slumber or sleep until they did so. Of this letter there is not the shadow of a ground for believing that any of the slave-holding states ever took the slightest notice. It had a great run in Gracechurch-street, however, where it was not likely to be of much service to the blacks; and so had another tract of Mr. Medlicott's upon the Mormonites—a sect to which he afterwards owned that he felt at one time a serious inclination to unite himself.

As to the ambitious book he published on his return, called "America Displayed," it was a curious and not very judicious mixture of florid descriptions of rivers and savannahs, declamatory chapters on liberty and education, zoological and geological discussions, and statistical tables and details, in the accumulation of which his industrious godson (aided by a pair of scissors) made himself remarkably useful. Mr. Medlicott paid particular attention, wherever he travelled in the States, to the schools and the prisons; in the latter of which establishments he witnessed, for the first time, the operation of the silent system, but expressed no desire to make trial of its benefits in his own person.

His travels made Mr. Medlicott more self-confident than ever, and his loquacity did not diminish, it will easily be believed, with the augmentation of his funds of discourse. If the Rhine or the Rhone often makes men over-talkative, you may fancy the effects of the mighty rivers of the American continent. He came back to England with all his foibles magnified on the scale of the face of nature beyond the Atlantic. His conversation now flowed like the Mississippi, spread out like the prairies, and was often as hard to penetrate as the great forests of the new world. He never was so great a lion as he was for some time after his return to England. Never before did he afford the eyes of friend Harvey such a feast. The Quakers now flocked about him in greater numbers than ever, and his connection with them became closer daily. They scarcely left him time to visit his wife and children, or look after his few private affairs. Teas and lectures were the order of the day. Philanthropists of all sects are notorious consumers of congo, and the Quakers exceed all other religionists in the love of lectures. America was an inexhaustible subject. Mr. Medlicott having lectured the Americans on England, now reversed the process, and lectured the English on America. He lectured in London, in Liverpool, in Birmingham, in Glasgow, and going over to Dublin, in company with Harvey, he lectured there also, eclipsing for a week all the ordinary lights of the Rotunda. From Dublin he proceeded on a tour to Killarney, from thence to Connemara, and the Giant's Causeway, after which a book on Ireland was a matter of course; and a remarkable book it was, for it settled every Irish question, probed the difficulties of Irish government to the bottom, and left nothing to be desired but that the writer should be made Chief Secretary, to set everything to rights by a short and simple Act of Parliament.

Mr. Medlicott, when in Dublin, honoured the lord-lieutenant of the day by attending his levee. The first person he met in the antechamber was Dr. Pigwidgeon; they conversed as if they had never been opposed, and the Doctor informed Reuben that he had just been appointed governor of some happy island belonging to the British Crown, and was on the point of resigning the borough of Blarney. While they were talking, who should come up, bustling through the crowd of sycophants, and place-hunters, but the foremost man in Ireland at that period, the leader of the Catholic body, and as great a borough-monger in his way as any duke in England. He was already acquainted with Mr. Medlicott, shook him cordially by the hand, was profuse of compliments upon the work on America, and finally invited him to dine that day, to meet Governor Pigwidgeon and other eminent public characters.

The dinner proved eventful, for it was arranged before the evening was over that Mr. Medlicott should try his luck again in the House of Commons, coming in for Blarney, as successor to the Doctor. It would only cost a thousand pounds or thereabouts; but it was indispensable that the new candidate should start at once and show himself in the first instance at the Corn Exchange.

On that conspicuous stage, accordingly, Mr. Medlicott the very next day played the mountebank to a large and an admiring audience. He praised the great Irish leader, and the great Irish leader praised him. Mr. Medlicott was only too happy and too proud to serve under the banner of so distinguished a chief, and that distinguished chief, upon his part, was equally ready to accept Mr. Medlicott for his captain.

These mutual flatteries having been exchanged amidst vociferous applause from the unwashed artificers of Dublin, our enterprising hero sent his address to the newspapers, and embarked immediately for England, sedulously attended by his new patron to the water-side.

The report of this most unexpected Irish freak, having preceded him to Salisbury and Chichester, threw the old Bishop into a short paroxysm of indignation, vexed the Vicar considerably, and gratified only the weakest of his friends, including that fondest and vainest of her sex, his mother.

"Again!" cried the Vicar; "after burning his fingers once, I was in hopes he would not be so rash for the future."

"I don't know," said Mr. Cox, after a moment's reflection, "I often hear it said that such a one, having once burned his fingers, will not be apt to burn them again. That is not my view of things. As far as my observation goes, the great mistakes of life are rarely committed only once. When I see a man make one imprudent marriage, I think it the more probable he will make another. If a man embarrasses himself by building a house, I don't expect him to give up building as soon as he is out of his difficulties; on the contrary, I am inclined to predict he will soon be in the mortar again."

CHAPTER V.

PEACE PROVES MORE FATAL THAN WAR.

MR. MEDLICOTT is now in the House again, but he treats the House with pretty much the same contempt that he formerly treated the University; writes M. P. after his name, enjoys the *éclat* and the precedence which the position brings with it, but only meditates appearing upon remarkable occasions, like a Cincinnatus to save his country, or a comet to make her tremble. His family, waxing larger at the rate of four new comers every three years, continued to reside in the house called the snuff-box, which they inhabited by Mr. Cox's never-ceasing kindness; Reuben lived there himself nearly as much as he did in London; and not being content with the enterprising outlay of a thousand pounds upon the representation of Blarney, he speculated now a little in agriculture, and bought a farm of twenty acres adjoining his rural abode, which, with the help of the Frenchman and his godson, he hoped to cultivate with credit and advantage.

There never was anything clearer on paper than the profits of this farm; but far from realising his anticipations, he soon found that it materially diminished his income, and that it was absolutely necessary to have some other iron in the fire. His wife being passionately fond of horticulture, it occurred to him to try the experiment of gardening upon a great scale: she would conduct the floral dapartment; he himself would manage the other branches, or his secretary and clerk under his control and superintendence. For the disposal of his flowers and vegetables, he opened negotiations with the most extensive green-grocers of Covent Garden, and he inaugurated the speculation with a lecture upon the history and philosophy of gardens, which was attended by all the nobility and gentry within twenty miles of Chichester.

The spot originally combined flower-garden with kitchen-garden; here a cherry-tree, there an acacia; the violets creeping amongst the lettuces, and the roses and gooseberries seeming to grow upon the same bushes. Never did old Matthew sleep so soundly as in the little dimity-curtained bedroom overlooking the cucumber-frame, or breakfast with such appetite as in the sunny parlour underneath it, enjoying the song of the thrushes as much as his chocolate, and the smell of the flowers in their season more than even the odour of the titillating dust by which he had made his fortune. There was, however, something perhaps of the love of property in the gratification which these snatches of rustic existence gave him, for he was fond of thinking, when the whiffs of sweetness came upon the wind, that they came from his own roses; and when the various birds were chirping, carolling, and cooing round about him, he was wont to distinguish what he called his own robins, or his own doves, from the cuckoo or the wood-pigeon that haunted the neighbouring grove, and were no tenants of his.

It was, indeed, a very pretty spot, and could not have been much more still had it been forty miles from any city, town, or borough. The nearest approach to hubbub ever heard there, was that of a rookery in an adjoining wood; or, if the wind was in a particular point, when the church-bells of the city rang out together upon any great occasion of civil or religious joy.

It was very good in Mr. Cox to surrender this place as he now did to Mr. Medlicott's use, not even reserving for himself the room that overlooked the cucumbers. Reuben now passed many of his days here, sometimes with his flageolet cheering his labourers, sometimes with his hoe in his hand, earthing his marrow-fats, while perhaps he meditated a speech or an enterprise, grafting the cares of the statesman upon the occupations of the farmer and the gardener. The Vicar, though growing unwieldy, was his grand vizier upon all horticultural questions, though no man saw more clearly than he did the wide difference between gardening for amusement and gardening for profit. His father, moreover, was no visionary even in matters of roses and rasp berries. He was for gardening very much in the good old English way. Reuben was a transcendental gardener, and among other extraordinary notions, he conceived the idea of cultivating certain species of flowering plants on the top of the house. For this purpose he went to the considerable expense of a new roof, with a very gentle slope to the south, which he then covered with a coating of soil of what he considered sufficient thickness and the proper composition for his purposes. Mr. Cox had a private opinion that as the house was his, he ought to have been consulted before it was remodelled for so odd a purpose; and both he and the Vicar suggested the possibility of the roof not proving strong enough to support the weight of the beds imposed on it, particularly as there was also a large leaden tank for water, not to speak of the occasional saturation of the earth with rain, and the corresponding increase of strain upon the rafters. Mr. Medlicott, however, was confident all was perfectly secure; he had not quite forgotten, he said, with an air of assumption, the mathematics he had read at Cambridge, and the strength of materials and doctrine of vertical pressure had been among the subjects to which his attention had there been directed. Upon this, the Vicar and the landlord drew in their horns and said no more, though the latter continued to harbour an unpleasant apprehension that the system of house-top gardening would break down sooner or later, with considerable injury to his property, if not more unpleasant consequences.

The life Mr. Medlicott led here, although eccentric, had a great many domestic comforts and social enjoyments. The place was picturesque; the operations going on had the attractions that rural operations always have; he had brought his library down; he was in the bosom of his family; some of his oldest associates were in his neighbourhood; upon the whole, except that his exchequer was low, and likely to be lower (which was, to be sure, a drawback), his position was by no means as unenviable as it was strange.

His wife, used to the country, and loving it, was many degrees a happier creature now, than she had been in her elegant little mansion in London. Now she was seldom daunted by moustache, or overawed by big-wigs. Moreover she was reunited to her mother, from whom it was marvellous how she ever tore herself. She was just such a comfort and a treasure to Reuben, as Mr. Cox had found in another member of the same religious community. Wherever Mary lived, her house shone like a mirror, both within and without. Her kitchen was always a place to dine in; all her domestic arrangements were neatness itself. The younger Mrs. Medlicott was at this time very generally admired: the consciousness of being the spouse of so distinguished a husband, communicated a dignity to her deportment; while her anxieties about his fame and prospects, as well as about her children, substituted an air of seriousness, almost of melancholy, for the excess of mirthfulness that formerly distinguished her. Both changes seemed to become her. She retained much of her primitive simplicity of costume, but its simplicity suited a style of beauty which had rather a tendency to the florid and exuberant, and Reuben took care to make up for the sobriety of the hues by the richness of the texture of her garments. As he was fond, however, of bright colours when pictorially combined, particularly in female dress, since he could not please his eye with them in that of his wife, he made himself compensation in the attire of two maidens who had been for some time in his service, and who opened his door and attended his table in gay boddices and petticoats, and ribbons of many a bright tint. Reuben's rural entertainments were generally more successful than his dinners in Piccadilly; and one of the circumstances that made them more agreeable was the absence of powdered footmen and black boys, and the substitution of those smiling girls, who glided and hovered about your chair, nimble as Hebe in handing a glass, and neat-handed as Phyllis at dressing a salad.

One of Mr. Medlicott's many amiable qualities was his vivid remembrance of old scenes and old acquaintanceships; of every little tie, however slight, that had once connected him with any one either in business or in pleasure. About a year after his union with Mary Hopkins, they had been prevailed on by Mrs. Wyndham to spend a short time with her at Westbury, where she occasionally went to manage matters, unaccompanied by the Bishop. There Reuben saw many a face he had formerly been familiar with; and among others, very little impaired by time, were those of Dorothy the gardener's daughter, and Jenny the maid of the dairy, both looking out for services. Mrs. Wyndham gave them such excellent characters, that Mary Medlicott carried them away with her back to town, and they had lived with her ever since, fully answering the promises made for them.

Mr. Primrose once amused himself by drawing a parallel, in the manner of Plutarch, between these two equally useful and ornamental members of Mr. Medlicott's establishment. Dorothy was a Devonshire lass, born in the orchards: Jenny a Welchwoman; her rude forefathers were goatherds on week-days and Jumpers on Sundays. Jenny was red-and-white: Dorothy was all red. Jenny was rather tall than short: Lorothy rather short than tall. The eyes of the Devon lass were blue: those of the Welch maiden hazel. Dorothy liked work well, but diversion better: Jenny seemed as happy at work as she could possibly be at anything. Dorothy wore pink boddices and blue petticoats: Jenny wore the same hues in the opposite order. Some people fancied Dorothy more than Jenny: some, Jenny more than Dorothy. Both were good-humoured and in good case, and looked particularly well of a morning whitening the steps of Reuben Medlicott's door.

It is possible, that if Mr. Medlicott had been left to himself, or let alone, he would have devoted himself more heartily and thoroughly than he did to his original kind of life, which had indeed many fascinations for him. It did not even want the charm of notoriety, for he contrived to make his undertakings well known to the public not only by his lectures, but by papers in the "Gardener's Journal," and by extensive correspondence with the most celebrated horticulturists in the kingdom. But the more ambitious of his friends and relatives had no notion of permitting a Pitt to sink into a Paxton. Harvey was wretched when Mr. Medlicott was out of his sight more than a week. Dr. Page wrote him short energetic letters, treating his cabbages with sovereign contempt. It was with difficulty Mrs. Primrose was restrained by her husband from sending him reproachful and stimulating letters; while a certain blue demon, in the form of a tall matron, with spectacles of the same hue, was always at his elbow leading him into temptation, and tempting him to commit the very sin, of all others, which led the holy angels astray.

But no doubt there was also that within his own breast which kept continually reminding him that his mission was not yet fulfilled; there was always the

"Nescia virtus stare loco,"

and even if that voice had been mute, and that principle dormant, the occasional calls of the House, and injunctions of Mr. Speaker, would of themselves have been enough to give him a fillip.

As member for Blarney he utterly failed to give satisfaction. He had consented to accept a jointship in the tail of the Liberator, but he performed as inefficiently as possible the duties of that office; forgot entirely that he was not an independant member, and absented himself from important divisions in defiance of priests and demagogues. The consequence was, that the power that brought him in had already threatened to turn him out, and angry letters had passed between him and the Irish Cleon, in which there was no question but that Mr. Medlicott got the worst of it.

In the hands of the Quakers he was always more pliable. Yielding to their earnest and united solicitations, he now promised to move a series of resolutions, with a view to pledge the House to the principles of the Peace Society. The very outline he gave of the propositions he intended to lay down produced not a little amusement. When the time was near at hand for making his motion, it was found to clash with arrangements for a debate upon a government measure of the greatest urgency. Mr. Medlicott refused to give way. His friend Winning, now Solicitor-General, begged him to postpone it as a personal favour, but the influence of friend Harvey was too strong. Reuben, in fact, wanted the moral courage to do what his natural sense of decorum prompted. On the morning of the day fixed, out came the *Times* with a thunderer of the justest severity, launched at the peace-mongers and their Coryphæus. The old caricatures appeared in the shop-windows. Thor and the elephant were once more in every man's mouth, and under these propitious circumstances Mr. Medlicott rose to make a six hours' speech upon a question almost too puerile for discussion in a debating society. The result need hardly be stated. Never did the folly of an individual bring down such speedy and crushing retribution upon his head. The smile grew into the laugh, the laugh changed to the cough, the cough passed into the groan, the groan rose and swelled into the shout—then laugh, cough, groan, shout, and all conceivable modes of expressing the determination of an assembly not to tolerate a speaker, were combined with a storm of noises that was fearful to hear. Long before the orator, who was as stubborn as he was rash, gave up the contest, his friend Winning left the house, so painful was it to him to witness the prostration of his old friend and schoolfellow.

Nor even with this amount of castigation did the unfortunate member for Blarney escape upon this occasion; for the minister, whose important motion had been kept waiting during this sad waste of public time, thought it his duty to make the strongest remarks upon the system of persecuting the House with frivolous and vexatious declamation.

"The honourable member," he said, "makes peace more formidable than war. He and the wild enthusiasts he represents lead us seriously to doubt whether peace is indeed so great a blessing as we have hitherto imagined it; we almost long for the roar of ordnance to silence this insufferable tongue-battery. We are told of the horrors of war, but at the present moment, after what we have witnessed to-night, I think the House has a much clearer idea of the horrors of peace. I will not call the honourable member an enemy to his country, but I will say that he has declared and levied peace against her. We shall henceforward associate peace with his harangues, and fly to the cannon's mouth to escape from his. What are the toils and troubles of war, of which the poets say so much, compared to the toil and trouble of sitting on these benches, condemned to the alternative of being deafened either by the honourable member himself, or the overwhelming majority of this House, determined, and properly determined, not to hear him? I heartily congratulate the House upon having finally wrested the olive-branch from the honourable gentleman's hands, for a more formidable instrument for the dispatch of public business, in the fatal sense of that word, was never wielded in this or any other country."

CHAPTER VI.

IN WHICH FORTUNE PROMISES TO COMPENSATE THE VICAR FOR HER TREATMENT OF HIS SON.

A THIRD caricature of Mr. Medlicott appeared the following day, representing him thrashing the Ministry with a huge olive-branch. He bought the engraving himself, and taking it down with him to Chichester, hung it on the walls of his breakfast-parlour, which had already (in the same spirit of bravado and contempt for public opinion), been decorated with the previous illustrations of his career in the senate. However, he did little or nothing in parliament after this; though the same obstinacy which would not allow him to sit down when the House ordered him to do so in a voice of thunder, led him to retain his seat to the last, in defiance of the loudest complaints from his constituents.

Probably few remained now of the once numerous band of believers in his genius, who expected great exploits in statesmanship from him. Perhaps his mother, perhaps friend Harvey, still hoped against hope; but if they did, they must have been almost the only people who did so. It was still possible, of course, that he had not hit upon the true sphere for his abilities. All the paths to eminence had not yet been explored; there were still roads to fame and fortune remaining to be travelled.

He was forty : a serious age; too late to become a physician, the only learned profession he had not yet turned his mind to. The army and the navy were out of the question for an apostle of peace, as he was. It was easier to see that something must be done, than to decide what the something was; for it was clear he could not live like a gentleman, and bring up his family respectably, by philosophical gardening, or as a gentleman farmer either.

In fact, his finances were much embarrassed just now, between his parliamentary and agricultural speculations; very little remained of the handsome legacy Mr. Broad had left him; it was as much as he could do to retain his godson in his service; and it was a great relief to him when M. Beauvoisin volunteered to leave him, for the purpose of going on the stage with his sister, who had already adopted that profession.

In this uneasy state of affairs, an incident occurred which promised first to give the Vicar a lift in the world, but ended in doing that service for his son, who, in truth, wanted it more.

When Madame Beauvoisin became an actress she assumed the name of Charmette, and by that name she was already extremely popular on the London boards, in nearly the same walk in which Vestris was so brilliant and successful. Mr. Medlicott went to London expressly to see her. The Wyndhams were in town, and the Primroses with them, of course. Reuben secured a private box, and all the party, except the Bishop, went to see Charmette. They found her equal to her reputation; she sang with great spirit, but it was more as an actress she shone, than as a vocalist.

"And who is Charmette?" said Mrs. Wyndham, observing that Reuben talked of her to his aunt as of an old acquaintance.

"Who is she!" repeated Reuben; "you have surely heard of her?"

"In the newspapers only."

"Well, you knew her brother, at Hereford."

"No!"

"Ah! I see you have forgotten a certain essay by an old acquaintance of yours,—an inexperienced young author,—an essay on shoemakers of genius! Now I have brought things to your memory."

"Perfectly!" said Mrs. Wyndham, laughing; "I shall never forget Adolphe and the pink satin shoe, and his theory of feet, which I suspect was more yours than his."

"Mdlle. Charmette is his sister."

"You don't tell me so! I trust she is not as great an object of interest with you as her brother was formerly?"

"What would Mary say to that?" said Mrs. Primrose.

The curtain now rose again, and when it fell, the second piece was over.

"What is the hour?" asked Mrs. Wyndham, anxiously.

"Half-past ten," said Reuben, looking at his watch.

"Oh, dear! and the House will be up early to-night, on account of the ball at St. James's."

The Primroses and Mrs. Wyndham hurried away, but Mr. Medlicott remained to see the third piece, in which Charmette was also to appear. She observed him in the course of her performance, and before it was over a slip of paper, with a few words in pencil, was put into his hands, inviting him to supper at her lodgings, to meet Henry Winning and De Tabley.

Charmette received him with the most enchanting cordiality. She had evidently at length discovered where her true force lay; everything about her was brilliant, her apartments, her servants, her table,—all the creation of her own energy and genius.

Beside Winning and De Tabley, she expected another guest that night, who, when he came, proved to be another of Reuben's old friends, Master Turner, still fresh and as well able to enjoy life as ever. The supper was so agreeable, that it was near three o'clock when the party broke up. Master Turner and Mr. Medlicott went away together, and the former, laying his hand on Reuben's shoulder, made precisely the same speech he had made more than once so many years before. "The Lord Chancellor told me that the best sermon he ever heard in his life was one your father preached before him at Chichester."

At breakfast the next morning with the Primroses, Reuben, after making a full confession of his dissipated proceedings on the previous night, mentioned the old Master's odd repetition of what the head of the law had said ever so long ago about his father's sermon.

"I think," said Mrs. Primrose, "since the Chancellor thought so highly of your father, he might have given him a living before this, or, at least, done something for his family."

"The probability is," said Hyacinth, "that the Chancellor never thought of the subject since he made the remark which Turner so absurdly repeats every time we meet."

"He might surely remind the Chancellor of the circumstance," she replied; "something good might come of it."

"But the misfortune is," said Reuben, laughing, "that the sermon was one of my grandfather's, so that my father would hardly think of accepting a living, if it was offered him under such peculiar circumstances."

"That would be rare Quixotism," said the chaplain. "Let us ask Mr. Turner to dinner at all events on an early day," said his wife, when her nephew was gone; "he is intimate with the Chancellor, and I think he would say a word in season to oblige me."

This was done. The Primroses had a little dinner of six in a few days, including Master Turner, Winning, and Mrs. Wyndham; the Bishop happening to dine at Lambeth.

"With the greatest pleasure imaginable," said the Master; "I'll probably have an opportunity to-morrow, after divine service at the Temple; the subject will be extremely apropos to a sermon from Benson."

A week elapsed, and nothing was heard from the Master in Chancery. Mrs. Primrose then had a note from him, requesting her to send him the Vicar's address. This was quite enough to set the hearts of his friends beating.

The Vicar received a letter with the great seal on it; at least if it was not the actual great seal, it was the greatest that had ever been seen in the parish of Underwood.

After puzzling himself to write a becoming answer, he gave it up, and protested it would save him time and trouble to go up himself to London. He came up to town accordingly, waited on the Chancellor the first thing he did, and after astonishing his Lordship by declining a much better living than Underwood, he entertained him by a narrative of the circumstances which led to his preaching a sermon of Bishop Wyndham's composition.

"Mr. Medlicott," said the Chancellor, "I respect your frankness as much as I admire your humour; you deserve a better living for your sincerity than I had it in my power to offer you for your preaching, but this is the best thing now at my disposal, and you will permit me to press you to withdraw your refusal, though dictated by so nice a sense of honour."

"I am sensible of your goodness, my lord," replied the Vicar; "but the very subject of the sermon I had the honour of preaching before you so many years ago would make my acceptance of your generous offer an act of peculiar and glaring inconsistency."

"Let me see," said the Chancellor, "it was upon the nature and office of conscience. I well remember a fine comparison of an accusing conscience to the statue of Juno in an ancient temple, which stared full upon her worshippers wherever they stood, and even when they had passed by, seemed to follow them with her eye still."

"Yes, my lord," said the Vicar, "my life would not be worth a week's purchase with that terrible eye upon me, as it would infallibly be, if I owed my preferment to another man's deserts."

This occurred in the Chancellor's chamber. He was in his robes, on the point of stepping into court. There was no time for further discourse, had there been occasion for it. The Chancellor shook his hand cordially, and in a few minutes was absorbed in the intricacies of a case, which had probably already ruined a couple of generations.

The Vicar went from the Chancellor direct to Pall Mall, where he found his son and the Primroses, who saw him enter with astonishment, but immediately guessed the reason of his journey to London.

"What are you, sir?" cried Hyacinth, warmly greeting him.

"Vicar of Underwood."

"Then you have not yet seen the Chancellor."

The Vicar then told his story, which variously affected his audience; Hyacinth was exceedingly displeased at what he considered an excess of scrupulosity: Reuben was delighted that his father had done exactly what he declared he would have done himself: Mrs. Primrose sometimes agreed with her husband, sometimes with her nephew; sometimes she was at a loss what to think or what to say, a natural and not unusual state of the feminine understanding.

CHAPTER VII.

MR. MEDLICOTT IN OFFICE.

"But surely," said Mrs. Wyndham, "there are other good things besides livings in the Chancellor's gift; perhaps while his heart is warm, he might be induced to do something for Reuben."

"I protest," said Mrs. Primrose; "I'll give Master Turner another hint."

"Give him another dinner," said De Tabley.

Mrs. Primrose wrote an invitation that instant.

"I should not wonder," said the chaplain, "if we have found out at last the situation in life that my clever and accomplished friend is best adapted for, a jolly sinecure under the Crown, like De Tabley's, one of those rosy bowers about the Court, or well-feathered nests at Somerset House, or Greenwich Hospital, where, blessed with emolument and unperplexed with duty, a man has time to think, which nothing interrupts like the hurry of business; and leisure to dine, which nothing spoils like the thought of to-morrow morning."

De Tabley never liked to be considered a sinecurist, and said he "knew of no such rosy bowers and cosy nests as Primrose spoke of. All non-officials talked in the same strain. He wished his friend Hyacinth would only try a week's duty in the Comptrollership of the Navy Victualling Department."

"Will you take the Bishop's chaplaincy for the same time?" replied Hyacinth.

De Tabley shook his head, laughed, and said "he had no doubt that was a post of considerable difficulty."

"You have no notion of it," said the other; "but when uncle Tom goes to school, the business will not be so heavy."

The Vicar meanwhile was paying his respects to the Bishop, whom he now saw for the first time since his elevation to the bench. Tom was rolling on the floor of the study, very busy, like a true "chip of the old block," building castles with the blue-books, and enlarging and altering them with parliamentary papers of all kinds. His cot with the purple velvet curtains stood in a corner, but he was now too great a fellow to sleep in it, and only used it as a general receptacle for the toys and bon-bons with which he was loaded by all his acquaintances, especially by the wives of the Shrewsbury clergy.

The kind reception old Mr. Medlicott met with from his venerable father-in-law affected him extremely. The Bishop thought he had been over-scrupulous in refusing the living, but highly commended his probity and disinterestedness, and hoped it would soon be in his power to offer him something in Shrewsbury worth his acceptance. The Vicar then said he regretted it had not been suggested to the Chancellor to provide for Reuben in some way or other.

The Bishop looked surprised at this suggestion, and at first the Vicar thought he was displeased at it; he rose from his chair, swung himself about the room, puffed his cheeks, protruded his lower lip, assisted Tom in his building for a moment; then pulled out his enormous watch, like the clock of a church, said he must go down to the House of Lords, and desired the Vicar not to fail to dine with him between six and seven.

The Bishop went straight to the point, while Mrs. Primrose was beating about the bush, with her diplomatic notes to Master Turner. Reuben was nominated that very day to an appointment of high respectability in connection with the Court of Chancery; the salary from seven to eight hundred a year, with a little patronage attached, and perquisites that brought it up to nearly the clear thousand.

"I know the office well," said De Tabley, "one of the very best things going."

"Except that, I fear, it leads to nothing," said Mrs. Wyndham.

"Leads to nothing!" exclaimed Hyacinth; "at the worst it leads to Blackwall and Richmond."

"Is it compatible with Parliament?" said Mrs. Primrose, aside to the Vicar.

"No, Catherine," he replied, "and so much the better upon many accounts."

There was some little apprehension, for various reasons, on the part of several of his friends, that Mr. Medlicott would hesitate to accept the appointment, great as its advantages were; in his embarrassed and critical circumstances nothing less than a splendid piece of good fortune. But, if he had his doubts, he kept them to himself, and upon the whole abandoned himself with wonderful resignation to the receipt of a handsome salary and the tranquil enjoyments of office.

The report at Chichester was that Reuben had joined the Cabinet. Alderman Cold met Mr. Pigwidgeon, and gave him an unctuous description of the emolument and dignity of the appointment. Mr. Medlicott, he understood, intended to give his friends a grand dinner,—turtle and venison and iced punch.

Mr. Pigwidgeon said he had no doubt the place was a rank sinecure, which ought to have been abolished long ago; but at the same time it was a wonderful come-down for a man who had cocked up his nose so high as Mr. Medlicott. He was sincerely sorry to see it. There was *his* son who had scorned to accept anything under the government of an island. He was now his Excellency Sir Theodore Pigwidgeon, and could hang anybody he pleased in the island without judge or jury.

"Be that as it may," said the Alderman, "turtle-soup is not a bad thing."

"Why do you talk of turtle?" said the Apothecary, "sure my son is in the place that turtle comes from."

One of the pleasant circumstances of Mr. Medlicott's new position was that it only involved personal attendance in term-time, so that it was not necessary to give up his gardening, or relinquish Mr. Cox's country-house, which he now held at a fair rent, but one which was never demanded nor paid. Another was the little patronage at his disposal. He was now enabled to provide for two of his godsons. Reuben Gosling was his first clerk and receiver of fees, with two hundred per annum; Reuben Medlicott Robinson his second, with half that salary. The former was a smart forward young man, not only clever at arithmetic and book-keeping, but sharp at everything; his travels in America and Reuben's favour had made him inordinately conceited; he thought no girl could withstand his charms, and laid out the greater part of his salary on finery to render himself still more attractive. The latter was an industrious, quiet, timid boy, proud of nothing but his name; he thought Mr. Medlicott the greatest man living, and would willingly have died in his service, which Mr. Gosling would not have done.

' It was curious to observe the different views which the relatives and friends of Reuben took of his present situation. His female friends in general were disposed to be uneasy lest the duties of his office should prove too severe for him; his wife was apprehensive of his suffering from mental anxiety; Mrs. Primrose was more afraid of sedentary habits and indigestion; Charmette warned him against corpulence; but his mother was haunted by errors of all sorts, particularly about his spirits and his lungs; she provoked the Vicar excessively by doubting whether, upon the whole, Reuben had acted wisely in accepting the place.

"If there are twenty right views of any subject," said the Vicar, "and only one wrong one, a woman will infallibly take the latter."

"I don't mean to say," said Mrs. Medlicott, "that the situation has not its advantages."

"And you may safely trust himself for discovering its advantages," said the Vicar.

There was one discovery, indeed, which Mr. Medlicott made before he was an official of three months' standing. This was the fact that, beyond signing his name a certain number of times in the day there was little or no duty which Mr. Gosling was not perfectly competent to discharge ; and he mentioned this to De Tabley in a tone of complaint, as if he had been betrayed into accepting that office by delusive representations.

De Tabley smiled, and said it was a singular complaint to make, even if the fact were so; but for his part, he added, he always found something to do in the Victualling Department, and he could hardly believe that in such a department as Chancery any place could be a complete sinecure. Why the very fleecing of the public to so great extent could not but be a work of considerable labour.

Reuben laughed at the word labour, as being ludicrously inapplicable to all the work done in the course of the week by himself and his godsons together.

"You will find more to do, when you have been longer in the office.—I speak from experience," said the other.

"Perhaps so," said Reuben. De Tabley, indeed, was that kind of man who in truth would have been content if his office had been discharged of all duty whatever; he would never have quarrelled with it on that account. At the same time he was not only most attentive to such business as he had to do, but he made it seem ten times as great as it actually was, by his leisurely and ostentatious manner of transacting it. He perfectly understood the art of seeming wise and appearing busy. He never wrote a short memorandum ; his minutes took hours to read ; he multiplied references, accumulated papers, used larger envelopes, greater seals, and more miles of red tape and green ribbon than anybody else in the public service. His table always suggested the idea of affairs the most numerous and weighty. He wrote all his private letters in office hours, upon official stationery, sealed them with official seals, and dispatched them by official messengers. There was always a difficulty about seeing him, and he was never surprised reading a newspaper or a novel, smoking a cigar, lunching, or taking a siesta in his easy chair. Then he never left his office without carrying away with him a box of papers, or a couple of blue-books, which impressed the spectators with the belief that even his private hours were encroached on by his public employments. He kept the messengers and junior clerks in a constant hurry and ferment, and by all these arts and contrivances, systematically practised, he convinced hundreds, and eventually persuaded himself, that he was a very hard-worked and meritorious public servant.

Business, however, grew so little upon Mr. Medlicott, that he had not only time enough on his hands to make long sojourns at Chichester, and pay occasional visits to his grandfather at Shrewsbury or Westbury, but ample leisure to renew his intercourse with his Quaker friends, who continued to believe him the foremost man of the age, and stuck to him the more firmly because they considered him a martyr to the envy or stupidity of the House of Commons. He now became treasurer to the Peace Society at Harvey's solicitation: but this gave him no increase of trouble, for Mr. Gosling took all the labour on himself, received the money, kept the books, prepared the accounts, did everything in fact that was to be done with an ease and cleverness that raised him still higher in his godfather's good opinion.

With all Mr. Gosling's cleverness, however, Reuben found at the end of a year that the profits of his office were not so considerable as he had been led to expect. This was a more unpleasant discovery than the first he had made. When he mentioned it to De Tabley, the latter hoped he had an efficient and trustworthy clerk to receive the fees.

"The cleverest fellow in England," said Mr. Medlicott, in everything connected with money; the best accountant, the best book-keeper; a most deserving and promising young man."

"I hope you audit his accounts, nevertheless," said his friend.

"Perfectly unnecessary," said Reuben; "he has such a luminous method of book-keeping that his accounts, in fact, audit themselves."

The clever young man in question came in at the moment with some papers for his chief's signature.

"Is that your Receiver?" said De Tabley, after having scrutinised the godson from top to toe with his eye-glass.

"I see," answered Reuben "you are surprised to see him

rigged out so smartly. Poor fellow, dress is the only indulgence he allows himself."

De Tabley was at Blackwall the following day, and noticed the Receiver at a table not far from his own, entertaining two companions at a regular white-bait dinner. He mentioned this to Reuben, who thought it his duty to speak on the subject to his godson. It was all a mistake. Mr. Reuben Gosling did not even know whether Blackwall was up the Thames or down the Thames. "And as to white-bait, sir," said he, "I do not know whether it is fish or fowl; I never tasted it in my life, and never hope to do so."

What could be more satisfactory? Indeed, there never was a public officer so happy in clerk or secretary, for Mr. Gosling soon showed him that by imitating his handwriting he could even save him the trouble of signing papers; the consequence of which was that in the second year of his placemanship Mr. Medlicott scarcely showed his face three times in the purlieus of the Court of Chancery.

CHAPTER VIII.

MR. MEDLICOTT RENOUNCES THE ERRORS OF BEEF AND MUTTON.

It was at this period, or thereabouts, that the still sanguine and ambitious Mr. Medlicott, applying his versatile mind to new objects of interest, was converted (through the exertions of Harvey principally) to the doctrines and practices of the vegetarians. He expatiated publicly on the subject in the Hanover Square Rooms to large audiences, chiefly composed of hypochondriacs who had lost their confidence in Parr's pills, and the regular dreary old pack of London lecture-goers, the same sort of people who are now to be seen flocking to lectures on animal magnetism and electro-biology. In his garden at Chichester he now devoted himself almost exclusively to the culture of vegetables, and announced himself to the world as an epicurean of the true school, and the only real possessor of the elixir of life. This was the only absurdity in which Mr. Medlicott was ever countenanced by his grandfather. The Bishop, now very old, was not the less disposed to live upon that account; but was determined, on the contrary, to live as long as he could, partly because he was thinking gravely of rebuilding the palace, partly because he was anxious to see his son well settled in the world.

Mr. Primrose beginning one morning to ridicule the vegetarian heresy, as he called it, got himself unexpectedly snubbed. The Bishop took up the cause of the peas against the ducks, and disparaged the lamb while he magnified the spinach. Nor was this mere table-talk. Tom was put upon vegetable diet soon after, Mr. Primrose began to tremble for his saddle of mutton and haunch of venison, and a feeling of alarm and insecurity, beginning with the chaplain, crept from parish to parish, and soon pervaded the whole diocese. Who could tell where such a revolution would stop? The larder in danger, would the cellar long be safe? Serious encroachments on the Protestant religion have often excited less apprehension in the minds of a portion of the clergy of the Church of England. Some of the very divines whose gorge rose upon this occasion at the idea of dining on a cauliflower, have since been known to swallow crucifixes and candlesticks, things the hardest, one would suppose, to be stomached by a clergyman of the Church of England.

After corresponding with his grandson for some time on the most improved modes of cultivating and cooking vegetables, to make them as worthy as possible of being used exclusively for the food of man, his lordship was seized with a sudden desire to see with his own eyes how Mr. Medlicott practised the system both in the garden and the kitchen, and announced his resolution to pay him a visit. No day however was fixed, nor could the Bishop be prevailed on to fix one, which was most uncomfortable for Mrs. Medlicott, for she was kept in a state of continual anxiety, not knowing the moment when a personage of such consequence would arrive. The house being so small, it was decided to remove to Mr. Cox's town residence (for he happened to be absent at the time), and surrender Virginia entirely to the Wyndhams during their stay. The Bishop for weeks continued shilly-shally, and at length arrived at the most unlucky of all possible moments. Mr. Medlicott and his father were dining with Canon Oldport, whose dining days were not yet over. Mary had gone with her children to her aged mother's cottage, leaving full instructions with her trusty maids how to act in case visitors should arrive, for it had been arranged that whenever the Bishop came, he should call first at the house in town. Dorothy and Jenny, however, saw no reason for expecting the Bishop on that evening more than another, and they thought they might very well venture to pop out for a quarter of an hour, to gossip with their acquaintances in the neighbourhood. They had not deserted their posts for five minutes, when a huge travelling coach-and-four drove up to Mr. Cox's, just such a coach as Squire Wronghead in the play travels up to London in. Old Matthew's door never experienced such a thundering salute. Again, again, and again, more like cannonading than knocking, with no reply but the echo of the empty house, while the choler of a very stout old gentleman, with a shovel-hat, who was mounted on the box, with a blooming boy at his side, rose at every unavailing application to the knocker. At length a little group of idlers collected, attracted by the noise, and curious to see a bishop on so unusual a bench.

Mr. Primrose alighted, and asked the civilest-looking of the bystanders whether this was not Mr. Cox's house.

"Yes."

"And is not Mr. Medlicott residing here at present?"

"What Mr. Medlicott?"

Primrose was amazed at the question.

"Such is popularity," growled the Bishop, unable to avoid philosophising, angry as he was. "Mr. Reuben Medlicott," said the chaplain.

"Is it the market-gardener?" asked another of the loungers.

"Oh, it's orator Medlicott the gentleman wants," said a third; "but he doesn't live here, sir, he lives at the Snuff-Box."

"We had better go at once to Virginia," said the sweet voice of Blanche from the inside; "Virginia is a prettier name than the Snuff-Box," she added, with a smile, aside to the chaplain.

"Drive to Virginia," called the Bishop to the postillions. The chaplain asked advice as to the road, and away dashed the coach-and-four up the green lane.

It was the same thing at Virginia; the bell that hung in the horse-chestnut was nearly pulled down with raging. The Bishop shouted to make himself heard, but there was nobody there to hear him, nor any rejoinder but the honest bark of Constable, who seemed to be the only officer in charge of the premises. In fact it was a very ugly business altogether, and there seemed no remedy but to return to Chichester and go to the Parrot. However, when they came back to Mr. Cox's house, all was right; Mr. Medlicott was at the door, just returned from Mr. Oldport's. There was no time, of course, to lecture the maids that night. It was almost dark. Reuben mounted the dickey, and con ducted the party back again to Virginia, where, before they were settled for the night, there was an hour of such fuss as that quiet retreat had never experienced before. Among other causes of confusion, it turned out that in place of a portmanteau with the Bishop's ordinary linen, a trunk with his lawn-sleeves and mitre had been brought down to the country. There was always some mistake of the kind wherever he went. Mr. Medlicott did the best he could to redress grievances, and then returned to town to rejoin his wife.

The overhauling of the delinquent maids at an early hour on the following morning was a sight worth the seeing. Old Matthew's wainscoted dining-room was the court of sessions: there sat the ex-member for Chichester in Mat's elbow chair (a chair from which justice had often before uttered her oracles), a self-constituted magistrate within his private domestic jurisdiction. Not far off sat his wife, in her semi-Quakerly habit, the gray silk gown, and the crisp white muslin, more than usually sedate, as became the gravity of the occasion. You heard the sighings and dolorous interjections of the offenders before they came to the bar. The meekest possible tap at the door heralded their appearance, and they entered in their neat tight jackets and gay petticoats, with their faces buried in their bosoms, their hands industrious with the strings of their snowy aprons, neither pressing herself forward, but rather wishing to prefer the other to the place of honor. One of the poor things was ordered to shut-to the door. Then Reuben began, and never did any justice of the peace paint crime in livelier colours, or so sting to the quick the conscience of the trembling criminals before him, as he did that morning in the rating he gave his delinquent handmaids; while at the end of every sentence his wife nodded her full approbation, as one judge upon the bench is seen to sanction in dumb-show the law as laid down by his learned brother. Reuben expounded the duties of domestics lucidly; what faith was reposed in them, what diligence and fidelity was expected from them; how they were trustees of their master's goods and chattels in his absence, how the safety of houses and the well-being of families depended upon their vigilance and good behaviour. Then he detailed instances of fires, and examples of robberies, which had taken place because maids preferred gadding to minding their business; and Mrs. Medlicott, as *amica curiæ*, reminded him of one or two cases in point which had escaped his recollection. If these topics made the guilty creatures tremble, imagine how they felt when ne went on to deliver the law of the land; with what eyes it regarded and with what correction it punished disorderly servants. Here he spoke with particular authority, for, as member for the city, he had been *ex officio* a visitor, and in some sort a controller of bridewells, and could reveal the secrets of the prison-house; but even this was not the climax of his address. It was not until, with artfully lowered voice and touching manner, he came to speak of the kindness and favour with which you Dorothy, and you Jenny, had been invariably treated by the mildest and best of mistresses, not overworked and under-fed like many of your degree, never grudged a holiday, never forbidden to see an aunt or a godmother,—it was not until he came to this that the grand effect was produced; and the fair penitents, unable to bear more, began to weep and sob so, that had their eloquent master intended to close his address with a sentence, the girls were scarcely in a condition to hear or understand it. However, even had the judgment-seat been so austere, the mercy-seat was there, with the gracious Mary upon it, to mitigate whatever doom should be pronounced. The girls had done wisely in throwing themselves upon the clemency of the court, and they were dismissed, still weeping, with the simple condition of never transgressing again while they wore petticoats, at least while they wore Mr. Medlicott's colours.

The day commenced early, because the Medlicotts were anxious to join their guests at the country-house. Thither they repaired immediately, laughing children, repentant maids, and all to be in time to receive the Bishop and his suite at breakfast. On the way, Mrs. Medlicott told her husband that she was very uneasy in her mind, having dreamed last night that the roof of the house had fallen in under the weight of the flower-beds, directly over the room occupied by the Bishop. Reuben smiled, repeated his conviction that all was perfectly safe, and in a few moments there was proof enough that his wife's dream had come through the ivory portal; for when they entered the grounds, the first person they saw was the glorious old prelate himself, going round the house and round the house, and planning and almost ordering some alteration or reconstruction of every part of it. At intervals he would pause, and scold either his chaplain or his wife about his shirts, desiring to know whether they intended him to walk about the fields in full canonicals, as if it was a coronation or the opening of Parliament.

Mr. Primrose ventured to observe that as the episcopal office was a pastoral one, there would be no great impropriety in his lordship wearing his lawn-sleeves in the meadows.

Mr. Medlicott said that Bacon's observations on the monarch's crown would apply equally well to the bishop's mitre, that to wear it with ease it ought to be worn every day.

The Bishop took no notice of what any of them said, but walked about with Tom by the hand, admiring the garden, which really deserved the praise he gave it, for between the finest of vegetables and the finest of flowers, it was nothing short of a wilderness of beauty.

"You have done well, sir," said the Bishop, "to couple Flora with Pomona; what can be more odoriferous than those beans? what gayer than those scarlet-runners? that cabbage-rose is not disgraced by growing beside the worthy vegetable from which it derives its name."

"Observe, sir, the extraordinary diameter of that head," said Reuben; "it measures nearly two feet from pole to pole. I am proud to have produced it; it makes me feel like the creator of a world."

"There is a world of nourishment in it," said the Bishop, "and as much wonder to the eye of the philosopher as in the great globe itself."

"Gardening, sir, after all, is a noble employment," said Mr. Medlicott.

The Bishop assented without speaking.

"Rather earthly, is it not?" said the chaplain.

"No, sir," said his master, turning round upon him with severity, "not earthlier than any other human employment, nor so earthly as many; it well represents the proper division of the mind of man between this world and the next. While the gardener digs the ground, his looks are fixed upon it; when he rests upon his spade, he lifts his eyes to heaven."

There was a sublimity not only in the thought, but in the Bishop's tone and manner of expressing it.

"*Os homini sublime dedit, cœlumque tueri*," said Mr. Primrose, to cover his defeat.

"Noble verse," said Reuben.

"It ought to be Virgil's," said the Bishop.

"Breakfast is ready," said little Chichester, creeping in among them all, a messenger from his mother, who had been busy all this time preparing the morning repast.

The first thing the Bishop thought of after breakfast was his shirts again. He told Reuben that he must get a shirt by hook or by crook. There was no great difficulty about it, because Mr. Medlicott was now himself a portly man, and his shirts promised to fit his grandfather fairly enough. He chose one of the newest, and gave it to the old man, who marched off with it to his chamber, crushing it in his hands as if it was no more than a napkin.

Ah, Dorothy, Dorothy, so soon to be in a scrape again, scarcely an hour out of the hands of justice, the tears scarce dry upon your cheek with which you implored and obtained mercy!

The Bishop no sooner entered his bedroom than he saw another member of the hierarchy standing in the middle of the floor, and in full pontifical attire, not only in his lawn-sleeves, but with his mitre on his head. He seemed to be admiring himself, too, in a large mirror, for he was looking over his shoulder, and was so intent on the prospect, that his brother of Shrewsbury was within a yard of him before his approach was noticed.

"How now, Mistress Curiosity!" shouted the Bishop, not long in discovering who it was that was dressed in his robes.

The maid screamed, pulled off the mitre and threw it on the bed, shuffled off the lawn with equal haste, and flew from the room almost into the arms of her master, who, hearing the girl scream, had hastened to the door, greatly shocked at his grandfather's behaviour in alarming his maids after such a fashion.

It was a serious misdemeanour on Dorothy's part, and greatly aggravated by the mercy so lately extended to her misdeeds; but, nevertheless, she got through this scrape easier than the last; the comic nature of her fault protected her from its just retribution; and had either her master or mistress proposed any form of penalty, there would have been an unanimous outcry in the offender's behalf.

Mr. Primrose was not long in giving her the title of the Bishop of Virginia; and the old gentleman meeting her again in the course of the day, sweeping the house very diligently, told her "he wished he could keep his diocese as clean as she kept hers."

CHAPTER IX.

IN WHICH ANOTHER BUBBLE BURSTS.

The Bishop, indeed, found himself so comfortable, and liked everybody and everything about him so well, that before dinner he announced his resolution to remain for a week under his grandson's roof, and even talked of leaving Tom behind him, which Blanche knew very well he would not do, when it came to the point. In fact he seldom let Tom out of his sight, and was miserable if he escaped for a moment to play with Chichester, lest he should be drowned in some duck-pond, devoured by Constable, or lost in some imaginary labyrinth of the garden.

"Depend upon it, sir," he said to Reuben, "you have hit upon the true mode of enjoying life at last; happiness depends upon three things (humanly speaking), health, contentment, and security: here you have all three; as to health, you have arrived at the great secret of preserving it; as to content, you have everything here that a man of sense and philosophy can require; and as to security (with that snug place in Chancery), I see nothing that is likely to interrupt it, until the hour comes that comes to all men, and you fall like a ripe pear, or the last leaf of October."

"Indeed, sir," said Reuben, "I think it highly probable that this will be the longest chapter of my life, if not also the last one. But I have now to put a practical question to you and to my other guests,—shall we dine in the usual apartment, or in the tower, or *speculum*, from which we command a most extensive and superb prospect?"

"Not in the *speculum*," said the Bishop; "I am not such a climber as I was in former days."

"As you were, sir," said Blanche, "when you took us all to see the new houses in Barsac Square, and made my poor father and uncle follow you up the ladders, at the risk of their lives. You remember that, Reuben?"

"That I do well, fair grandmamma," said Mr. Medlicott.

"No," continued the Bishop, "order the table to be laid under the trees; the wasps are not come yet; and remember!—no compromise, no infraction of the system,—neither fish, flesh, nor fowl,—if Primrose will not feast with us and Epicurus, let him have his dinner with Aristippus in the buttery, or at the sideboard."

"My wife has arranged all that," said Reuben; "the cloth shall be spread, sir, where you propose, and as soon as my father and mother arrive, the gong shall toll, and we shall go to dinner."

The Vicar and old Mrs. Medlicott did not keep the company long waiting. *Eheu fugaces!*—they were both much altered since we first introduced them to the reader's acquaintance. The Vicar's head was now very hoary; his teeth were fewer in number; his gait much tardier; his rosy cheeks and the sly humourous twinkle in his eye, were the only respects in which he was not greatly changed. His wife was more changed still, but the change was, on the whole, to her advantage; she had expanded comfortably in sundry directions; her hair was now pure silver, without being diminished in quantity; and though she still had the didactic air of the schoolmistress, she was altogether a comelier woman in the winter than she had been in the summer of her days.

But there goes the gong, sounding the tocsin of conviviality! To the pastoral table, with the blue above and the green below, the portly and handsome Reuben conducted the fairest and youngest of grandmothers, the steadiest of friends, the best of little women. The veteran prelate (fine old oak that he was of the English forest) escorted his meek, amiable, semi-Quakerly hostess. To the Vicar's share fell the goodly prize of his buxom sister-in-law, in whom (although no Dryden has commemorated her worth) there dwelt as many virtues as in Eleanora herself, or Mrs. Killigrew. The chaplain had Hobson's choice, and led the senior Mrs. Medlicott to the board, where he took his seat with wonderful good grace, considering the bleak prospect before him; but then he had a glimpse of a cold sirloin on a side-table not far off, which probably helped to preserve his serenity.

The table, spread on a patch of smooth emerald sward, in an open space near the house, was as perfect as neatness could make it without splendour or expense. The only piece of plate was that which the electors of Chichester had presented to Mr. Medlicott when he retired from the representation. A few vases of Mary's finest flowers were the only other ornaments. At each corner stood a great crystal or glass jug of the brightest water. Mr. Primrose and the Vicar had no objection to the brightness; but they would both have been better pleased if the taste in colours displayed in the costume of the maids had also prevailed in the contents of the decanters. The company stood. The chaplain pronounced the benison, but probably would have pronounced it with more unction, had he not but too clearly foreseen what the uncovering of the dishes would reveal. Dorothy and Jane performed this part of their duty with as much gravity and importance as if they were ministering at the most formal dinner. At the head, before the master of the feast, stood a dish of enormous cauliflowers, like the wigs of chancellors, garnished with Brussels sprouts, arranged with evident attention to pictorial effect. At the foot, before Mr. Primrose, were parsnips and carrots, also artistically combined, the parsnips arranged in a circular heap, from which the carrots radiated like spurs; indeed the dish resembled nothing so much as an immense sunflower. On the left was spinach without lamb, and beans without bacon; on the right, peas separated from ducks, and turnips divorced from the leg of mutton. Potatoes dressed in six different ways were distributed at intervals. There were salads with oil for people who knew what salads ought to be, and salads with cream for people who did not. There were removes of asparagus and artichokes; and the second course consisted of peas of younger growth, mushrooms variously cooked, and several new species of vegetables which Mr. Medlicott was endeavouring to naturalise in England.

The Bishop had always been a lusty diner, and he now dined as lustily and voraciously on all manner of vegetables as he had ever done in his life on more savoury and substantial things. He commended everything in succession, and only paused in his commendations to eat again. All his intolerance of character came out upon this occasion; he was angry when anybody refused an artichoke or declined a second helping of peas; and he never saw Jenny or Dorothy stealing a slice of the sirloin on either the Vicar's plate or his chaplain's, but he scowled at the poor girl from under his grizzly brows, called the taste for animal food a deplorable bigotry, and spoke in the most unhandsome and unbecoming terms of the roast beef of old England.

"Now, my lord Bishop," said the host, after he had pretty well distributed his fine cauliflowers, "good eating, says the adage, requires good drinking; let me call your attention to the sparkling flask near you; I have the honour to pledge you in a glass of it."

The Bishop crowned his glass, quoting Pindar in praise of the virtues of cold water with a jovial air, and pushed the croft to the Vicar, who (being less subservient than the chaplain) honestly confessed that his tastes were more Anacreontic than Pindaric, adding a sly remark, that Pindar after all was a Bœotian, and consequently no very great authority with him.

"A fair hit," said the Bishop; "you deserve a glass of port for it."

"You shall have it, father," said Reuben; and handing a key to Dorothy, he instructed her to fetch the wine.

The wine came; Mr. Primrose quietly seconded the Vicar in disposing of it, while the host and his grandfather adhered to the more innocent beverage in the croft, which certainly could not have promoted loquacity more, had it been Bourdeaux or Burgundy. Reuben talked largely (and on the whole with magnanimity) of the House of Commons; his grandfather talked of both Houses when it came to his turn, and although the old stager talked too much, he was certainly the least garrulous of the two. The rest were mere listeners, though perhaps only the senior Mrs. Medlicott listened with profound attention. She thought her son much too lenient in his criticisms on the Lower Chamber; and from her father's observations on the Upper one, satisfied herself thoroughly that Reuben had only failed in Parliament because he had not the good fortune to have been born a peer.

Once or twice the Bishop forgot himself, and filled his glass from the bottle of port, but by tacit consent the mistake was connived at by the company. In short, he so thoroughly enjoyed his vegetarian entertainment, that, although the shades of evening had begun to prevail, he could not be induced to rise, until numerous great drops of rain foretold the approach of a heavy shower, and rendered a precipitate retreat within doors advisable.

"We shall have a wet night," said the Bishop, looking at the barometer, which was falling rapidly.

It proved the wettest night he ever passed in his life, but the weight of moisture in the clouds was not altogether to blame for it. With the greatest difficulty did Reuben and his wife effect their return to Chichester in safety; and it was also as much as the Vicar could do to get back to Underwood without being drowned. Reuben slept soundly. His wife did not sleep for many hours, not so much thinking of her dream as of the natural and only too probable effect of such weather upon the roof of her country house. At length she began to doze, but it was only to dream again of the same perils, and before long the images of terror which filled her mind began to be mingled with strange, sharp, intermitting sounds. She awoke in terror, and sat up in the bed; the sounds were too real; it was a loud knocking at the street door. With no little difficulty she awakened her husband. He threw the window open and inquired who the disturber was, and the cause of this untimely visitation. It was one of his gardeners from Virginia, with the news that the tank on the roof had either overflowed, or given way (the exact nature of the disaster was as yet unknown), and that the whole house had in a moment been deluged with water. The fright which this intelligence caused her proved nearly fatal to poor Mrs. Medlicott. Reuben was unable to leave her for nearly an hour, urgently as his presence was required in the country. When he got to Virginia, he found the house empty. The Bishop and his family, having narrowly escaped with their lives, had taken refuge at the Vicarage, which was the nearest asylum to them, and there Reuben (after a rigid inspection of his hydraulic arrangements, too late to be of use to anybody) found them all in a most dismal and uncomfortable pickle, drying their clothes at a great fire in the kitchen, and relating the particulars of their several adventures and escapes. The Bishop, with Tom in his arms, had actually escaped with only his old dressing-gown and a blanket to cover him.

Nothing could exceed the good nature of Mrs. Primrose and Mrs. Wyndham; they felt for Reuben much more than for themselves, and tried to speak of what had occurred as people do of that class of fatalities to which it is commonly said that the best regulated houses are subject. The Bishop was in a different mood; had he stormed ever so furiously, it would have alarmed Reuben less than the savage silence which he obstinately maintained the whole morning; not that he so much minded the wetting he got, although at his age it was a serious matter; but it was through the ceiling of the room where Tom and his nurse slept that the water had forced its passage: the wonderful child of his old age had been saved by little short of a miracle; so that it was very well his lordship governed his tongue as he did, for he not only severely blamed himself for his foolish journey to Chichester, but even repented that he had ever made up his quarrel with his unlucky grandson.

The Bishop never opened his lips until he heard Reuben say

to Mrs. Wyndham, that unfortunate as the accident was, it was no more than a carpenter and a plumber would easily set to rights in a few hours, so that all would be snug again before night. Then his lordship called to his servant, and directed him to order post-horses to be ready to start the moment their clothes were dry and breakfast was over; nor was much said by any one to alter his resolution. Reuben merely repeated his regret that a visit from which he had promised himself so much pleasure had terminated so abruptly.

"Abruptly, indeed!" muttered the Bishop; "I know nothing more abrupt than a water-spout in the middle of the night. It came down, sir, over Tom's bed like the falls of the Rhine at Schaffhausen!"

"Those are disasters, sir," said Mr. Medlicott, in a philosophising and soothing tone of voice, "which rarely happen twice in the course of a man's life."

"Not to the same person," said the Bishop.

Nobody, however, caught a fever, or even a cold, from the accident of the night. When the clothes were all dry, they sat down to breakfast, and as cheerless a meal it was as ever a family circle sat down to. It was dismal out of doors into the bargain; the rain continued to pour, but without the least effect upon the Bishop's determination to set out. Mr. Medlicott was really the only person to be pitied of the party. He felt more prostrated by this spiteful little freak of Fortune, than he had often been by some of her heaviest blows. His female friends embraced him tenderly; and perhaps his grandfather himself felt at the last moment that his conduct had been too harsh, for he shook him by the hand just before he drove off, gave him his blessing, and advised him not to think of patching his roof, but to take it all down and put on a new one.

To a man of ordinary steadiness of purpose, such an incident as we have just recorded, far from discomposing the whole tenor of his existence, would have been no more than a slight temporary derangement, such as everything is liable to beneath the moon. The annoyance of to-day would have been the jest of to-morrow. Such a man would have straightway repaired his house, and resumed his ordinary routine of living, nor would all the rain in the clouds, or all the morose old bishops and grandfathers in the world, have pushed him out of his track for the space of twenty-four hours. But there was no firmness in the mind of Mr. Medlicott, and consequently no stability in any course he adopted, or in the scheme of his life itself. He was just the kind of person for Fortune to crack her jokes on, and knock about at her caprice and pleasure. His grandsire had never hazarded a more unlucky prophecy than when he foretold the permanence of the system which he found instituted, and seemingly so flourishing, among the flowers and herbs of the garden at Virginia. It may be said to have died while the soothsayer was predicting its longevity. Mr. Medlicott, indeed, directed the necessary repairs to be executed in the dwelling-house, but he never returned to it. His wife remained seriously indisposed for some time, having had a premature confinement in consequence of the fright she had received; and upon her recovery he took her with him to London, where he continued to reside as long as his official connection with the Court of Chancery lasted. The profits of that place continued to disappoint his fair expectations; and again and again did De Tabley and other friends remonstrate with him on the imprudence of placing too much reliance on his subordinates, particularly on Mr. Gosling, who had for some time been running a rig which might well have excited the suspicions of the most confiding of human beings. He had chambers in the Albany, kept a cab and a tiger, occasionally drove a tandem, was a member of Crockford's, and was even rapidly becoming a noted character on the turf. If all was honest and straight, there certainly was not a young man in England did half so much with two hundred a-year as he did; but Mr. Medlicott was either not to be shaken in the confidence he placed in his dashing godson, or he could not bring himself to make the exertion necessary to overhaul his accounts. The Peace Society, however, whose funds were also at Mr. Gosling's control, was not so negligent of its affairs; and several irregularities having been detected by Mr. Harvey in the way the moneys were lodged and the books kept, a committee was named to scrutinise everything; and at the conclusion of a strict audit, a deficit was discovered and declared against the treasurer to the extent of several hundred pounds. There did not exist a doubt on the mind of any man of business that Gosling had embezzled this sum; but Mr. Medlicott was urged in vain to hold him accountable for it. He refused to be convinced that his officer was morally responsible; the money might have slipped through his fingers, but he felt assured it had never stuck to his hands; nay, so positive was he upon the subject, that he replaced the deficit entirely out of his own pocket, not even requiring Mr. Gosling to contribute a single shilling.

Folly succeeded folly, in a quick march. The salary grew "fine by degrees and beautifully less," until at length it fell to little more than four hundred a-year; when Mr. Medlicott, with a wife and five children, found it more difficult to provide a plain dinner for them, than his clerk did to entertain a party of twenty fast men like himself at Lovegrove's or Richardson's. Reuben now bethought him of those mines in Brazil, in which he had a few thousand pounds invested; and the secretaryship of the mining company falling vacant, he applied for it, and obtained it easily. This set him up again in the world, for the salary was seven hundred a year, and there was a commodious residence attached, which saved him the rent of a house, and other incidental expenses. So completely was he engrossed by this new employment, into which he entered with scientific ardour, as well as with official enthusiasm, that he now treated the place in Chancery more carelessly than ever, and left the management of everything to Mr. Gosling, who soon evinced his gratitude, no less than his ingenuity, in a very striking manner.

The house where Mr. Medlicott now lived was in Duke Street, Westminster. One morning, just as Reuben rose from the breakfast table, a gay cab drove up to the door, with a gay horse and a gay tiger; but neither cab, horse, nor tiger was half so gay as the young man who jumped out and inquired for Mr. Medlicott. Reuben had not seen his right-hand man for several months, and received him with the utmost graciousness and cordiality. Mr. Gosling came with a carefully-matured plan for securing his chief the enjoyment of his present salary for life, and at the same time relieving him from even the shadow of duty and responsibility. The scheme was this. Mr. Medlicott was to resign, and Mr. Gosling, having interest to obtain the appointment, was to succeed him, entering at the same time into a private compact to pay him a yearly sum equal to the existing emoluments of the office during his natural life. In fact, this ambitious and enterprising young man only wanted rank and position; salary was a secondary consideration with him. He doted on business, idolised nothing but his desk; he was in his element, he said, in the midst of that dull official routine, which (he could well understand) must be so unspeakably disgusting to a man of Mr. Medlicott's splendid abilities. Strange to say, the principal objection Reuben saw to this project was, that Mr. Gosling proposed to deal too handsomely with him in a pecuniary way. If that point could be equitably adjusted, and if his godson really had the interest he spoke of, the arrangement would be to himself an extremely agreeable one.

"It would in fact, sir, be to you the same as a perfectly well secured annuity of between four and five hundred a-year."

"I should be only too well off," said Mr. Medlicott, "as things are now; but the office was worth more than eight hundred a-year when I was prevailed on to accept it."

"It was always utterly beneath you, sir," said his flattering godson.

"Why, so I thought myself at the time," said Reuben; "but I was married, and my friends got about me and insisted that a certainty of even eight hundred a-year, was better than an income of a couple of thousands at the end of a vista of hopes and imaginings."

"Will you believe me, sir," said Mr. Gosling, "I never could bear to hear you called a clerk in Chancery."

"You say you have interest to obtain the place?"

"Beyond all doubt, sir, if there is faith to be placed in human promises. My friend, the member for Newmarket, will vote against Government if they refuse me; and another most particular friend of mine, member for some place in Connaught, who asks for everything and gets everything he asks for, is ready to go to the Chancellor to-morrow, if I have only the good fortune to obtain your consent to the arrangement."

"All I will say to you now," said Reuben, "is that there are points of view in which I like what you propose; but there are others which, to say the least of them, require very mature consideration. I will reflect upon the matter, consult friends, and in a few days acquaint you with the result."

With that result we shall make the reader acquainted at once. In the teeth of the strenuous advice and remonstrance of every friend he had in the world, capable of advising him on the subject, Mr. Medlicott, within a few months of the opening of the negotiation, accepted the terms offered him by Mr. Gosling; and not only gave up his lucrative situation upon no better security than the honour of a scapegrace, but actually obtained the appointment for him, through his influence with his old friend Lord Appleby.

It was singular, but from the moment that Mr. Gosling became the head of that office in Chancery the fees returned; the tide of emoluments began to flow rapidly again. Indeed, Mr. Gosling made no secret of it, and for a couple of years he made his quarterly payments to Mr. Medlicott, according to their private agreement, with a punctuality that did him the greatest credit. One of these years was passed by Reuben in Brazil, on a special mission from the company, to examine and report on the state of the mines in their possession. He learned Portuguese expressly for the society of Buenos-Ayres, and contrived to make a good deal of noise on his return to England, by means of his contributions to the principal museums and scientific societies of the metropolis. Among other things, he presented the menagerie in the Regent's Park with a splendid collection of macaws and parrots, one of which proved a singularly eloquent bird; and, having been taught, during the voyage, to pronounce the name of the donor, helped to extend Mr. Medlicott's notoriety among a very numerous section of the public.

BOOK THE TENTH.

"*Therefore I perceive a man may be twice a child before the age of dotage, and stand in need of Æson's bath before threescore.*"—*Religio Medici.*

ARGUMENT.

It is not the phenomenon of a few gray hairs, nor the stolen march of a wrinkle, that marks the melancholy turning of the tide of life, but the first overshadowing of the mind with despondencies and self-upbraidings, the first sense of the difficulty of hoping, and the vanity of intending and designing; when to purpose and to dream, once our easiest and most delightful occupations, have become a Sisyphian labour. Then have we begun to grow old, when the first sigh escapes us for the pledges of youth unredeemed, or when we look into the kingdom within us, and perceive how few of its abuses we have reformed in the palmy days of our power; then shuddering think that the time of the fulfilling of promises and the correction of faults has passed; that the day is far spent and the night is at hand;—

> "When thoughts arise of errors past,
> Of prospects foully overcast,
> Of passion's unresisted rage,
> Of youth that thought not upon age."

These are the reflections that extinguish the "*purpureum lumen,*" that put out the youthful fire; he that is acquainted with remorse, whether it comes of folly or of crime, is already stricken in years, as old as Priam, though he may bear himself as gallantly as Paris. But some there are to whom these dreary thoughts come late, and who uphold themselves with wondrous strength and bravery under the weight of misspent hours. Hope is often an Atlas that will bear a world of disappointments on his shoulders; and should he ever totter, Vanity is at hand, like another Hercules, to relieve him. How many men do we not see in the world more confident after a thousand failures, than others after a large measure of success! Men, who never know that they are conquered, but imagine themselves still mounting, and crow and clap their wings, as if the firmament was still their own, when with their heavy or broken pinions the height of the barley-mow is almost beyond their flight. Folly is attended by a troop of spurious merits, the apes of Wisdom's body-guard, a false fortitude which is nothing but groundless self-assurance, a bastard industry which is only a fatiguing idleness, a magnanimity from which nothing comes that is great. Ardelio grown old, and with one foot in the grave, is Ardelio still.

> "Tu secanda marmora
> Locas sub ipsum funus, et sepulcri
> Immemor struis domos."

A species of happiness follows, no doubt, in the train of the mimic virtues, which strutting Folly trails behind her in her conceited progress to the last. The man who has disappointed the world has thoroughly deceived himself, and fancies he is still the admiration and the hope of his age, when he has only earned the "monstrari digito," to be pointed at as one example more of the downcome of overweening confidence, with the additional moral of many shining talents lost for the want of a few plain ones.

How benevolent is Hope, however, which, if it betrays a man in his early hours, cleaves to him often so faithfully in his latter days—

> "Hope! of all ills that men endure,
> The only cheap and universal cure!
> Thou captive's freedom, and thou sick man's health,
> Thou loser's victory, and thou beggar's wealth,
> Thou manna which from heaven we eat,
> To every taste a several meat!
> Thou strong retreat!—thou sure-entailed estate
> Which nought has power to alienate.
> Thou pleasant, honest flatterer, for none
> Flatter unhappy men, but thou alone."

CHAPTER I.

THE LAST EFFORT OF GENIUS.

THE reader may probably recollect Barsac Square, in the environs of Hereford—one of the joint building-speculations of Bishop Wyndham and Mr. Barsac. Only three houses had ever been finished, and these, with other property of the same nature, had passed into the hands of Mr. Cox, in the final settlement of his pecuniary transactions with the Bishop. In one of these houses Mr. Medlicott took up his residence at a nominal rent, shortly after his return from Brazil. It was furnished with more expense and ostentation, than propriety or comfort; for the Barsacs themselves had occupied it for a season, and had fitted it up with their usual taste in such matters. Among other things, they had brought down from London that magnificent bed with the purple velvet curtains fringed with gold lace, which had been bought for their venerable son-in-law, at the time of his advancement to the mitre. It was placed in the principal bedroom, and actually slept in by Mr. Medlicott himself, although too stately a couch for the Bishop.

Old Hannah Hopkins was no more, when Reuben returned from South America, and he had previously tried whether the cottage which she had long tenanted would suit him; but whether it was that its accommodation was defective, or that he found living at Chichester unpleasant, associated as that place was with the most signal failure of his life, he was certainly well pleased when the handsomer and more spacious dwelling at Hereford was placed at his disposal. There was probably a good deal of morbid pride in this preference of the three-storied house in Barsac Square, to a simple cottage in a quiet green lane. Time was when Mr. Medlicott's affectation would have led him to make the very opposite choice. Then, he fancied himself important enough to exalt and dignify the humblest abode. Now, he had probably some secret misgivings on that point, and felt no longer conscious of the power to elevate a cottage into a great house by conferring upon it the honour of his residence.

How he carried on the war of life at this period—that is to say, how the sinews of war were provided—was a mystery to everybody; for his connection with the mining company ceased in consequence of his report, which offended a majority of the directors; and his receipts from Mr. Gosling had dwindled to zero—a quantity on which only mathematicians can operate with success. Yet he continued, one way or another, to hold up his head in the world, and there was nothing of seediness about him, no symptom as yet of bleakness; on the contrary, there was much more of the air and appearance of the prosperous than the decayed gentleman. As to external appearances, indeed, he seemed more careful about them now than ever, His family made as great a show in the cathedral on Sundays, as the Barsacs were wont to do when he was a boy; and though he adhered himself to the vegetarian diet (upon which he seemed to thrive uncommonly well), his mode of living was costly enough in other ways; his house was always open to his fanatical admirers from London, who made no scruple of Pigwidgeoning him as he had Pigwidgeoned them on many a former occasion; and he manifestly spared no expense, either in the education of his children, or on their dress and amusements, all of which were upon a scale which required a good fortune to support it. It was his taste, evidently, that predominated in all these matters. Everybody who knew his wife knew very well that it was not for her gratification little Chichester and his sisters were fantastically habited in scarlet tunics, with caps and feathers, and trotted about Hereford and its suburbs on minute cream-coloured ponies, attended by a black groom (the same Pompey who had lived with him in Picadilly), as if they were the children of a millionnaire, or the progeny of Ducrow or Astley. It was very well known that these were altogether Mr. Medlicott's whims and follies, and there was many a speculation upon the source that supplied such extravagance, as well as upon the issue and results of it.

The Finchley school still existed; nay, was more flourishing than in former times, although Mr. Brough was now stricken in years, and beginning to be talked about as too old for the management of a large seminary. Mr. Medlicott was very kind to his ancient master, possibly a little too patronising—an air which had much grown upon him of late, and offended many of his acquaintances, while it merely curled the lips of others with a contemptuous smile. The older Mr. Brough grew, he was naturally only the more wedded to the system of instruction over which he had presided the greater part of his life; and as Mr. Medlicott had his mind full of a hundred new-fangled ideas on the same subject, some of which he had brought home with him from his visit to the United States, while others he was probably the author or inventor of himself,—there was ample subject for controversy between old pupil and old master, and many a discussion they had upon such matters, sometimes calm and sometimes stormy enough. Harvey, the Quaker, happening one day to be present at a conversation of this kind, Reuben held forth with more than his usual ardour, upon what he considered the true code of educational principles, lamented that they had never been tried upon a sufficiently large scale, spoke of the experiment as the noblest that could engage the mind of the philosopher or the philanthropist, and prophesied splendid moral revolutions and glorious intellectual millenniums, to date from the happy day of the realisation of his views. Harvey listened, as usual, with his eyes and mouth, no less than his ears, drinking in all these fine phrases and admirable speculations, as if he was sitting at the feet of a Plato or an Aristotle. Poor Mr. Brough was overwhelmed with the fluency of his opponent, and could only reply by shaking his hoary head sceptically, and entering a general protest against what he called quackeries, meaning thereby every departure from the method of his own institution.

This little conversation—if conversation it can fairly be called, in which hardly anybody talked but Mr. Medlicott—led to the last public undertaking of any consequence in which that gentleman took an active and leading part. Shortly after Harvey returned to London, he addressed a rigmarole letter to Reuben upon the general subject of middle-class education, conjuring him to take it up with energy, assuring him that no other man living was equal to so mighty a task, and ending with a proposal for some sort of a joint-stock educational company, with a governor, a board of directors, and a capital of fifty thousand pounds. The answer which Mr. Medlicott returned was an elaborate specimen of his imposing quasi-philosophical, chiaro-oscuro style; and both epistles were immediately published by Harvey, not only in the newspapers, but in the form of a penny tract, as easily disseminated as a pinch of thistle-down, to which, indeed, in point of weight and practical usefulness, it bore no faint resemblance. It told, however, with the desired effect upon a sufficiently large portion of the public to answer Harvey's purposes completely. Letters of cordial approval came rapidly pouring in from enthusiasts, fanatics, zealots, dupes, and blockheads, of both sexes and all persuasions; and these were soon followed by the tender of such liberal subscriptions to raise the necessary funds, that in a few weeks there was a sufficient sum in the bank to make an immediate commencement of the enterprise feasible.

However, the commencement was deferred, in order to afford Mr. Medlicott time to agitate upon the subject in England, Ireland, and Scotland, a mission upon which he was sent by the unanimous vote of a public meeting, and which he undertook with all the fervour and excitement of his early days. Now was he in his congenial element once more, wielding his old hammer daily, surrounded by a swarm of wild admirers and blind worshippers; a prophet, or a mountebank, according as he fell in with a mob of hot-headed enthusiasts or a few discreet people, in the course of his rambles.

It was probably a most convenient arrangement, just at this crisis, for Mr. Medlicott to turn schoolmaster, although, of course, it was not a thing to be done without a flourish of trumpets, and a great deal of previous parade, to throw the air of a grand enterprise over the acceptance of such an employment. Soon after his return from his speechifying tour, he was again commissioned to select a proper site for the projected establishment. It had been decided to purchase some large mansion, with a park or extensive grounds surrounding it: and after visiting and inspecting a great many country-seats which were then in the market, he was making up his mind where to pitch his choice, when his grandfather, being anxious to dispose of Westbury, offered it to the company for so moderate a sum, that Reuben recommended them to purchase it: and accordingly at Westbury the Grand Joint-stock Liberal and Enlightened Education Company was established, and in a very short time in actual operation, under Mr. Medlicott as Preceptor-General, for such was the imposing title he assumed.

The Bishop had no notion of encouraging the scheme, when he offered his house to the projectors; indeed he had tried in vain to comprehend the principles set forth in the prospectus, and after reading some of Mr. Medlicott's speeches declared that they only rendered the obscurity still more obscure. But Friend Harvey and some of his broad-brimmed brethren were so hot upon the subject, and proportionably unscrupulous, that they gave out in all quarters that their institution had the sanction and patronage of the learned Bishop of Shrewsbury; whereupon the latter (as pugnacious at fourscore and ten as at forty) published a letter of contradiction, in which he unfortunately committed himself by speaking most contemptuously of the project, at the same time affirming that he knew no more about it than the babe unborn. This led to a stiff reply in Harvey's name, but written by Mr. Medlicott; and to this reply the Bishop rejoined, all which was as favourable to the projectors as possible, for it excited public curiosity, and gave that notoriety to their establishment which to quacks of all descriptions is an object of so much importance. Another circumstance also, which took place at the same time, tended to the same result. Mr. Medlicott, on leaving Barsac Square, sold his stud of little cream-coloured ponies to Mr. Leadenhall, who had married one of Mrs. Wyndham's sisters. A warranty was given in the usual way with the ponies, upon which a dispute arose, and there was an action and a trial about it, which involved a great many curious and amusing circumstances, and caused Mr. Medlicott to be a great deal talked about, which was desirable at the moment, and, indeed, was never at any time very disagreeable to him.

The Westbury Collegiate institution for the education of youth upon the most enlarged principles of mental and moral philosophy—such was the announcement of its pretensions—opened with one hundred boys; but after all the fuss made about the novelty of its system and regulations, there was nothing in them for the first year that was either very attractive to the lovers of novelty, or very formidable to those who were partial to old methods. Lectures in a great measure superseded tasks. Botany, geology, and natural history were combined with exercise, and communicated peripatetically. Modern languages were taught in a manner little more oppressive to the students; and remonstrances, either private or public, were introduced in place of the punishments commonly resorted to in schools.

But the mind of the Preceptor-General was not long content with deviations so modest as these from the ordinary system of education. After long brooding upon the subject, not without too much reference to what he considered due to his own reputation for originality, he convened a meeting of the committee of directors, and propounded a scheme for what he called a new organisation of the establishment.

It was quite as radical a scheme for a school as Henry Hunt and other political visionaries were broaching at the same time for the nation. Several pupils were withdrawn on the first intimation that such a plan even existed on paper. Some of the directors thought Mr. Medlicott stark mad; but the faith of the majority in him was not so easily shaken. A man of his stamp must be allowed to have original ideas; and it was only fair to give whatever he might propose the fullest and maturest consideration. Repeated meetings were held in the board-room at Westbury, and at the end of the discussions the directors divided on the question of adopting or rejecting the innovations. They were carried by a majority of six to three, and two of the minority immediately threw up the undertaking.

Reuben carried another favourite point of his on the same occasion, the appointment of his old friend Doctor Page to the situation of physician to the institution, with a salary, apartments, and coals and candles. A more injudicious appointment could hardly have been made, for Page was now a prosy old man, and had latterly forfeited his reputation for good sense and medical skill by running wild after homœopathy, and professing to cure all human distempers, no matter how inveterate or malignant, with pills of too minute a size to be seen without the help of a powerful microscope. To this egregious system he was not long in making Mr. Medlicott a convert, and Mr. Medlicott in return made Doctor Page a proselyte to his vegetarian and aquarian practices. The two luminaries, thus happily reunited after a separation of many years, used to sit over their crofts of an evening, glorying in their common absurdities, and praying for the time to come when all the world would be as absurd as themselves.

CHAPTER II.

FOLLY INTERRUPTED BY SORROW.

The Westbury Institution, on the new model, was a free school in the strictest sense of the word. It was expressly established on the principle of unlimited confidence in the honour of the scholars, or *alumni*, as they were designated. The compulsions were altogether of a moral nature. Task-work was almost entirely superseded by lectures, which were to be either aulic, or peripatetic (signifying in plain English, in-doors, or out-of-doors), according to the season and the nature of the subject. The classes, or chambers, as they were called, were formed upon psychophrenological principles, which, as the phrase vastly delighted old Mrs. Medlicott, we must charitably hope that she understood what it meant. The Preceptor-General was, of course, the principal lecturer himself. It was his prerogative to lecture at all hours and upon all topics; but the subjects he reserved especially for himself were Rhetoric, the Conduct of the Understanding, and the Spirit of the British Constitution. The latter was one of the peripatetic courses; for, as our Anglo-Saxon liberties originated in the forests, Mr. Medlicott was of opinion that there was a peculiar propriety and advantage in explaining the nature of them walking in the woods, surrounded by the sylvan influences. But he also proposed to instill the spirit of our representative institutions in a practical manner, and for this purpose he ordained that all the games and festivals of the school should be settled by a council elected annually by universal suffrage and the ballot. The meals were to be on a model something between an Attic symposium and the convivial usages of the Utopians. The bill-of-fare for each week was to be fixed by an elective committee, within certain limits of variety and expense. Grace was to be said by the students in rotation, but never any two days in the week in the same language; and there were to be Italian, French, and German tables, where such students as desired to improve themselves in those languages, by using them exclusively, might sit, if they pleased. A corps of readers and declaimers was appointed monthly, who were to have their meals earlier than the rest, in order to be at leisure to recite pieces of poetry, or declaim passages from the ancient or modern orators, to entertain their fellow-students at dinner. It was also to be the duty of these declaimers, when any charge was brought against a cook, to send for the delinquent, and remonstrate with her in full symposium; a pleasant institution, attended with the advantage of accustoming the boys to speak at a moment's notice upon questions, not of imaginary, but real interest. On certain days of peculiar festivity, the *alumni* were to be encouraged to trifle elegantly and classically with anagrams, riddles, impromptu verses, and Spartan repartees. There were even prizes for distinguished merit in these exercises, the highest being for the best extempore iambics on a cook found guilty of over-seasoning, excessive boiling, or any similar misdemeanour. Dorothy, who was always in scrapes, was twice roasted for over-roasting, and Jenny herself was more than once in a stew.

Proficiency in general was tested by quarterly "investigations of progress," held at the equinoxes and solstices—words which pleased a multitude of fathers and mothers infinitely more than the vulgar names of the seasons. To the solstitial investigations, all the learned men in the kingdom were to be invited, and formed into a court or jury, which (after hearing a charge from the Preceptor-General) was to proceed to the performance of its duties. The occasions for haranguing created by the fundamental rules were amusingly frequent. The system of remonstrance was eminently favourable to the gratification of the Preceptor-General's ruling passion. After two private remonstrances, the student was liable to a public one; and after a second infliction of that kind, the offender was to be proclaimed to be "at large," which was the courteous phrase for a boy's expulsion. One of the oddest of all the regulations, but growing naturally out of the principle of confidence, was the following: any student might absent himself from lectures upon a certificate signed by two other students of the same chamber to the effect that he was indisposed, or pre-occupied by distressing or interesting news from home. But as this usage was obviously open to abuse, it was guarded by the delivery, once a quarter, of a grave address to the students, in full assembly, upon the beauty of truth and upon moral obligations in general, which furnished the eloquent head of the establishment with one periodical opportunity more for addressing his ever-attentive and submissive audience.

Mr. Medlicott, in fact, realised in this institution what may be said to have been the great idea of his life, namely, that everything in this world is to be done best by talking.

Few sane people, it will easily be believed, sent their sons to Westbury, when the system we have described was published abroad. But there were fools enough to admire, applaud, and patronise it with all its absurdities, and it actually stood its ground against a prodigious amount of ridicule for nearly three years, during which some changes, no doubt, were made in the details of the management, but with very little tendency to more rational regulations. There was something to fascinate various fanatical sections of the public. Mr. Medlicott personally adhered to the vegetarian system, and presided himself at a table expressly set apart for those scholars whose parents wished to bring up their children in blissful ignorance of beef and mutton. The Peace Societies were gratified by a fundamental ordinance against fighting of every kind, and the use of gunpowder, for any purpose whatever, even to fire a sixpenny brass cannon. A boy was solemnly remonstrated with, soon after the establishment opened, for letting off a squib; and the Preceptor-General availed himself of that opportunity for explaining the proper method of receiving an invading army, should the shores of England ever be outraged. This method consisted simply in resolutely ignoring the military character of the transaction, persisting in looking at it in the light of a friendly visit paid by some fifty thousand men of a particular nation, in a particular costume, to the people of another nation, and considering only how to make such an unexpected number of guests as comfortable as possible during their stay.

"For my own part, gentlemen," said the Preceptor-General, at the close of his remonstrance, "should a French army ever come to Westbury, I promise them as warm a reception as my kitchen can afford. I shall open my whole *batterie-de-cuisine* upon them. They shall not have to say that they had no English host to encounter, for they shall find a host in me at all events. As many as are vegetarians we will regale with the produce of our garden; those who hanker after the flesh-pots shall have the best mutton from yonder downs; we will meet them with our spits and pot-hooks; and if they come in September, when the woods are pleasant to stroll in, why we will invite them to come with us and hear a lecture on the laws and institutions of England."

Had everything gone on smoothly in this extraordinary college, Mr. Medlicott would probably have got tired of his position sooner than he did; but although there never assembled round a table a weaker-headed set of men than the board of directors consisted of, their imbecilities were sufficiently diversified to create innumerable disputes among them, which kept the Preceptor-General, who was a member *ex officio*, effectually from falling asleep. They quarrelled about religion among other things, the first bone of contention being the erection of a sort of pulpit for the public remonstrances, which gave them some resemblance to sermons, particularly as Mr. Medlicott had fallen much of late into a drawling mode of delivery that savoured more of the clerical profession than any other. Some members of the board were in favour of his actually taking orders, and pressed that step upon him. Others, including the Quakers, declared they would retire from the institution if he did. Compromises took place upon these several points. The pulpit gave place to an elevated platform, or dais; and instead of becoming a doctor of divinity, Mr. Medlicott repaired to his university and got himself dubbed a doctor of laws. He was thenceforward styled in his prospectuses Reuben Medlicott, Esq., LL.D., late member of Parliament for the city of Chichester, with several *et ceteras* appended; and as it was very soon discovered by his friends and his pupils that it tickled his ear to be addressed by the name of Doctor, he got doctoring enough from everybody about him, particularly from the *alumni*.

He had been about two years at the head of this odd institution, when he was summoned to his native city upon a no less melancholy occasion than to pay the last honours to his father, who died after a short and rather sudden illness, in the fulness of years, leaving behind him many friends who sincerely respected and loved him, and the well-earned reputation of one of the most honest and single-minded men in the Church. The Vicar had been an affectionate and faithful shepherd for nearly half a century to his little flock at Underwood; and had particularly endeared himself to them by his refusal to accept the Crown living, and by also subsequently declining to change his vicarage for one or two better things which he might have had in the diocese of Shrewsbury. He always said he was too old to move, and sometimes appealed to Sirach, who seemed to express by his croak his unwillingness to see a new incumbent.

When Reuben reached Underwood, he found his mother in a very nervous state, and gladly accepted the kind offer of a farmer in the neighbourhood to receive her into his house, until she was strong enough to bear removal to Westbury. She left Underwood for this temporary residence on the evening of her son's arrival there.

A numerous train of friends attended the excellent Vicar's funeral, but some of our own old acquaintances were not among the number. Mr. Oldport, the jovial canon, was no more; and Mr. Cox, although still living, was bowed down by the multitude of years and disorders, and devoutly waiting for that last and only universal remedy, which "to prepared appetites" (as Sir Thomas Browne beautifully expresses it) "is nectar, and a pleasant potion of immortality." The last time Reuben ever saw Mr. Pigwidgeon, the apothecary, was at the dismal breakfast upon this occasion. He had passed his seventieth year, was bent almost double, and had only two thin white locks of hair left, one over each temple: but his appetite was anything but decrepit, and not until he had satisfied its cravings, on pretence of keeping out the cold air, did he indulge his sorrow for his departed friend. To do the apothecary justice, he spoke with warmth and sincerity, when he did speak; not omitting the praise of the Vicar's hospitality, among his numerous other virtues, but frankly confessing how much of it he had enjoyed himself, and how unlikely it was he should ever see such a hospitable vicar of Underwood again. Mr. Medlicott was attentive and good-natured to the old man, who no longer cherished any hostile sentiments towards Mr. Medlicott; in fact, the comparative success of his own son in the world had completely extinguished the paltry little sorenesses, chiefly arising from wounded paternal pride, which had all along been at the bottom of his grudge to Reuben.

The Vicar fell with the leaf. It was a chill damp day, towards the close of October, when his remains were committed to the earth, within a dozen yards of the spot whose tillage had been his innocent amusement for forty years.

"The last words I ever heard him speak," said the old sexton, talking with Reuben in that melancholy deserted garden, when the ceremony was over,—"he was standing just where you are standing at this moment,—were these: 'Thomas,' he said, ' you and I cultivate the same ground, but you are the superior gardener; for what you sow will be immortal, and will blossom hereafter in heaven.' His reverence had a cough upon him at the time; you see he never finished planting out those young cabbages."

Reuben looked, and saw a bed recently dug, but only partially planted. A little bundle of the plants that remained unset was lying on the walk almost at his feet, and against the trunk of the pear-tree, mentioned before in this history, a spade was leaning; telling the story most distinctly of the abrupt summons which his father had received.

Men of sterner nature than Mr. Medlicott's would have been moved by this; he was powerfully affected, and turned away to indulge his grief in solitude. How neglected, how bleak, how utterly forlorn was all that once exquisitely cultivated rood of earth, associated in Reuben's mind with so many happy days of his childhood, with so many eventful periods of his maturer years, with the chief objects of his love and honour, with his early studies, and the recollection of all he had imagined that never was realised, and all he had hoped that never was fulfilled? Everything to both his eye and his heart was inexpressibly sad. A cold mist hung in the perfectly still air; the yellow leaves were dropping listlessly to the ground; those of the old walnut-tree covered the rustic table that stood beneath it. The last time Reuben had ever sat with his father at that table was the day of his return for Chichester, and the birth of his son. There were birds, but they were silent; the walks wont to be so trim were grass-grown in many places; here and there they were strewn with fallen apples, over which the slugs crawled; the last crop of peas had come to maturity in vain, the pods were swollen and growing brown,—the straw should have been removed a week before.

Returning to the place where he had talked with the sexton, Reuben found him engaged in setting the remainder of the plants, which, though they had lain there a fortnight, had the principle of vegetation still in them. It was an instinct of affection and duty in the old man that impelled him to undertake this little office; he felt himself a sort of executor in a matter of this kind of the last unaccomplished purpose of his deceased master.

Sirach was perched in the fork of the pear-tree, and seemed to be intently watching what the sexton was doing, as if it was incumbent on him, also, to see the intentions of the late Vicar carried out. Upon Reuben's approach he spread his wings, and with a low shuffling flight close to the ground penetrated the line of yews, and presently was heard mournfully croaking in the churchyard.

Reuben moved slowly to the door in the hedge. The sexton followed and opened it for him. He loved the old man for loving his father, thanked him cordially, and, bidding him an affectionate adieu, went to mingle his tears with his mother's at the neighbouring farm-house. His mother was never destined to see Underwood more; but it was Reuben's lot to visit it again after many years.

CHAPTER III.

PROGRESS OF MENTAL INFIRMITY.

THE death of the worthy Vicar was fraught with results very little to have been expected from it. Our Protean hero was now upon the verge of that curious religious metamorphosis to which he had been tending for many years, and to which his grandfather had always predicted he would come at last.

He had, indeed, exhibited through his motley life (though not in so prominent a manner as to arrest the attention of the public) no less infirmity of purpose in spiritual than in secular concerns. We saw him when a mere stripling almost turning his back upon the Church of England, because his grandfather had obtained a bishopric in a manner of which he disapproved, and he never entered again into very cordial relations with her. This estrangement was, of course, increased by his subsequent close connections with the Society of Friends, above all by his marriage with a member of that persuasion. However, his wife's religious zeal was far enough below that degree of heat which impels people to make proselytes; had it reached that boiling-point, she would never have left the Meeting to follow Reuben through the world; neither, in all probability, did the Harveys and Wilsons lay themselves out deliberately to convert him, for if they had done so, it is unlikely they would have failed in that more than in their other practices upon his weakness. He was certainly not entangled doctrinally with the Quakers when he first went to America, for we have seen that he was so much taken with the creed of the Mormonites as to have actually felt some disposition to attach himself to their wild community; and from the time of his return to England to the present period, it would not have been easy to determine to what denomination of Christians he belonged, for though he never sat "in the seat of the scorners," he frequented no particular place of worship, but roved hither and thither, not so much blown about by the winds of divers doctrines, as led to and fro by the fame of preachers noted for their eloquence, whenever such preachers were to be heard.

Perhaps, however, he would never have openly revolted from the Church of England if certain incidents that occurred after his father's death, and in consequence of that event, had not involved him in warm disputes about ecclesiastical matters. There were charges for dilapidations against the Vicar's representatives, which Reuben considered unjust and even monstrous; but whether they were unjust or not, he had no alternative but to submit to them, or risk the expenses and hazards of litigation in the spiritual courts. His old friend, Mr. Fox, the Proctor, strongly recommended resistance, and by his advice Doctor Medlicott did resist, and had eventually to pay upwards of three hundred pounds above the demand for dilapidations, which did not amount to a hundred and fifty. This made him sore enough; but another quarrel, in which he was involved at the same time by his mother, put him in still worse temper with the Church and its officers.

Like many other ladies, Mrs. Medlicott had been somewhat blind to the virtues of her spouse during his life-time; and as to talents she never allowed that he possessed any at all; but no sooner was he taken from her, than her heart grew soft, her eyes were opened, and she discovered that she had been wedded for nearly forty years to a man of the rarest merits of every kind. In short, she thought it incumbent on her to indite an epitaph on her deceased husband, and in the act of composing it, excellencies of all kinds sprung up under her pen, with a profusion that was perfectly astonishing. Reuben extolled her production with becoming filial enthusiasm, and offered a prize to his scholars for the best Latin and Greek translations of it. Two tolerable versions were produced; but what was the use of inscriptions? On what were they to be inscribed? Epitaphs in general are made for monuments, but in the present instance the monument had to be made for the epitaph. Mrs. Medlicott, encouraged by her son, and assisted by the subscriptions of her sister, and many other friends of her late husband, employed an eminent sculptor to express her high-flown ideas in marble; and when the work was executed, she wrote in a most ostentatious strain to the authorities of the cathedral of Chichester, proposing to do them the honour of having it erected there. She received an answer in a very different style, the most business-like conceivable, inclosing a scale of the fees payable upon the several descriptions of monuments, and naming the specific charge for that which she proposed to erect.

"All England shall hear of this," vowed Doctor Medlicott, who had received upon the same day disagreeable tidings of the dilapidation suit; and all England did hear of it, for he threw aside all other business for the time, and not only attacked the Dean and Chapter of Chichester, but all the deans and chapters in the kingdom, denouncing them in newspapers, belabouring them in pamphlets, and presenting petitions of interminable length against them to both houses of Parliament; hashing up his other grievances with that of the monument, and not even sparing the doctrines and liturgies of the Church in the unreasoning violence of his resentments. Among his other extravagancies, he had the extreme folly to prefix to one of his libels on the deans and chapters an engraving of the proposed mausoleum to his father, with the elegy composed by his mother, and its translations into the learned languages by his own wonderful scholars. It was in the same pamphlet that he entered his grand protest against the Established Church, and gave the first intimation of his resolution to take signal vengeance upon her for her manifold iniquities, by formally withdrawing himself and his family from her pale.

If the Church of England had at this period been as angry with Doctor Medlicott as he was with the Church, and, above all, if she had gone the length of excommunicating him with bell, book, and candle for his undutiful behaviour towards her, she would have just taken the very course that would have delighted him most, for his passion for notoriety was now an incurable disease. But that venerable establishment was not so accommodating to his foibles. The Vicar's successor in the parish of Underwood quietly received the sum for dilapidations which the law decreed in his favour; the Proctor and his brother officers pocketed their fees and costs with the same coolness: the Dean of Chichester adhered to the usages of the cathedral relative to monuments; and, unless laughter is a passion, nobody (out of the circle of his own fanatical followers) was seriously disturbed by all that Doctor Medlicott wrote and stormed about the church and his parents, his intolerable grievances and his terrible resolutions.

The resolution he took was formally to join the Quakers, and he only suspended the execution of this great design for an opportunity of making the change in the most public and conspicuous manner at the next annual meeting of the Society in the month of May. His friend Primrose, now the venerable archdeacon of Shrewsbury, wrote him the kindest letter of remonstrance, in the hopes of restraining him from the commission of this incredible extravagance; but his interposition was unavailing, and only brought upon the archdeacons the same description of ill-usage which the deans had already experienced.

Before the merry month of May came, Doctor Medlicott had ceased to be the head of the Westbury institution, and that notable institution itself had ceased to exist. It was not its absurdities that destroyed it, for it was established to carry out the views of the most absurd people upon earth, and its folly was really the only element of success it contained. The circumstances are only worth relating because they arose from that amiable trait in Mr. Medlicott's character which we have already noticed more than once, the strength of his private attachments and his vivid recollection of old associations and old times. We have related how comfortably Doctor Page was settled at Westbury, with a salary, apartments, and other advantages, as resident physician and professor of homœopathy to the institution. Whether this was a job, or not, it certainly looked very like one. When old Mrs. Medlicott, after the Vicar's decease, came to live with her son, it was so natural an arrangement that no difficulty was made about it in the first instance; at the same time it was another encroachment, and the subject no doubt of unpleasant remarks in private. The old lady ought to have kept herself as quiet as possible under the circumstances; but she was not that sort of woman; she soon made herself obnoxious to her son's assistants by tampering with the heads of the boys, and objecting to regulations which were not sufficiently preposterous to please her. But this was not the worst: she persuaded Reuben that he wanted a register, and actually sent to Chichester for one of his remaining godsons to fill that office. There was a great battle about this at the Board, but Friend Harvey bore down all resistance, and by a narrow majority a small salary was voted to the godson. This transaction wore unquestionably an ugly aspect; yet if the system had stopped here there would probably have been no serious outcry; but just at the same moment it happened that a professor of French was wanting. A professor was advertised for; he must be a gentleman, he must be a Parisian, and the advertisement was not long unanswered.

Doctor Medlicott was sitting with his wife and mother, his register and physician, at breakfast, when Dorothy, now a corpulent dame of forty, but still dressed in all the colours of the rainbow, entered with a card in her hand for the Preceptor-General. The card bore the address of "M. Adolphe Beauvoisin, Chevalier de la Légion d'Honneur, Professeur des Langues Modernes, &c., &c."

"This is wonderful!" cried the head of the college, rising: "I had almost forgotten my old friend's existence. What a Proteus he is! what a strange chameleon! Dorothea, show in the Chevalier."

Adolphe was now a meagre, sharp-visaged old fellow: he entered the room with twenty bows and grimaces, his seedy black coat buttoned up to his chin, and another old parapluie under his arm; it was manifest he had not thriven on his versatility, as well as other people. The Chevalier, as he styled himself, looked very like a man who was at his last shift, or on his last legs; much in the state of the unfortunate fox in the fable, hunted down in spite of all his tricks, while his companion the cat, who had but the one gift of climbing a tree, escaped scot-free by its timely exercise. Of course he had a theory, cut and dry, as usual, to account for the new character in which he now made his appearance. He had discovered his true talent at last; nor did he seem in the least conscious what a melancholy thing it is to make that important discovery at sixty. On the contrary, he extolled his own sagacity highly; and old Mrs. Medlicott, on being appealed to by her son, scrutinised his organ of language, and pronounced it admirably developed; at the same time ascertaining the distressing fact that the accomplished Chevalier had no shirt.

Reuben first gave the impudent pretender his breakfast; then he supplied the defects of his wardrobe; and thirdly, he promoted him to the vacant professorship, introducing him to the students that very day at dinner, with an elaborate eulogy on his talents, and a touching allusion to the circumstances of their original acquaintance. Before the subject of these encomiums was a week in his situation, his kind and generous patron had to remonstrate with him seriously for teaching the alumni to smoke; and before the expiration of a month, it was ascertained that he also gave private lessons to the senior students in that practical branch of the science of probabilities commonly called gaming. This was too grave a matter to be passed over even with the dismissal of the offender. Mr. Medlicott was formally called to account for making the appointment, and the opportunity was seized upon for accusing him of having corruptly turned the institution into a comfortable asylum and snuggery for himself, his family, his relations, and friends. He made a long speech in his own defence, and Friend Harvey stuck to him to the last; but a resolution of censure was passed, and Doctor Medlicott threw up his place in disgust, and removed his family immediately to London.

CHAPTER IV

THE LAST FOLLY AND THE LAST SPEECH.

It was the first of May (or Fifth Month, as the Quaker almanack terms it), not very long after the break-up at Westbury; and a large majority of the disciples of Fox and Penn resident within the sound of Bow bell, with many of the same fraternity from far beyond the reach of that celebrated tongue of Time, were gathered together in Finsbury, in an unusually crowded yearly meeting. Upon one side were arrayed the solemn males of the community, upon the other sat the formal females; the separation between them reminding one of the original creation of the various species of living things after their sexes and kinds; while the unjoyous colouring that reigned (if colouring it could be called with propriety) led the spectator to congratulate himself that the same harsh taste in tints did not prevail at the era of the Creation; for then had the face of nature wanted its loveliest varieties, the rainbow had never spanned the sky, the peacock spread his starry train, or "the firmament glowed with living sapphires." A Quaker Iris would ill have symbolised the vivid hues of Hope; a Flora of the same persuasion would never have eclipsed the glories of the court of Solomon.

It was a favourable moment for studying the Society, had you been disposed to publish a little book about them, of the kind which the French have lately entitled "Physiologies." The present meeting was a sort of prim parliament, very fairly representing all the varieties of Quakerism. There were English Quakers, Scotch Quakers, Irish Quakers, and even Yankee Quakers. There was the Quaker as brown as a Moor; the Quaker as grey as morning; the drab Quaker; the snuffy Quaker; and the Quaker as white as snow. There was the dreary sort and the sprightly; the coarse and the cultivated; the mild and the morose. You could see where the bigoted hue was only external, and where the heart itself was drab. You saw the old dry variety, and the modern wet one. There was dismal devotion and cheerful; piety obviously unaffected, and piety conspicuously assumed. There was no priest among them, but there were probably some pharisees and hypocrites. It is still more certain, however, that there was many a meek publican and many a good Samaritan in the throng.

Observing the fair side of the meeting particularly, you might almost have classified the Quakeresses by their silks. The maidens were generally dove-coloured; the mothers silvery, fleecy, or bluish-grey; the grand-dames olive and dun. The far-poking bonnet seldom concealed a pretty face; nor did the comeliest figures seem to be those which availed themselves of the uncouthest garbs to hide them. There was not much beauty, perhaps; but what there was stood independently on its personal merits, and proved what sparkling eyes will do without other brilliants; bright hair, without flowers or pearls; a beautiful arm, without a bracelet; and white tapering fingers, without a ring. Nor yet had either the dove-coloured damsels, or the matrons of silver-grey, so utterly neglected their personal decoration as to select the harshest materials for their habits, or enjoin upon their milliners total inobservance of shapes and forms; on the contrary, if there was no clothing of wrought gold, there was much raiment of elaborate needlework; where the tint was very sad, the texture was apt to be very rich; and you sometimes felt inclined to remark of piety, what the poet does of ambition, that it "should be made of sterner stuff."

It was not, however, upon the female side alone that these symptoms of human weakness were to be detected. The more you attended to minutiæ upon both sides, the more you were convinced that, while the founders of the sect had triumphed to a wonderful extent over the love of pomp and vanity—even over the feminine passion for dress and ornament,—the victory was not complete; nature was not conquered: you saw by the hats of many brims, the coats of many cuts, the bonnets of many pokes, and the silks of many a shade,—that even the Jacobs and Obadiahs had their Mirror of Fashion, and the Rebeccas and Ruths their *modistes*.

Unless the observer, too, was much deceived, he detected on the present occasion a gloss upon the broadcloth, a novelty in the silks, and a crispness in the cambrics, which bespoke something more than usually exciting, nay almost festive, in the season, or the day. Although it was one of those annual gatherings, when they assemble not only from far cities and countries, but even from far distant regions of the globe, to exchange looks of kindness, and silent breathings of peace and good-will,—it was impossible not to conclude, from the crowded state of the benches, the abundance of new dresses, and the extraordinary intentness of all eyes—but particularly those of the fair sex,—that something was about to happen out of the usual course of events in the Quaker world.

There was evidently a greater throng than usual, for the men sat with their arms pinioned to their sides, and their knees in contact; while the matrons and maidens were penned so close together, that the countenances of some, who were not so unworldly as the rest, exhibited manifest tokens of chagrin at the unavoidable rumpling of their gowns.

Prominent among the males were Friends Harvey and Wilson, particularly the former. Harvey was all brown; Wilson was all drab. The progress of time had made Wilson drier and sourer and stiffer than ever. Upon Harvey, years seemed to have had the opposite effect—increasing his smoothness and briskness. Although stock-still, he seemed to be all in motion; and if you can imagine a talkative silence, it was that which he was keeping with his lips, out of which his tongue was continually making little excursions; while his eyes rolled about with the most fidgety anxiety, as if they expected to see an angel come down from heaven, or something of that sort. Harvey was now a sexagenarian, and sat with the reverend elders of the meeting. Behind him were his sons, now men of ripe age, still not easy to be known asunder, except by the habit, in which one of them kindly persevered, of keeping his mouth wide open, to give the flies a hospitable reception.

The cause of this extraordinary stir in so calm a community was not very long a secret. Presently, as if by one accord, or by a simultaneous movement of some spirit, peradventure only that of curiosity, all eyes were turned to one point, and that point was the door of the Meeting-house. It opened and opened again, but nothing satisfactory made its appearance, only grim old Isaac Hopkins, the rich brewer, or one of the dismal pieces of female antiquity which we may recollect having formerly seen at the Meeting in Cavendish Square.

At length, however, came the desire of all eyes. Harvey's seemed to be starting from their sockets. The mouth of Jonas opened to its extreme width. The silks rustled; the crisp muslins rose and fell over the agitated bosoms. With a slow, measured, solemn, and not unstudied step, in strict but not painfully rigid Quakerly attire, carrying his new glossy broad-leaved white hat in his hand, and wearing in his button-hole a bouquet of the gravest flowers of the season, entered a tall portly man, but with faded cheek, and past the meridian of his days, showing an evident struggle in every feature between the desire to appear meek and subdued, as became a novice, and the conceited consciousness that he was the admired of all beholders. A more severe costume might perhaps have disguised Reuben Medlicott for a few moments, but the deviation from his ordinary dress for many years was not considerable: and the eternal bouquet, emblem of his undying coxcombry, was sufficient of itself to establish his identity. His wife and children, however, were there to vouch him, and he wanted vouchers. His wife crept beside him, as conscious of being disregarded and unwelcomed, as her husband was of being received with rapture. Mary had left the Meeting to follow the lover without a regret, and she now returned to it to obey the husband without a particle of enthusiasm. He was no proselyte of hers; no triumph was visible in her deportment: on the contrary, had not her poking bonnet and white veil nearly concealed her countenance, you might have detected an affecting change in its once so radiant and joyous features, an anxious expression in her eyes, and the traces of much care upon her brow—the consequences, undoubtedly, of long and painful solicitude for her husband's interests and the fate of his children. She was accompanied by three of them, two girls in their teens, and Chichester, also coming on rapidly, though, in his full-dress suit of drab, he looked by no means so fast a young man as when he galloped about Hereford in scarlet uniform, on his cream-coloured pony.

Husband and wife—the new prize and the regained property of the Society—separated when they reached the centre of the open space that divided the sexes. Friend Reuben was admitted, with every demonstration of mute greeting, into a place that had been carefully reserved for him between Harvey and Wilson; while, on the opposite side, the matrons of the sect, with infinitely less ardour and cordiality, received the poor downcast Mary into their demure ranks.

Mr. Medlicott did not preach on the first day of his admission into the Society of Friends. It would have been a variance with their discipline, or he would probably have done so. There were some of the fraternity who would willingly have set all rules aside upon so great an occasion, but they were overruled by the sterner members of the body. The neophyte, however, was enrolled, in an unusually short time, among what are termed "the acknowledged ministers;" and soon attained a melancholy eminence as the most powerful—which meant the longest-winded —of them all. Some of his rhapsodies are better recorded than even Mrs. Fry's most attractive addresses, or even than Hannah Hopkins's famous sermon on Daniel in the den of lions, which Matthew Cox remembered to have heard. One of Reuben's outpourings is still considered by the survivors of the Harveys and the Wilsons as having been, not only the most wonderful effort of eloquence that ever broke the silence of the meeting, but as having partaken in some measure of the prophetic strain. It was a discourse in which, amid a labyrinth of metaphorical prolixities, he introduced a highly-wrought description of a figurative olive-tree, that was to be planted hereafter in the heart of the great metropolis, under which all the nations of the earth were to be gathered in peace and amity, to celebrate the triumphs of knowledge and industry, arts and sciences, concord and civilisation. This is now considered, by the faithful few in whose memory he still flourishes, as a distinct and most remarkable prediction of the Palace of Crystal, and the great event in the history of civilisation connected with that magic edifice. Mr. Jonas Harvey, whose shop and whose mouth are still open, has no doubt whatsoever of the inspiration of his father's friend.

While Mr. Medlicott continued a Quaker, he was a thorough-going one. He did not quake by halves, but went the whole hog with the most strait-laced, the most broad-brimmed, and the most fanatical of the sect. When they sent their spiritual envoys abroad, he was always in the commission. When ministers were appointed to go from house to house, "dealing" with perverse or delinquent brethren, Friend Reuben was seldom omitted from the number. These pious peregrinations were unhappily from the first only too convenient to him in a pecuniary point of view; but eventually they became almost his only means of subsistence, and he passed a great part of every year going to and fro with his family, quartering himself freely in the snuggest houses, and paying for his substantial entertainment with a profusion of vapoury discourse. In fact he was growing bleak; and it was now beginning to be noticed that he no longer held up his head with the self-assurance which he had hitherto so well preserved, as if he hoped against hope, and held the faith in himself unshaken. There were, however, occasionally—even now—flashes of the once wonderful Reuben, who had given his friends such promises of success, and pledged himself to the world for such great performances. Now and then, in some comfortable house where he was received with more than ordinary warmth, and still listened to as an oracle, he would pour himself out at dinner, or more frequently at the tea-table, with all his characteristic exuberance of metaphor, allusion, quotation, and anecdote, with no drift and to no end. But then again he would collapse for weeks into a state of almost stupidity, as if he had talked himself down and had need of repose and refreshment before he was able to commence again.

Often at this period would his family in London have wanted bread, if the Primroses and the Harvey family had not been very kind to them. His wife did not long survive her return to her old communion. Setting out upon one occasion to attend a quarterly meeting in the North of England, to which he had received an invitation from some enthusiastic friends, he left Mary behind him laboring under what seemed a slight indisposition. It turned rapidly to a fatal illness. On his return to town he found himself a desolate and dreary widower.

In three months after this event he looked ten years older. Now, for the first time in all his life, to speak was visibly a labor to him. He was the eloquent preacher and powerful minister no more; and when he was no longer actively serviceable to the Meeting, the Meeting naturally ceased to employ and honor him as before.

He was now advised to leave England for some time, and, in change of scene and of climate, to seek the repair of his spirits and his health. While he was hesitating what to do, the Society of Friends in London were on the point of sending out a few of their most distinguished members to represent them at the annual meeting in Pennsylvania. Reuben was most anxious to be one of the mission; but he was not among the chosen, which so offended and mortified him, that he abruptly left the Society, and was seen the next day in the streets of London wearing his old Babylonish garments.

Not even this could alienate the ever-devoted Harvey. He took one of Mr. Medlicott's daughters to live in his house. Mr. Primrose undertook the maintenance and education of the other. A subscription was raised to place Chichester at a public school. The unfortunate father retired, with his aged mother, to the neighborhood of Hackney, where he tried to make out a livelihood by re-editing his travels and collecting those miscellaneous essays of which we have given the reader a specimen. When this failed, he published the prospectus of a course of lectures on mesmerism and other kindred quackeries; but before the day came for the first exhibition, he was seized with a partial paralysis of his limbs, and continued a wretched invalid, generally creeping about London to the close of his unprofitable, yet exemplary, life.

A very short time since, two students of the same college where Reuben Medlicott received his university education, sauntering one fine evening on the banks of their famous stream, observed a melancholy man, with a frame broken down more by grief and malady than by years, his cheek hollow, his eye dim, and his lip quivering, moving feebly beneath the willows. Something intellectual in his countenance, faded and worn as it was, together with an air of distinction about him, the remains of former consequence, whether real or imaginary, excited their curiosity and tempted them to address him. Feebly, but politely, he received and even encouraged their advances, evidently pleased to talk and perhaps flattered by their willingness to listen. He inquired about their studies, then spoke about his own formerly; began by relating his college recollections, and at length proceeded to unfold the history of his life. He surprised them by the abundance of his knowledge of many subjects, and even professions; delighted them by the variety and often the brilliancy of his language; perplexed them by the extent of his experiences as a lawyer, an author, a traveller, a politician, a divine. They marvelled, as he talked, who the man could be; seemingly possessing every talent and all accomplishments, yet wandering there forlorn, needy, and unknown. The mood of his narration changed often; now it was calm, now excited, but most frequently it was in a tone of deep pathos, as if there was always some regret uppermost, some painful emotion even when he recalled his triumphs. At length he stopped suddenly in his tale, and, leaning on his staff, regarded his hearers earnestly, and bade them mark his counsel, for it was the province of age to instruct youth.

"I have excited your admiration, young men," he said, "while I only merit your compassion. You see in me a signal example of what little is to be done in this busy world, by much knowledge, much talent, much ambition, nay, even by much activity, without singleness of aim and steadiness of purpose. For want of these two undazzling qualities, my life has been a broken promise and a perpetual disappointment. My views also were too exalted. I aimed too high and overshot the mark. Like Percy's, my heart was great, too great; and Harry's farewell may be my soliloquy:—

> "Ill-weaved ambition, how much art thou shrunk!
> When that this body did contain a spirit,
> A kingdom for it was too small a bound,
> But now two paces of the vilest earth
> Will soon be room enough."

A tear rolled down the old man's hollow cheek when he came to the last words of the quotation. The young men were greatly affected, and waited in respectful silence for him to resume his discourse; but he broke it off abruptly, with an ejaculation in so low a tone that it scarcely reached the ear. "Alas," he sighed, "what I might have been!"

Not many weeks later the same old man was seen in one of the green lanes in the neighbourhood of Chichester. He took up his abode as a lodger in a small cottage, from which he only removed to lie in the same grave with his father in the quiet churchyard of Underwood, where an aged raven, hopping from an adjoining garden through a stately row of yews, croaked his requiem.

THE END.

www.ingramcontent.com/pod-product-compliance
Lightning Source LLC
Chambersburg PA
CBHW022135300426
44115CB00006B/194